African Voices

African Voices

AN INTRODUCTION TO THE LANGUAGES AND LINGUISTICS OF AFRICA

EDITED BY

Vic Webb and Kembo-Sure

OXFORD
UNIVERSITY PRESS

OXFORD
UNIVERSITY PRESS

Great Clarendon Street, Oxford OX2 6DP

Oxford University Press is a department of the University of Oxford.
It furthers the University's objective of excellence in research, scholarship,
and education by publishing worldwide in

Oxford New York

Athens Auckland Bangkok Bogotá Buenos Aires Calcutta
Cape Town Chennai Dar es Salaam Delhi Florence Hong Kong Istanbul
Karachi Kuala Lumpur Madrid Melbourne Mexico City Mumbai
Nairobi Paris São Paulo Singapore Taipei Tokyo Toronto Warsaw

with associated companies in Berlin Ibadan

Oxford is a registered trade mark of Oxford University Press
in the UK and certain other countries

Published in South Africa
by Oxford University Press Southern Africa, Cape Town

**African Voices: An Introduction to the Languages
and Linguistics of Africa**
ISBN 0 19 571681 7

© Oxford University Press Southern Africa 2000

Editor: Helen Moffett
Designer: Mark Standley
Cover designer: Mark Standley
Cover artwork: Profiles of Africa (private collection)
Indexer: Jeanne Cope

Published by Oxford University Press Southern Africa
PO Box 12119, N1 City, 7463, Cape Town, South Africa

Set in 10.5 pt on 12 pt Minion by RHT desktop publishing, Durbanville
Reproduction by RHT desktop publishing
Cover reproduction by The Image Bureau
Printed by Creda Communications, Eliot Avenue, Epping Industrial II, Cape Town.

Contents

List of contributors

VIC WEBB is a professor in the Department of Linguistics and director of CentRePoL at the University of Pretoria, 0001, Pretoria, South Africa.

KEMBO-SURE teaches in the Department of Linguistics and Foreign Languages at Moi University, PO Box 3900, Eldoret, Kenya

HERMAN BATIBO is a professor in the Department of African Languages and Literature at the University of Botswana.

ALBINA R. CHUWA is attached to the Institute of Kiswahili Research at the University of Dar es Salaam, Tanzania.

HILTON HUBBARD is a professor in the Department of Linguistics at the University of South Africa.

NKONKO M. KAMWANGAMALU is a professor in the Department of Linguistics at the University of Natal.

JANE KEMBO teaches in the Faculty of Education at Moi University, Kenya.

OSWALD K. NDOLERIIRE is a professor in the Department of Languages at Makerere University, Uganda.

D. OKOTH OKOMBO is a professor in the College of Education and External Studies at the University of Nairobi, Kenya.

DANIE PRINSLOO is a professor in the Department of African Languages at the University of Pretoria.

ELSABÉ TALJARD teaches in the Department of African Languages at the University of Pretoria.

Introduction

Most introductory textbooks in linguistics are (understandably, we suppose), shaped by North American or British/European perspectives. This generally means that:

- the conceptual framework within which they define linguistics as a field of study is non-African;
- the concepts with which they work are not contextualized within African cultural traditions;
- their definition of what constitutes a linguistic problem is determined by Western academic perspectives;
- the languages and linguistics of Africa are not centralized, with most of their illustrative material coming from outside Africa;
- the language and language-related problems typical of the comprehensive and complex multilingualism of Africa are not dealt with substantially;
- the background knowledge assumed in these textbooks is Western in nature, and the information they provide and the skills they develop are not specifically directed at African conditions; and
- very little reference is made to the work of African linguists.

African linguistics cannot, of course, divorce itself from the linguistics of Europe, the United Kingdom, or North America, and it is essential for linguistics students in Africa to be acquainted with this work. However, Africa has its own typical linguistic problems and its own typical language situations, and linguistics students in Africa need more African-oriented training programmes; that is, programmes that provide information about the languages of Africa, that are directed at problems common to African societies, and that enable students to analyse and handle these problems in ways appropriate to Africa. Students of linguistics in Africa need, in addition to the knowledge, insights, and skills of general linguistic theories, knowledge, insights, and skills relevant to Africa.

Two examples illustrate the point. Firstly, the two most important language problems common to almost all African states are (a) the role of the languages of power in Africa (generally English, French, and Portuguese) and the lack of proficiency of the majority of African people in these languages; and (b) the low esteem in which speakers of the African languages generally hold their own languages. It is generally true that less than 25 per cent of the African people know the ex-colonial languages well enough to be able to develop educationally, economically, socially, and politically. Consequently, these languages are barriers to effective access to information and to participation in educational, economic, and political processes and decision-making. Similarly, the striking preference in African communities for English, French, and Portuguese as languages of learning and teaching in pre-tertiary education suggests that Africans generally regard their languages as less fit for use in formal contexts. Given the extreme seriousness of these problems, they should be urgently addressed in every relevant context. These are complex and comprehensive problems, however, and interact with factors in various non-linguistic domains. If linguistics students are to be trained to handle these problems, they need to be equipped with specific knowledge, skills, values, norms, beliefs, and attitudes. They need to be able to identify these problems in their specific contexts of work, to tease out their linguistic aspects, to know what has been done elsewhere, and to realize what they as linguists can do to contribute to solving the problems.

Secondly, a general theme in training programmes in Departments of Linguistics in African countries is the history of English (or French, or Portuguese). However, in the case of English, for example, discussion often focuses mainly on the European and North American history of English (with some mention of the English of Australia and New Zealand). But the appearance of English in Africa, its structural, functional, and pragmatic adaptation to the African world, and the way it came to acquire such a strong hold on the psyches and minds of the African people, dominating their educational, political, and economic lives, is given almost no attention. We believe this situation is imbalanced, particularly as the dominant roles of the ex-colonial languages in Africa are, at least to some degree, causally involved in a number of serious problems in Africa. An African-oriented linguistics training programme must, we argue, discuss the history of English (and French and Portuguese) from the perspective of this continent.

Given the basic orientation of this book, *African Voices* wishes to achieve two major goals:

- to introduce students to theoretical linguistics – its concepts, theories, ways of argumentation, data collection, data analysis, and data interpretation; and
- to introduce them to the languages and linguistics of Africa, thus providing them with the knowledge and skills required to handle the language and language-related problems typical of African conditions.

In addition to these two goals, *African Voices* also aims at involving African scholars in a joint venture, thus constructing a network of African linguists.

Conversely, it also wishes to contribute to the world of linguistics outside Africa, and to enrich European, British, and North American linguistics with perspectives from Africa.

African Voices is characterized by a number of features:

- It is an introductory text to linguistics in general, aimed at the first years of tertiary study, which means that the linguistics of Europe, Britain, and North America won't be ignored.
- It has a specifically African orientation, but is not meant to be a textbook on African languages.
- It intends to introduce students of linguistics to the technical aspects of the discipline, hoping to indicate how skills and knowledge of these technical aspects can contribute to handling the language and language-related problems of Africa.
- It presents a holistic picture of language. In other words, it is not devoted to formal linguistics only, seeing linguistics as an end in itself, but also covers aspects of pragmatics (for example, interactional sociolinguistics, discourse analysis, and the like), as well as the politics of language and applied linguistics (language teaching). It looks at language as a fundamental tool in the lives of people – used for communication, giving access to knowledge and privileges, binding and separating communities, functioning as a factor in identity construction, and so on. This book is thus sensitive to the social meaning of languages in the lives of their speakers (for example, English, Kiswahili, Dholuo, and Suba in the lives of the people of western Kenya).

African Voices is structured as follows. It begins with a discussion of the language-related and language problems of African countries, thus providing the broad framework within which a training programme in African linguistics could be developed, given the perspectives of the contributors (Chapter 1). Chapter 2 introduces the languages of sub-equatorial Africa, and in Chapter 3 a brief introduction is provided to the study of languages (linguistics). This chapter also introduces the concepts and terms required for reading the more technical chapters, such as Chapters 4 and 6 to 12. Chapter 4 contains an overview of the nature of languages in contact, while Chapter 5 deals with the nature of languages in competition. In Chapters 6 to 10, the linguistic tools needed to deal with language phenomena are introduced: phonetic and phonological tools (Chapters 6 and 7), morpho-syntactic tools (Chapter 8), lexical and semantic tools (Chapter 9), and discourse analytical tools (Chapters 10 and 11). Chapter 12 discusses language in education.

We conclude with some explanatory remarks about several of the editorial decisions which guided the preparation of the text:

- Each chapter starts with a list of the expected learning outcomes it hopes to achieve. Generally, these outcomes are of three types, namely the knowledge students are expected to have acquired by the end of a chapter, the linguistic skills which a chapter seeks to develop (or contribute towards developing), and the values, standards, and attitudes it wishes to inculcate. Examples of these three types of outcomes are: knowledge of the concepts and terms (definitions) of the sub-discipline, and the basic facts that have been established; skills such as being able to define a linguistic problem, collecting relevant data on it, analysing and describing the data, interpreting it, testing hypotheses, being able to make generalizations, writing grammatical rules, and arguing for or against linguistic claims or propositions; and values, standards, and attitudes such as accepting the equality of all languages and their varieties, rejecting the validity of subjective evaluations of diverse linguistic accents, and defending the adequacy of all natural languages to express the communicative intentions of their speakers. In addition to the list of outcomes, the editors have also inserted a number of tasks and exercises into the chapters provided by the contributors.

- Where important technical terms are used in the chapters, they are printed in bold characters and briefly defined in the course of the subsequent discussion.

- The names of the languages of Africa are given in the forms used in their own speech communities, and not in their English form. For example, the usual English form of the South African language Zulu is *Zulu* (for the same reason that French is not referred to as *le Francais* in English). In this book, however, the indigenous form *isiZulu* is used. The reason for this decision is that the editors believe that this practice will give further emphasis to the African orientation of the book. (It is certain that we have made mistakes in the spelling of the names of the African languages, in spite of our best efforts. In such cases, we would like to extend our apologies, and to request readers to submit corrections to us.)

- Finally, a remark mainly for the benefit of South African users: the term *Bantu* languages and linguistics is used for two reasons. Firstly, it is internationally the normal reference term for these languages, and, secondly, the Bantu languages need to be distinguished from the other African languages, which include the Khoisan languages, the Nilo-Saharan languages, and the Afro-Asiatic languages, as described in Chapter 2. (For non-South African readers who are puzzled by the need for an explanatory note, it should be added that in South Africa the term *Bantu* became stigmatized as part of apartheid terminology, in which it was used as a racially offensive term to distinguish black South Africans from white South Africans.)

A last editorial observation: as *African Voices* is a group production, each author obviously takes responsibility for his or her own views, and not, of course, for the views of others. Similarly, the two editors are not responsible for the content of chapters they did not write.

African Voices is an experimental venture in several senses. To our knowledge, it is the first time that a wholly African-oriented introductory linguistics textbook has been compiled; it is the first attempt at covering the languages of Africa; and it is the first time that linguists from across the continent have co-operated in a joint enterprise. It is therefore highly unlikely that this textbook will be without serious shortcomings. In light of this, the editors therefore invite critical comment as well as any information that may contribute towards a more comprehensive and more adequate linguistics training product, should this book be followed by further editions. The addresses of the editors can be found at the beginning of the book.

To conclude, we will be pleased if *African Voices* can contribute in some small way to promoting an attitude which is being expressed more and more in African circles: that Africa must begin to take responsibility for herself, for her own destiny, thus becoming less reliant on others.

Vic Webb, Pretoria
Kembo-Sure, Eldoret

November 1998

Political map of Africa

1 Language as a problem in Africa

Vic Webb and Kembo-Sure

Expected outcomes

At the end of this chapter you should be able to:

1 List the language-related problems typical of African countries, give examples of such problems from the country in which you live, and explain the possible role of language in each of these problems.

2 Identify the linguistic information and tools needed to address these problems, and describe how a linguist would try to resolve them.

3 Convince linguistically untrained persons that all languages are equal from a linguistic point of view, and that English, French, or Portuguese are therefore not superior to any other language in Africa; also that languages which presently have not yet been expanded to the same degree as the ex-colonial languages can be similarly developed.

4 Demonstrate that all living languages are equipped to serve the communicative needs of their speakers.

5 Describe what language development means in linguistic terms.

The perspective of *African Voices*

Language is seldom thought of as a problem. As long as people are able to communicate with one another, and can get answers to their questions or can provide information to others, they are happy. As long as we can understand what someone else is saying, and are able to read a newspaper, listen to the radio, or watch television, we are satisfied. As long as our immediate communicative needs are met, language is not experienced as a problem.

However, if we think a little more deeply about language and its role in society and the lives of people, we discover that language can indeed be a problem. Perhaps students will understand this better if we first consider the social functions of languages.[1]

The **social functions of language**, that is, the role of language in society, can be described in terms of two properties: the instrumental and the symbolic functions of language.

The **instrumental function** of language is its use as a tool, an instrument; languages can be used to do something, such as giving or receiving information or expressing emotions or desires. This is called the **informative function** of language, and it is very important for interpersonal and social interaction. Language can also be used as an instrument which people use to group themselves together or to separate themselves from others. This is called the **binding** or **separating function** of language. Finally, language can be an instrument that allows people to participate in activities and enjoy certain privileges. This is called the **participatory function** of language.

Language can also have a **symbolic function**. Usually, language symbolizes identity; for example, the language Kikuyu symbolizes being a member of the Gikuyu people or cultural group. In this sense, language functions like the national flag or the national anthem of a state. Some African states have national languages, which are said to represent the political identity of the people of that state. For example, Chishona and isiNdebele have been designated the national languages of Zimbabwe, which means that they symbolize being Zimbabwean, or holding Zimbabwean citizenship.

Our discussion of the social functions of language has been presented with the emphasis on the positive value of a language. However, it is possible for language to be used negatively. This occurs when language is used to deny people access to information, to manipulate people (for instance, to force people who speak a certain language to behave in a certain way), or to separate one group of people from another. If language is used in these ways, it can lead to problems.

The symbolic meaning of language can also have serious consequences, as happens in ethnic killings, when people are killed for speaking a certain language (because it symbolizes their membership of specific communities and therefore, supposedly, their political or ethnic loyalties). This happened in Kenya in 1992 and 1998, for example, when hundreds of people were killed during conflicts between the Gikuyu and the Kalenjin – because they belonged to the 'wrong' ethnolinguistic group. It is clear, therefore, that languages can play a role in social and political problems.

Now, if these problems become serious and the authorities want something to be done about them, the question is, who should handle them? Politicians will naturally be centrally involved. However, insofar as these problems have a linguistic facet, linguists will be needed to make a contribution. But in order to be able to contribute, linguists need to be specially trained.

A training programme that prepares linguists to help resolve language-related societal problems will entail, firstly, a study of the link between

language and society, and, secondly, a detailed study of the structural, functional, and social nature of languages. We can solve language-related societal
problems only if we understand how language works in society.

This, then, is the perspective from which this book operates. It follows a
'problem-solving' approach to linguistics, and, through that approach, seeks to
remove the discipline from the ivory tower, where it is mainly an intellectual
pursuit, and demonstrate the relevance of linguistics to resolving fundamental
problems in society. Furthermore, as said in the Introduction to this book,
African Voices is explicitly directed at Africa and aimed at equipping students
with the knowledge, skills, and attitudes necessary for tackling the continent's
many problems.

The instrumental and symbolic functions of language will be discussed in
the rest of the chapter. First a number of serious language-based problems
will be mentioned, followed by a discussion of the role that language plays in
these problems. Then some of the more important language problems will be
given attention. (The structural and functional character of languages will be
discussed in Chapters 6 to 11.)

Before discussing language-based problems and language problems, it is
necessary to distinguish clearly between them.

Language-based problems are not actually language problems, as will be
made clear in the following section. Rather, they are problems in the domains
of education, the economy, politics, or social life, but with a clear language
component. In other words, language plays a central role in their occurrence.
Language problems, on the other hand, are linguistic by definition; that is,
they have to do with the nature of language directly. Some examples are the
uncertainty some people feel about the appropriate way to speak in formal or
public situations, or the appropriate way to write formally (language standard-
ization/the norms of language); the unwillingness some people feel about
using their own languages in public places; the fact that some languages are not
yet adapted for use in certain domains, such as that of technology (a temporary
problem); and the social connotations of some languages. More information
on language problems will be given later in this chapter.

We end this first section with a series of questions that we hope will get you
thinking. In responding to these questions, make sure that you can provide
motivation for your views. Also try to support your views by providing facts
(or data) which are relevant to your argument. Refer, where possible, to the
functions of language, as discussed at the beginning of this section.

Questions

1   What was the language of instruction in the school you attended? Did you know it well? Or did you sometimes believe that you were at a disadvantage because you felt your knowledge of that language was inadequate?
2   Can the citizens of your country participate freely in its political life? And in economic life? Do you think that language plays a role in this regard? How?
3   The country you live in is almost certainly multilingual. What does this mean in individual and in societal terms?
4   Do you know anyone who tries to hide the fact that he or she is a speaker of a certain language? Or who has changed his or her name into a form that creates the impression that he or she is from a different linguistic community? If so, why did he or she do this?
5   Have you ever had the experience of someone refusing to talk to you in a certain language? If so, how can such behaviour be explained?

Language-based problems

In this section, four serious problems will be discussed. All four are aspects of the same larger problem, namely the inadequate development of Africa's human resources – educationally, economically, and politically. The discussion in this section will be largely based on information about South Africa, as the necessary information was readily available to the authors. It is likely, though, that the discussion will be applicable to the majority of African states.

In working through this section, you should make sure that you can perform the following three tasks:
• explain what the central issue is in each case;
• describe the role of language in the case of each problem; and
• give an appropriate example from the country you live in that illustrates the role of language in the occurrence of the problem.

The four language-based problems are:
• restricted access to knowledge and skills;
• low productivity and ineffective performance in the workplace;
• inadequate political participation by the public, manipulation, discrimination, and exploitation by the ruling powers, national division and conflict;
• linguistic and cultural alienation.

Restricted access to knowledge and skills

South Africa is ranked ninety-third in the *Global Human Development Ratings* by the United Nations Development Programme (Africa Institute 1996: 24) with a Human Development Index (HDI)[2] of 0.65 (0.462 for black South Africans), as compared with first-ranked Canada's figure of 0.932. This is not surprising, if one considers the following facts:

- In 1993, there were 15 million illiterate people in South Africa, measured in terms of those who had not completed seven years of formal education.
- The drop-out rate in 1988 for the first school year in black schools was 16.2 per cent (South African Institute of Race Relations 1990: 828).[3]
- In 1992, the mean period of schooling for the population over 25 years of age was 3.9 years.
- In 1994, approximately 5 million South Africans (of whom 3.5 million were black) above the age of four years had had no education at all, and only 1.7 million had some form of post-matriculation training. Only 1 per cent of the population had degrees.
- In 1993, the matriculation[4] pass-rate for black pupils was 39 per cent. In 1994, only 13 per cent of black pupils in their final school year passed well enough to be admitted to university.
- In 1992, 14 per cent of the teachers in black schools did not have a teaching diploma, and 57 per cent were underqualified.

Clearly, therefore, the cognitive development (the stock of knowledge and the mental skills) of many black South Africans was far below its potential. The same probably applied to their affective and social development.

Of course, there are a number of reasons for this educational underdevelopment, such as the fact that many schoolchildren grew up (and still do) in an illiterate or semi-literate environment, with almost no exposure to the world of learning, that their daily chores kept them from studying, that the educational system within which black South Africans were educated in the apartheid era was not conducive to the development of their full potential, that teachers were underqualified, and that school classrooms were overcrowded. Another contributing factor in South Africa is language.

The question we are concerned with is the role that language plays in educational underdevelopment.

It is generally accepted that cognitive development can occur effectively only in and through a language the learner knows very well. Cognitive skills, such as

- the ability to understand the central purpose of a text or to summarize its main line of argument;
- the ability to select information and to organize it into a new coherent whole;

- the ability to discover and formulate generalizations;
- the ability to understand abstract concepts and to manipulate them in arguments; and
- the ability to recognize relationships between events (for example, cause and effect)

can develop only in and through a familiar language. Such a language is generally the learner's first (or primary) language, the language he or she learnt as a child in his or her home.[5]

In spite of these generally accepted findings, black parents in South Africa overwhelmingly prefer English as the language of learning and teaching for their children, even in primary schools. The reasons for the preference for English among black South Africans are fairly self-evident: English is a world language, it provides access to almost all the sources of knowledge (school textbooks) and entertainment (literature, television, films), it is the most important language of work in the country, it allows one to communicate with billions of people all over the world, it is the language of the most successful people in the Western world, and it was the language of the struggle against apartheid.

These facts about English are clearly valid,[6] and it is essential that all South Africans be given the opportunity to acquire English to the best of their abilities. The high value placed on English, however, has led educational authorities and parents to decide that it has to be used as the language of learning and teaching (the medium of instruction) in schools as early as possible. In some schools, English is even used from the first day of primary education.

This decision has most likely contributed to the unacceptably low level of individual educational development in the country, since most black schoolchildren in South Africa simply don't know English well enough to be able to use it effectively as a language of learning and cognitive development. It has been argued (Webb 1996) that only 25 per cent of black South Africans are **functionally literate** in English (know it well enough to be able to use it effectively in public life) and can thus 'control' their destinies through the language.

The inadequacy of schoolchildren's English proficiency has been demonstrated in research findings. For instance, in a research project in primary schools in the former Zululand in 1987, it was found that Grade 5 pupils could generally not understand questions such as 'Where is your home?', 'Have you come (from) far?', 'What does your father do?', and 'In what standard are you?'; and 83.5 per cent of them could not understand their textbooks, according to their teachers. In another research project conducted in 1996 among teacher trainees in the four northern provinces of South Africa, it was found that, although English was to be their language of formal learning, only 5 per cent of them were functionally literate in English.

Quite clearly, therefore, in spite of a history of 150 years of English teaching in South Africa and vast expenditure on the English language business ($10 billion in 1989 internationally), proficiency in English is still inadequate in the case of black South Africans, preventing them from using it as an instrument of meaningful access to education.[7] Knowledge, skills, and opportunities have not been accessible to many, partly because they do not know the language they use for learning well enough.

The decision of school authorities and parents to use English as the language of learning in schools (especially primary schools) has definitely contributed to the underdevelopment of the South African people. One of the tasks that linguists in South Africa need to undertake is to persuade parents that the answer to their needs and those of their children lies in the use of a language of learning which their children know well, together with high-quality teaching of English as a subject.

Sociolinguists in other African countries, such as Nigeria, Cameroon, and Kenya, have expressed exactly the same views. It is also interesting to note that most non-English-speaking countries outside the African continent (such as Europe, China, and Japan) also do not use English as a language of learning and teaching, without their citizens being any less successful or civilized than other nations. However, they do invest strongly in the teaching of English as a second or foreign language.

Low productivity and ineffective performance in the workplace

South Africa is characterized by an unequal and uneven distribution of wealth. About half the population is considered to be poor, while 40 per cent of total consumption is accounted for by less than 6 per cent of the population. The country's economic development is thus not equitable. There are many reasons for this, one of which may be linguistic in nature.

The fact is that English is the dominant language of economic activity (almost exclusively so), yet less than 25 per cent of the black population know it well enough to be able to use it to participate in the economic life of the country. Similarly, the languages of 75 per cent of the country's people do not play any serious role in its economic activity. Either way, language is a barrier to the meaningful participation in the economy of South Africa by the vast majority of her people.

To get some idea of the seriousness of the situation, note the following research findings from the Eastern Cape in South Africa, where the dominant language is isiXhosa, a Nguni language closely related to isiZulu:

- Eighty-five per cent of the communication between employers and employees was between white and black respectively, yet only 4 per cent of the white workers knew isiXhosa.

- Nearly 50 per cent of the training officers couldn't speak isiXhosa, and 22 per cent used only English for training purposes.
- Half the organizations did not make information on pension schemes, insurance, or savings available in isiXhosa. (Some of the reasons given were that translation was time-consuming and costly, that black people were in any case illiterate, and that isiXhosa was not a technical language!)

It is clearly important from the perspective of redistributing wealth and facilitating access to occupational opportunities that the use of African languages in all areas of work life (training and skills development, work communication, contracts, public notification, and work-related documentation such as conditions of employment) should be seriously considered.

Unless African languages are used far more comprehensively in the economic life of South Africa, and African countries in general, the majority of citizens will remain outside the mainstream of economic life.

The important question to consider from the perspective of this book is what linguists can contribute to resolving the problem. (The answers will be given later on.) It is clear, however, that linguists need to become involved in language policy development and the adaptation of languages into effective instruments of technical and economic usage.

Inadequate political participation

From the perspective of democracy, Africa is underdeveloped not only educationally and economically, but also politically. For example, in spite of the fact that South Africa now has a democratically elected government and that its second democratic elections took place in 1999, there is as yet little evidence that the basic elements of a democratic state are significantly present in the country. For example, there is very little meaningful citizen participation in political decision-making; there are very few signs that the basic values and beliefs of democracy (such as respect for fundamental human rights, respect for opposing points of view, and the acceptance of decisions that may be contrary to sectarian interests) are operational to a meaningful extent; and the national community is still deeply divided, with strong potential for inter-group conflict.

One of the reasons for this underdevelopment is that the major language of political debate is English, which, as has been said, 75 per cent of the country's black citizens do not know adequately. In addition, language has been a useful tool for purposes of political manipulation, discrimination, and exploitation.

The strongest demonstration of the use of language for manipulative purposes was, of course, the policy of apartheid. While pretending that the philosophy of separateness was culturally based, the Nationalist government divided culturally similar black people into nine groups on linguistic grounds. Each of these groups was to be governed in a separate 'state' (the infamous 'Bantustans'). The culturally fragmented whites, on the other hand (and also the culturally disparate Indians), were politically grouped together. The policy of apartheid was a clear case of dividing people in order to retain control over them (the 'divide-and-rule' principle), and it is a good example of language-based political manipulation. The same can be seen in Kenya, where administrative districts are established on the basis of linguistic differences. For example, the Kuria are separated from the Luo, and the Teso from the Bukusu, for political reasons, while language is used as the criterion for marking these boundaries.

Discrimination on linguistic grounds is also easy to illustrate from South Africa. The fact that Afrikaans[8] (the main language of the former white government) and English have both been so dominant has led to their use for discriminatory purposes. This is especially true of the restriction of particular occupations (such as radio and television reporting, teaching, and the public service) to those who were fully proficient in the formal standard varieties of these two languages. These attitudes have begun to change with the recent democratization of the country, and public political figures, their spokespersons, and media people are no longer expected to follow the norms of Standard South African English exclusively. Yet, given the tendency of the privileged classes to protect their position, there is a very real chance that knowledge of English, given its exceptionally high status in both political circles and the general community, may continue to be used as a basis for potential discrimination. The implications of such a scenario are quite serious if one considers that almost the entire Asian population, 85 per cent of the 'coloured' population,[9] and probably 95 per cent or more of the white Afrikaans-speaking population of South Africa know English reasonably well. These groups will obviously once again be placed in an advantaged position.

The same situation exists in Kenya, where the language of political administration is English (although Kiswahili is used in communication between the ruling elite and the majority in the rural areas). Unfortunately, Kiswahili itself is as alien to most rural people as is English, and, even among those who claim to speak it, only a small proportion are fluent enough to engage in serious discussions with the police or the courts. The neglect of local languages thus puts those who speak them at a serious disadvantage when it comes to participating in official and public affairs.

As regards exploitation on linguistic grounds, there was the practice in the South African gold mines of using Fanagalo (a pidgin that apparently developed on the Natal sugar farms) as a medium for worker communication

(see also Chapter 2). Given that mineworkers usually come from diverse linguistic backgrounds in the southern African region, this policy was aimed at
increasing efficiency and therefore production. However, it also meant that, as
workers were not given the opportunity to learn English (or Afrikaans) adequately, they were severely restricted with respect to job prospects. This can
certainly be interpreted as exploitation. As an alternative, the mines could have
taught all their workers English, which would probably also have served the
interests of productivity, while at the same time increasing the miners' occupational (and social) opportunities. Today, another option could be to use the
indigenous African languages as the working languages of the mining industry,
particularly, in the short term, at the lower and middle levels. This would mean
that white foremen and managers would have to become relatively proficient
in the major Bantu languages of the mining industry.

Obviously, there are many more areas in which we will find general unfair-
ness, such as the courts of law, where all the proceedings were (and often still
are) only in Afrikaans and/or English (in spite of the opportunities to use
interpreters in other languages); in rural health services, where medical doctors
and psychologists are usually unable to speak to their patients in a language
with which the latter are familiar; and in farming, where farm labourers are
expected to use the language of the farmer.

Problems of conflict and nation-building

Language has also played a role in South Africa in the occurrence of conflict
and in the lack of national unity.

Conflict

In spite of the advent of political democracy in 1994, South Africa is still a
deeply divided and complex society, and there is still evidence of tension
between races and ethnic communities. This is partly due to pre-colonial
conflicts (between the Khoikhoi,[10] the San, and the Bantu-speaking people), as
well as the conflicts during colonial rule and the apartheid era. In all these cases
of conflict and division, language played some part. In apartheid South Africa,
as we have seen, language (together with race) was a basic divider of society. As
Herbert (1992) points out, some language boundaries in South Africa were
consciously created for political reasons. He shows that Sepedi (also called
'Northern Sotho'), one of the eleven official languages of democratic South
Africa, is actually a fiction. It was created by the Nationalist government, and
then standardized and adapted for higher-function use, to justify the apartheid
policy. It subsequently became the official language of Lebowa, the designated

'homeland' of the 'Sepedi-speakers'. Herbert argues that the linguistic differences between Sepedi and Setswana, its geographical and genetic neighbour, are smaller than the differences between some of the dialects within Sepedi itself. Linguistic autonomy therefore had more to do with socio-political criteria than with linguistic considerations.

Social divisions and potential for conflict are often fuelled by language as a symbol of socio-cultural identity. This seems to be a problem in many African countries, for example Nigeria (where the predominantly Igbo-speaking Biafra wanted to secede from the country), Angola, and the Democratic Republic of Congo (former Zaire). Language is not, of course, the direct cause of these conflicts, but it is a useful political tool, as it can easily be developed into a symbol of a particular political movement.

Nation-building

Most African states have experienced serious problems with the construction of national integration (or 'nation-building', as it is also called), and it is often argued that indigenous languages cannot play a role in national integration because of their divisive potential. As a result, political leaders usually decide to promote the ex-colonial language of the pre-independence era (English, French, or Portuguese) as the 'language of national integration', arguing that these languages are socio-culturally neutral and do not have the potential for stirring up conflict, as they are 'nobody's primary language'.

The exact role of language as an element of socio-cultural identity in African communities has not yet been adequately investigated. However, using South Africa as an example once again, a number of observations can be made about the social meaning of languages.

For example, the perception of language as an identity marker in South Africa differs between communities. In some Afrikaans-speaking communities, for instance, Afrikaans is regarded as an indispensable part of socio-cultural life (a belief expressed through statements of extreme language loyalty and 'language love'), while in others it is perceived merely as a tool or means of interaction. In many black communities, Afrikaans is regarded as a symbol of oppression, triggering anger and even resistance. These differing views lead to conflict, as can be seen in the recent tensions over the demand for single-medium Afrikaans schools, and for control of school curricula, prescribed texts, and the appointment of teachers, between the government and educational and cultural leaders in the white Afrikaans community.

The social meaning of English in South Africa is also ambivalent. On the one hand, it is a symbol of liberation, but, on the other, it is becoming a site of contestation, particularly because of the insistence that a specific set of language norms (namely 'British English') be applied.

In the Bantu language communities, ethnic self-awareness (and perhaps even linguistic nationalism) also seems to be emerging little by little. One example is the recent formation of a committee for marginalized languages. In spite of the recognition of Xitsonga, Tshivenda, and siSwati as national official languages, these three language communities, along with the isiNdebele-speaking people, have formed the Committee for Marginalized Languages, because of the sense they have of being threatened by Afrikaans and English, as well as by the other five 'big' Bantu languages. The seriousness of their intentions becomes apparent in the statement by their chairperson, in which it is said that the present debate on language policy and planning in South Africa

> implicitly tells the people who speak these [marginalized] languages that their languages are of very little, if any value at all. This could further stigmatize the people who speak the 'minor' official languages, hence perpetuating tribalism. To succeed in social and economic life, people who speak the 'minor' official languages will be increasingly under pressure to run away from their languages and cultural practices to associate themselves with one or two of the 'major' official languages. Alternatively, this may lead to a rise of **ethnic demagogues** among the people who speak the marginalized languages, unleashing extreme forms of ethnic chauvinism that may result in unwanted ethnic clashes. (Page 6 of a submission presented to the Language Plan Task Group (LANGTAG), a committee appointed by the government to develop a framework within which a national language policy could be developed)

A second, less overt, but equally dramatic example of the politicization of the South African languages was provided by a colleague, who reported that it is not unusual in the metropolitan areas of Gauteng (one of the provinces of South Africa), to find a speaker of isiZulu in conversation with a speaker of Setswana, each speaking their own language and refusing to accommodate the other in any way.

The possibility of linguistic and cultural alienation

The symbolic meaning of languages also plays a role in linguistic and cultural alienation in Africa. As pointed out above, African communities seem generally to be characterized by an exaggeratedly high esteem of the ex-colonial languages and an unwarrantedly low opinion of their own languages. This, plus the process of language contact and the asymmetric nature of the power relations between linguistic communities,[11] has the potential to lead to language shift, or reculturalization, and language death, hence the loss of cultural diversity. Many Africans want to be 'English', 'French', or 'Portuguese', and gradually begin using these languages more and more, and their own less and less – thus losing their African languages and identities.

The term **language shift** refers to a process in which the speakers of one language begin to use a second language for more and more functions, until they eventually use only the second language, even in personal and intimate contexts. Language shift becomes total when the second language becomes a symbol of the socio-cultural identity of these speakers. **Language death** occurs when all the speakers of a language have totally shifted their language behaviour, so that there are no persons left who still speak the original language as a first or primary language.

South Africa provides several examples of language shift. A first and extremely striking example is the almost total loss of the 'first languages' of southern Africa – the Khoikhoi and San languages – as distinct entities. Almost as dramatic is the shift in the Indian communities of KwaZulu-Natal away from Hindi, Gujarati, Urdu, Tamil, and Telegu to English (see Mesthrie 1992, 1995.) A third, rather ironic example is provided by Davey and Van Rensburg (1993), who discuss the elimination of Afrikaans as the primary language of a Tswana community near Rustenburg in the North West province. Although the people of this community were native speakers of Afrikaans (and could not speak Setswana), they were forced to relocate to a Setswana-speaking area by the Group Areas Act of the apartheid government. As a result, the children lost their native language and gradually (and against the wishes of their parents) became Setswana-speaking. Today, practically no one in the community speaks Afrikaans. The irony lies in the fact that the previous government was set on protecting Afrikaans, but in this case its political policies clashed with its language policies.

The language policy of a country can also sometimes cause language shift. In Kenya, English is the only language of instruction after the first three years of school, and is also the language of officialdom (together with Kiswahili). Kembo-Sure (1997) shows that this policy has led to a dramatic increase in the preference for and use of English, and has become a threat to the indigenous languages of Kenya, possibly leading to language shift away from them.

Since language and culture are closely connected, the occurrence of linguistic shift may lead to cultural shift: the alienation of people from their cultural identity, and, eventually, perhaps even the 'death' of a particular way of life. When this happens, a society seems to lose direction, often becoming victim to the twin evils of poverty and crime.

In bringing this section to a close, we would like to pose a number of questions, with the aim of helping you to develop your skills in collecting information and linguistic argumentation.

Questions

1 How many languages are spoken in your country of residence/citizenship?

2 Is there a link between any of these languages and the different social classes in your community? And is there any link between language and ethnic identity?

3 Are these languages regarded as 'major' or 'minor' languages? If so, what grounds are used to classify them in this way?

4 Have you experienced any social pressure to use a particular language in public, or not to use a particular language in public? If so, what could the reasons be?

5 In many societies in the world, people are said to be socially mobile, moving up the social ladder, or down it. Very often language plays a part in social mobility, for instance by acting as a barrier or a facilitator. Does language play this role in your society? Could you say that languages in your community or country restrict people's access to social rights and opportunities?

6 What is/are the official language(s) of your country? How well do you know it/them? How well do you know the other languages?

7 Can you think of any examples in your country of language(s) being used for purposes of discrimination, manipulation, and exploitation?

8 Have you ever felt that the language you speak in your personal life (with your family and your friends) is threatened in any way?

9 What can it mean to say that a language is threatened?

10 Sociolinguists often talk about language rights. What do you think they mean? Can you think of any rights we might call 'language rights'?

11 Consider the example mentioned above of an isiZulu-speaker and a Setswana-speaker who refuse to use each other's language, but continue to talk to each other. It could be argued that this situation sends a message of linguistic tolerance rather than conflict. Would you agree? If so, what are the reasons for your view?

12 The four language-related problems we have discussed here are not, of course, restricted to South Africa. They occur to greater or lesser extent in every African country. Look for examples of each in your own country, and write an essay, explaining the role of language in each case. South African readers might like to look for further examples in their own communities.

Language problems

The second main issue to be introduced in this chapter is the matter of language problems – in particular, language phenomena that have an impact on society. There are a large number of problems of this nature, and it is important that students of linguistics are made aware of them, and that they be provided with the knowledge, understanding, and skills needed to handle these problems.

As we cannot cover all the many different language problems in this chapter, we shall focus on three major ones: the insufficient adaptation of African languages, the politicization of languages, and language standardization.

Insufficiently adapted African languages

In general, African languages have an extremely low status, as shown above. Those who speak them do not believe that they can be used in public (or secondary) domains of life, as instruments of learning, economic activity, social mobility, or for any other serious public business. They often argue that their primary languages do not have the necessary vocabulary and speech styles, or sufficient status to be used spontaneously in public domains, and that it therefore makes no sense to study them at school. It is suggested that they are only useful as instruments of interpersonal social interaction and cultural expression within the community (the private or primary domains of life).

There are a variety of possible reasons for Africans' tendency not to believe in the value of their own possessions – their languages. According to Omotoso (1994: 15 and elsewhere), these reasons could include long-term factors such as slavery, the culturally destructive impact of the work of Christian missionaries, colonialism, and, in South Africa, apartheid. Because of the power of the colonial masters, it seems that everything associated with them, including their languages, became objects of great admiration.

Considered linguistically, these views are simply not justified. All languages are of equal value in the sense that they are perfectly adequate instruments for the expression of whatever their speakers wish to communicate, and in the sense that they are linguistically all equally complex. Unfortunately, however, linguistically uninformed persons lack this information; which is part of the reason so many Africans seem to have a firm belief in the inferiority of their languages.

Given that language plays such a fundamental role in the lives of people, it is important to ask what can be done about this problem. One answer is that a major programme of **language revalorization**[12] is necessary. Such a programme would be designed to raise both the functional usefulness and the prestige – the social status – of African languages (see Webb 1994). In order to design such a programme, we need comprehensive linguistic knowledge and skills. For example, we must understand the relationship between language and society, and what language means in the lives of people. We must also know how languages can be adapted in terms of vocabularies and functions (see Chapter 5).

The adaptation of languages forms part of what is often called **corpus** and **status planning**. Corpus planning refers to the determination of standards and norms for a language, as well as the introduction of new words and technical terms; status planning refers to authoritative decisions to use a language for important official functions, thereby enhancing its social prestige.

The politicization of a country's languages

It is fairly common for languages to become associated with particular political philosophies or programmes, and thus to attain particular political meanings. When this happens, they are said to have become 'politicized'.

The problem of politicized languages (and unequal or asymmetric power relations, mentioned above) in South Africa manifests itself in many ways. These include the unevenness in the knowledge of the country's languages; the strong ethnic nationalism associated with Afrikaans in particular, and the negative socio-political connotations of Afrikaans for many communities; the generally extremely positive socio-political status of English; the generally very low socio-educational status of the Bantu languages; and the strong drive towards linguistic 'purism' (in Afrikaans, English, and isiZulu, as well as some of the other languages). In Kenya, this problem is seen in the reluctance to use community languages in public places, even when those speaking share a mother tongue. This is particularly true of the urban centres. It is interpreted as a sign of tribal chauvinism (see also Chapter 3).

In general, there is some degree of ethnolinguistic intolerance in most multilingual African countries, with stigmatization and stereotyping of some language communities by others. In South Africa, this has been particularly true of the different racial groups, but it is also found with regard to language communities. Many white Afrikaans-speakers are markedly antagonistic towards their English-speaking cohorts, whereas white English-speakers can be highly contemptuous in return, with negative references to Afrikaans-speaking persons formulated in 'linguistic' terms (for example, 'There's this Afrikaner cow at work...'). Ethnic intolerance is also mirrored in racially directed reference terms. Given South Africa's history of racial conflict, the terms used to refer to the different racial groups have become extremely problematic.

For instance, Afrikaans-speaking whites are called *Boers*, which has a pejorative meaning for some, but evokes fierce pride in others; English-speaking South Africans are negatively referred to as *rooinekke* (which translates as *rednecks*) or *the English*; black South Africans as *kaffirs* (a name publicly banned by the president of the country); Indians as *coolies*; and coloured people as *boesmans* ('Bushmen') and *hotnots* (from 'Hottentot', a name formerly used to describe the descendants of the Khoikhoi). Even terms such as *Bantu*, *Khoikhoi,* and *San* have negative connotations, and it has been pointed out, for example, that *San* is a Khoikhoi word which formerly meant 'tramp', 'rascal', 'vagabond', or 'forager'. Naming is thus always an instrument in the exercise of power, and as such needs to be dealt with in public education programmes.

Afrikaans provides a strong example of linguistic nationalism. Although the language has deep historical roots in the country's coloured (formerly largely Khoikhoi and slave) communities, it was appropriated[13] by the white political intelligentsia of the past as an instrument of political mobilization. In the process, Afrikaans was ideologized and mythologized into a 'White Man's Language'. In the process of its 'standardization', its non-white speakers were reclassified as speakers of non-standard Afrikaans, the language was purged (supposedly purified) of foreign elements (especially English elements), and it became a symbol of a particular socio-cultural identity (that of the Afrikaner). This latter association has become so strong that Afrikaner leaders often see any changes relating to Afrikaans (for instance, regarding its public functions, or the acceptance of supposedly non-standard elements) as a threat to the integrity of the cultural identity of the Afrikaans people. Hardly surprisingly, Afrikaans has become schizophrenic, with increasing alienation between 'cultured' – or, more accurately, culturalized – formal standard Afrikaans on the one hand, and colloquial Afrikaans on the other. This internal division has led to internal language conflict, which has had serious educational consequences for children who grew up in coloured working-class families, as the language they grew up with in the intimacy of their homes and friendships is not the same as the rigidly standardized 'white' language insisted upon in the schools. These children therefore have a legacy of being constantly told that they do not 'speak properly', and that if they speak in 'that way', they are displaying their backwardness. (See Chapters 5 and 11 for a further discussion of the relationship between language and culture.)

The politicized nature of South African languages has several significant consequences. Firstly, it means that these languages can't perform their social functions fully (such as serving as instruments of national integration, or effective instruments of access in public domains). Secondly, it obstructs both horizontal and vertical lines of communication (for example, communication between coloured and white speakers of Afrikaans, or between lower-level speakers, such as factory workers, and higher-level speakers, such as managers). Thirdly, it means that languages may well play a role in future conflicts.

The politicization of the country's languages has also led to the politicization of other language-related phenomena, such as the issue of the language of learning and teaching (in particular, the principle of mother-tongue instruction) and ethnicity. The extent and degree of this politicization makes these issues extremely contentious, so that it is difficult to debate them publicly, as any support for the use of a first language as a language of learning and teaching, or concern expressed about threats to the country's linguistic and cultural diversity, is immediately interpreted as an attempt to divide people, to continue holding back the disadvantaged, and to keep political control in the hands of whites, thus reinstating apartheid.

The same phenomenon can be seen in Kenya, where two people from one language background are forced to use English or Kiswahili when speaking in public to avoid being branded as tribalists. Speaking one's mother tongue in the presence of those who do not speak it is considered politically imprudent; in other words, it has become stigmatized.

It is worth noting that in multilingual societies that have reached a high degree of sophistication, and where language groups do not feel insecure or threatened, language choice does not appear to be an issue when people talk to each other. In Switzerland, for instance, French-speaking Swiss are said to switch to German in German-speaking communities without any hesitancy, and vice versa. Swiss society seems to have reached a remarkable level of linguistic tolerance. The same tolerance is shown towards English in Switzerland, as recent investigations show that English is being used more and more in the business world. In fact, secretaries who are proficient in English earn considerably more than their counterparts who do not know English well.

Language standardization

Language standardization is the process by which an authoritative language body (such as a government-appointed body) prescribes how a language should be written (its orthography – see Chapter 6), how its sounds should be pronounced, how its words should be spelt, which words are acceptable in formal situations, and what the appropriate grammatical constructions of the language are. This body thus intervenes in the regularization of the grammar, vocabulary, pronunciation, and writing system of the language. The basis upon which language bodies make their decisions is very often the linguistic behaviour of the dominant community in the society, and it is the variety spoken by these people that generally becomes the standard language of the broader community.

The term **language codification** is also used in conjunction with standardization. Codification refers to the description of the norms and standards of a language in dictionaries, grammar books, manuals, and thesauruses.

For example, in East Africa, the Kiswahili that was spoken on the islands of Zanzibar and Pemba (and which is called Kiunguja) was selected in 1927 as the standard for the whole region. The chosen form was then taught in schools and used in the mass media and in all public official communication. Kiunguja thus became the standard for Kiswahili throughout East Africa, although people have retained their local varieties in private communication at home and in their neighbourhoods.

The issue of standardization is crucial for more reasons than simply its function as a set of practical guidelines for appropriate public verbal behaviour. Given the politicization of languages, language norms determine the content of language teaching programmes, can determine career appointments, can act as a basis for discrimination, and can affect the degree to which people are taken seriously in public debate.

In South Africa, the recent heated public reaction to the use of radio broadcasters whose English was not considered standard 'British English' is a good example, and this is still a major issue. While English is generally accepted as the language of public preference, there are differences about 'what English' should be used. At a recent conference (Johannesburg, 1997), a young black South African delivered a paper entitled 'English? Yes. But whose English? Your English? Or mine?' His message could be summed up as follows: 'We are governing this country now, and we will decide what English is acceptable. If you don't like our decisions, you can leave the country quite easily. There are no lions at the Johannesburg International Airport, and an air ticket to London is relatively cheap.' This attitude is, of course, extreme, but it does illustrate the intensity of the debate – which is understandable, given the colonial history of the country.

A second emotive issue in South Africa is the debate about the **harmonization** of the languages of the two main language families in the country, the Nguni (isiNdebele, siSwati, isiZulu, and isiXhosa) and the Sotho languages (Sepedi, Sesotho (also called 'Southern Sotho'), and Setswana). About sixty years ago, a proposal was made that the Nguni and Sotho languages should be harmonized internally. In other words, a single variety common to all the languages within each of these families should be developed, as a way of facilitating closer unity between the different language communities in the black sectors of the population. This suggestion has recently been revived, and has since been heatedly debated and rejected by many language workers. One problem is that the call for harmonization is often wrongly interpreted. In fact, the proposal envisages the creation of a common written variety for each of the two major Bantu language families, to be used in school textbooks and in formal documents. The proposal certainly has political undertones (those of 'black unity'), but also has clear economic advantages. It has the support of some sociolinguists, but has been rejected by many leading figures in the Bantu language communities, mainly, it seems, because harmonization is perceived as a threat to their socio-cultural (and perhaps their political) identity. This perception is unfounded, because the proposal is not intended to take anything away from any community. Rather, it intends to add something, by creating a language variety that will make it possible to publish all educational material for Nguni and Sotho pupils, respectively, in one written language, thus making possible a considerable saving of time, effort, and cost.

A third example of problems with standardization concerns the selection of the basic variety for the standardization of the Bantu languages. In most cases, the 'natural' standardization route was chosen, and a dominant dialect was used as the basis for standardization. This was the case with Sepedi (which was based on the Pedi dialect) and Tshivenda (which was based on Tsiphani). However, as a result of this approach, internal language tension is building up, with speakers of the non-standard dialects feeling marginalized.

Any linguistic discussion of the problems relating to standardization should look into the underlying factors. These could include the colonial past of the African states; the grouping of linguistically disparate communities into the same states, and linguistically related groups into separate states; and the development of economically and politically powerful communities alongside economically and politically powerless communities, leading to asymmetric power relations between neighbouring communities.

An important linguistic factor is the extremely multilingual nature of African societies, in the form of both individual and societal multilingualism (respectively, the fact that individuals know more than two languages, and the fact that more than two languages are used in a particular community). As pointed out above, this forms the roots of problems such as internal language conflict, the overvaluation and undervaluation of certain languages, the appropriation of standard languages, and ineffective second- and third-language acquisition, as well as issues such as language shift, language maintenance, language death, and linguicide. Multilingualism also has linguistic consequences, which may or may not be regarded as problems. Some of these are discussed in Chapter 5.

Once again, we close this section with a number of questions and tasks.

Questions and tasks

1   Do you think that African languages are inferior to English, French, and Portuguese? What arguments can you provide to support your answer? Are your arguments valid from a linguistic perspective?

2   The success with which people learn foreign languages is sometimes explained with reference to the market value of these languages: English, French, and Portuguese are acquired relatively easily because people who are proficient in them know that they can get better jobs or higher wages; in other words, they satisfy people's economic and social needs. Is this true in your country? Is there a pattern in the acquisition of foreign languages that can be explained in this way?

3   Discuss the level of ethnolinguistic tolerance in your country. Be sure to provide factual support for every statement you make. Also try to give reasons for your views.

4   Is there any evidence of purism in your language community? Can you explain its presence or absence?

5   Who decides on the norms and standards in your language community? Is there any disagreement among the members of this community about these standards and norms?

6   In the section on the politicization of languages, three consequences were mentioned. Can you illustrate each of these consequences? How, for instance, can language politicization obstruct horizontal and vertical communication?

7   Are there any signs in your country of ethnic consciousness? If so, why? Is this a positive phenomenon? If not, why not?

8   Are there people in your community who are considered not to speak 'properly'? If so, is this sometimes attributed to lack of intelligence?

9   Can the attitudes of people towards languages be changed? How? (An adequate answer to this question will clearly illustrate the importance of linguistics in society, as attitudes are deeply embedded in the human psyche, and cannot easily be changed. To work out a strategy for doing so requires an insight into the place which language occupies in human life.)

10   Give examples from the region in which you live of (a) disparate language communities grouped together in one country, and (b) language communities broken up by political boundaries. What are the linguistic consequences of these groupings and divisions?

11   Would you say that the study of ritual language can contribute in any way to our understanding of how language works in society?

Conclusion

To conclude this first chapter, it is necessary to discuss the task of the linguist in contributing to the resolution of language-based problems and language problems. The role of the linguist will of course vary in these two cases.

In the case of language-based problems, the linguist's main task should be to provide information about relevant language issues to the decision-makers (the parents of schoolchildren, educational authorities, economic leaders, the government, and so forth) – about, for instance, the role of language in educational development, economic performance, access to social rights and privileges, and political participation. In order to make a convincing case, linguists will need a thorough understanding of the relationship between language and society. They will also have to obtain the relevant information, either through a detailed study of the applicable literature or by conducting research. They need to know what knowledge is available, what still needs to be uncovered, how the necessary information should be gathered, how the collected data should be analysed and interpreted, and so on.

In the case of language problems, an understanding of how human languages work, what they consist of, and how the different constituent parts fit together is indispensable. This can be illustrated with two examples. Firstly, if a community whose language does not yet exist in written form wishes to learn to read and write, the assistance of a linguist is necessary to develop an appropriate orthography, to analyse and describe the grammar of the language, to produce dictionaries, to develop the appropriate norms for reading and writing, and to develop literacy programmes.

Secondly, if a linguistic community wishes its language to be adapted so that it can be used in the modern technological world, it is necessary to know how technical words can be borrowed or formed, and how they can spread through the community for general use. It will also be necessary to understand that the existence of technical terms is not enough, and that technical ways of thinking and speaking must also be developed, which means that the members of the linguistic community must acquire the necessary technical literacy.

If students of linguistics therefore wish to be able to contribute to resolving the language problems of Africa, and its language-based problems, they need to acquire a basic knowledge of linguistics and language study, and to be trained in linguistic skills, such as identifying and defining linguistic problems, and analysing and describing language phenomena. They also need a working knowledge of linguistic research methodology, and the ability to find available knowledge about the languages of Africa.

As an introductory textbook, *African Voices* hopes to equip its student readers with the rudiments of the necessary knowledge and skills. In addition, we want to make students aware of higher-level sources of information in Africa.

We thus provide a list of some associations which focus primarily on African languages, and a brief list of some basic reference works.

The associations are: Afrilex, which focuses on the lexicography of the African languages (see Chapter 8), the African Languages Association of Southern Africa (ALASA), the Linguistics Association of SADC Universities (LASU), the West African Linguistics Society (WALS), the World Congress of African Linguists (WOCAL), the Annual Conference on African Linguistics (ACAL), and the Summer Institute of Linguistics (SIL).

Endnotes

1   Languages also have other types of functions. For instance, when they are used to express emotions or attitudes, they can be said to function psychologically, and when they are used to make sense of one's thoughts or to give order to one's arguments, they can be said to function cognitively.

2   The HDI is based on longevity, knowledge (adult literacy, mean years of schooling), and the standard of living (purchasing power).

3   The term *black* is used here (and elsewhere in this book) when discussing South Africa, mainly because race was (and still is) such a basic determining factor in the country, due to its political policies since 'union' in 1910. The term is also used because many of the differences between South Africans (in terms of education and wealth, for example) are race-related.

4   *Matriculation* means, strictly speaking, passing the final school examination well enough to satisfy the entrance requirements for university admission. In South Africa, the word is also used to refer to passing the examination in the final school year (Grade 12, or Standard 10).

5   The term *mother tongue* is often used to refer to this language. We avoid this term because its meaning in the African context is not clear, and because it has negative connotations in South Africa, having been misused in apartheid ideology.

6   The value of English is often overestimated, and a simple knowledge of English is often equated with 'success' and 'being civilized', as can be seen in the following quotation:

'[T]o be educated and trained means having acquired knowledge and expertise mainly through the medium of English' (Professor Abram L. Mawasha, University of the North, South Africa).

7   The reasons for the poor knowledge of English are clear: a restricted exposure to English (especially in rural areas), lack of motivation to learn English (an inevitable result of the preceding reason), generally inadequately trained teachers, inappropriate second-language teaching methodologies, inadequate educational facilities and learning materials, and overcrowded classrooms. It is clear that the apartheid system of education wreaked total havoc in the country.

8   For readers not familiar with South Africa, about six million people in southern Africa, of whom 50 per cent are white, speak Afrikaans. Afrikaans has its origins in the Dutch spoken by the seventeenth-century settlers, which then spread (and was shaped) through contact with the aboriginal Khoikhoi peoples and the slaves imported from various parts of Africa and the East.

9   Non-South African readers should note that the term *coloured* refers to people of mixed racial descent, and not to all black people, as is the case in the UK and North America. (In South Africa, it is also less pejorative than in North America.) There are about three million people in South Africa who were classified as coloured during the apartheid era, 85 per cent of whom are Afrikaans-speaking, with the remainder being English-speaking.

10 There is some disagreement about the most appropriate form of this name, with some scholars using the form *Khoen*. In this book, the form *Khoikhoi* will be used.

11 The term *asymmetric power relations* refers to the inequality between two (or more) social groups in terms of their relative power, for instance their economic or their political power. In South Africa the English-speaking community (including anyone who knows English well) 'controls' the economy, entertainment, sport, and so forth, and is extremely powerful, whereas communities who are speakers of a Bantu language are relatively weak in all public domains, and 'control' a very small portion of public life.

12 The prefix *re-* is used here since African languages presumably did have value for their speakers before slavery, colonialism, and the impact of Christian missionaries took their toll.

13 The term *appropriate* as used here means 'taking over as an exclusive possession'. In the case of Afrikaans, the white rulers ignored the fact that three million coloured South Africans also 'owned' Afrikaans.

Basic linguistic reference books

ADEGBIJA, EFORUSIBINA. 1994. *Language Attitudes in sub-Saharan Africa*. Clevedon: Multilingual Matters.

ALEXANDRE, P. 1967. *An Introduction to Languages and Language in Africa*. Nairobi: Heinemann.

BAMGBOSE, AYO. 1991. *Language and the Nation: The Language Question in sub-Saharan Africa*. Edinburgh: Edinburgh University Press.

HARTMANN, R. 1990. *Lexicography in Africa*. Exeter: Exeter University Press.

HERBERT, ROBERT K. (ed.). 1992. *Language and Society in Africa: The Theory and Practice of Sociolinguistics*. Johannesburg: Witwatersrand University Press.

KASHOKI, MUBANGA E. 1990. *The Factor of Language in Zambia*. Lusaka: Kenneth Kaunda Foundation.

LADEFOGED, PETER, RUTH GLICK, and CLIVE

CRIPER (eds.). 1972. *Language in Uganda*. Oxford: Oxford University Press.

MAZRUI, ALI, and ALAMIN MAZRUI. 1995. *Swahili State and Society*. Nairobi: East African Education Publishers.

OHANNESSIAN, SIRARPI, and MUBANGA E. KASHOKI. 1978. *Language in Zambia*. London: International African Institute.

POLOMÉ, EDGAR C., and C.P. HILL (eds.). 1980. *Language in Tanzania*. Oxford: Oxford University Press.

RUBAGUMYA, C.M. (ed.) 1990. *Language in Education in Africa: A Tanzanian Perspective*. Clevedon: Multilingual Matters.

SCHMIED, J. 1986. *English in Africa: An Introduction*. London: Longman.

SPENCER, JOHN. (ed.) 1963. *Language in Africa*. Cambridge: Cambridge University Press.

WHITELEY, W.H. (ed.) 1974. *Language in Kenya*. Nairobi: Oxford University Press.

Bibliography

AFRICA INSTITUTE. 1996. *Africa at a glance. Facts and Figures. 1995/6*. Pretoria: Africa Institute of South Africa.

DAVEY, L., and M.C.J. VAN RENSBURG. 1993. 'Afrikaans, sy ondergang in Thlabane' [Afrikaans, its demise in Thlabane]. *Tydskrif vir Letterkunde* [Journal for Literature] 31, 3: 25–40.

KEMBO-SURE. 1997. *English in Kenya*. Unpublished manuscript.

MESTHRIE, RAJEND. 1992. *English in Language Shift: the History, Structure and Sociolinguistics of South African Indian English*. Cambridge: Cambridge University Press.

———— (ed.) 1995. *Language and Social History: Studies in South African Sociolinguistics*. Cape

Town and Johannesburg: David Philip.

OMOTOSO, KOLE. 1994. *Season of Migration to the South*. Cape Town: Nasionale Pers.

SOUTH AFRICAN INSTITUTE OF RACE RELATIONS. 1990. *Race Relations Survey. 1989/90*. Johannesburg: South African Institute of Race Relations.

WEBB, V.N. 1994. 'Revalorizing the Autochthonous Languages of Africa.' In Martin Pütz (ed.), *Language Contact and Language Conflict*. Amsterdam: John Benjamins, 181–203.

——— 1996. English and language planning for South Africa. In Vivian de Klerk (ed.), *Focus on South Africa*. Amsterdam/Philadelphia: John Benjamins, 175–190.

2 The languages of Africa

Vic Webb and Kembo-Sure

Expected outcomes

At the end of this chapter you should be able to:
1 Draw a map of Africa, indicating the constituent states and showing where the major languages of the continent are to be found.
2 Discuss the number and locality of the languages of the continent.
3 Begin to construct a description of the origin of the languages in your country.
4 Explain the grip which English, French, or Portuguese has on the people of your country.
5 Provide information on the social functions of the major languages in selected African states.
6 Construct a sociolinguistic profile of your country.

In this chapter, we want to introduce you to the languages of Africa. Given the restrictions of an introductory text, we cannot, of course, provide full information on all the languages of the continent. So we have made our own selection, based on the information readily available to us. As you will see later, however, one of the tasks we suggest that you undertake is to compile descriptions similar to the ones we provide, of the countries you know well.

The following questions will be discussed in this chapter:

- How many languages are there in Africa, and where are they located?
- Are they related in any way?
- Why do the ex-colonial languages have such a grip on the African people?
- What is the general sociolinguistic[1] character of the African states?

The chapter ends with brief sociolinguistic profiles of selected African countries.

How many languages are there in Africa?

In order to obtain a proper perspective on the languages of Africa, the larger linguistic picture must be taken into account; we must first take note of the languages of the world. Table 2.1 shows information provided by the British linguist David Crystal about the number of languages spoken in the world as first languages, arranged according to the size of their speaker numbers, for a world population of more than 5 000 million (Crystal 1997: 286).

TABLE 2.1 Number of languages in the world by size of speaker numbers (as first language)

More than 1 million speakers	283
100 000–1 million speakers	616
10 000–99 999 speakers	1 364
1 000–9 999 speakers	1 631
1–999 speakers	1 495
Extinct languages	310
No estimate of speaker numbers	905
TOTAL	6 604

As a matter of interest, Mandarin Chinese has the largest number of first-language speakers in the world (726 million),[2] with English second (427 million) and Spanish third (266 million). Of the other major ex-colonial languages of Africa, Portuguese is sixth (165 million) and French eleventh (116 million) in the world (Crystal 1997: 289). If second-language speakers are taken into account, English then occupies first place, with more than 800 million speakers.

In Africa, about 2 000 languages are spoken as first languages by more than 480 million people (Crystal 1997: 316). Seventy-two of these languages have more than 1 million speakers each (Crystal 1997: 443–451). Sixteen are spoken by 5 million or more people. The ten most extensively spoken languages are Arabic (180 million speakers worldwide, with the exact figures for Africa not provided; spoken mainly in Morocco, Algeria, Tunisia, Libya, and Egypt); Hausa (25 million, Nigeria); Yoruba (20 million, Nigeria); Amharic (14 million, Ethiopia); Igbo (12 million, Nigeria); Oromo or Galla, a Cushitic language (10.6 million, Ethiopia and Kenya); Malagasy (10 million, Madagascar); Lingala (8.4 million, Democratic Republic of Congo, Congo, and Central African Republic); isiZulu (8 million, South Africa); and, in joint tenth position, isiXhosa (7 million, South Africa) and Chishona (7 million, Zimbabwe and adjoining regions). Following these are Luba-Kasai (6.3 million,

Democratic Republic of Congo); Kinyarwanda (6.2 million, Rwanda); and Afrikaans (6 million, South Africa).

If speaker numbers are calculated in terms of second-language knowledge, a different picture emerges. Arabic, Hausa, and Lingala are still major languages, but languages such as Bambara-Malinka and Wolof (both spoken in West Africa), and Kikongo (central Africa) become significant, as they are widely used for communication between speakers of different languages. In East Africa, Kiswahili (which has about 5 million first-language speakers) is used by about 30 million people, and in South Africa the Nguni languages (isiZulu, isiXhosa, and others) are used by at least 25 million people. Besides these aboriginal languages, English, French, and Portuguese must also be mentioned as second languages. At certain levels of public communication, one can probably get by with one of these ex-colonial languages almost anywhere in sub-Saharan Africa. Languages like these, which are used widely for inter-group communication, are generally called **languages of wider communication** (LWC), and sometimes **lingua francas**. (A lingua franca is a language that is used as a medium of communication by people who speak different first languages.)

The previous two paragraphs may give the impression that the number of languages in Africa and the numbers of their first- and second-language speakers can be determined quite accurately. This is not the case, however; there is in fact quite a large degree of uncertainty about these figures, and many linguists differ in their views regarding the identity of the languages of Africa, their number, and their speaker numbers. Why is this so?

The first and most practical reason is that the available information is simply not adequate. If we consider the inaccessibility of some communities deep in the rural areas of Africa, it is easy to understand why it is difficult to obtain accurate information.

Secondly, the concept of **language** has not yet been defined,[3] that is, described in such a way that the definition enables one to decide unambiguously which forms of human communication can be categorized as belonging to the same 'language' and which as *not* belonging to the same 'language'. There are several problems in this regard.

In the first place, the term *language* is often used (particularly by linguistically untrained people) to refer to what is regarded as 'proper language' or 'correct language', which is usually a variety prescribed by language teachers as the appropriate form for communication in formal situations. Such a view usually excludes **vernacular** forms of speech: the varieties used in everyday life, often containing features not regarded as 'proper' or 'correct'. In a similar vein, the term is sometimes taken to mean what linguists call **standard language**, which is the variety accepted by various groups as the appropriate form of speaking or writing. (This term should not be confused with the sense described first, as, technically, standard language is not necessarily regarded as strictly 'proper' or 'correct'.) If the term *language* is used to refer only to the standard variety, all the **non-standard varieties** of a language are obviously excluded, thus directly affecting a language count.

Thirdly, there is the matter of **dialects**. Dialects are varieties of a language used in specific geographical areas or by particular social groups, and the speakers of the dialects of a particular language can usually understand one another even though each speaks his or her own variety. The criterion for classifying dialects as varieties of the same language is thus **mutual comprehensibility** (or intelligibility). Given how hard it is to exactly determine mutual comprehensibility, the boundaries between varieties are vague, which means that it is often difficult to be definite about the mutual relationship between dialects. A particular linguistic variety may thus be categorized by one linguist as a language and by another as a dialect. (See also the discussion in Chapter 4, as well as the remarks quoted from Herbert in Chapter 1.)

Fourthly, the enumeration of languages is affected by the existence of **pidgins**, which are 'incidental' modes of communication that usually arise in situations where people from three different language communities (who do not share a language) need to communicate with one another – for purposes of work, for instance (see also Chapters 3 and 4). Examples of pidgins are Kisettla, which black workers and white farmers in Kenya used to communicate with each other, and Fanagalo, spoken on the mines in South Africa. Pidgins are not spoken as first or primary languages, and they are nobody's mother tongue. Can they then be said to be languages, and counted as such in language surveys? Or are they just ways of speaking, of communicating in specific contexts? Let's look a little more closely at Fanagalo, the vehicle of communication between mineworkers and mine managers in South Africa. Fanagalo came into existence when people from India arrived in the country to work on the sugar-cane farms on the east coast, and needed to communicate with both the isiZulu-speaking local population and the English-speaking farmers. In this three-way contact situation, a pidgin arose. As it was easy to learn, Fanagalo soon spread to the gold mines of the Johannesburg region, and came to be used as a vehicle of communication in this particular context. The mining authorities realized its value as a cross-linguistic means of communication, and decided to teach it to all new mineworkers, which meant that grammars and dictionaries were compiled, and educational material was developed. Should Fanagalo now be counted as a language? Millions of black South Africans would be unhappy if this were to happen, as Fanagalo is a highly stigmatized phenomenon, associated mainly with situations in which black people are in subordinate positions and white people in superior positions as employers (see also Mesthrie 1995). Given views such as these, it is uncertain whether these instruments of communication should be regarded as languages or not.

Finally, the concept of language is largely a 'political' concept; this means that its status depends on its 'official' recognition as a language (in schools, in the media, or in government circles). For example, Afrikaans (spoken in South Africa) and Dutch (spoken in the Netherlands) are linguistically reasonably similar and are mutually comprehensible (in writing and through careful speech). So it could be argued that they are one and the same language. However, members of both language communities would strongly protest against such a classification, largely for cultural and political reasons, and because they are used in vastly different geographical areas.

Given these problematic issues, the numbers quoted above must be seen as tentative. They are estimates or rough guides. This point is neatly illustrated by the following cases. According to the Africa Institute in Pretoria, South Africa, the 2 000 languages in Africa can be reduced to a few hundred if related languages are grouped together. For instance, their research shows that there are 22 language clusters spoken by ten million people each, and 85 languages spoken by more than one million speakers each. The number of languages with at least two million speakers each is less than 100. Secondly, research being undertaken in Cape Town under the supervision of the Ghanaian sociologist Kwasi Prah places the number of African languages in the hundreds (rather than the thousands), on the basis of the criterion of mutual comprehensibility.[4]

A final consideration that makes it difficult to give an exact figure when counting languages is the uncertainty about whether all languages should be counted. Should we count the 143 extinct languages that Crystal mentions? Or the San languages in South Africa, which were almost extinct, but which now seem once more to be returning due to migrations from Namibia and Botswana? And what about languages spoken in a country by migrant workers or illegal immigrants? Should we count languages spoken per state, and then simply add together state totals, or should we count a language spoken in more than one state as one language? Trying to specify how many languages there are in Africa is therefore a rather intricate task.

Are the languages of Africa related to one another?

When we talk about languages being 'related' to one another, we mean that they are lexically and structurally similar; words referring to the same objects sound similar (are 'phonetically related' – see Chapter 6), and their words and sentences are formed in similar ways (see Chapter 8). For example, Afrikaans and English are related, as can be seen from the following examples:

My pen is in my hand. (Afrikaans)
My pen is in my hand. (English)

These two sentences have exactly the same lexical items, the same word order, and exactly the same meaning. (Phonetically, however – that is, in terms of the pronunciation of the words – they are different.) Languages that are lexically and structurally similar, like Afrikaans and English, are thus said to be related, and to belong to the same **language family**.

Many of the languages of Africa are related in this way. Generally speaking, they are grouped into four language families. These are Afro-Asiatic, Nilo-Saharan, Khoisan, and Niger-Congo. The latter family is in turn divided into two sub-families, here called Niger-Congo A and Niger-Congo B (Bantu). The linguistic diversity of Africa is shown on the map below.

As it is necessary for you, as apprentice linguists in Africa (and elsewhere), to know something about the four language families on the continent, brief notes about each are provided.

1 The **Afro-Asiatic languages** (previously called the Hamito-Semitic languages) include the Semitic languages, the Cushitic languages, Berber, and the Chadic languages. The major Semitic language is Arabic, which is the language of Islam, studied and used throughout the Islamic world. Amharic, an official language of Ethiopia, is also a Semitic language. The Cushitic family includes Oromo (also called Gala) and Somali (spoken in Somalia, Ethiopia, Kenya, and northern Tanzania). The best-known Chadic language is Hausa, which is spoken in West Africa, particularly in Nigeria. The 300 languages of this family are spoken by 250 million speakers, and were introduced into Africa in the seventh century, after the Islamic invasions.

2 The **Nilo-Saharan languages** are spoken, as the name of the family suggests, along the higher reaches of the Nile River, and are found in Sudan, Ethiopia, Uganda, Kenya, and northern Tanzania. They include Turkana, Samburu, Kipsigis, and Nandi (spoken in Kenya); Dholuo and Maasai (spoken in Kenya and Tanzania); Padhola and Acholi (spoken in Uganda); and Dinka, Pari, and Nuer (spoken in Sudan). In total, 30 million people speak the hundred or more Nilo-Saharan languages.

3 The **Khoisan languages** of the Khoikhoi (called Hottentots in colonial times) and the San (also called Bushmen), number about fifty, each spoken by 1 000 people on average. They are regarded as the 'first languages' of southern Africa, having been spoken there for 8 000 years. Today they are used mainly in Namibia, Botswana, and Angola, but are also found in Tanzania. Since this language family consists of such distinctive and rather rare (in fact, almost endangered) languages, we want to provide slightly more information about them.

FIGURE 2.1 Africa's linguistic diversity

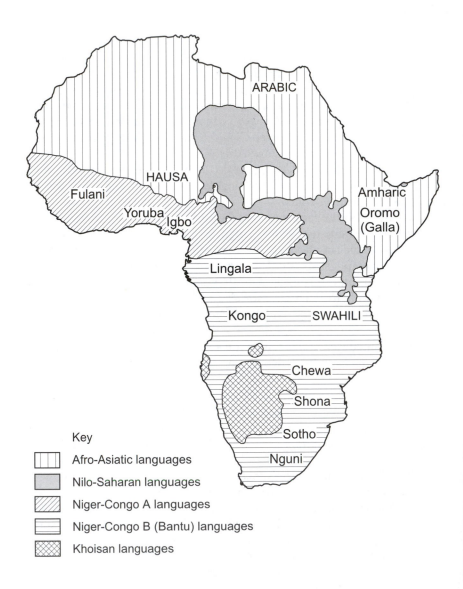

Key

Afro-Asiatic languages

Nilo-Saharan languages

Niger-Congo A languages

Niger-Congo B (Bantu) languages

Khoisan languages

These languages are sharply distinguished by the presence of clicks (which were later borrowed into isiXhosa and isiZulu in South Africa). However, the Khoi and San languages do not seem to be genetically related, and the lifestyles of their speakers were also significantly different, the San being mainly hunter-gatherers and the Khoikhoi nomadic cattle herders.

About 350 years ago there were between 10 000 and 20 000 San-speakers in southern Africa, but by the mid nineteenth century, they had almost vanished due to pressure from the Khoikhoi and Baster[5] communities, as well as the white frontier farmers and the in-migrating speakers of isiXhosa.

In the early seventeenth century, there were about eleven Cape Khoi varieties in what was later to be the Cape Province of South Africa, spoken by between 100 000 and 200 000 people. Within sixty years of the arrival of the Dutch in southern Africa (in 1652), their economic, social, and political order had almost entirely collapsed, due to conflict with the Dutch and the Xhosa, and the smallpox epidemics of 1713. Khoi was absorbed into isiXhosa in the east, and Cape Dutch/Afrikaans in the west, and today lives on in the sounds, words, and grammatical constructions of these two languages (15 per cent of Nguni lexical items, for instance, are said to contain clicks).

Since the coming of democracy in South Africa in 1994, the descendants of the San, who had almost vanished from the country and were living mainly in Namibia and Botswana, have gradually begun to return to South Africa, so that they are once again a presence in that country. Given that the new South African Constitution makes special provision for the promotion of the Khoi and San languages, it is possible that they will once again become part of the linguistic scene in South Africa. Though not a clear-cut case of language revitalization or revival/revalorization, this is an example of the reintroduction of a language into a state.

4 The **Niger-Congo languages** form the largest language family in sub-Saharan Africa. It consists of more than a thousand languages, which are spoken by 260 million people in western, central, eastern, and southern Africa. A sub-group of these languages, known as the **Bantu languages** of central and southern Africa, numbers about 500 (Crystal 1997: 316). The largest of these languages (in terms of user numbers) are Yoruba (with 20 million first-language speakers in Nigeria), Igbo (12 million first-language speakers, also in Nigeria), Kiswahili (5 million first-language speakers and 30 million second-language speakers in central and eastern Africa), Kikongo (7 million), Kinyarwanda (7 million), Makua (6 million), and isiXhosa and isiZulu (with over 7 million first-language speakers each and 24 million second-language speakers combined in southern Africa).

As the languages of this family are so dominant in sub-Saharan Africa, we want to pay more attention to them, and to discuss their spread from their place of origin.

The Bantu languages originated in the Cameroon area, and spread eastwards and southwards from there, as shown on the following map.

FIGURE 2.1 The origins and spread of the Bantu languages

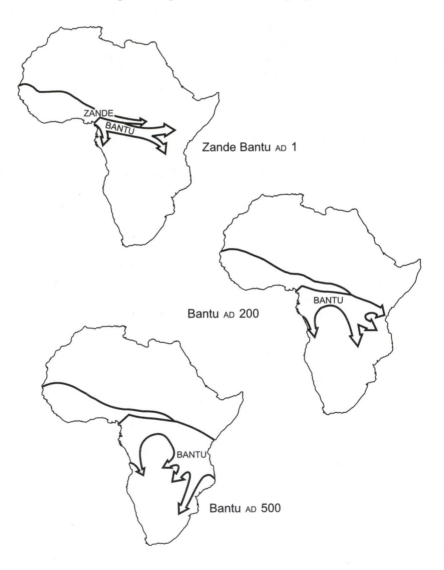

The Bantu languages of sub-equatorial Africa

The Bantu languages of sub-equatorial Africa can be categorized as follows:
- the north-eastern group, with Kirundi and Kinyarwanda in Burundi and Rwanda, Runyoro, Rutoro, and Luganda in Uganda, and Kiswahili, Kikuyu, Luluhya, and Kikamba in Kenya;
- the central-eastern group, with Chichewa-Nyanja, Chitumbuka, and Chiyao in Malawi, Chibemba, Lozi, and Tonga in Zambia, Kisukuma, Kinyamwezi, and Tonga in Tanzania, and Xitsonga and Imakwa in Mozambique;
- the central-western group, with Kimbundu-Chokwe in Angola, Mongo, Kiluba, and Kiswahili in the Democratic Republic of Congo, Kikongo and Kituba in the People's Republic of Congo, Angola, and the Democratic Republic of Congo;
- the south-western group, with Umbundu, Lunda-Chokwe, Otjiherero, Kavango, and Oshiwambo in Angola, Zaire, Zambia, and Namibia; and
- the south-eastern group, with Chishona, Sotho (Sepedi, Setswana, and Sesotho), Nguni (isiZulu, isiXhosa, siSwati, and isiNdebele), Lozi, Ila-Tonga, Xitsonga, and Tshivenda in Zambia, South Africa, Lesotho, Swaziland, Zimbabwe, and Botswana.

This may create the impression that the Bantu languages can be neatly sub-divided into exact categories. This is not the case, as languages are constantly in contact with each other (see Chapter 4), which leads to language change. This is especially the case in large urban areas, where urban varieties often arise. A good example of this phenomenon is Pretoria Sotho, which is said to be so different from Sepedi (from which it is derived), that it is not imme-diately intelligible to rural speakers of Sepedi (although this may be a partly psychological barrier).

Common linguistic features of the Bantu languages

A characteristic of these languages is the fact that their nouns are subdivided into classes, each class being marked by a particular word segment (called a morpheme – see Chapter 8). The isiZulu word for 'boy', for example, -fana, is a member of class 1, which is marked by the class marker u-, thus umfana. The Bantu languages are furthermore characterized by the requirement that verbs which combine with nouns to form a sentence must agree with them in the sense that the noun-class-marker must be added to the verb as a prefix. For example, to form the sentence The boy runs in isiZulu, the noun umfana must be joined with the verb gijima ('runs'). When this happens, the u- of umfana must be fixed onto the beginning of gijima, producing Umfana ugijima.

Although the ex-colonial languages also have noun classes (for example, English has count nouns, such as 'boy', and non-count nouns, such as 'water'), they are not formally marked to indicate this property, and do not function in the same way as in the Bantu languages. And although they have agreement rules, as is shown in sentences such as *The boy runs* as opposed to *The boys run*, their rules for agreement between the nouns and the verbs in a sentence work differently.

Other characteristic features of the Bantu languages relate to their sound patterns (the Bantu languages are tonal and prefer syllables consisting of a consonant and a vowel – see Chapters 6 and 7); the nature of their vocabularies (lexicons – Chapter 9); the order of words (syntax – Chapter 8); and the way in which certain functions are expressed, such as 'the subject of the sentence' and 'the object of the sentence' – see also Chapter 8).

Other language families in Africa

The four language families mentioned so far obviously do not cover all the languages spoken in Africa. They represent the 'original' languages of this continent. Over the past three or four centuries, however, Africa has experienced a large influx of people from other parts of the world, and their languages have now become an integral part of life on this continent. It is therefore necessary to study these languages as well. Four of the most widespread language groups in this category are outlined below.

The European languages

The European languages that are currently most prevalent in Africa are Portuguese, French, and English (Afrikaans, spoken mainly in southern Africa, is a derivative of Dutch).[6] These languages became part of the African scene in colonial times, and are therefore generally called **ex-colonial languages**. As Romance languages (French and Portuguese) and Germanic languages (Afrikaans and English), these languages are structurally non-African. However, in terms of their borrowings, the meanings of their words, and the pronunciation of their sounds, they can be regarded as Africanized languages. In fact, they have developed distinctive varieties, with Nigerian English, for example, being clearly distinguishable from Kenyan English or the English of black South Africans. The case of Afrikaans is also interesting, for in spite of its obvious European roots and close similarity to Dutch, it is not used in any significant way outside Africa, and is arguably an 'African' language.

Indian/Dravidian

Another important group is represented by the Indian languages, which are either Indo-Iranian or Dravidian in origin. These languages are found throughout sub-equatorial Africa. In Mauritius 50 per cent of the population is Hindu, and Hindi, Urdu, and Tamil are important languages. In Kenya, Uganda, and Tanzania there are significant minority speakers of Hindi, Gujarati, and Punjabi. In South Africa, which has about one million citizens of Indian origin, the speakers of these languages have almost totally shifted to English, and languages such as Hindi, Urdu, Telegu, and Tamil are now used mainly for cultural and religious purposes.

Chinese languages, though not part of the Indian or Dravidian language families, should also be mentioned here. Chinese languages are used in some African countries, notably Mauritius.

Austronesian

Another language family that appears in Africa is Austronesian, represented by Malagasy, which is spoken in Madagascar.

Pidgins/creoles

These languages, though hardly qualifying as a 'group', are found in different parts of Africa. Some examples are Nigerian Pidgin, Krio (in Sierra Leone), Fanagalo (in South Africa), Sango (in the Democratic Republic of Congo), and Kreol (in Mauritius, Reunion, and the Seychelles).

In this context, the development of 'mixed languages' (such as Sheng in Kenya, and 'tsotsitaal' in South Africa) in urban centres must also be mentioned. These languages cannot be categorized as pidgins or creoles, but they do have pidginized and creolized features. They often also have the social meaning of 'young, modern city-dweller with no links with traditional African culture.'

Why do the ex-colonial languages have such a grip on the African people?

Courses in the history of English at many African universities often discuss only the European and North American history of this language, with almost no reference to its history in Africa. This is strange because English (like French and Portuguese) has obtained an extremely strong grip on Africa, with significant consequences for the people of the continent. How did this come about? And why?

An introductory textbook in linguistics cannot give a full account of this fascinating and complex topic, and students should begin tracking this history on their own. Some of the questions they should try to answer are: how did these languages get to Africa? How and why did they spread? Can they give expression to the African way of life?[7] What are the advantages and disadvantages of the ex-colonial languages for the indigenous African communities? What role do they play in the lives of Africans? What are the structural, functional, and social features of their Africanized varieties? Have they become indigenized? What are their linguistic relationships with their cognates in their countries of origin? Are the norms set for their public use appropriate for African people (who are generally third-language speakers of these languages)? What should the bases be for setting these norms? Should these include international comprehensibility, or the requirement of non-discrimination (in other words, that African speakers of these languages should not be penalized in their own countries for speaking a variety of a European or colonial language that is different from the standard in non-African countries)? Is it in the interests of the African people that these languages should be the main languages of learning and teaching for their children?

These questions are vital to the linguistics of Africa, but are very difficult to answer. To illustrate the history of the ex-colonial languages in Africa, a brief overview of English and Afrikaans in South Africa is given. (Perhaps you might like to relate the history of these languages in South Africa to the histories of the ex-colonial languages in your own country, focusing especially on the economic and political aspects. You can begin this task by consulting history books and talking to anthropologists and specialists in literature.)

The British arrived in the Cape at the end of the eighteenth century, and immediately took over the government of the country, then a Dutch colony, gradually establishing administrative control over the Cape Colony and Natal. By 1907, they controlled the whole of present-day South Africa. As part of this process, they used military force to gain control of the state administration, divided the country into administrative districts, collected taxes from local tribes, established trade (mining and the ivory trade), and set up their system of justice. Within a century, they had complete control over every aspect of public life in the country. Today, although South Africa no longer belongs to Britain, the overwhelming anglicization of everyday life suggests that, culturally and linguistically, it is still colonized.

Although English is spoken by less than 10 per cent of the South African population as a first language, and is known well enough to function fully in public life by less than 25 per cent of black South Africans, it is practically the only language used in all the important domains of public life. Secondary and tertiary education (almost all textbooks, for example), economic opportunities (most jobs), political participation, and so on are only really accessible to those who speak, read, and write English. If you aren't proficient in English, you are barred from these domains, and English then becomes a barrier. At the same time, English proficiency (or lack thereof) becomes a basis for discrimination, and an instrument of inclusion and/or exclusion from rights and privileges.

English in South Africa has, naturally, become 'indigenized', at least in the sense of becoming the 'property' of many non-native speakers, and of developing distinctive structural and semantic features. Certain varieties of the language can therefore be seen as 'African'. However, this indigenization has also led to conflict between what the 'custodians' of the language regard as 'proper', which is the 'British' or the so-called 'international' form of English, and the way in which it is typically spoken by most black South Africans and also by certain white South Africans. This debate deals mainly with linguistic issues, but should also take note of the communities involved. In this regard, one argument could well be that South Africa, like all other African countries, 'belongs' firstly to its indigenous people, and that they therefore have the right to decide what is appropriate, and cannot be dictated to by people who historically come from elsewhere.

Although political, educational, and economic leaders do not seem to be particularly aware of the conflict between English and the other languages of South Africa, it is worth paying attention to this issue and exploring it thoroughly, as this conflict might well lead to problems later on (see Chapter 1).

The position of Afrikaans is also interesting from a sociolinguistic perspective. Many South Africans regard Afrikaans as an ex-colonial language. However, although it developed out of the language (Dutch) of an ex-colonial power (Holland), Afrikaans in its present form is not strictly speaking an ex-colonial language. It developed from the Dutch spoken by the people who established a refreshment station at the Cape in 1652, and who later gained administrative and economic control of the region, much as the British did 150 years later. Because the Dutch possessed the necessary regional power, their language became the dominant language, and had to be acquired by everyone who needed to deal with them. Out of this grew Afrikaans, a form of Dutch found mainly in the mouths of Dutch soldiers, sailors, Khoikhoi herders and labourers, and the slave community of the Cape. It was a language that arose at a grassroots level and thus grew, so to speak, out of the African soil. A number of its phonological, grammatical, and semantic features are not found in Dutch, the language from which it evolved. It contains sounds and intonation patterns, as well as forms for expressing intensity (by the reduplication of a word) and negation,[8] that were introduced through the 'broken Dutch' spoken by Malay slaves and Griqua companions. The Afrikaans vocabulary similarly contains large numbers of words that are completely foreign to Dutch. Afrikaans is 'African' by nature, and it gives expression to an African world. In this sense, it is an African, not a 'European', language.

Today, Afrikaans is spoken by about six million South Africans, of whom over 50 per cent are not white. However, as is well known (see also Chapter 1), Afrikaans was gradually appropriated – 'taken over' – by its white speakers and claimed as their exclusive property, and finally used as an instrument to gain political power. This development was successful; in 1948, the white speakers of Afrikaans took control of the country and established the policy of apartheid, leading to immense pain, hardship, and loss for most other citizens, including many other Afrikaans-speakers. Ironically, apartheid was also the (short-term?) death knell for the language, as Afrikaans became strongly stigmatized as the language of the oppressor, and was to be totally rejected by many black South Africans, in spite of the fact that it was also an effective language of struggle against apartheid. Today, many sociolinguists are arguing for the 'democratization' of Afrikaans; in other words, they propose 'giving the language back to the people who are its rightful owners'.

The story of Afrikaans, therefore, is not quite the same as the story of English, or of French and Portuguese.

What is the general sociolinguistic character of the African states?

African states do not all have the same sociolinguistic character. However, it is possible to make some general observations.

If we look at the table provided at the end of this book (Appendix), we notice a number of features that are, generally speaking, common to all the countries of Africa. We list some of these here.

- Practically all the states are (complexly) multilingual. This is important, and will be discussed in more detail below.
- English, French, and Portuguese are widespread. The striking thing is that, although these three languages are known well by only 10–20 per cent of the inhabitants of African countries, they are often the (only) official languages of the countries, and are the main languages of learning and teaching. In fact, these languages are so strongly established that some countries are referred to as 'English-speaking', 'French-speaking', or 'Portuguese-speaking'. Practically all these states have just one official language.
- Political borders cut through language borders, so that many languages are spoken in more than one state as a first language. For instance, Galla and Somali (both Cushitic languages, members of the Afro-Asiatic family) are spoken in Somalia, Ethiopia, and Kenya. Further examples are Setswana,

which is used in Botswana, South Africa, and Namibia; and Chichewa, spoken in Malawi, Mozambique, Zambia, and Zimbabwe.

- Some languages have spread beyond the borders of their first-language communities as second languages, even crossing state borders. They have thus become lingua francas. Kiswahili is a good example. It is spoken by about 30 million people in ten eastern African countries (not, of course, with the same concentration: Kiswahili is significantly present in only six of the ten, namely Tanzania, Kenya, Uganda, the Democratic Republic of Congo, Rwanda, and Burundi). The Nguni languages of southern Africa (isiZulu, isiXhosa, and others) are common to about 30 million people in South Africa, Swaziland, Zimbabwe, and elsewhere.

The multilingual nature of the African states

The multilingualism of the African states occurs at the levels of both the individual and society. Many African people know or speak five or more languages in the course of daily life, and most countries house many languages within their borders. Multilingualism is the norm in Africa.

The existence of multilingual societies in Africa has had a number of consequences, some of which are linguistic, while others are political.

The linguistic consequences include:

- the growth in lingua francas, which develop because of a need for cross-group communication;
- the development of mixed languages, mainly due to intense language contact, which results from urbanization and industrialization, as well as migrant labour;
- the development of cross-cultural communication skills; and
- the development of cross-linguistic communication strategies, such as code-switching and code-mixing (see Chapters 4 and 5).

The political consequences relate to the fact that the languages of African states are generally embedded in the political and economic orders of their countries. This results in some languages being 'powerful' (and so empowering their speakers) and others being 'powerless' (thus offering their speakers no power). The first type of language is called a majority language, and the second a minority language. It is necessary to distinguish between these two categories of language power in Africa.

Majority and minority languages

The concepts majority and minority are often understood in quantitative terms; that is, a language with a million speakers is regarded as a major language. This is not generally the case in Africa, however, because speaker size is just one dimension of the phenomenon. The functional value (what functions it can perform) and the prestige of the language also play a role. So, for example, isiZulu in South Africa has more than 8 million first-language speakers, and is used by at least 16 million more as a second language. Yet, during the apartheid regime (and even today), it was considered a minority language. It had neither the functional value nor the general social status (prestige) that majority languages generally have. English, on the other hand, is the first language of only about 3.5 million South Africans, yet is clearly a majority language. (Afrikaans, which was a majority language before the democratization of South Africa, is rapidly becoming a minority language.)

The recognition of the difference between majority and minority languages allows us to explain all sorts of phenomena: for instance, the differential incidence of multilingualism in communities. In South Africa, for example, societal multilingualism is extremely restricted in the so-called coloured, Asian, and white communities; all the members of these societies know English and/or Afrikaans, but very few know any Bantu languages. Most black South Africans, however, know five or six languages, including Afrikaans and English. The reason for this is clear: it's a matter of power. People tend to learn only the languages that are socially and economically useful to them. This is the linguistic version of the law of maximum returns.

Linguistic tools for the study of multilingualism

The existence of extensive and complex multilingualism presents many challenges to linguists. Because multilingualism can have serious consequences for countries, linguists need a variety of analytical and descriptive tools with which to investigate it. For instance, they need an instrument that can be used to characterize different types of multilingualism (compare, for instance, the difference between multilingualism in Britain or the USA and in most African countries); they need tools to measure people's knowledge of different languages; and they need tools for dealing with inter- and intra-language conflict. (**Inter-language conflict** refers to conflict between languages, and **intra-language conflict** to conflict between varieties of the same language. Conflict is the presence of tension, whether linguistic, psychological, or social.)

Linguists also need an instrument with which they can classify the languages of multilingual societies along the 'power dimension', thus locating them on the scale that runs from majority to minority. A tool such as this would help to describe the multilingual character of their countries (or regions and communities).

Such an instrument (or formula) would have to refer to the speaker size of a language, its functional value, and its social status. These three features do not have the same role, and therefore cannot have an equal value in determining the 'majority-ness' of a language. It is difficult to decide what the relative weights of these three features should be. As a tentative proposal, we suggest the following: that the total quantity of the speakers of a language forms 20 per cent of its 'value', that its functional value constitutes 50 per cent, and its prestige 30 per cent. If this is found to be an acceptable distribution, we would be able to develop an index that could express the relative 'majority-ness' or 'minority-ness' of a particular language.

As an illustration of how this idea can be applied, three South African languages (English, Tshivenda, and isiZulu) are taken and (subjectively) awarded values for each dimension. A simple aggregation of these values yields power indices for each, as shown below.

	Speaker size (as first language)	Functional value	Prestige	Index
English	10 (3.5 million)	40	30	80
isiZulu	20 (8.5 million)	20	15	55
Tshivenda	5 (0.75 million)	10	5	20

Multilingualism as a resource

Finally, an important task that faces linguists is to persuade the decision-makers in their countries that multilingualism is not merely a source of problems, but in fact a valuable resource. Besides the fact that a knowledge of more than two languages allows us to communicate with so many more people (in both personal and professional contexts), the vast amount of knowledge that people and communities possess is often only effectively accessible through a particular language. A knowledge of the indigenous African languages provides access to a vast reservoir of wisdom and skills contained in their body of speakers.

The sociolinguistic profile of African countries

The term **sociolinguistic profile** is used to refer to a characterization of the language situation in a state, region, or community, or the language world of an individual. If we want to give a full sociolinguistic profile of a country, we need information on the following features:
- the population of a country, its major regions/provinces, and its major metropolitan areas/cities;
- the number of languages in the country, their genetic relationship, and their names;

- the geographic distribution of the languages;
- the demographic distribution (urban and/or rural, by socio-economic class, age, and gender);
- the functional distribution (or distribution by domain) of the languages, including which languages are designated as official languages and national language(s), and which are used for (a) low functions: home, friendship networks, and (b) high functions: governance, parliamentary debate, legislation, administration (record-keeping purposes, internal communication), the courts of law, education (as a medium of instruction, as a subject of study at school, and for certification requirements), science and technology, economic activity, trade and industry, the media (print, radio, television), religion, cultural activity, public entertainment, and sport;
- the state of language knowledge in the country: the number of primary speakers per language, the number of non-primary speakers per language, the degree or incidence of multilingualism, and the levels of literacy;
- general language preferences among the people of the state, particularly in specific domains and for particular functions (for example, the national political debate, secondary and tertiary education);
- the social or symbolic meanings of the different languages, the incidence of language loyalty, language-based ethnic nationalism, the social attitudes (including prejudices) towards non-primary languages, and the instrumental value of the languages; and
- the degree of standardization, codification (descriptive and prescriptive grammars, dictionaries), and technologization (availability of technical terms and registers); the corpus development[9] of each language, the provision of language services by the state (translation, interpretation, terminographical development, and so on), and the number of language promotion agencies in the country.

In the section that follows, brief sociolinguistic profiles of selected African states are provided. In these profiles, very little attention is given to aspects such as the symbolic and social meaning of languages, and their geographic, demographic, and functional distribution. Besides the fact that including this information would take up far too much space, the relevant information is not available to us. These aspects of a sociolinguistic profile can thus be illustrated only with reference to the language situation in South Africa.

Language status/prestige

The language with the highest status in South Africa is English. It is the major economic, educational, and social language, and during the years of the struggle against apartheid it came to be seen as the language of liberation. English is thus the lingua franca of the national political debate.

The socio-political status of Afrikaans is ambivalent. On the one hand, it is a powerful symbol of ethnic identity in some sectors of the white community, thus becoming an important factor in ethnic/socio-cultural mobilization and conflict. However, it is also stigmatized in many communities for its association with apartheid, the political ideology of the National Party, which governed South Africa for nearly fifty years, and which was supported mainly by Afrikaans-speaking whites. Instrumentally, Afrikaans has been an important language of the workplace and in administration, but with the demise of the political power of the Afrikaner this may be changing.

The Bantu languages are widely used for personal and domestic communication, and cultural and religious expression, but have a very low public status in general.

As described in Chapter 1, the major South African languages are strongly politicized, mainly because of their use in political manipulation (Afrikaans and isiZulu), political division (the so-called 'homelands' policy of apartheid), cultural domination (Afrikaans in the former Bantu Education system), discrimination, and exploitation (Fanagalo, the pidgin used in the mining industry).

Geographic distribution

There is a weak correlation between geographic location and language in South Africa, with the Bantu languages being the most clearly delineated geographically: Xitsonga and Tshivenda are concentrated in the Northern Province, bordering on Mozambique and Zimbabwe, Sepedi in the central areas of the Northern Province, and Setswana in the North West province. The Nguni languages (respectively isiNdebele, siSwati, isiZulu, and isiXhosa) range along the east coast of southern Africa, from Swaziland down through KwaZulu-Natal to the Eastern Cape. They are also all found in urban areas, but to different degrees.

Afrikaans is distributed across the country, with concentrations in some urban areas (mainly Bloemfontein and Pretoria), whereas English is mainly an urban language, and is found in particular in Cape Town, Durban, and Johannesburg.

Demographic distribution

Demographically, English is a middle- and upper-middle-class language, Afrikaans is found throughout the socio-economic classes, and the Bantu languages are used mainly by the working classes. Linguistic and religious divisions correlate weakly, and the country's languages are spread evenly over both age and gender groupings.

Functional distribution

As a broad generalization, Afrikaans and English are the high-function languages of South Africa, while the Bantu languages are mainly low-function languages, used in interpersonal communication and for religious and cultural purposes. They are also, however, used by the radio and television media. The main languages of government, parliamentary debate, legislation, state administration, the courts of law, education, and economic life are English and Afrikaans (but with English rapidly replacing Afrikaans in all these domains).

Standardization and codification

The major languages of public resource in South Africa are Afrikaans and English, both being highly standardized, codified (with dictionaries, terminology lists, and normative grammars), and technicalized, with wide registral[10] scope. The Bantu languages are far less standardized, codified, and technicalized. Given the democratization of South Africa in 1994, this situation is bound to change.

Sociolinguistic profiles of selected countries of Africa

Students should try to construct similar profiles for their own countries.

ANGOLA

Population: 11.5 million
Number of languages: 11
Dominant languages:[11] Umbundo: 1.5 million first-language speakers; Kimbundu: 1 million; Kikongo: 0.5 million (also spoken in the Democratic Republic of Congo); Lundo: 0.4 million; Ngangela: 0.4 million
Other languages: Chokwe (also spoken in the Democratic Republic of Congo and Zambia); Oshiwambo (also spoken in Namibia)
Official language and only language of administration: Portuguese
Language of learning and teaching at all levels: Portuguese[12]
Literacy in indigenous languages: 10%; literacy in Portuguese: 58% (1990)
Most books are published in Portuguese, with only a few on religion in local languages.

Portuguese is the prestige language in the country, and is used as a lingua franca in the urban areas, in fact becoming the first language of younger urbanized people. It is not known[13] as well in rural areas, or by people with only primary school education or less

BOTSWANA

Population: 1.5 million
Number of languages: 25
Dominant language: Setswana (spoken by 90% of the population)
Official languages are English and Setswana, with Setswana also the national language
Languages of learning and teaching: Setswana in the primary schools; English at all three levels
Literacy rate: 70% (1995); 30 Setswana literacy programmes exist
Literature has been produced in both Setswana and English
Newspapers and radio broadcasts in both languages

CAMEROON

Population: 13.5 million
Number of languages: 240, grouped into three families: Bantu (e.g. Fulani, in the southern and western parts of the country); Nilo-Saharan (Kanuri); and Afro-Asiatic (about 10% of the adult males can read and write Arabic). Hausa, Bura, Musei, and Njai are Chadic languages
Dominant languages: the Bamileke languages (Banjun, Bangangte, Dschang), Fulfulde (in the north), Ewondo, Bassa, and Douala
Official languages are English and French
Languages of learning and teaching: both English and French are used in the primary schools (some schools are bilingual); English and French at all three levels
Literacy level: 63%
Literature has been produced in both French and English
Newspapers, radio, and television mainly in English and French

KENYA

Population: 24 million
Number of languages: 42
Dominant languages: Kikuyu (spoken by 20%), Dholuo (14%), Luluya (13%), Kikamba (11%), Kalenjin (11%), Ekigusi (6.5%), Kimeru (5%)
Others: Maasai, Galla, Rendile, Turkana, Somali
National language: Kiswahili (known

as a second language by 65% of the nation)

Official languages: English (known as a second language by about 16% of Kenyans) and Kiswahili

Language of learning and teaching: most of the indigenous languages during the first three years of primary education, with English and Kiswahili as subjects; English from the fourth year of primary school onwards

Language study: Kiswahili and English are studied throughout the school system. No indigenous language is studied after the third year

Literacy level: 78%

Literature: most literature is in English, but there is also a growing literature in Kiswahili. Some indigenous writing is available in Dholuo, Kikuyu, and Luhya.

Media: most newspapers are in English; there is only one Kiswahili daily now (there used to be three a few years ago). Radio and television use English and Kiswahili. Some channels are English only

LESOTHO

Population: 2 million

Number of languages: 3

Dominant language: Sesotho (spoken by 99%)

Official languages: Sesotho and English

Language of learning and teaching: Sesotho for the first four years of primary school; English at all three levels

Literacy level: 71%

MALAWI

Population: 10 million

Number of languages: more than 12

Dominant languages: Chichewa/ Chinyanja (spoken by 80%) (*nyanja* means 'lake'), Chiyawo (19%), Chilomwe (15%), Chitumbuka (9% and apparently growing in importance)

Others: Chisena, Chitonga, Chilambiya, Chingonde, Chingoni (originally from the Nguni people in South Africa, but today used only in traditional dances and ceremonies)

National language: Chichewa

Official language: English (known as a second language by about 6% of the Malawians) and Chichewa

Languages of learning and teaching: indigenous languages during the first four years of the school programme (with English as a subject of study), and English thereafter up to tertiary level

Literacy rate: 56%

Media: the printed media is English, with the radio using indigenous languages as well

MOZAMBIQUE

Population: 18 million
Number of languages: about 24
Dominant languages: Imakwa (spoken by 38%), Tshitsonga (24%), Chisena (10%), Chishona (10%), Kiswahili (6.4%)
Also: Xironga, Xichangana, Cicopi, Cikunda, Ciyao, Shimakonde
Official language: Portuguese
Language of learning and teaching: Portuguese, at all educational levels
Literacy rate: 40%
Media: almost entirely Portuguese

NAMIBIA

Population: 1.6 million
Number of languages: More than 14
Dominant languages: Oshiwambo (Ndonga, Kwanyama) (spoken by 50.6%), Nama/Damara (12.4%), Kavango (Mbukushu, Kwangali, Gciriku) (9.6%), Otjiherero (9.6%), Afrikaans (9.5%), Caprivi (4.6%), Bushman (1.9%), German (0.9%), English (0.8%), other African (0.6%), Setswana (0.4%), other European (0.4%), other languages (0.1%)
Official language: English
Language of learning and teaching: English, at all educational levels
Literacy level: 38%
Media: printed media in English, Afrikaans, and German

NIGERIA

Population: 111 million
Number of languages: 400 (representing three of the generally recognized language families: Niger-Congo, Nilo-Saharan, and Afro-Asiatic)
Dominant languages: Hausa (spoken as a regional lingua franca by more than 25 million people), Yoruba, Igbo, Edo, Efik-Ibibio, Fulani, Nupe, Tiv, Urhobo, Nigerian Pidgin
Official language: English, with Yoruba, Hausa, and Igbo the national languages
Languages of learning and teaching: mother tongues/the language of the immediate community in junior primary school; English at senior primary, secondary, and tertiary levels
Language study: English, a national language (Hausa, Igbo, and Yoruba), and a language of the local community
Literacy level: 57%
Literature has been produced in English as well as the indigenous languages
Newspapers, radio, and television mainly in English, but also in the indigenous languages

SOUTH AFRICA

Population: 40.5 million

Number of languages: between 25 and 80

Dominant languages: isiZulu (spoken as a first language by 22.7% of the population, but known by 24.2 million), isiXhosa (17.76%, but known by 18 million), Afrikaans (14.34%, but known by 16.5 million), Sepedi/Northern Sotho (9.12%, but known by 12.6 million), English (8.53%, but known by 18.5 million), Setswana (8.15%, but known by 11.3 million), Sesotho/Southern Sotho (7.66%, but known by 10.5 million), Xitsonga (4.33%, but known by 4.7 million), siSwati (2.5%, but known by 3.4 million), Tshivenda (2.16%, but known by 2.5 million), and isiNdebele (1.44%, but known by 2.2 million); four of the Bantu languages belong to the Nguni sub-family (isiNdebele, siSwati, isiXhosa, and isiZulu), three to the Sotho sub-family (Sepedi/Northern Sotho, Sesotho/Southern Sotho, aand Setswana), while two belong to neither – Xitsonga and Tshivenda

Other languages: European languages – Portuguese (57 000 speakers), Greek, Italian, German, Dutch, and French; Asian – Hindi (26 000), Gujarati, Tamil, Urdu, and Telegu; in addition, there are a number of urban 'mixed' varieties (Fanagalo, and an urban youth vernacular, Flaaitaal/Tsotsitaal/Iscamtho), as well as Arabic, Hebrew, and Greek, which are used as church languages

Official languages: all 11 of the dominant languages; no designated national languages

Languages of learning and teaching: any of the official languages (but with English overwhelmingly the first choice) in primary school; mainly Afrikaans and English at secondary and tertiary levels

Literacy level: 82%

Literature has been produced in all the main languages, but with a large majority in English and Afrikaans

Newspapers, radio, and television in English, Afrikaans, Zulu, and Xhosa (in that order)

SWAZILAND

Population: 0.95 million

Number of languages: 2

Dominant language: siSwati (spoken by 91%)

Official language: English

National language: siSwati

Language of learning and teaching: siSwati at junior primary level; English at all educational levels

Literacy level: 77%

Media: mainly English, but with siSwati used in all the media

TANZANIA

Population: 29 million
Number of languages: between 135 and 150
Dominant languages: Kisukuma (spoken by 12.5%), Kinyambwezi (4.2%), Kiswahili (10%, but known as a second language by 90% of the population)
Other languages: 15 other languages are spoken by between 0.5 and 1 million speakers each
Tanzania's languages mainly belong to four language families (Bantu, Nilotic, Cushitic, and Khoisan)
National and official language: Kiswahili; English as an official language (known by 20% of the population)
Language of learning and teaching: Kiswahili at primary level and English at secondary and tertiary levels
Literacy rate: 68%
Media: Printed and radio media in both English and Kiswahili

As Kiswahili is such a well-known language in southern and eastern Africa, some further information on it may be useful. It is a Bantu language with strong Arabic influences. (The name 'Swahili' derives from an Arabic word meaning 'coast'.) It originated in the seventh and eight centuries along the coast, and spread from about 1 000 AD southwards along the trading routes, becoming the lingua franca for trade between the Arab merchants and the local population. In the eighteenth and nineteenth centuries, it spread inland along the caravan routes. Today Kiswahili is the official language of Tanzania, the co-official language of Kenya (where it is used for administration and education), and one of the national languages of the Democratic Republic of Congo. It is also a lingua franca in Uganda, Burundi, Rwanda, and Djibouti

UGANDA

Population: 20 million
Number of languages: more than 30; 12 are Bantu (Luganda, Runyoro, Runyankore, Runyarwanda), 11 are Nilotic (e.g. Acholi), and 7 are Sudanic (e.g. Lugbara)
Dominant language: Luganda (spoken by 39%), with Kiswahili (35%) dominant in the police force and army. Knowledge of English rises according to level of education, youth, and occupational level
Official language: English

Languages of learning and teaching: local languages during the first years of the primary level; English at all educational levels
Literacy rate: 62%
Literature has been produced in English as well as the local languages (Luganda in particular)
Media: newspapers, radio, and television mainly in English, but also in some local languages, including Kiswahili

ZAMBIA

Population: 9.5 million
Number of languages: 80
Dominant languages: Icibemba (spoken by 56%), Cinyanja/Chichewa (42%), Citonga (23%), Silozi (17%)
Other languages: Luvale (8%), Kikaonde (7%), and Lunda (5%)
Official language: English, known by 26% of the population as a second language

National languages: The major indigenous languages
Language of learning and teaching: English from the outset of the school programme, and at all educational levels
Literacy level: 78%
Media: the printed media and television are mostly English, with local languages used on radio

ZIMBABWE

Population: 11.2 million
Number of languages: More than 8 (including Tshivenda, Setswana, Shangani, Afrikaans, English, Indian languages)
Dominant languages: Chishona (an amalgam of mainly three 'dialects' – Manyika, Karanga, and Zezuru, but also Korekore and Ndau), spoken by 75% of the Zimbabwean people; isiNdebele (spoken in the western part of the country, originally from

Zululand)
Official language: English
National languages: Chishona and isiNdebele
Language of learning and teaching: indigenous languages during the first four years of the primary level; English at all educational levels
Literacy level: 85%
Media: the printed media is mainly English, with the local languages used on radio and television

Endnotes

1   The term *sociolinguistics*, which will be discussed more fully in Chapter 3, refers to a particular approach to linguistic work, namely the study of language in its social context. Language can also be studied in other ways, for example without reference to any of its contexts (usually called *linguistics*), or with reference to its psychological context, called *psycholinguistics*.

2   If all the Chinese languages are counted as one (which should not be done as they are

mutually unintelligible), the figure rises to 1 071 million.

3   Note that the term *define* is used as a technical term; in this case, it means to 'describe in such a way that the description is true of all phenomena it is meant to cover, and of none it is meant to exclude'.

4   As we have seen, mutual comprehensibility is not a decisive criterion for enumerating languages. A number of other factors should also be considered.

5   The term *Baster* (originally *Bastaards*) refers to people originally of mixed race, descended from white frontier farmers and Khoi women. They developed a strong pride in their European ancestry, using this to justify their 'superiority' over the aboriginal communities.

6   There are others too, of course, such as Spanish in Equatorial Guinea and German in Namibia.

7   This issue is particularly contentious. You might like to consider the following question: do the novels (in English) of the Nigerian writer Chinua Achebe and the Kenyan writer Ngugi wa Thiong'o give adequate expression to life in African communities?

8   For example, reduplication can be seen in the words *nou-nou* ('now' or 'soon') and *fluit-fluit* (literally 'whistling-whistling', with the meaning 'easily'); negation is also 'doubled', as in *ek kan nie sien nie* (literally 'I cannot see not', with the meaning 'I cannot see').

9   *Corpus development* is a term from language planning. It refers to the development of the linguistic equipment (such as technical terms) required by the speakers of a language to give adequate expression to their communicative needs.

10   The term *register* refers to 'ways of talking' in particular situations, usually occupational situations. For instance, the ways in which motor car mechanics or medical practitioners talk to each other (as opposed to talking to laypeople), are called registers. Registers have both a lexical aspect and a discourse aspect (see Chapters 9 and 10 respectively).

11   The languages mentioned here exclude the ex-colonial languages, which are generally the significant 'dominant' languages.

12   Generally speaking, the language policies of the Portuguese and French colonial governments were directed at assimilation, and thus Portuguese and French became the languages of learning and teaching from the first day of formal education. (Even the study of the local languages as subjects was disallowed!) The British colonial governments, on the other hand, adopted an 'indirect' approach, which meant that local languages (called *vernacular languages* at the time) were used during the first three or four years of primary school, with a gradual transition to English later on in primary education, and continued throughout secondary and tertiary education.

13   By now it should be clear that the expression *knowledge of a language* is imprecise, referring to a wide spectrum of linguistic proficiency, ranging from a very basic knowledge (the ability to ask questions or directions) to a level almost equivalent to first-language proficiency.

Bibliography

ALEXANDRE, P. 1972. *An Introduction to Languages and Language in Africa.* London, Ibadan, Nairobi: Heinemann.

CRYSTAL, DAVID. 1997. *The Cambridge Encyclopaedia of Language.* Second edition. Cambridge: Cambridge University Press.

DALBY, D. 1977. *Language Map of Africa and the Adjacent Islands.* London: International African Institute.

GROBLER, E., K.P. PRINSLOO, and I.J. VAN DER MERWE. 1990. *Language Atlas of South Africa.* Pretoria: HSRC.

HERBERT, ROBERT K. (ed.) 1992. *Language and Society in Africa. The Theory and Practice of Sociolinguistics.* Johannesburg: Witwatersrand University Press.

LANHAM, L.W., and K.P. PRINSLOO. (eds.) 1978. *Language and Communication Studies in South Africa: Current Issues and Directions in Research and Inquiry.* Cape Town: Oxford University Press.

MANN, MICHAEL. 1990. 'A linguistic map of Africa.' In R.R.K. Hartmann (ed.), *Lexicography in Africa. Exeter Linguistic Studies,* vol. 15, 1–7.

MESTHRIE, RAJEND. (ed.) 1995. *Language and Social History. Studies in South African Sociolinguistics.* Cape Town and Johannesburg: David Philip.

MIDDLETON, JOHN. (editor-in-chief). 1997. *Encyclopedia of Africa South of the Sahara,* vols. 1–4. New York: Charles Scribner & Sons.

SOW, ALFA I., and MOHAMED H. ABDULAZIZ.
1993. 'Language and social change.' In Ali A.
Mazrui (ed.) and C. Wondji (asst. ed.),
*General History of Africa. VIII. Africa since
1935.* California: Heinemann and UNESCO.
WEBB, VICTOR N. (ed.) 1995. *Language in South
Africa. An input into Language Planning for a*
post-apartheid South Africa. Pretoria:
University of Pretoria.
———— (in press) *Language in South Africa. The
quest for a future. The role of language in
national reconstruction and development.*
Amsterdam: John Benjamins.

3 Linguistics: an overview

Kembo-Sure and Vic Webb

Expected outcomes:

At the end of this chapter you should be able to:

1 Explain what the concept of a language system means, to someone who has not studied linguistics.
2 Explain what is meant by linguistic structure, with an illustration from a language you have studied.
3 Describe the organization of a grammar.
4 Give a list of a number of linguistic universals.
5 Distinguish between human languages and the communication systems of non-humans.
6 Describe what we know when we 'know a language'.
7 Identify and discuss the various functions of language.
8 Outline the various branches of linguistics and describe the differences between them.

Introduction

Scholarly concern with language – its nature, its functions, its origins, and its link with how we think – has a long history. However, the study of language as a separate discipline, what is now called **linguistics**, is relatively young. In many universities, the study of language was a sub-branch of anthropology or psychology. Even today, many prominent linguists still consider the study of language to be a legitimate branch of cognitive psychology, as they see language as a special mental endowment with which all humans are born, and which makes us distinctively different from all other forms of life on this planet.

The aim of this chapter is to introduce you to linguistics, its object of study, and its various fields of enquiry. We believe it is necessary for linguists in train-ing to have a holistic grasp – a bird's-eye view – of the discipline. Obviously, we cannot cover the topic comprehensively, as this would require far more space than we have available. This chapter therefore aims to provide only a brief and relatively superficial overview of the field. More details about most of the topics dealt with here are covered in other chapters, and we will refer readers to those chapters where applicable.

This chapter will deal with the following issues:

- language as system;
- the distinctive features of human languages;
- the functions of language; and
- approaches to language study.

Language as system

Linguistics, as we have said, is the study of language. Some people would prefer to add the word 'scientific', so that linguistics would be referred to as 'the scientific study of language'[1] (Lyons 1981). This sounds straightforward until we are faced with the question 'What is language'? Matters now become a little complicated. Language is all around us; we use it all the time; but to define it calls for more than we assume we know about it.

An attempt at formulating a comprehensive definition of language that captures all its important and distinctive attributes has been dismissed by linguists as futile. In order to avoid the pitfalls involved in finding a single definition, we shall discuss some of the properties of language that are considered to be universal, as well as those that make it distinctively different from other communication systems.

We have already used the term **system** to refer to language, and many definitions of language tend to include it as a necessary attribute. The term *system* refers to a collection of entities organized into a whole and arranged in such a way that they work together to achieve a particular aim or perform a particular function. This is also true of language; all languages consist of entities (or parts) such as sounds and words, which can be arranged in such a way that they can successfully perform a particular function, such as conveying information. Let's look at an illustration of the systematic nature of languages.

Each language has a clearly distinguishable pattern of sounds. In other words, every language has a set of sounds, which are combined and distributed in a particular way that makes each language different from others. Note the following examples from Kiswahili and English:

Kiswahili		*English*
kisu	('knife')	king
ngombe	('cow')	struggle

While the sounds used in the two Kiswahili words and the two English words exist in both languages, they are arranged differently in each language. While the sound 'ng', which in Kiswahili starts the word *ngombe*, occurs in English (as we see in the word *king*), the sound cannot occur in the initial position in an English word. That is, there is no English word that starts with the sound 'ng'. Kiswahili and English thus may share sounds, but these sounds do not necessarily pattern in the same way.

A second difference is illustrated in the English word *struggle*. This word starts with three consonant sounds that follow each other (s, t, and r). This kind of combination is not possible in the sound patterns of Kiswahili. Therefore, we cannot find a Kiswahili word that has two or more consonant sounds following each other at the beginning of a word. So we can deduce that there is a systematic way in which each language arranges its sounds, and that behind each arrangement there is a pattern allowing or prohibiting certain sound combinations and distributions.

The notion of pattern can be formulated in a different way; we can say that the combination and the distribution of linguistic elements (for example, sounds) exhibit a particular structure. The linguist can break down a word (a combination of sounds) into its constituents and describe their arrangement or patterning.

As we shall see in later chapters, there are also unique systems of word formation, word arrangement, and conversational structuring in all languages. Given this, we can say that language is a **system of (sub-)systems**. This means that language as a communication system is composed of sub-systems: a system of sounds (a phonological sub-system), a system for forming words (a morphological sub-system), a system for word arrangement (a syntactic sub-system), and a system for the construction of conversations (discourse analysis). (See Chapters 6 to 11.)

Language is rule-governed

A fundamental property of languages as systems is the fact that they are **rule-governed**; the combination of their elements follows particular rules. To illustrate this property, here are some examples from Dholuo, a Nilotic language found in Kenya:

Singular	Plural	Gloss
tado	tedni	roof
pala	pelni	knife
mesa	mesni	table
simba	simbni	boys' hut
dirisa	dirisni	window

If we study these examples carefully, we discover that the singular and plural forms are related in a regular and consistent way. When the plural form of a word is formed, the vowel in the first syllable of the singular noun changes to 'e' (except when this vowel is already an 'e' or is an 'i'), the vowel in the last syllable is deleted, and the element *ni* (called a suffix) is inserted at the end of the word. This regularity can be formulated in the form of a rule, thereby illustrating the rule-governed nature of Dholuo. Similar exercises show the same for any human language.

The rule-governed nature of human languages means that linguists can predict the form of linguistic entities. If we are given a Dholuo noun in the singular, and we know the underlying rule, we can predict its plural form. In other words, there are processes in human speech that are controlled by a set of rules, and it is this set of rules that linguists seek to identify and to describe.

If languages were wholly rule-governed, they would be fairly easy to learn. Unfortunately, they are not entirely rule-governed. Look at the following Dholuo singular nouns and work out what their plural forms are, given your knowledge of the relevant rule: *dhako, siro, dala, ndara,* and *pado.*

You probably decided that the plural forms of these nouns are as follows:

Singular	Plural	Gloss
dhako	dhekni	woman
siro	sirni	pole
dala	delni	homestead
ndara	nderni	path
pado	pedni	piece

If you produced the word forms in the second column of this table, you would have been quite close to being correct. However, the forms *dhekni and *delni are not grammatical. (In linguistics, ungrammatical and non-occurring forms are usually indicated by placing an asterisk [*] directly in front of them.) The plural of *dhako* is *mon* and that of *dala* is *mier*. These examples do not obey the generally applicable rule; they are exceptions to the rule. In other words, they are irregular. This is also reflected in their acquisition; they must be learnt separately.

There is another feature of human languages that we can learn from these examples. The fact that someone learning Dholuo as a foreign language, as well as a Luo child learning it as a first language, would produce the wrong forms *dhekni and *delni points not only to the existence of a rule, but also to the creativity with which the rule is applied by the speakers; speakers and learners can create forms which have not been heard or used before.

Language creativity can be illustrated by the fact that, each time we speak, we do not try to repeat sentences we have spoken before, or which we have heard uttered before by other speakers. Each sentence we utter can be said to be novel. For example, the following sentences could each be produced in the same situation, and mean the same thing:

Could you close the window?
Juma, could you? [pointing at the window]
You can close that window, can't you, Juma?
Could we have that window closed?
Close the window, Juma.
Oh, that breeze is chilly, Juma. [when Juma is seated next to an open window]

The fact that we can produce different sentences to say the same thing means that what we say at any particular moment is not predictable. Whereas we can accurately predict what kind of noise a cat will make when stroked, or when it is hungry and wants to be fed, this is not possible in the case of human language use.

The fact that language is governed by rules can also be demonstrated by the process of language learning. Children do not usually receive any formal instruction from their parents or older siblings when they are in the process of acquiring their first language. Parents do not explain to their children, for example, that in Dholuo gender-marking occurs in colour adjectives, as in the following cases:

nyako-ma-lando	(girl-who-brown)	a brown girl
wuoi-ma-silwal	(boy-who-brown)	a brown boy
nyaroya-ma-dibo	(heifer-which-white)	a white heifer
nyaruath-ma-rachar	(bull-which-white)	a white bull

As you can see here, the Dholuo words for 'brown' and 'white' depend on the gender of the noun: *lando* :: *silwal*, and *dibo* :: *rachar* respectively. This pattern – that masculine and feminine nouns require different colour terms for the same colours – is 'discovered' by learners on their own.

To get back to the main topic of this section, we can say that linguistic forms are structured. This means that they can be analysed in terms of their constituents, and the relationships between these constituents can be described. The notion of structure can be illustrated quite simply by using the example of a four-legged table. If we were to describe the structure of such a table, we would have to say that it consists of five parts (or constituents): one table top and four legs; then we would have to describe the relationship between these five constituents, by noting that the four legs are each placed vertically, with the table top placed on top of the legs, each of which is placed in a specific spot. Once these two dimensions of an object have been described (its constituents and their interrelationship), its structure can be said to have been analysed. The structure of linguistic forms works in exactly the same way. For example, the English word *tables* consists of two constituents: *table-* and *-s*, with the latter following the former (*table+s*, and not **s+table*).

The grammar of a language is also structured

The totality of the units (or elements) in a language, together with the rules that govern their use, is called a **grammar** of the language.

The grammars of languages are usually organized into sub-components, one for each of the different types of linguistic units and the rules that pertain to them: the sounds and sound rules of the language (the phonological component); the word-formation units and the rules which govern their combination (the morphological component); the sentence units and the sentence-formation rules (the syntactic component); and the words of the language (the lexicon). These components of a grammar are arranged together into the whole. The grammar of a language is thus also a structured entity.

The various components of the grammars of African languages are discussed in the second half of this book: the phonetics and phonologies of African languages in Chapters 6 and 7, the morphology and syntax in Chapter 8, and the lexicon in Chapter 9.

Language allows variation and change

Human languages do not have only one fixed form that never changes. No language has an internally controlled resistance to change. Languages change as regards the forms of their units, the rules that govern the use of these units, the meanings of their words, and so on.

Some of these changes may result from the separation of the speakers of a language. For instance, there are variations that arise because of the physical separation of the members of a speech community. One group of speakers may be separated from another by a range of mountains or a body of water, and this physical barrier leads to their speech forms developing in different ways. Varieties that arise in this way are normally called **regional dialects**. This is what has happened in the case of the Dholuo spoken by the Padhola and the Acholi of Uganda and that of the Luo of Kenya. These varieties are now regarded as separate languages, even though, like British and American English, they are mutually comprehensible. Speakers of a language may also become separated because of differences of class, race, age, or religion. When this happens, we have the development of **social dialects**.

Language variation (and ultimately language change) also comes about through contact between different languages. Such contact often leads to borrowing (especially of words). It can also lead to what is called interference (or negative transfer). When people know two languages very well, they may construct forms (sentences, for example) in one of these languages on the basis of the sentence-formation rules of the other. This also happens when people learn a second language; the grammar of their first language interferes with that of the one they are acquiring. This is how the varieties of English spoken by many African communities have acquired their characteristic forms.

The variation in linguistic communities, particularly variations in dialect, gives rise to a rather serious linguistic problem (one that was raised in Chapter 2 with regard to counting languages): when do we count a variety as a language, and when as a dialect of a language? Where do we draw the line between dialect and language? This matter is discussed below with reference to the Zambian varieties Chibemba and Lamba (see Kamwangamalu, forthcoming.[2])

Linguists usually describe dialects in neutral terms, seeing them (as pointed out above) as regionally or socially distinct varieties of one language that are mutually intelligible. In other words, when linguists describe something as a dialect, they do not mean that it is inferior. However, as Wiley (1996: 105) explains, in addition to mutual intelligibility, dialects (and other varieties) that coexist within the same environment may have different social values, particularly if one variety is used as a medium of wider communication. The variety that has the higher social value is usually called a language, while the one with the lower social value is called a dialect.[3] Hudson (1980: 31–2) adds that, in terms of size, a language is assumed to be larger than a dialect; in other words, a variety considered a language contains more items than one classified as a dialect. As an illustration of how thin the line can be between language and dialect, let us consider the language situation in the Congo–Zambia border area, with a focus on what is known in Zambia as the Chibemba cluster.

Chibemba and Lamba: different languages or varieties of one language?

The Chibemba cluster includes the following languages: Chibemba, Lamba, Lala, and Lima. Chibemba is one of Zambia's seven official indigenous languages. The others are Nyanja, Tonga, Lozi, Kaonde, Lunda, and Luvale. Chibemba has the widest demographic distribution and is used across the country as the medium of instruction in the early years of primary education. The question of interest here is, to what extent are Chibemba and Lamba, both of which belong to the Chibemba cluster, separate languages as they have been claimed to be? To see whether this is the case, and to determine the similarities and differences between Chibemba and Lamba, let us look at some features of both languages, with a focus on the lexical, phonological, and syntactic features. (The discussion that follows is fairly technical, and students are advised to study it more closely after working through Chapters 6 to 9.)

Lexical features

As far as the lexicon is concerned, the data shows that in most cases Chibemba and Lamba share a common vocabulary, as is evident in Table 3.1. (Lima and Lala are included in the table to provide a complete representation of the varieties that make up the Chibemba cluster.) Of all the items collected, the only minor difference between Chibemba and Lamba is found in the morphological structure of the Chibemba and Lamba equivalents for the English word *man*; Chibemba has *umwa-ume* while Lamba has *-lalu-ume*. Note, however, that in spite of this difference the stem *-ume* remains the same in both Chibemba and Lamba (as well as in Lala and Lima). The claim that Chibemba and Lamba share a core vocabulary is further shown in Table 3.2. (This table does not include Lima and Lala.) The data shows that, although for some English lexical items Chibemba and Lamba have different words (for example, *oka/omo* 'one', *tamba/-kasa* 'foot'), most of the remaining vocabulary items are identical in both languages.

TABLE 3.1 The Chibemba cluster

English	Chibemba	Lamba	Lima	Lala
sky	umulu	umulu	umulu	umulu
world	icalo	icalo	icalo	icalo
chicken	inkoko	inkuku	inkoko	inkoko
house	inganda	inganda	inganda	inganda
man	**umwaume**	**-lalume**	-lalume	umwaume - (mu)lume
woman	-kashi	-kazi	-kashi	-kashi -(mu)kadzi
love	-temwa	-temwa	-temwa	-temwa
marriage	-cupo	-cupo	-cupo	-cupo
death	umfwa	umvwa	umfwa	umfwa

TABLE 3.2 Lexical similarities between Chibemba and Lamba (compiled from Kashoki and Mann 1978: 82–93)

English	Chibemba	Lamba
all	-onse	-onsi
animal	-nama	-nyama
ashes	-to	-toi

belly	-fumo	-kati
big	-kulu	-kulu
bone	-fupa	-fupa
breathe	-peema	fuuta
buy	-shita	kala
child	-ana	-ana
cold	-talala	-talala
eat	-lya	-lya
father (my)	-taata	taata
father (his)	-wiishe	wiisi
head	-twe	-tu
mother (my)	-maayo	maai
mother (his)	-nyina	yina

Phonological features

Phonologically, the difference between Chibemba and Lamba is marginal, and is limited mainly to vowel height and consonant sonority. The following examples, taken from Table 3.2, show that, for instance, where Chibemba has a mid-vowel at the end of a word, Lamba tends to have a high vowel (for example, *wiishe/wiisi* 'his father'; *onse/onsi* 'all'; *koko/kuku* 'chicken'). Similarly, the information in Table 3.3 shows that where Chibemba has a voiceless fricative, e.g. [s, f, sh], Lamba tends to have a voiced counterpart, e.g. [z, v, dz].

TABLE 3.3 Phonological differences between Chibemba and Lamba

English	Chibemba [s, f, sh]	Lamba [z, v, dz]
hand	-sansa	-zanzala
wife	-kashi	-kazi
to hear	-mfwa	-vwa
name	-shina	-zina
water	-inshi	-inzi
rain	-fula	-vula

Syntactic features

In order to determine syntactic similarities or differences between Chibemba and Lamba, the following syntactic phenomena were considered in both languages: tense-marking, negation, and question formation. These are illustrated in the four examples given below. The a-sentences are Chibemba, and the b-sentences are Lamba. These show that both Chibemba and Lamba use the morpheme -*li*- to mark past tense, -*ka*- to mark future tense, -*sha*- to mark negation, and *ninani* to mark interrogatives (singular form). Note the agreement between the subject and the verb in each of the structures under consideration, and also the fact that, in terms of word order, both Chibemba and Lamba are SVO (subject, verb, object) languages. We must admit, however, that the data presented here is limited, and that further investigation is needed to determine whether the syntactic structures of Chibemba and Lamba are in all cases as strikingly similar as the data here suggests.

Tense marking:

1 I went to visit my brother yesterday
(a) Na-**li**-ya mukutandalila muninane mailo
(b) Na-**li**-le mukutandalila umukwasu mailo

2 I will go to visit my brother tomorrow
(a) N-**ka**-ya mukutandalila munyinane mailo
(b) N-**ka**-ya mukutandalila umukwasu mailo

Negation:

3 I did not go to visit my brother yesterday
(a) N-**sha**-ile mukutandalila munyinane mailo
(b) N-**sha**-ile-po mukutandalila umukwasu mailo

Question formation:

4 Who's crying in the house?
(a) Ninani ulelila munganda?
(b) Ninani ulukulila munganda?

Given the lexical, phonological, and syntactic similarities between Chibemba and Lamba outlined above, and the consequent degree of mutual intelligibility between these two languages, it can be concluded that Chibemba and Lamba are not two separate languages, and that, notwithstanding the distinction between language and dialect, Lamba is a dialect of Chibemba. Therefore, for purposes of standardization, for instance, Chibemba would serve as the basic variety. The following section discusses briefly what standardization would entail for Chibemba and Lamba.

Standardization

Crystal (1985: 286) defines **standardization** as the natural development of a standard language in a speech community, or an attempt by a community to impose one dialect as standard. For Hudson (1980: 32), standardization is a direct and deliberate intervention by society to create a standard language where before there were just 'dialects' (i.e. non-standard varieties). Standard languages are usually associated with prestige and cut across regional differences, providing a unified means of communication and thus an institutionalized norm that can be used in the mass media, for teaching the language to foreigners, and so on. Standardization, argues Trudgill (1983: 161), is necessary in order to facilitate communication, to make possible the establishment of an agreed orthography, and to provide a uniform form for educational material. Standardization involves the following processes, as suggested by Haugen (1966), and cited by Hudson (1980: 32–33) and Wardhaugh (1986: 30–31).

Firstly, a particular variety must be selected as the one to be developed into a standard language. The selected variety can be an existing variety, such as the one used in an important political or commercial centre, as is the case with Chibemba in Zambia, or it could be an amalgam of various varieties. The selection has political significance, as the selected variety gains prestige, so those who already speak it share in this prestige (Hudson 1980: 31).

Secondly, the selected variety must be accepted by the wider community and thus serve as a strong unifying force in the state or region. Acceptance also means that a measure of agreement must be reached about what is included in the language and what is not (Wardhaugh 1986). In this regard, Romaine (1982: 46) notes that one of the characteristics of standardization is that it is intolerant of, for instance, wide variation in phonology and the overlapping of phonemes in phonetic space. In other words, standardization requires an orthographic system in which each sound is represented by a single phonetic symbol. Ferguson (1959), quoted by Wiley (1996: 192), advises that establishing such a system is a crucial basis for developing a modern literate and literary tradition in any language.

Thirdly, the selected variety must be codified: grammar books and dictionaries must be written to 'fix' the language so that everyone knows what is 'correct'.

Finally, the functions of the selected variety must be elaborated or expanded; that is, once accepted as the standard language, the variety should be used in all the functions associated with central government and with writing, for example in parliament, the courts, education, administration, commerce, mass media, and in various forms of literature (Hudson 1980; Wardhaugh 1986).

These four processes, namely selection, acceptance, codification, and elaboration of a variety, must be ordered. The selection and acceptance of a variety, for instance, must precede its codification and elaboration. This is because, as Haugen (1966) points out, if the community cannot accept and agree on which variety is the standard, then neither codification nor elaboration is likely to proceed very far, let alone get off the ground.

If we apply the above processes to Chibemba and Lamba, the following picture emerges. Chibemba is more likely serve as the basis for standardization because it is widely spoken and accepted as the medium of communication by the majority of Zambians, including those living in the Congo–Zambia border area. If this premise is accepted, then where Chibemba and Lamba diverge morphologically (see Tables 3.1 and 3.2) or phonologically (see Table 3.3) the features of Chibemba would prevail over those of Lamba and thus become part of the standard language.

Questions

1   When, and why, do you think, did the standard languages in your country of residence arise? In your search for a possible answer, consider the fact that African communities had no need for such varieties European colonial rule. (Neither were they needed in Europe until after the Middle Ages.)
2   In South Africa, the question of standard Afrikaans and standard English have been or have become serious issues of debate, because standardization has been used as an instrument of political control (see Chapter 1). Does the issue have similar implications in your country?

All languages are equal

Every human language is adequately equipped to meet the demands made on it by its speakers. This means that all of them, and all their varieties, have the words and sounds necessary to express whatever their speakers wish to say, and all of them have the linguistic structures and rules needed to speak about any topic. All languages are equally structurally complex, and all, therefore, are linguistically equal. This means that there are neither 'primitive' nor 'advanced' languages. Every language is flexible enough to admit new elements to enhance its efficiency. Dholuo, for example, has borrowed words like *mitoka* ('motor-car'), *buk* ('book'), *sati* ('shirt'), and *direba* ('driver') from English so that it can express new concepts as they are introduced into that society.

It is true, of course, that some languages have a higher prestige value than others, so that all languages are not seen as socially equal. English, French, and Portuguese, for example, have a higher social value in Africa than most of the indigenous languages,[4] but this does not mean that they are in any way 'better' languages. The fact that one language has a word for a certain concept while another lacks such a word does not mean that one is superior to the other. For example, Kiswahili has three words for rice (in various stages of preparation), whereas English has only one. *Mpunga* is rice in the field, *mchele* is uncooked rice, and *wali* is cooked rice. All these terms translate into *rice* in English. This does not mean that Kiswahili is superior to English; it simply suggests that rice is revered as a staple food in the Swahili community. On the other hand, English has the general term *vehicle* and many specific ones, such as *bus, bicycle, boat,* and *plane.* In fact, this category of words leads to even more specific ones, such as *jumbo jets, racing bicycles, double-decker buses,* and so on, which Kiswahili 'lacks', although it has borrowed some of these words to enrich its vocabulary. Again, this is not to say that English is the superior language. The fact is that all languages have an inherent capacity to accommodate new items by means of different strategies, borrowing being just one of them. Language can thus be described as a self-regulating system that keeps adjusting itself to maintain its efficiency, an attribute that is lacking in other communication systems.

The most important point here is that the cross-cultural and cross-linguistic differences between languages should not be used to judge languages as 'primitive' or 'superior'. The value judgements we hear from time to time about languages are matters of personal taste, or cultural or group prejudices. Any scorn for a language is actually a masked form of scorn for its speakers. Such judgements are therefore social, not linguistic.

Linguistic universals

Now that we have discussed a number of features that are common to all languages, we can introduce the notion of **linguistic universals**.

A striking property of human languages is the existence of features that are common to all languages. For example, all naturally acquired human languages operate with speech sounds and sentence-formation units (such as words); all languages are rule-governed; and all languages function on the basis of the same principles of organization. In addition, all languages are acquired in the same way, change in the same way, perform the same functions (see below), and have the same design features (see below). These common features are generally called linguistic universals.

Language is culturally transmitted

Whereas puppies are born with the innate ability to bark like adult dogs, and goat-kids bleat like adult goats from birth onwards, human children learn only the language or languages spoken in their direct surroundings. This means that, while animal communication systems are instinctive, human language is culture-bound; it is learnt from the community in which a person is born.

It is worth noting that children are born with a capacity to learn any language. For example, a South African child born of Afrikaner parents in a Kiswahili-speaking environment in Kenya will acquire Kiswahili with the same ease, efficiency, and speed as a Kenyan child of Swahili parentage, if both children are given the same amount and quality of exposure to Kiswahili. This underlines the fact that, although the capacity to acquire language is innate, language is not genetically transmitted from parents to their children.

This distinguishes humans from all other creatures. No matter how long a kitten plays with puppies, it will not learn dog noises, and no matter how much exposure animals are given to humans and their languages, they never really master human language.

This highlights two facts: first, that all human children share a universal characteristic that predisposes them to acquire language(s); and, second, that this natural predisposition is present only in the human species. So children acquire language without any conscious effort, seemingly as spontaneously and naturally as growing, while adults' efforts at formal instruction seem to yield negligible results.

Language knowledge

The final point in this discussion of language as a system concerns the question, what is it that we know when we 'know a language'?

Up to now, we have probably given the impression that language and grammar are more or less equivalent. If this were true, knowing a language would mean knowing (only) the grammar of a language. This is not the case, however. Knowing a language, in the sense of having the proficiency to communicate in it, involves much, much more than knowing its grammar. According to Brown (1997: 228–9), an American applied linguist, being able to communicate effectively in a language presupposes at least the following types of communicative knowledge:

- grammatical competence, i.e. knowing how to combine the units of a language into grammatical wholes (words or sentences);
- textual competence, i.e. knowing how to combine sentences into effective texts or conversations/discourses;

- pragmatic competence, i.e. the ability to use language to perform a chosen function (conveying information, manipulating people, and so on), as well as the ability to select the appropriate way of speaking in specific situations; and
- strategic competence, i.e. the ability to manipulate linguistic forms to achieve one's communicative intention (for instance, selling something or persuading others).

Questions

1   What is meant by language as a self-regulating system? Give examples from your mother tongue.
2   Many schoolteachers say that the indigenous languages of Africa cannot be used to teach subjects such as Mathematics or Physics. What are their reasons? Do you agree with them? From where did English get its medical terms? And the names for plants, insects, and animals?
3   Most of the computer terms we use today are borrowed from American English. Is there any reason why these terms can't simply be borrowed from English and used even when we are talking in our own mother tongues?
4   Why aren't English, French, or Portuguese better languages than others?

How else do human languages differ from the communication systems of non-humans?

Language is a human phenomenon that we usually take completely for granted. Yet it is the one capacity which sets us apart from other living creatures. We seldom stop to think about how impossible it would be for us to tell stories, explain to the doctor how we feel, give directions to a traveller, or plan a hunting expedition, without the facility of language. In this section, we shall discuss some of the fundamental **design features**, which can be seen as the unique properties of human languages (see Hockett 1953, cited in Lyons 1977). Some linguists list up to sixteen features, but we shall discuss only four, which we consider to be basic for the study of language in Africa.

Arbitrariness

Language is said to be arbitrary because the words of any language bear no physical resemblance or correspondence to the things they describe, except for a few onomatopoeic expressions such as (in English) *crash*, *mumble*, and *bang*. (And even onomatopoeic words are not similar in all languages. For example, the sound of a gunshot is represented as *bang* in English, *pum* in Spanish, and *tup* in Dholuo.) Let us look at the following examples of arbitrariness:

English	Kiswahili	French	Dholuo
dog	mbwa	chien	guok
water	maji	eau	pi
table	meza	table	mesa
boy	mvulana	garçon	wuoi

Each of the four items is represented differently in each language. Even in the case of *table*, where the French word resembles the English one, and the Kiswahili word is similar to the Dholuo equivalent, the pronunciations are quite different. This means that, even when words are borrowed, the physical representation is often altered so that the word becomes incorporated into the new language and represents meanings in a way that is characteristic of that language.

The point is that there is no logical connection between these words and their meanings. The relationship is thus said to be arbitrary and conventional. There is no reason at all why English has the sound sequence *water*, while Dholuo has *pi* for the same meaning. It is simply a question of members of a speech community agreeing that a particular sound sequence will carry a particular meaning. Once this agreement has been reached, it becomes a convention and therefore everyone follows it, or is expected to do so.

Arbitrariness is also demonstrated in the multiplicity of meanings a sound sequence can convey. For example, in English, the word *round* has various meanings, or, more accurately, there are several English words that share this form. Also, the English sound sequences *tin*, *sand*, and *pat* in Dholuo mean *small*, *persecution*, and *slap* respectively. Such coincidences occur because these elements of language do not bear meanings of their own. They are mere tokens that a language adopts, to which any meaning value can be assigned.

This property is one of the most important and widespread features of human languages. Because of it, however, learning the vocabulary of a language is slow and difficult. There is no discernible rule to guide a learner; every word has to be learnt separately. Nonetheless, it is because of its arbitrary quality that language is flexible and thus capable of signalling meaning without restriction. This would not be possible if every word had a necessary connection with the object or idea it represents in the world. We wouldn't, for example, have words with multiple meanings or different words expressing one meaning.

Productivity

Speakers of any language have the ability to use their language to say anything, including things they have never heard anyone utter before. In other words, it is this property of language that enables native speakers to make and understand an indefinitely large number of sentences, some of which may not ever have been spoken before. Consider the following sentences in English:

> The haughty spider demanded to be supplied with a ton of Viagra.
> Mrs Thatcher was spotted hobnobbing with Maasai morons at Lelmolok.

These two sentences can be understood by any speaker of English, although we are sure no one has ever heard them spoken before. Imagine what the world would be like if there were only a fixed (or finite) set of utterances in each language from which we had to select what to say. One of the most wonderful human qualities is our capacity to construct and understand novel utterances, while other creatures are confined to a limited set of signals, which they have to produce in given situations.

Imagine how long it would take to learn a language if a child had to learn by heart all the sentences in his or her language. Communication would be extremely difficult, if not impossible, if we could only talk to those who had learnt the same sentences we had learnt. This characteristic feature of language is also called open-endedness; it means that we are not constrained in the number of sentences we can produce or in what we can understand.

Displacement

Human language allows us to talk about present events, but we can also talk about events to come and those that have taken place in the past with equal ease. We can also discuss things that are 100 miles away as easily as we speak about things that are present around us. In other words, human language is not restricted in terms of time and place. This means that we can use language not only to discuss what we are doing in the present, but also to tell stories about our ancestors, and to plan for the future.

Although vervet monkeys make several different noises to signal meanings, we have yet to see them using these noises to discuss the effect of illegal logging in their habitat, or a fire that destroyed trees the previous night. Neither would we expect flamingos to use their system of sounds and calls to plan their next migration.

The only evidence of the quality of displacement in other systems is the bee dance, which takes place when the honey bee returns to its fellows in the hive and does a dance to indicate the direction and distance of the source of nectar it has discovered. This is a unique case of displacement in a non-human system, but considering the rigidity with which the dance is performed and the fact that the response of the other bees is regulated and very limited, it is remarkable only in the animal world. Compared to human languages, it lacks the novelty and complexity that are evident in all human language systems. For example, it is highly unlikely that the honey bee can arrive at its hive and wait three hours before delivering the message. The message is invariably delivered during the first few seconds of its arrival back at the hive.

Stimulus-freedom

The fact that we are free to say anything in any context is to say that our utterances are stimulus-free. Consider the following dialogue:

1   A: Good morning.
2   B: Good morning.
3   A: I'm trying to get to St Michael's Cathedral.
4   B: It's about 300 metres down the road, on your left after the clock tower.

Although B's answer in line 2 is predictable, there is nothing to stop him from saying something different. Similarly, what B says in line 4 is not constrained by A's request. He could choose to say, 'I don't know', 'St Michael is dead', 'Three hundred metres ahead', or he could just remain quiet.

However, when a vervet monkey sees a snake approaching, it will make a stereotyped warning noise to alert the others. There is no chance of it making the same noise when it sees a leopard approaching. In other words, the vervet monkey's cries are controlled by the kind of stimulus available; in this case, the specific dangerous animal approaching. The noise is instinctive and fixed, which means that the monkey is entirely powerless in the choice of which noise to make when.

The fact that human language is stimulus-free also makes it possible for us to tell falsehoods, whereas it is unknown for animals to deliberately mislead others by giving a false signal. Prevarication – the deliberate distortion of the truth – is therefore a unique feature of human communication systems not known to exist in animal communication.

The four properties of language outlined above are some of the unique features of human language that make us different from other living creatures. We take them for granted, but if we take a critical look at them, we discover that they are so remarkable that, without them, the line between us and other animals would probably be quite faint.

Questions

1 We know that different language communities use different onomatopoeic forms to refer to the sounds made by animals, birds, vehicles, and so on. In English, a motorcycle 'goes *brrm-brrm*' and a dog 'goes *woof*'. These forms are also often used to refer to these objects in 'baby-talk'. Is this true of other languages you know? Can you give examples?
2 Using the examples you collected for the previous question, discuss how arbitrariness makes language communication special.
3 Would you consider sign language to be a true natural language?

Functions of language

When we speak about language and its meaning, we often do so from the point of view of what it does or what we use it for – its functions. Any layperson's definition of language would most definitely include the attributes concerning the uses of language. In this section we are going to discuss five functions of language. (You might like to turn back to the discussion of the social functions of language in Chapter 1.)

Giving information

One of the basic uses of language is to communicate information. This function is so basic that many people regard it as the only one. It is, therefore, common to come across claims that language is the means by which members of society communicate, or that language is a system of communication. This use of language is called the **informative** or sometimes the **representational** function.

As a medium of communication, language can be used to affirm or refute propositions, to present arguments, to make suggestions, and so on. We thus use language to describe our world and to reason. Our arguments and descriptions can be either correct or incorrect; they involve not only information but also misinformation. In fact, the ability to give incorrect or false information is often cited as one of the distinguishing features of human language. As we've said before, animals are not capable of deliberately sending false signals. Let's look once more at the example of the honey bee. When a hunter bee discovers a source of nectar, it flies back to the hive and performs an intricate dance, watched by other bees. The movements in the dance vary according to the distance to the source of the nectar, its direction, and even the quality of the nectar. A bee dance therefore conveys a great deal of information. However, a bee cannot come back to the hive and perform a dance that misinforms the other bees about the nectar it has discovered. The dance is strictly regulated by the bee's instincts. There is no possibility that individual bees might consciously vary it. This clearly differs from human language use.

Expressing feelings and emotions

Language not only enables us to talk about the world and to display our knowledge and thoughts; it also provides us with a facility to express our intimate feelings and attitudes. The following lines from Okot's *Song of Lawino* illustrate this well:

> Ocol is no longer in love with the old type
> He is in love with a modern girl,
> The name of the beautiful one
> Is Clementine,
> Brother, when you see Clementine!
> The beautiful one aspires
> To look like a white woman;
> Her lips are red-hot
> Like glowing charcoal,
> She resembles the wild cat
> That has dipped its mouth in blood.

Here the primary intention of the poet is not to communicate factual information or to display knowledge of the world, but to convey his feelings and attitudes. Symbolically, he wishes to express his dislike of Clementine (or women like her), and he uses the voice of another woman to convey this. His object is to woo the reader into sharing his perception of the Clementines of this world. In cases like this, language enables us not only to express our emotions and attitudes, but it also makes it possible for us to influence other people to feel as we do. This is called the **expressive** or **imaginative** use of language, and when it is primarily directed towards influencing others, it is known as **conative**.

Expressive language, unlike informative language, is not viewed as either correct or incorrect. A person's emotions cannot be judged as true or false, although we may or may not agree with them. Furthermore, expressive language is not necessarily aimed at an audience. Someone saying a sorrowful prayer in solitude, or writing a love song or poem that they don't intend showing to anyone, is still using language to satisfy their innermost yearnings or to gratify themselves in a personal or private way. In contrast, a persuasive orator at a public meeting aims at winning the support of his or her listeners. In both cases, however, language is being used to express personal feelings, opinions, or attitudes.

Establishing rapport

We often ignore the power of language in bringing people together to start a social interaction. For people to meet and start talking is so normal that we tend to assume that it happens naturally, without any deliberate action by the participants. We are familiar with fixed expressions, such as the greetings that are exchanged between people, but we seldom give any thought to what they are meant to do for us. Let us look at the following Kiswahili conversation, for example:

A:	Shikamoo!	('How are you?')
B:	Marahaba.	('Fine.')
A:	Habari ya bibi?	('How is your wife?')
B:	Hajambo.	('She is fine.')
A:	Na watoto?	('And the children?')
B:	Hawajambo wote.	('They are all fine.')
A:	Na mbuzi?	('And the goats?')
B:	Ni wazima pia.	('They are also fine.')

This exchange sounds like idle chat, especially when A asks B about the health of goats; but in this culture it is perfectly normal to ask after the well-being of domestic animals as if they are part of the family. This is acceptable and respectable. However, as is the case with greetings in all languages, A does not seek factual information about the members of B's family (such as 'Has your wife recovered from her fever?' or 'How many kids were born to your goats this spring?'). The questions, like their answers, are stereotyped and highly predictable. Their real value is to help the speakers make certain that their relationship has not changed since the last time they spoke, and that they can therefore engage in conversation with one another once more. The function of the exchange is thus to initiate the dialogue, and to prepare the stage for the other language functions to follow. Compare the Kiswahili example with the following English conversation:

ANDREW: Daddy, this is my friend, Patrick.
FATHER: How do you do, Patrick.
PATRICK: How do you do, thank you.

On the surface, this exchange is empty of any useful information, but culturally it has significance, something all native speakers recognize as part of their linguistic competence. It is a useful 'starter' before other linguistic transactions begin. This is normally called **phatic** communication. It provides the vital social contact and psychological atmosphere that the participants need before information exchange can take place, and ensures that other communicative transactions proceed smoothly. The phatic function is found in greetings in all languages, and their meanings are culturally determined (see Chapter 11).

Exercising authority

The power relationships between participants in a conversation can be detected in the selection of words, pitch levels, and loudness of voice. The more powerful a participant is, the more latitude he or she has in the choice of what to say, and, more importantly, how to say it. In a multilingual community, the range of choices includes the appropriate language for a given occasion. That is, a speaker must know which language to use when, where, and with whom.

For example, in most families in Kenya, it is considered extremely impudent for a son or daughter to address his or her parents in English, even if the parents are regular users of English. This is not to say that the child cannot use English at all, but when this happens it is usually only after prompting by the parent. So those who hold power normally decide which language is to be spoken in specific situations. This is most apparent when parents switch to English when they wish to chastise or to give strict instructions. This switch is interpreted as a means of asserting authority, and underlines the seriousness of an occasion, situation, or topic of conversation.

Associated with the use of language to exercise authority is its use to regulate the behaviour of others. We give commands and orders, or persuade people to do what we want. We also prohibit people from doing or saying certain things. We do all this by deliberately manipulating our linguistic knowledge. The following English utterances illustrate this:

If I hear you say that again, I will smack you!
Get out of here at once!
You don't talk like that to your little sister!
Girls do not sit like that!

All these utterances are aimed at influencing the actual behaviour of those addressed, so this type of language is known as **regulatory**. It performs the function of regulating what others do or say. It is meant to enforce acceptable standards in the community, and eventually this becomes part of the speakers' knowledge of their language.

Identity marker

The often ignored function of language as a symbol of individual and group identity is probably its most important feature in multilingual and multicultural societies. At an individual level, children use language from a very early age to define their personalities in relation to others, and to separate themselves from objects in the physical world. It is difficult to imagine how children would develop any sense of their individuality without the intervention of language.

Later on in life, we continually make use of language to define ourselves as we play various roles in the community. For example, as a managing director in an office, we would use a variety of language that carries with it the authority inherent in one's position and social status, whereas at home we would adopt a variety that suggests relative equality with our family, the sort of language that enables us to withdraw from the pressures of the workplace. The former would thus be strictly formal and controlled, while the latter would be casual, friendly, and much more relaxed.

These varieties are usually mutually exclusive, or, to use a technical term, they are in **complementary distribution**. In other words, where one is used, the other is either forbidden or completely inappropriate. As part of their mastery of a language, speakers know which variety is to be used where. In a multilingual community, the choice is also between one language and another, and competent bilinguals know which is the appropriate language to use in every situation.

For example, a Kenyan professor of medicine will certainly use English with his or her students, but will use either Kiswahili or English with his or her patients at the surgery, depending on their educational background. At home, our professor can choose between Kiswahili and English (which are home languages for only a few families), or one of the many mother-tongue languages. If the professor plays golf, he or she will most likely speak English with fellow golfers in the club lounge, but will probably use Kiswahili to talk to the caddy on the golf course. When visiting the rural home, he or she will probably use only the mother tongue in conversation with relatives and neighbours, as a way of signalling cultural solidarity.

It would be most unfortunate if our professor had only one variety or language to use in all the situations listed above. This is because there are social rewards and sanctions associated with proper language or variety choice, and all members of the speech community know them. The switches from one variety (or language) to another define the shifting identities of each individual. To give another example, at a funeral Requiem for the first author's father-in-law, the presiding priest approached the daughter of the deceased and humbly asked if she was able to read in Dholuo. (The service was to be conducted in Dholuo and she had been assigned a reading from the Bible.) The priest was greatly relieved to learn that she could read Dholuo, because, as she was a learned woman who taught at a university, her competence in her mother tongue could not be assumed.

Finally, one is a member of a social group, and one of the most telling indices of group identity is language. Language is often used for purposes of inclusion or exclusion from a group. Let us look at the following text from a conversation between Kenyans in their capital city, Nairobi (Myers-Scotton 1993: 40). The setting is the main Nairobi post office. Kiswahili is used, except for switches to Dholuo, which are italicized.

CLERK: Ee. . . sema.
              ('OK. What do you want?')
CUSTOMER: Nipe fomu ya kuchukua pesa.
              ('Give me the form for withdrawing money.')
CLERK: Nipe kitabu kwanza.
              ('Give me your passbook first.')
CUSTOMER: Hebu chukua fomu yangu.
              ('OK, take my passbook.')
CLERK: Bwana, huwezi kutoa pesa leo kwa sababu hujamaliza
              siku saba.
              ('Mister, you can't take out money today because you
              haven't yet finished seven days.')
CUSTOMER: [Switching to Dholuo]
              Konya an marach.
              ('Help me, I'm in trouble.')
CLERK: [Also switching to Dholuo now]
              Anyalo konyi to kik inuo kendo.
              ('I can help you, but don't repeat it.')

The conversation starts off in Kiswahili, the neutral lingua franca used in the cities for cross-ethnic communication, as is the practice between two Kenyans who do not know each other. But the conversation moves to Dholuo when the customer realizes he is dealing with a fellow Luo. He does this to announce his other identity, which he knows carries with it some social obligations and expectations, which are unavailable to him in Kiswahili. This knowledge is shared by the clerk as a speaker of an ethnic language, and so he quickly changes his position and offers to give his 'brother' money even though this goes against the official instructions. Here language is used to evoke group solidarity in order to change the behaviour of one of the parties participating in the conversation.

Questions

1 Choose a piece from any newspaper, and analyse it, describing the language functions in it.
2 What functions does English (or French or Portuguese) perform in your personal life? And your mother tongue? If there is a difference, why is this so?
3 If you live in East Africa, and an unknown white person addresses you in Kiswahili, in what language would you respond? Why? (Or, if you live in southern Africa, and an unknown white person addresses you in a Bantu language such as Setswana, Sesotho, or isiZulu, in what language would you respond? Can you explain your linguistic behaviour?
4 What language (or variety) would you be likely to use when talking to the following people:
   - your mother
   - your father
   - your brothers or sisters
   - your best friend
   - an unknown person of your own age from another part of the country
   - an unknown person from another racial group
   - a friend who speaks the same language as you do, in the presence of someone who doesn't know your language
   - a medical doctor in his or her consulting rooms
   - a professor from your university
   - a former teacher of yours at a chance meeting in the streets?

   Can you give linguistic reasons for your choices?

Branches of linguistics

Since the beginning of the twentieth century, linguistics has grown from an appendage of disciplines such as philosophy and anthropology into a fully-fledged area of study with its own branches. In this section, we shall discuss some of the major branches that you will come across in the course of your studies.

Theoretical linguistics

One of the most important branches of linguistics from the perspective of linguistics in general is **theoretical linguistics**. Theoretical linguistics is concerned with the construction of theories about the nature of human language, its underlying system, its structure, its basic units and rules, and so on. Theoretical linguistics studies language in general, not any particular language. It is primarily concerned with the theoretical framework within which the grammars of particular languages can be analysed and described, and therefore with the concepts and linguistic categories needed for this task. In other words, theoretical linguistics is concerned with the universal properties of language – those properties believed to be present in all natural languages. For example, theoretical linguistics may hold that all languages have sound units called phonemes that signal changes in meaning, and that a combination of these phonemes gives higher-level units of meaning called morphemes. This hypothesis may be tested using data from particular languages. We may come across a language that does not have such categories, and then the hypothesis will be proven wrong.

The analysis and description of particular languages is called **descriptive linguistics**. The aim of the descriptive linguist (usually known as a grammarian) is to produce a grammar of a particular language. While the field of descriptive linguistics relies on theories from theoretical linguistics, theoretical linguists in turn rely on descriptive linguistics for data to validate their theories.

Theoretical linguistics is usually subdivided into sub-disciplines called phonetics and phonology, morphology, syntax, semantics, and lexicology (see Chapters 6 to 9).

Over the past century, there have of course been various approaches to languages. These different perspectives on the nature of human languages have different names. Three of the most influential approaches have been structuralism, generative linguistics, and functionalism.

Structuralism

The term **structuralism** is used in linguistics to refer to an approach that emphasizes the organization of linguistic forms as structures, and which is concerned with determining the constituents of these forms, and the patterns according to which they are combined. The proponents of structuralist linguistics are called structuralists.

Let us look at the following sentences in English:

1. Kamau loves Maria.
2. Kamau loves the girl dearly.

We can analyse the first sentence as having a subject (*Kamau*), a verb (*loves*), and an object (*Maria*). The second sentence has the same pattern, but adds a new element – an adverb (*dearly*). The basic structure of these sentences is: S + V + O + (Adv). This exercise aims to discover the smaller units of language or grammatical categories that combine to give us the bigger unit we call the sentence. This is only one of the ways in which a sentence can be analysed; there are others which are equally valid, but which we won't discuss here (see Chapter 8).

Structuralism is associated with the Swiss linguist Ferdinand de Saussure, who worked at the beginning of the twentieth century, and who is often referred to as the 'father of modern linguistics'. According to Saussure, linguistic items do not exist as isolated entities, but perform their role as part of larger systems, and in relation to other, similar units.

Structuralism is no longer regarded as a separate school of linguistics. Its principles and approaches are still followed, as the structure of linguistic forms still has to be analysed, whatever our theoretical framework may be.

Generative linguistics

This approach to language is associated mainly with the American linguist Noam Chomsky, who developed the theory of **transformational-generative grammar** from the mid-1950s onwards, partly as a response to the influence of earlier linguists who studied language from the perspective of behaviourism. One of the most influential of these linguists was another American, Leonard Bloomfield, who regarded language as something learnt by imitation, arguing that children learn language by habit formation, and explaining language behaviour in terms of stimulus–response patterns. According to this view, a child listens to adults speak (stimulus), responds to what she or he hears (response), and, if the response is positively received (and thus reinforced), she or he repeats the same performance later (repetition/habit formation) until it becomes part of her or his usual speech.

Chomsky, however, argues that children learn language on the basis of an innate faculty designed to enable them to acquire human language. Language acquisition is inborn; it is biologically determined. Children are born with a blueprint of language, as it were, in their minds. Once a child has acquired the grammar of a particular language (its units and rules), she or he is able to produce grammatical sentences at will, even sentences she or he has never heard before. Similarly, she or he can understand any grammatical sentence, even sentences never heard before. Chomsky calls this ability a **generative** ability – an ability that human children use creatively to generate ('produce' or 'understand') utterances. For example, a child learning English could utter the following:

1   I runned very fast.
2   The sheeps are eating grass.

In the first example, the child has learnt the past-tense-formation rule and has used it to produce 'runned', whereas in the second example the child has used the plural-formation rule to produce 'sheeps'. Since no adult uses these forms, it is plausible to argue that the child has discovered the rule, but has **over-generalized** it; in other words, he or she has not yet learnt that there may be exceptions to rules. The child can thus be said to be using these rules creatively to produce novel utterances, rather than merely reproducing what he or she hears from adults. The 'deviations' found in languages spoken by learners are evidence that humans learn languages by 'discovering' the rules of their languages, and not by memorizing 'correct' utterances.

The fact that these rules can help children to produce and understand an indefinite set of utterances, some of which they have never heard before, points to the productivity of language, discussed earlier in this chapter. Moreover, stimuli received from adults do not control what children say. This means that what children produce is 'unpredictable' and does not necessarily resemble what they hear in their environment. But, as their utterances follow particular rules, their creative behaviour is called **rule-governed creativity**.

Functionalism

While structuralism emphasizes the relations that exist within and between linguistic forms, **functionalism** has as its focus the use of languages to perform particular functions. According to this school of thought, structures derive their forms from the functions they perform in the speech community. According to Halliday (1973: 10), 'The child knows what language is because he knows what language does'; elsewhere he says, 'language is as it is because of the functions it has evolved to serve in people's lives' (1978: 4). He postulates that by the time a child is five years old, she or he has identified seven functions that can be performed with language. Let us look at examples of three of these functions:

1   I want a banana. (instrumental)
2   Don't do that! (regulatory)
3   Mummy, what is that? (heuristic)

In the first example, the child knows she or he can use language to satisfy some of her or his material needs; in the second, she or he is using language to control the behaviour of others; and, in the third, she or he is using language to seek information or an explanation about an object in the environment. It is the need for an instrument to perform particular functions that motivates a child to learn and use language, and it is these functions that determine the form or patterning of the linguistic structures. For example, the instrumental function determines the structure of the first sentence, making it a request, whereas the regulatory function makes the second sentence an imperative that conveys a command or order.

There are, of course, many linguistic strategies with which different functions can be performed. In the examples above, the strategies used were mainly the ordering of words (statement, command, or question), or lexical (the use of particular words – *want, don't, what*). Another strategy would be the use of pronunciation to convey attitudes and feeling, for example, through the use of tone or stress.

Historical linguistics

The approaches to linguistics discussed in the previous section are characterized by their not considering language change as a central feature of language. The temporal context of language is left out of reckoning.

In the nineteenth century, however, students of language believed that languages have their present form because of the effect of internal and external forces that changed them over a period of time. This approach meant that all explanations about the nature, structure, and function of language could be found only in the history of the language, and was called **historicism**. The study of language therefore focused on comparing the current state of a language with its earlier forms. **Historical linguistics** is therefore mainly concerned with describing the changes which have occurred in the sounds, the meanings of words, and the grammar of a language over time, and the possible causes of these changes.

The historical linguist collects data from early records of written languages, uses this information to trace the development of languages, and looks for reasons for changes over time. In the case of unwritten languages (as is the case with many African languages), the linguist analyses consistent similarities and differences in present-day languages of the same family, and then tries to uncover an underlying form that might reflect earlier versions of the parent language or **proto-language**. When a linguist tries to reconstruct the earlier stages of a language by using data from the current forms, he or she is engaged in what is called **linguistic reconstruction**.

Sociolinguistics

The simple definition of **sociolinguistics** is 'the study of languages in relation to society' (Hudson 1980: 1). The study of society – its structures, beliefs, traditions, and practices – belongs to the discipline of sociology, and sociolinguistics is thus a hybrid discipline, which combines sociological and linguistic concepts and techniques to study the role and function of language in society. For example, sociolinguists are interested in the social significance of language varieties such as dialects, accents, and idiolects, which (as we have already seen) denote social status and roles, and reflect social relationships between speakers and between social groups.

Different branches of sociolinguistics have developed, and we distinguish between **variation linguistics** (which focuses on the social patterning of linguistic forms), **interactional sociolinguistics** (the study of the use of language for interaction within and between social groups, such as age groups or racial groups), and the **sociology of language**, which studies the interaction between languages as large entities and societies as macro-entities. Furthermore, there are a number of linguistic phenomena that have a social aspect but fall into the categories of pidgin and creole studies, or code-switching and code-mixing (see Chapters 4 and 5).

Concerning the complex relationship between language and society, there are many issues on which scholars differ, or about which they simply do not yet know enough. For example, the Pare of Tanzania and the Taveta of Kenya speak more or less the same language, but because they live in separate states they are regarded as two independent language communities. However, in their dealings with each other in cross-border social and trade transactions, the international political boundary is irrelevant. This calls into question the classical definition of dialects as mutually intelligible varieties of a language, as shown earlier in this chapter. Are Pare and Taveta two languages or are they dialects of the same language? The answer depends on many factors and is not straightforward. Each community might wish to be recognized as culturally autonomous and also as politically distinct. If this is the case, they will demand to be considered as each speaking a language of their own, and not a dialect.

Remember that the classification of a language is often a question of attitude. For example, the former colonial governments referred to African languages as 'vernaculars', a stigmatized term that implied that these were somehow not proper languages. Recently, however, this became a political issue, and the label was dropped (see note 3 below.)

Ethnolinguistics

Ethnolinguistics is the study of language with specific reference to its cultural context, and is related to sociolinguistics. Ethnolinguistics focuses on the interaction of language and culture, and makes use of knowledge and methods of enquiry from the fields of ethnology, anthropology, and linguistics. Ethnolinguists are, for instance, interested in discourse rules in a particular society – how is turn-taking organized in a conversation? Who speaks first when a man and a woman meet, or an elder and a child? (In Chapter 11, for example, we are told that Baganda women kneel when greeting their men.) The ethnolinguist is involved with the identification of these cultural variables, which are the social basis of communication. However, the emphasis is on the description of linguistic interaction as conditioned by these cultural features and not the cultural interactions per se. Ethonolinguistics is also interested in how meaning is structured and negotiated in different cultural settings.

Psycholinguistics

Psycholinguistics is the branch of linguistics that is interested in the relationship between language and psychological phenomena, such as the way in which the human child acquires language **(language acquisition)**, the localization of language in the brain **(neurolinguistics)**, the link between language and mental/cognitive processes (such as memorization, thinking/reasoning, perceiving), and the way in which language is processed in the brain during linguistic production and interpretation.

The best-developed area in psycholinguistics is the study of language acquisition, which combines general theories of learning with linguistic theories about the nature of language. For example, do children learn language by imitation or are they born with a natural capacity for language learning, which only needs to be activated, with the child then able to construct an internal grammar with minimal external influence? As in other areas of linguistic study, there is no agreement on this and other issues. This is partly because it is not possible to be certain what goes on in the human mind.

Discourse analysis and pragmatics

In the first half of this century, linguistics was almost exclusively directed at the study of language as a system. More recently, however, attention has also been given to the use of language in interpersonal communication. The principles underlying human discourse, the factors that play a part in the verbal communication process, the nature of communicative competence, and the structure of discourse/texts (both spoken and written) are coming under increasing scrutiny (see Chapter 10). One topic that has received particular attention, given the increasing globalization and international migration, is cross-cultural communication (see Chapter 11).

Applied linguistics

When theories and findings from linguistic research are applied in solving practical tasks, this is called **applied linguistics**. For example, the linguistic theories about how a child acquires language are used in the development of language teaching methodologies and syllabuses for teaching language, especially foreign-language teaching. **Educational linguistics** focuses on solving language problems in education, for example, mother-tongue instruction and bilingual education programmes in multicultural and multilingual countries (see Chapter 12).

The linguistic analysis of language disorders is also developing into a distinct area of applied linguistics called **clinical linguistics**.

Recently the line between pure and applied linguistics has become increasingly blurred, and whether this distinction is still necessary is currently a matter of controversy.

Endnotes

1 We would have liked to include a discussion of the scientific character of linguistics in this chapter. However, the topic is extremely complex and we have far too little space. We therefore can offer only a short list of some of its criteria here. As a *science*, linguistics requires its hypotheses, its generalizations, its analyses, and its descriptions of linguistic phenomena to be systematic and testable, and to be constructed on the basis of factual data collected with methods whose validity can be checked.

2 The section that follows was written by Professor Kamwangamalu, the author of

Chapter 4.

3 In a 'fact file' about Congo-Kinshasa (former Zaire), *The Saturday Paper* (17 May 1997) uses the term *language* to refer to French, but *dialect* to refer to the Congo's indigenous languages.

4 The social value of a language is determined by historical and political factors that differ from place to place; Portuguese, which has a high social value in some African countries, has a lower social value (compared to English and Spanish) in North America, for example.

Bibliography

BROWN, H. DOUGLAS. 1997. *Principles of Language Learning and Language Teaching.* New York: Prentice-Hall.

CHOMSKY, NOAM. 1972. *Language and Mind.* New York: Harcourt Brace Jovanovich.

CRYSTAL, D. 1985. *A Dictionary of Linguistics and Phonetics.* Oxford: Basil Blackwell.

FERGUSON, C.A. 1972. *Language Structure and Language Use.* Stanford: Stanford University Press.

HALLIDAY, M.A.K. 1973. *Explorations in the Functions of Language.* London: Edward Arnold.

———— 1978. *Language as Social Semiotic.* London: Edward Arnold.

HAUGEN, E. 1966. *Language Conflict and Language Planning: the Case of Modern Norwegian.* Cambridge, Mass.: Harvard University Press.

HUDSON, R.A. 1980. *Sociolinguistics.* Cambridge: Cambridge University Press.

KAMWANGAMALU, N.M. (forthcoming). 'Language frontiers, language standardization, and mother tongue education: The Zaire–Zambia border area with reference to the Chibemba cluster.' *South African Journal of African Languages.*

KASHOKI, M., and M. MANN. 1978. A general sketch of the Bantu languages of Zambia. In S. Ohannessian and M. Kashoki (eds.), 9–46.

LYONS, J. 1977. *Semantics,* Vol. 1. Cambridge: Cambridge University Press.

———— 1981. *Language and Linguistics.* Cambridge: Cambridge University Press.

MYERS-SCOTTON, C. 1993. *Social Motivation for Code Switching.* Oxford: Oxford University Press.

OKOT P'BITEK. 1966. *Song of Lawino.* Nairobi: East African Publishing House.

ROMAINE, S. (ed.) 1982. *Sociolinguistic Variation in Speech Communities.* London: Edward Arnold.

TRUDGILL, P. 1983. *Sociolinguistics: an Introduction to Language and Society.* Harmondsworth, Middlesex: Penguin Books.

WARDHAUGH, R. 1986. *An Introduction to Sociolinguistics.* New York: Basil Blackwell.

WILEY, T.G. 1996. 'Language planning and policy'. In S.L. McKay and N.H. Hornberger (eds.), *Sociolinguistics and Language Teaching,* 103–47. Cambridge: Cambridge University Press.

4 Languages in contact

Nkonko M. Kamwangamalu

Expected outcomes

At the end of this chapter you should be able to:
1 Define the following concepts: borrowing, code-switching, code-mixing, language change, pidginization, creolization, and diglossia.
2 Collect examples of these phenomena in the language behaviour in your community, and then classify these on the basis of the different types of contact phenomena (in other words, label the phenomena).
3 Analyse the collected examples as cases of contact phenomena.
4 Determine the possible reasons for the relevant cases of borrowing and/or code-switching, motivating your views linguistically.
5 Collect examples of conversations in different languages from a multilingual community.
6 Determine the possible reasons for the particular choices of language in the examples you have collected.

Introduction

Africa is so linguistically complex that it has been likened to the Tower of Babel (see, for example, Mühlhäusler 1995). Contact between languages is common-place. In South Africa, for instance, Sesotho, Tshivenda, English, Afrikaans, and isiXhosa come into contact with one another daily as their respective speakers meet and mix. The same is true for Portuguese, xiTswa, xiTsonga, and giRonga in Mozambique; French, Lingala, Ciluba, and Kiswahili in the Democratic Republic of Congo; English, ciNyanja, ciChewa, and ciTumbuka in Malawi; English, Yoruba, Igbo, and Hausa in Nigeria, to name but a few. When two or more languages come into contact, as is the case in multilingual communities in Africa and elsewhere in the world, they colour one another. This colouring, which Haugen (1972) has termed **interlingual contagion**, manifests itself in language contact phenomena such as borrowing, code-switching, code-mixing, language change, pidginization, creolization, and diglossia. This chapter describes these phenomena and examines some of the issues to which language contact can give rise.

Questions

1 How many languages are spoken in the locality where you live? Do they have names?
2 If your community is multilingual, how did this happen? (What is the history?)
3 Is there a pattern in the use of the different languages? Are some languages spoken by certain groups in the community, and other languages by other groups? Do people who speak the same language tend to live in the same area? Is language a social divider in your community?
4 Are there any 'mixed' languages in your community? If so, which languages have contributed to the mixture? Who uses these mixed languages? Why?
5 What is your intuitive or gut reaction to these languages? Are they good or bad? What do other people in your community think of them?

Some basic concepts in language contact studies

Borrowing

Borrowing is defined as the introduction of single words or short, frozen, idiomatic phrases from one language into another (Gumperz 1982: 66). While not everyone agrees on exactly what does or does not constitute borrowing, most investigators agree that when a linguistic item is borrowed, it is integrated into the grammatical system of the host or borrowing language (see Weinreich 1964; Poplack et al. 1989). In some cases, integration of a linguistic item from one language into another entails adapting the borrowed item to the phonological, morphological, and syntactic patterns of the borrowing language. For instance, the words listed in 1, 2, and 3 below were originally English. However, as a result of language contact, these words have been introduced into Ciluba, Kiswahili, and isiZulu. Similarly, contact between French and Ciluba in the Congo has resulted in the importing of French words into Ciluba, as illustrated in 4. The English and French loan words presented here can be referred to as **borrowing proper** or **nativization** (according to Kachru, 1983).

1   *Ciluba*   *English*
    mbeketshi   bucket
    mbulanketa   blanket
    kanife   knife
    kandeya   candle
    obiside   offside

2   *Kiswahili*   *English*
    dereva   driver
    shati   shirt
    cheki   cheque

3   *isiZulu*   *English*
    isikholo   school
    isiphuni   spoon
    ibhola   ball
    iayani   iron

4   *Ciluba*   *French*
    kalande   canal d'eau   ('drainage tube')
    kaye   cahier   ('notebook')
    tabulo   tableau   ('blackboard')
    shimishi   chemise   ('shirt')

In other cases, however, the borrowed units may resist the type of integration just described, as can be seen in the case of English numbers and expressions for indicating time (for example, *ten o'clock, five cents, twenty rand, half-past nine*) used in South African languages such as isiZulu, Sesotho, and Tshivenda, among others, or French numbers and expressions for indicating time (for example, *trois heures du matin* 'three o'clock in the morning', *cinquante makuta* 'fifty makuta') used in the languages of the Congo such as Ciluba, Kikongo, and Cibemba. Compare the responses to an African-language equivalent of the English question *How much are the bananas?* or to the French question '*Quelle heure est-il?*' ('What time is it?') In each case, the response is invariably an expression borrowed from English or French respectively, regardless of the African language involved.

English: How much are the bananas? Two rand.
siSwati: Umalini banana? Two rand.
isiZulu: Imalini ubanana? Two rand.
isiXhosa: Zibiza ntoni ezibanana zako sana? Two rand.

French: Quelle heure est-il? ('What time is it?') Cinq heures. ('five o'clock.')
Lingala: (Tozali) ntango nini? Cinq heures. ('five o'clock.')
Ciluba: (Tudi) diba kayi ? Cinq heures. ('five o'clock.')
Kiswahili: Saa ngapi? Cinq heures. ('five o'clock.')

In the literature on code-switching, examples such as the French and English numbers and expressions for indicating time mentioned above are known as **nonce borrowing**. Poplack (1978) defines nonce borrowing as the use of linguistic items from one language (such as English or French) in discourse in another language (such as siSwati or Ciluba) that show no signs of adaptation to the linguistic system of the latter language. Such non-integrated loans are sometimes mistaken for code-switching, which will be discussed in the next section. This is because, as in the case of code-switching, linguistic units that qualify as nonce borrowings retain their original phonological and morphological aspects. It seems that the distinction between nonce borrowing and code-switching lies in the level of social integration. Hasselmo (1972: 180) interprets social integration as a function of the degree of consistency, regularity, and frequency with which linguistic items from one language are used in discourse in another language, in a given context. In this sense, then, nonce borrowing refers to linguistic items that are socially integrated, while code-switching refers to those that are not.

Questions and tasks

1 Collect examples of borrowing from the everyday speech of people in your community, and classify them on the basis of (a) their frequency of occurrence, (b) whether they have been nativized or not, and (c) the word classes they belong to (nouns, verbs, and so on).
2 What are or were the reasons for these borrowings? Did they have to do with the introduction of new concepts or technologies (such as computers)? Do people sometimes use foreign words or phrases to make an impression?
3 Which language is the borrowing language and which the providing language? Is there a reason for this difference? Do you think the economic, political, or social power of the two language communities plays a role?

Code-switching and code-mixing

The alternating use of two or more languages within the same conversation is a hallmark of the linguistic behaviour of bilingual speakers around the world (see Gumperz 1974; Kachru 1978; Poplack 1978; Myers-Scotton 1988; Milroy and Muysken 1995; and Kamwangamalu 1996). Traditionally, the terms code-switching and code-mixing are used to label subtypes of such linguistic behaviour. **Code-switching** refers to language alternation across sentence boundaries, and **code-mixing** to language alternation within sentence boundaries. The data in examples 1 and 2 below illustrate code-mixing (Kamwangamalu 1989a: 239), while those in 3 and 4 illustrate code-switching.

Code-mixing

1 Lingala–*French*

Okomona soki azongi mosala boye akokota na *chambre a coucher* mpo na *ko-se-changer*. Nsima azongi na *salon* nde abandi kosala ngai *ba-remarques* ya mike mike, o eloko oyo *il fallait* osala boye, oyo boye *ca va mais*... o boye na boye. Mokili abalukeli biso awa na *Amerique*, tosala boni kasi.

('You notice that when she comes back from work, she goes to the bedroom to change her clothes. Then she comes back to the living-room and starts making minor remarks to me: Oh, this thing here you should have done it this way; that thing over there is okay but... and so on. America has turned the world upside-down against us. What else can we do?')

2 Kiswahili–*French*

Hakuweza kumtumia *toutes les choses* alimuomba kwa sababu *a-li-mu-sur-prendre* wagati alikua *na-preparer voyage* ya kwenda Bulaye.

('He could not send her all the things she asked for, because her request came as a surprise to him at a time when he was preparing for a trip to Europe.')

Code-switching

3 Afrikaans–*English*–*Sesotho*–**isiZulu**

Ek wil net graag vra ... my naam is K. Makhudo. Ek werk vir die Suid-Afrikaanse Uitsaaikorporasie maar ek teenwoordig hulle glad nie. Ek wil net vra hoekom gebruik ons nie die ander tale vir hierdie program? Hoekom? Is dit want onse gedagte, elkeen van ons, ons dink Engels is hierdie groot magtige taal wat nie ... ons kan nie doen sonder daardie taal nie. En dit is verkeerd. *We are still thinking along compartmentalized ways and that's terrible! I think that symbolic things must happen in this country. We must begin to use these languages. We can't say it's impractical all the time. We can't say we don't have enough money for the tertiary institutions not to use these languages. We have not even tried. We have not begun yet. We don't have a plan.* **Ha re etse letho. Re olutse feela ... rea tseha, re re ha hona chelete. Ha re khgone ho lefa. Lento uyazi isifaka ihlazo ngampela, Sikhathele ...**

('I just want to ask ... My name is K. Makhudo. I work for the South African Broadcasting Corporation. But I do not represent them at all. I just want to ask ... Why do we not use other languages in this programme? Why not? It's because our thoughts, each of us, we think English is a big powerful language that doesn't ... We can't do without this language. And that's wrong. *We are still {...} have a plan.* **We are not doing anything. We are just sitting. We are wringing our hands. We are laughing. We are saying there is no money. We can't afford to pay. This thing is truly embarrassing! We are tired ...**')

4   English–*Siswati*

He is talking about two schools out of how many? *Kudlalelwani kojwa vele ngabatali labangasebenti?*

('He is talking about two schools out of how many? *Why are unemployed parents made fools of?*')

Although earlier studies (see Espinosa 1917; Gumperz 1974; Kachru 1978) distinguish between code-switching and code-mixing, as mentioned above, current studies (see Myers-Scotton 1993; Heller 1995; and Auer 1997) tend to use code-switching as a cover term for instances of both code-switching and code-mixing, and this will be our practice in the rest of this chapter. The linguistic units (words, phrases, and sentences) used in code-switching preserve their original phonological and morphological aspects. This point has been widely observed in many studies (see Gumperz 1982; Kachru 1983; Gibbons 1987). It constitutes one of the criteria that sets code-switching apart from the language contact phenomenon – non-integrated or nonce borrowing – discussed earlier. Other criteria include those presented by Sridhar and Sridhar (1980: 204), who note that code-switching is different from borrowing in the following important respects. In code-switching, first of all, the switched elements do not fill 'lexical gaps' in the host language; secondly, they are not restricted to a more or less limited set of lexical items accepted by the speech community of the host language; and thirdly, they are not necessarily assimilated into the host language by regular phonological and morphological processes. Also, as Pfaff (1979: 295) rightly points out, the two terms, code-switching and borrowing, make totally different claims about the competence of the individual speaker. Borrowing can occur in both monolingual and bilingual speech, while code-switching is necessarily a product of bilingual competence. In other words, code-switching presupposes competence in at least two languages (or two distinct varieties of a language), while borrowing does not.

A note on research on code-switching

As a final comment on the preceding discussion, it is worth pointing out that code-switching has become one of the most intensively investigated topics in studies of language contact phenomena. This research can be divided into two main perspectives: the pragmatic and the syntactic perspectives.[1] The pragmatic perspective has been concerned with explaining why bilingual speakers engage in code-switching (see Nartey 1982; Goke-Pariola 1983; Heller 1992; Meeuwis and Blommaert 1994). The syntactic perspective has focused on determining whether there are structural constraints on code-switching (see Poplack 1981; Lin and Stanford 1982; Sobins 1984; Berk-Seligson 1986; Clyne 1987). Briefly, contrary to earlier studies, such as those of Espinosa (1917) and Lance (1972), which claimed that code-switching was random linguistic behaviour, research into the pragmatics of code-switching has convincingly shown that it is not an end in itself, but that it can serve a wide range of functions in the interactions of bilinguals, such as in-group identification, modernization, confidentiality, eliteness, and so on.[2] Similarly, syntactic research has likewise shown that code-switching is not random, and that there are constraints on when switches are or are not allowed to occur in code-switching utterances. However, defining such constraints has remained a thorny issue in code-switching research (see, for instance, Bentahila and Davies 1983, Khati 1992, and Kamwangamalu 1994 for discussion of constraints on code-switching with English or French in African languages).

As a last example, let us look at the following example from Parkin (1974: 210). (The main language is Dholuo; Kiswahili is indicated by italics, and English by bold italics.)

1　1ST LUO:　Onego ikendi. ('You ought to marry.')
2　2ND LUO:　Kinyalo miya dhok. ('If you can give me the cattle.')
3　1ST LUO:　Dhi penj wuoru. ('Go and ask your father.')
4　2ND LUO:　*Baba bado anasema niko **young**.* ('My father still says I am too young.')
5　1ST LUO:　In-**young**-nadi? Itiyo-*umetosa kuwa na watoto-* **and every thing**. ('How are you young? You are working. You have

reached a stage when you should have children and everything.')

6 2ND LUO: Nyaka ayud nyako maber. ('I have to get a good girl.')
7 1ST LUO: Karang'o masani to ichiegni bedo-*mzee*-ni? ('But when? You
            are soon becoming an old man.')

This conversation takes place between two adult speakers of Dholuo who live
in Nairobi. They are both tailors, a trade dominated by not very highly educated Kenyans. However, they both have some knowledge of English and
Kiswahili besides their mother tongue. The switch to Kiswahili and English in 4
can be interpreted in many ways, and one plausible explanation is that the second Luo would like to reinforce his claim to youthfulness by using the language
generally associated with the youth, particularly in rural areas. Most of the tailors in Nairobi are migrant workers from the countryside, and these two
probably moved to Nairobi as adults looking for work. The language usage
here is perhaps meant to ward off the challenge that the second speaker is
growing old and should marry and start a family. When the first Luo retorts in
the same languages in 5, the second speaker advances another reason for his
delay in getting married; this time, it is not that he is still too young, but that he
is still looking for the right partner. What started as a moment of teasing in the
intimate mother tongue thus develops into a rather more competitive verbal
exchange that calls for the use of other linguistic codes.

The use of three languages may not reflect any serious social meaning
beyond the skilful stylistic variations demonstrated by the two speakers, who
draw on their rich language repertoires to enliven the conversation. At the marketplace where these two men work, it is usual for people gathered there to
engage in conversation as they wait for their garments to be mended or
finished. When the tailors have no company to chat to, they find all kinds of
topics to keep them engaged in various linguistic exchanges – what Parkin calls
language games. It is within this social context that we should interpret the use
of different languages in a single conversation by people who share a mother
tongue. Here conversation is an art to be learnt, mastered, and used with dili-
gence and style.

Questions and tasks

1 Collect examples of code-switching from the everyday speech of
   people in your speech community. (If you can't find any examples of
   code-switching, look at why there are none.)
2 Do the transitions occur at specific places in the sentences and the

discourses? If so, where do they take place?

3 Why do these transitions occur at these places?

4 Do you think the switching occurs because the discourse participants want to accommodate each other (facilitate communication, or 'be nice' to each other)? Or does it rather have to do with the respective statuses of the languages involved?

Code-switching and language change

The use of code-switching by bilingual speakers, whether for purposes of confidentiality, in-group identification, or for any other reason, is often accompanied by change and innovation in the structures of the languages involved. This may involve, as D'Souza (1987: 197) points out, the creation of new styles and registers, the introduction of new grammatical features, the introduction of new discursive and stylistic devices, the introduction of new sounds, and expansion of the vocabulary, to name just a few examples. This section presents some instances of language change in Lingala and Kiswahili as a result of Lingala–French and Kiswahili–English code-switching in the Democratic Republic of Congo and Tanzania respectively (Kamwangamalu 1989b: 327–329).

Lingala–French

French has been used for over a century as the only official language in the Congo. Given this status, French has had considerable influence not only on socio-political life, a point to which we shall return later (see the section on diglossia), but also on the structure of local languages, especially Lingala, Kiswahili, Kikongo, and Ciluba. Traces of French influence on these languages can be found at all linguistic levels: phonology, lexicon, morphology, and syntax. The data in example 1 below (Sesep 1978: 7) illustrates some aspects of this influence on Lingala, which has acquired from French new features it originally did not have in its phonological and morpho-syntactic structures. These features include new sounds and consonant clusters, a double plural, and a double infinitive.

1 L'heure ya kala *trois quarts* ya *ba-jeunes* bazali *ko-comprendre avenir* te, *mais* sikoyo na *quatre quarts, trois quarts* baza *ko-comprendre l'avenir* mpe *la plupart* bakoti kelasi.

('In the past, three-fourths of young men did not care about the future, but now, three out of four-fourths do care and most do go to school.')

Phonologically, the sound [r] (as in *trois, comprendre*), which Lingala did not originally have, is being introduced into the Lingala sound system as a result of Lingala–French code-switching. Other potential phonological innovations include consonant clusters such as [pl], as in *plupart*; and [kr], as in *krize*. Over time, these clusters might become part of the Lingala phonological system.

Morphologically, code-switching has led to the development in Lingala of the use of a double plural-marking, as can be seen in words such as *ba-jeunes* ('young men') and *ba-cahiers* ('notebooks'). *Ba-* is a plural human class noun prefix in Lingala. The French word *jeunes* is the plural form of the corresponding singular noun *jeune*, as is *cahiers* of *cahier*. However, these French plural nouns are used with the Lingala plural prefix *ba-*. The combination of these elements has created a double plural, a feature that is not inherent in either Lingala or French. Also, the use of *ba-* with French words such as *cahiers* has been overgeneralized[3] to Lingala non-human class nouns. Examples of these are *ndako/bandako* ('house/houses'), *nsoso/bansoso* ('chicken/chickens'), and *kiti/bakiti* ('chair/chairs'). Usually, nouns such as these should have the same form for both singular and plural, the difference between the two being marked only by the verbal-agreement prefix as in examples (a) and (b) respectively:

(a) Nsoso ezali awa. ('The chicken is here.')
(b) Nsoso izali awa. ('The chickens are here.')

Syntactically, code-switching has introduced double infinitives into Lingala. For instance. the word *ko-comprendre* (see example 1) consists of two elements: the Lingala infinitive marker *ko-* ('to') and the French infinitive verb *comprendre* ('to understand'). The combination of these elements has resulted in a double infinitive, a feature that did not previously exist in Lingala. In addition, words in Lingala (and related Bantu languages) do not end with an open syllable. However, code-switched items such as *jeunes* in *ba-jeunes* retain their plural marker *-s*. For example, the word sequence in sentence (a) below is unacceptable because this marker has not been retained, while sentence (b) is considered well formed for the opposite reason:

(a) **Ba-jeune* bakokota te.
(b) *Ba-jeunes* bakokota te. ('Young men will not enter.')

Although cases such as (b) are not a problem in spoken Lingala, since *-s* is not pronounced when in word-final position anyway, they present a problem in the written language.

From a lexical standpoint, thousands of French words have been nativized and entered into the Lingala lexicon. These cases are, strictly speaking, examples of borrowing rather than code-switching. Some of these words are *mersi* (from the French *merci* 'thank you'); *fami* (*famille* 'family'); and *bonane* (*bonne anne* 'happy new year'). The massive nativization of French words into Lingala has created a homonymic clash between native words and imported ones. The original Lingala words for the above (*eboto*, *libota*, and *mbula ya sika*) have been displaced by borrowed French words and are now part of Lingala–French speakers' passive knowledge of Lingala only, whereas the corresponding words *mersi*, *fami*, and *bonane* are more common in colloquial Lingala.

Kiswahili–English

Kiswahili and English have been in contact for over a century in the East African countries of Tanzania and Kenya. The Kiswahili–English code-switching resulting from this prolonged contact has had a considerable influence on the linguistic structure of Kiswahili, especially on Kiswahili lexicon and syntax. In Tanzania, for instance, the influence of code-switching is marked by an extension of the inherent meaning of Kiswahili words to match their English counterparts. Mkilifi (1978: 140) discusses, for example, the utterance *Umenunua fruit* ('Did you buy fruit?'), which was produced by a Kiswahili–English bilingual speaker. When asked why he used the English word *fruit* instead of the Kiswahili *matunda*, he responded that *matunda* referred to fruit on trees for picking, whereas *fruit* referred to *matunda* bought in the market. According to Mkilifi, the use of *fruit* rather than *matunda* in this context is an innovation that extends the meaning of the existing term *matunda* or gives it a new meaning altogether. Mkilifi points out that many new political, economic, and scientific terms have been added to Kiswahili in this way. The following Kiswahili–English extract from a tape-recorded verbal report by a research assistant (Mkilifi 1978: 140) includes a number of such terms (such as *kustandardize* ('to standardize'), *kuyasolve* ('to solve'), *dictionary*, *Research Bureau*, and so on):

Inakuwa maana yake *they go against their own wishes kustandardize*, maana wengi katika *legal affairs hawajastandardize* bwana, matatizo haya wameweze *kuyasolve* kwa kutumia *dictionary* mpya *published by the legal Research Bureau of the University*.

('This is because they go against their own wishes to standardize everything, while in the legal affairs no standardization has taken place. This can be solved by using the new dictionary published by the legal Research Bureau of the University.')

From a syntactic point of view, adverbs in Kiswahili traditionally occur in sentence-final position, but not in sentence-initial position. However, there is now in various registers of Kiswahili a tendency to use adverbs in sentence-initial position. The following is a case in point:

(a) Jambo hili nizuri *kielimu*. (Kiswahili syntax)
     ('This (matter) is an advantage, educationally.')

(b) *Kielimu* jambo hili nizuri. (English syntax)
     ('Educationally, this (matter) is an advantage.')

Here, the adverb *kielimu* should normally occur at the end of the sentence, as in (a). However, due to the influence of code-switching, (a) is commonly rendered as in (b), with the adverb occurring in sentence-initial position.

Questions

1   If you live in an urban area, do the people in your community use 'mixed' languages? If so, do these have names? Can people outside your community understand them?
2   Are there particular groups of people who speak these languages? Can you give the reasons why they use them?
3   If these mixed languages do occur, are they regarded as an indication that the original language is degenerating?
4   Do you think such languages cause any problems, for example in schools? If so, what should teachers do about these problems?

Language choice in multilingual communities

In a discussion of languages in contact, it is important to ask what criteria people use when choosing between various languages in everyday conversations in multilingual societies (or what governs their choices in situations of code-switching). This issue will be discussed with reference to Kenya.[4]

In Kenya, more than forty languages are spoken besides English and Kiswahili, which are the official languages and the main lingua francas. In most urban centres, speakers of a wide range of languages meet in government offices, marketplaces, schools, churches, and so on. The urban centres are therefore multilingual, and urban dwellers need to master the use of more than one language in order to operate effectively and confidently in the various situations they encounter every day.

In the rural communities, the situation is a little different. Depending on factors such as the neighbouring language communities, the existing communications network, distances from the nearest administrative centre, and so forth, most rural people learn English and Kiswahili at school alongside their mother tongues, and also come into contact with a variety of other Kenyan languages.

An urban Kenyan boy will wake up on a Sunday morning and use his mother tongue (maybe Kikuyu, Dholuo, Suba, Maasai, or Tugen) with his family, go out to buy bread from a nearby shop and use Kiswahili to negotiate the purchase with the vendor. On his way home from the kiosk, he meets a friend with whom he might speak Sheng, or a mixture of Sheng, Kiswahili, and English. After breakfast, he goes to church, where the service may be in English or Kiswahili, depending on the socio-economic status of the family and the surrounding community. At school the next day, he speaks English in all his lessons except for the Kiswahili lesson. On the playground, depending on the type of school he attends, he uses Kiswahili or English. If it is a high-cost private school, the usual playground language is English, whereas at the less expensive public schools it may be either English or Kiswahili. When he goes to the headmaster's office, the boy may use Kiswahili to address the secretary, but he will certainly speak English to the headmaster.

This clearly shows that language choice changes according to the various situations that arise and the different people to be addressed. The situations here can be summarized as those involving family, commerce, friendship, religion, education, recreation, administration, and hierarchy. These are called **domains**, and the people spoken to are known as **addressees** (Fishman 1972: 22. Table 4.1 below, taken from Fishman, shows some domains of language use.) Language choice can thus be said to depend on both the domain of usage and the particular addressee. This is a rather simple way of explaining how we decide which language to use when, where, and with whom, but it helps to illustrate the connection between our knowledge of language and the context of language use. (See also Chapter 10, where the ideas of the educational sociolinguist Dell Hymes are discussed.)

TABLE 4.1 Domains of language use

Domain	Addressee	Setting	Topic	Variety/code
Family	Parent	Home	Planning a family party	
Friendship	Friend	Beach	How to play beach tennis	
Religion	Priest	Church	Choosing Sunday liturgy	
Education	Teacher	School	Solving a maths problem	
Employment	Employer	Workplace	Applying for promotion	

Pidginization/creolization

Wardhaugh (1992: 58) defines a **pidgin** as a language that has no native speakers; it is no one's first language, but a contact language instead (see also Chapter 2). It is a language that, according to Holm (1988: 4–5), results from extended contact between groups of people who have no language in common, that is, whose languages are mutually unintelligible. A pidgin evolves when such people need some means of verbal communication, perhaps for trade purposes, but no group learns the native language of any other group, for social reasons that may include lack of trust or motivation or insufficient contact. A pidgin differs from a 'normal' language both in terms of function and structure. In terms of function, a pidgin is used mainly for intertribal communication. So it is not used, for instance, in government, administration, education, or the media, and it has a low social status in the community. In terms of structure, a pidgin is characterized by a limited vocabulary and a simplified grammar. For instance, nouns are not marked for number and gender, and verbs lack tense-markers and inflectional morphemes. Fanagalo in South Africa and Lingala (in its original form) in the Congo are examples of pidgins. Fanagalo was created by speakers of isiZulu, English, and Afrikaans (as well as various Indian languages) after British settlers arrived in Natal together with indentured Indians brought to work in the sugar-cane fields of Natal, in the mid-nineteenth century. It was later adopted for use in the mining industry. Adendorff (1993: 24) remarks that Fanagalo can be put to many uses; in some contexts, it can serve as a marker of asymmetrical power relationships, usually that of master and servant (particularly between black servants and their white masters or mistresses), while in others it can be used as a marker of solidarity (see also Chapter 1).

Like Fanagalo, Lingala originated as a pidgin created in the 1890s by speakers of Bantu languages such as Libinza, Liboko, and Dibaale, and non-Bantu languages such as Zande, Ngbandi, and Ngbaka in the Congo's Equator province to enhance intertribal communication, commerce, and trade (Yanga 1980: 124). The pidgin origin of Lingala is reflected in its vocabulary and grammatical features, which many Bantu linguists believe to be more heterogeneous than homogenous, as they are represented in varying degrees in each of the local languages listed above, the closest being Dibaale and Libinza (N'sesep 1978; Odhner 1981). Because of the heterogeneous origin of Lingala, no one in the Congo has ever claimed ethnic or tribal ownership of this language. Rather, many of those who speak Lingala consider it to be distinct from their native tongues, but the common property of all the ethnically related tribes living along the Congo River from Lolango to Mobeka (Polome 1968: 298–299).

Unlike a pidgin, a **creole** is defined as a pidgin that has become a native language for a new generation of speakers (see Wardhaugh 1992: 59). Like any 'normal' language, it has native speakers, complex grammatical structures, expanded vocabulary, and can be used in formal and public spheres such as government and education. The case of Lingala is illustrative here. Remember, Lingala was originally a pidgin created over a century ago by speakers of mutually unintelligible languages to facilitate intertribal communication. Since then, the evolution of Lingala has been dramatic: it has become one of the four national languages in the country; there are millions of Congolese who speak Lingala as a native language; it has a complex grammatical system; and, because of its association with the ruling party (since ousted), it was granted more prestige than any other national language, and was at times targeted to replace French as the official language. It remains to be seen whether Lingala will maintain a high status, especially in the light of the recent political changes in the Congo. The new ruling party, the Alliance of Democratic Forces for the Liberation of the Congo, seems to favour Kiswahili (and, to some extent, English) as the language of government and administration. Notwithstanding these changes, the current relationship between Lingala and its sister national languages (Ciluba, Kiswahili, and Kikongo) can be described in terms of diglossia, a phenomenon that will be explained in the next section.

Diglossia

The term **diglossia** was first used by Ferguson (1959) to refer to a situation where two varieties of a language, one identified as the H(igh) variety and the other as the L(ow) variety, have clearly distinct social functions in the community. In other words, where the H variety is used, the L variety is not used, and vice versa. Ferguson (1972: 236) notes that the H variety is used for giving sermons in churches or mosques, speeches in parliament, formal lectures at universities, broadcasting the news on radio and television, and for writing editorials in newspapers. In contrast, the L variety is used for giving instructions to servants, waiters, workers, and clerks; in captions in political cartoons; in conversations with family, friends, and colleagues; and in folk literature and soap operas on the radio. Anyone who uses H while engaged in an informal activity like shopping, or who uses L during a formal activity like a parliamentary debate, runs the risk of ridicule. Generally, H is learnt at school, while L is more spontaneously acquired in informal settings. H is generally perceived as more aesthetically pleasing, and has more prestige than L. H has a literary tradition, whereas L does not. And if there does exist a body of literature in L, it is usually written by foreigners rather than by native speakers. Taking the above characteristic features of diglossia into account, Ferguson defines diglossia as a relatively stable language situation in which, in addition to the primary dialects of the language (which may include a standard or regional standards), there is a very divergent, highly codified (often grammatically more complex) superposed variety, the vehicle of a large and respected body of written literature, either of an earlier period or in another speech community, which is learned largely by formal education and is used for most written and formal spoken purposes but is not used by any sector of the community for ordinary conversation. (Ferguson 1972: 245)

Although Ferguson's definition of diglossia is concerned specifically with two varieties (H and L) of the same language, Fishman (1971: 75) extended the definition to include situations where two different languages are used in the community, one in formal settings (such as churches, parliament, and media broadcasts), and the other in informal settings (in the family home or the playground). The language situation in Africa can be used to illustrate both the original and the extended definitions of diglossia.

In Africa, it is generally true that any indigenous language with a literary tradition, such as isiZulu in South Africa, Kiswahili in Tanzania, Cibemba in Zambia, and Yoruba in Nigeria, has two varieties; one High and the other Low. The variety of isiZulu that is used in church or taught at school, for instance, is not the same as the variety that is spoken at home or in the marketplace. In light of this and other characteristics of diglossia, it can be said that the isiZulu-speaking community is diglossic, as are the Kiswahili-, Ciluba-, Cibemba- and Yoruba-speaking communities. The relationship between African languages and former colonial languages is diglossic as well, as will be explained below.

Questions

1 Is there any evidence of diglossia in your speech community? Have you heard, for example, schoolteachers using a language for formal meetings that they almost never use when talking to friends and family?
2 If you have been able to find such examples, why is there this functional differentiation?
3 Do you think that diglossia is a sign that the L(ow) language is losing ground, and perhaps even in danger of dying out? If so, do you think this would be detrimental to its speakers?

Diglossia, African languages, and former colonial languages

In Africa, the colonial languages have been put on a pedestal and enjoy far more prestige than indigenous languages. Bearing the characteristic features of diglossia in mind, English, French, and Portuguese can be characterized as H languages, and indigenous African languages as L languages. The social status of the Congo's four national languages (Ciluba, Lingala, Kiswahili, and Kikongo) vis-à-vis French, for instance, proves this point. The national languages are used for intra- and inter-ethnic communication. They have also served, in the regions where they are spoken, as the medium of instruction during the first two years of primary education (years during which French is taught as a subject). French remains a status symbol. It is the language of administration, the media, education, diplomacy, social mobility, inter-ethnic communication, and international business transactions. English plays similar roles in anglophone Africa (e.g. Nigeria, South Africa, Zimbabwe, Kenya, and Tanzania), as does Portuguese in Angola and Mozambique.

In the absence of competition from the indigenous languages, English, French, and Portuguese enjoy much popularity in Africa and are perceived as the only languages that can open up job opportunities and allow for upward mobility. It is worth noting, however, that the social distribution of these languages in African communities remains very limited and is usually restricted to a minority elite group. In the Congo, for instance, it is reported that only one person out of every twenty-five can speak French correctly; and only one out of every thirty can write correctly in French (Rubango 1986: 267). In anglophone Africa, reports indicate that only between 5 and 20 per cent can communicate in English (Samuels 1995: 31). In Zambia, for instance, Siachitema (1992: 19) and Tripathi (1990: 38) report that since independence the number of Zambians competent in English has shrunk. Therefore, given that competence in English is a prerequisite for participation in the national political and economic system, the majority of the people (especially those who live in rural areas) have been left out in the cold, on the fringes of privilege and political action. The situation in Angola and Mozambique is no different. Heine (1992: 27) notes that less than 10 per cent of these citizens are able to use Portuguese well enough to function (see also Chapter 1).

Because of diglossia and the attending prominence given to English, French, and Portuguese in Africa, the indigenous languages have been rendered almost instrumentally valueless. This situation calls for a closer examination of the language policies adopted by African states, especially in education, with a view to reformulating or changing these policies for the benefit of the population. This is a very important issue, but is beyond the scope of this chapter. However, the issue is addressed elsewhere (see Chapter 1).

Conclusion

The main objective of this chapter has been to describe and illustrate some of the phenomena that language contact brings about, such as borrowing, code-switching, code-mixing, pidginization, creolization, language change, and diglossia. These phenomena raise doubts about certain beliefs that many people have about language, in particular the notion that languages are 'pure,' homogeneous, and unvarying. It is quite clear that all dynamic languages contain elements that originate from other languages, are vibrantly diverse, and are subject to change.

Endnotes

1   There are two other perspectives in research on code-switching: the neurolinguistic and the psycholinguistic perspectives. The former tries to determine the number of grammars that a bilingual speaker has internalized and which allows him or her to produce code-switching speech. The latter is mainly concerned with the issue of code-switching processing, i.e. whether code-switching sentences take a longer time to process than monolingual sentences. It is worth noting that studies on these two perspectives are few and far between compared with studies on the pragmatics and syntax of code-switching.

2   For a discussion of the functions of code-switching in the African context, see Parkin 1974; Agheyisi 1977; Mkilifi 1978; Nartey 1982; Myers-Scotton, 1976, 1983, 1993; and, for a selected bibliography of studies of code-switching across cultures, see Kamwangamalu 1989c.

3   As described in Chapter 3, the term *overgeneralization* is used in linguistics to refer to the application of a rule to forms to which it does not apply; i.e. forms that are exceptions to the rule. For example, if a learner of English were to use the form *goed* as the past-tense form of *go* (instead of the irregular *went*), a linguist would say that the learner had overgeneralized the English rule for past-tense formation.

4   This section was written by Dr Kembo-Sure.

Bibliography

ADENDORFF, R.D. 1993. 'Ethnographic evidence of the social meaning of Fanagalo.' *Journal of Pidgin and Creole Languages* 8, 1: 1–27.

AGHEYISI. R. 1977. 'Language interlarding in the speech of Nigerians.' In P.F.A. Kotey and H. Der-Housikian (eds.), *Language and Linguistic Problems in Africa*, 99–110. Colombia, SC: Hornbeam Press.

AUER, P. (ed.). 1997. *Code-switching in Conversation*. London: Routledge.

BLOM, J-P., and J.J. GUMPERZ. 1972. 'Social meaning in linguistic structure: code-switching in Norway.' In J.J. Gumperz and D.H. Hymes (eds.), *Directions in sociolinguistics*, 407–434. New York: Holt, Rinehart and Winston.

BENTAHILA, A., and E.E. DAVIES. 1983. 'The syntax of Arabic-French code-switching.' *Lingua* 59, 4: 301–330.

BERK-SELIGSON, S. 1986. 'Linguistic constraints on intra-sentential code-switching: a study of Spanish-Hebrew bilingualism.' *Language in Society* 15: 313–348.

CLYNE, M.G. 1987. 'Constraints on code-switching: how universal are they?' *Linguistics* 25: 739–764.

CRYSTAL, D. 1985. *A Dictionary of Linguistics and Phonetics.* Oxford: Basil Blackwell.

D'SOUZA, J. 1987. *South Asia as a Sociolinguistic Area.* Unpublished doctoral dissertation, Department of Linguistics, University of Illinois at Urbana-Champaign, Illinois.

ESPINOSA, A. 1917. 'Speech mixture in New Mexico: the influence of the English language on New Mexican Spanish.' In H.M. Stephens and H.E. Bolton (eds.), *The Pacific Ocean in History,* 408–428. New York: Macmillan.

FARDON, R., and G FURNISS. (eds.). 1994. *African Languages: Development and the State.* London and New York: Routledge.

FERGUSON, C.A. 1959. 'Diglossia.' *Word* 15: 325–40. (Also in P.E. Giglioli, 1972 (ed.), 232–251).

———1972. *Language Structure and Language Use.* Stanford: Stanford University Press.

FILLMORE, C.J. 1997. 'A linguist looks at the Ebonics debate.' *Applied Linguistics Forum* 17, 1: 13–16).

FISHMAN, J.A. 1971. *Advances in the Sociology of Language.* The Hague: Mouton.

GIBBONS, J. 1987. *Code-mixing and Code Choice: a Hong Kong Case Study.* Clevedon: Multilingual Matters.

GIGLIOLI, P.E. (ed.) 1972. *Language and Social Context.* Harmondsworth, Middlesex: Penguin Books.

GOKE-PARIOLA, A. 1983. 'Code-mixing among Yoruba-English bilinguals.' *Anthropological Linguistics* 25, 1: 39–46.

GUMPERZ, J.J. 1974. 'The social significance of conversational code-switching.' *Working paper* 46. Berkeley: Language Behavior Laboratory.

——— 1982. 'Conversational code-switching.' *Discourse Strategies,* 59–99. Cambridge: Cambridge University Press.

HASSELMO, N. 1972. 'Code-switching as ordered selections.' In E.S. Firchow (ed.), *Studies for Einar Haugen,* 261–280. The Hague: Mouton.

HAUGEN, E. 1966. *Language Conflict and Language Planning: The Case of Modern Norwegian.* Cambridge, Mass.: Harvard University Press.

——— 1972. 'The stigmata of bilingualism.' In A. Dil (ed.), *The Ecology of Language.*

Stanford: Stanford University Press.

HEINE, B. 1992. 'Language policies in Africa.' In Robert K. Herbert (ed.), *Language and Society in Africa: the Theory and Practice of Sociolinguistics,* 23–36. Johannesburg: Witwatersrand University Press.

HELLER, M. 1992. The politics of code-switching and language choice. *Journal of Multilingual and Multicultural Development* 13, 1 & 2: 123–142.

——— 1995. 'Language choice, social institutions, and symbolic domination.' *Language in Society* 24: 373–405.

HOLM, J. 1988. *Pidgins and Creoles.* Cambridge: Cambridge University Press.

HUDSON, R.A. 1980. *Sociolinguistics.* Cambridge: Cambridge University Press.

KACHRU, B.B. 1978. 'Code-switching as a communicative strategy in India.' In J. Alatis (ed.), *International Dimensions of Bilingual Education,* 107–24. Washington, D.C.: Georgetown University Press.

——— 1982. 'The bilingual's linguistic repertoire.' In B. Hartford, A. Valdman, and C. Forster (eds.), *Issues in Bilingual Education: the role of the vernacular,* 25–52. New York: Plenum.

——— 1983. *The Indianization of English: the English Language in India.* Delhi: Oxford University Press.

KAMWANGAMALU, N.M. 1989a. *Code-mixing across Cultures: Structure, Functions and Constraints.* Unpublished doctoral dissertation, University of Illinois at Urbana-Champaign, Illinois.

——— 1989b. 'Code-mixing and modernization.' *World Englishes* 8, 3: 321–332.

——— 1989c. 'Some morphosyntactic aspects of French/English-Bantu codemixing: evidence for universal constraints.' *Chicago Linguistic Society* 25: 2: 157–170.

——— 1994. 'siSwati-English code-switching: the matrix language principle and linguistic constraints.' *South African Journal of African Languages* 14, 2: 70–77.

——— 1996. 'Sociolinguistic aspects of siSwati-English bilingualism.' *World Englishes* 15, 3: 295–306.

——— (forthcoming). 'Language frontiers, language standardization, and mother tongue education: the Zaire-Zambia border area with reference to the Cibemba cluster.' *South African Journal of African Languages.*

KASHOKI, M., and M. MANN. 1978. 'A general sketch of the Bantu languages of Zambia.' In S. Ohannessian and M. Kashoki (eds.), 9–46.

KHATI, T. 1992. 'Intra-lexical switching or nonce borrowing?' In Robert K. Herbert (ed.), *Language and Society in Africa*, 181–196. Johannesburg: Witwatersrand University Press.

LANCE, D. 1975. 'Spanish-English code-switching.' In C. Hernandez-Chavez and A. Beltramo (eds.), *El Lenguaje de los Chicanos*, 138–153. Arlington, VA: Center for Applied Linguistics. (First published in 1972.)

LIN, J.S., and L.M. STANFORD. 1982. 'An experimental reappraisal of some syntactic constraints on code-switching.' In J. Morreall (ed.), *The Ninth LACUS Forum*, 474–483. Columbia, SC: Hornbeam Press.

MEEUWIS, M., and J. BLOMMAERT. 1994. '"The Markedness Model" and the absence of society: remarks on code-switching.' *Multilingua* 13, 4: 387–42.

MILROY, L., and P. MUYSKEN (eds). 1995. *One Speaker, two Languages: Cross-disciplinary Perspectives on Code-switching.* Cambridge: Cambridge University Press.

MKILIFI, A.M. 1978. 'Triglossia and Kiswahili-English bilingualism in Tanzania.' In J.A. Fishman (ed.), *Advances in the Study of Societal Multilingualism*, 129–149. The Hague: Mouton.

MÜHLHÄUSLER, P. 1995. '"Babel Revisited."' *Bua!* 9, 4: 4–7.

MYERS-SCOTTON, C. 1976, 1983. See Scotton

———1988. 'Code-switching as indexical of social negotiations.' In M. Heller (ed.), *Code-switching: Anthropological and Sociolinguistic Perspectives*, 151–86. Berlin: Mouton de Gruyter.

———1993a. *Social Motivations for Code-switching: Evidence from Africa.* Oxford: Oxford University Press.

NARTEY, JONAS N.A. 1982. 'Code-switching, Interference or Faddism? Language use among educated Ghanaians.' *Anthropological Linguistics* 24, 2: 183–192.

ODHNER, J.D. 1981. *Lingala–French manual.* Washington, D.C.: University Press of America.

PARKIN, D.J. 1974. 'Language Switching in Nairobi.' In W. Whiteley (ed.), *Language in Kenya.* Nairobi: Oxford University Press.

PFAFF, C. 1979. 'Constraints on language mixing.' *Language* 55: 291–318.

POLOMÉ, J.E. 1968. 'The choice of official languages in the Democratic Republic of the Congo.' In J.A. Fishman, C.A. Ferguson, and J.D. Gupta (eds.), *Language Problems of Developing Nations*, 295–312. New York, NY: John Wiley & Sons, Inc.

POPLACK, S. 1978. 'Syntactic structure and the social function of code-switching.' In R. Duran (ed.), *Latino Language and Communicative Behavior*, 169–184. Norwood, NJ: Ablex Publishing Corporation.

———'Sometimes I'll start a sentence in Spanish y termino en Espanol: toward a typology of code-switching.' *Linguistics* 18: 581–618.

POPLACK, S., S. WHEELER, and A. WESTWOOD. 1989. 'Distinguishing language contact phenomena: evidence from Finnish-English bilingualism.' *World Englishes* 8, 3: 389–406.

ROMAINE, S. (ed.) 1982. *Sociolinguistic variation in speech communities.* London: Edward Arnold.

RUBANGO, N.YA. 1986. 'Le Francais au Zaire: Langue "superieure" et chances de "survie" dans un pays Africain.' *Language Problems and Language Planning* 10, 3: 253–271.

SAMUELS, J. 1995. 'Multilingualism in the Emerging Educational Dispensation'. *Proceedings of SAALA* 15: 75–84. University of Stellenbosch.

SCOTTON, CAROL MYERS. 1976. 'Strategy of neutrality: language choice in uncertain situations.' *Language* 52: 919–41.

———1983. 'The negotiation of identities in conversation: a theory of markedness and code-choice.' *International Journal of the Sociology of Language* 44: 115–136.

SESEP N.B. 1978. *Le metissage Francais-Lingala au Zaire: essai d'analyse differentielle et sociolinguistique de la communaute bilingue.* Unpublished doctoral dissertation, University of Nice, Nice.

SIATCHITEMA, A.K. 1992. 'When nationalism conflicts with nationalist goals: Zambia.' In

N.T. Crawhall (ed.) *Democratically Speaking.*
Cape Town: National Language Project.

SOBINS, N.J. 1984. 'On code-switching inside
NP.' *Applied Psycholinguistics* 5, 4: 293–303.

SRIDHAR, S., and K. SRIDHAR. 1980. 'The syntax and psycholinguistics of bilingual code-
mixing.' *Studies in the Linguistic Sciences* 10,
1: 203–215.

TRIPATHI, P.D. 1990. 'English in Zambia: The
nature and prospects of one of Africa's "new
Englishes."' *English Today* 6, 3: 34–8.

TRUDGILL, P. 1983. *Sociolinguistics: an
Introduction to Language and Society.*
Harmondsworth, Middlesex: Penguin Books.

WARDHAUGH, R. 1986. *An Introduction to
Sociolinguistics.* New York: Basil Blackwell.

——— 1992. *An Introduction to Sociolinguistics*
(2nd edition). Oxford: Blackwell Publishers.

WEINREICH, U. 1964. *Languages in Contact.* The
Hague: Mouton.

WILEY, T.G. 1996. 'Language planning and policy'. In S.L. McKay and N.H. Hornberger
(eds.) *Sociolinguistics and Language Teaching,*
103–47. Cambridge: Cambridge University
Press.

YANGA, T. 1980. *A Sociolinguistic Identification of
Lingala.* Ann Arbor, MI: University
Microfilms International.

5 Languages in competition

Kembo-Sure and Vic Webb

Expected outcomes

At the end of this chapter you should be able to:
1 Analyse a language user's repertoire, and identify the main factors which influenced it.
2 Explain how you, as a parent, would intervene in your children's language learning processes to make sure they reaped the maximum benefit from the languages spoken in the community.
3 Define the notion of languages in competition (or conflict).
4 Explain, from the perspective of languages in competition, the meaning of the concepts language attrition, linguistic hegemony, and language shift.
5 Explain the role of integrative motivation in determining how well and quickly we learn a new language, and indicate whether you think that this consideration is applicable in the case of the language used in education and government administration in your country.
6 Distinguish between attitudes and opinions/views, and explain the role of attitudes in language choice and learning in multilingual communities.
7 Discuss the identity implications of multilingualism and the cultural consequences of losing one's community language.

Introduction

In the previous chapter, the emphasis was on contact phenomena in multilingual situations – code-switching, code-mixing, language change, pidginization, creolization, and diglossia. In this chapter, we will focus on languages in 'competition' or 'conflict' in multilingual societies, and the linguistic consequences of such situations.

The field of study called **conflict linguistics** (here referred to as **competition**

linguistics) generally deals with situations in which two or more languages or varieties of languages that are in contact with each other (used in the same communities), are also in a state of competition, that is, in a relationship of tension. This tension usually suggests that the speakers of one of the languages or varieties feel threatened. Examples of situations in which there is language competition or conflict are those where there is a relationship between a dominant (or major) language and a dominated (or minority) language; where there is tension between the standard variety of a language and its non-standard varieties; and where indigenous linguistic features (such as inherited vocabulary) are threatened (or perceived by members of that linguistic community to be threatened) by borrowings. Of course, it is not the languages, the varieties, or the linguistic features that are in contact or in conflict. Linguistic phenomena do not have lives of their own. It is the people who use these languages, varieties, and features that are in contact or conflict. It is they who feel threatened, dominated, or marginalized. For example, in South Africa, there is a great deal of conflict between Afrikaans and English. This is manifested in the refusal by some to use English (in an effort to keep Afrikaans 'pure' – free from the taint of English elements), the insistence on the recognition of the rights of Afrikaans-speakers, and the derogatory terms of reference some members of each language group use for the other. This state of tension, however, has nothing to do with the two languages as such. It is the users of these languages, and in particular the white Afrikaans-speaking community, who experience feelings of threat. Thus, when we speak about languages in competition, we are speaking metaphorically.

So Chapters 4 and 5 deal with similar topics and issues, but approach these from different perspectives.

The main topics of this chapter are:
- the concepts of language shift, language loss, language death, linguicide, linguicism, language maintenance, and language revitalization;
- the nature and role of language attitudes; and
- language and identity.

The following anecdote will help to set the stage for further discussion of these topics.

Othoro and Tiktik are two teenage boys born to a mother whose native language[1] is Dholuo, and a father whose native language is Suba. The two boys use English and/or Kiswahili when they are alone, with Kiswahili predominating when they are teasing or quarrelling. However, to add humour and light-heartedness when teasing, they use a sprinkling of Sheng, a mixed code with lexical items from English, Kiswahili, and other Kenyan languages (mainly Dholuo and Kikuyu) superimposed onto the Kiswahili way of building sentences.

When addressing their parents, they use either English or Dholuo, or both. Code-mixing involving English and Dholuo is thus the norm in family conversation. It is important to note that although all the members of the family speak Kiswahili, it is seldom part of their repertoire in family conversations.

The two boys were born in a Kikuyu-speaking environment, and by the time they were five and three they spoke Kikuyu with the same proficiency as Gikuyu children of their age. Since the parents did not speak any Kikuyu, it remained the language of the playground and was not used in their home. A few years after the parents were transferred from the Kikuyu-speaking region, the boys lost their Kikuyu, which was soon replaced by Kiswahili as the peer language (in which they chatted to friends and so forth).

In primary school, they learnt English and Kiswahili as subjects, with English as the general medium of instruction. Outside the classroom, they spoke both languages. Since they now live on a university campus with a large non-Kenyan population, the dominant languages of the neighbourhood are English and Kiswahili. English is used to include non-Kenyan children, although nearly all of the non-Kenyan children of all races quickly learn Kiswahili and use it fluently in peer interactions. (All of them have to study it as a school subject.)

The boys attend National Schools. In Kenya, this refers to those secondary schools that admit candidates from all the districts in the country. This means that the scholars come from different linguistic backgrounds. English is thus the preferred language in many situations in these schools, although Kiswahili is still widely used by pupils in informal interactions. Our two boys both take French as a school subject, which means they can read elementary French literature and follow a simple French conversation.

When they visit their rural home, they use Dholuo of necessity, but are quickly identified as speaking it with the hesitancy of foreigners. They often grope for the appropriate words or stumble over sentence structures, but somehow they get by. The truth is that they are now fluent in English and Kiswahili, but less than fluent in Dholuo, which is technically their home language, given that it is their mother's home language and their father's adopted language.

A summary of the boys' repertoire looks like this:

1   Their main and best-mastered language in most of their dealings both within and outside the home is English, which is used for the greater part of their written and spoken communication.
2   Kiswahili is very well mastered, but used in restricted areas, generally informally. The variety they speak is not strictly the standard variety learnt at school, but the accepted variety widely spoken away from the coastal region.
3   The boys speak Dholuo at a basic level that enables them to get by; however, they are not proficient enough to use it in any serious spoken or written

communication. Even when used with their parents, it is mostly code-switched with English, so that in serious family discussion English is the preferred language. It is therefore doubtful whether the boys will ever teach Dholuo to their children.

4   Sheng is a developing code used mainly to signal solidarity among young-sters, but it is still rather unstable as a linguistic medium. There are some 'crude' dictionaries of Sheng, but nothing to point to serious codification. Nevertheless, it comes in handy for casual peer interactions, and as a code for excluding parents and other adults when they so wish.

5   French is generally known as a school subject, but hardly ever used in con-versation, even between the two boys at home. They may occasionally use isolated French phrases or expressions, but mainly to show off, especially in the hearing of their parents.

6   Suba, their father's native language, is spoken neither by the boys nor their parents. Suba is an endangered language (a phenomenon we shall discuss later in this chapter), but still has a fair number of people speaking it active-ly. The father still identifies himself as a Suba, and would like his sons to be identified likewise.

How can we explain the boys' linguistic repertoire? And why does it differ from that of their parents? The reasons clearly have to do with the 'market value' of the different languages in their society, especially in the communities in which the boys find themselves. English is clearly the most highly valued language (they can do more with English than with any other language; it 'buys' them the most), while Suba has the least value, even though in theory it should have cultural and symbolic value for the boys.

This anecdote shows that languages do not exist independently of their users. Languages are directly connected to those who use them, and this means that there are 'strong', influential languages and 'weak', uninfluential languages. This phenomenon – the power relations between languages – obviously war-rants analysis and description. This will be the focus of the remainder of this chapter.

Basic concepts

If we want to analyse and describe the competition between languages, we obviously need to know the basic concepts and terms involved.

In our story of the two boys, we see how a foreign or additional language learnt after or alongside a home language gathers more strength and begins to acquire more functions for an individual at home and in the public domain. In the case of these boys, the conscious effort by their parents to use Dholuo at home is a deliberate attempt at language maintenance so that the boys do not lose the linguistic aspect of their cultural identity (an issue we shall discuss in detail later). If members of a speech community insist on using their language of cultural identity for at least some important functions in the home and elsewhere, then the language is assured of continued active existence in spite of the learning of other languages for additional uses.

For the boys, however, the native language is used in very restricted areas, and, even then, not with native fluency. It is not even used domestically for serious communicative events. Since Kiswahili and English have replaced Dholuo in all of the important functions for these boys, we say that a **language shift** has occurred. (This is a process whereby members of a speech community abandon the use of one language for certain functions and adopt another; the former is often a native or home language.) This does not mean that Dholuo is a threatened language, however. It is still spoken as a primary language by over three million people in Kenya and parts of northern Tanzania. As an ethnolinguistic group, the community is still alive and active. Rather, the case of the two boys is typical of urban children who do not have adequate opportunities to actively use the native languages spoken in their original rural homes. They are beginning to experience **language loss**, a situation in which members of a community experiencing language shift begin to lose fluency in their native language. Language loss does not necessarily mean language death, as the language could still exist in a robust state elsewhere. Millions of Kenyan children in the urban centres can barely speak their native languages, but these languages nevertheless remain potent media of many forms of communication for rural populations.

Language death occurs when a language ceases to have any speakers anywhere in the world. This may occur suddenly; for example, when invaders exterminate a whole speech community, as was the case with many Native American languages, whose speakers experienced genocide at the hands of white immigrants. A community may also be wiped out by an epidemic, leaving no one to pass on the language to the next generation. However, it is more usual for languages to die out gradually. This can happen when their speakers are assimilated into another speech community of numerical and/or technological superiority. An example of language (near) death is that of the Khoisan languages, which were lost due to genocide, epidemics, and domination. The Khoisan eventually adopted Afrikaans, isiXhosa, or Sesotho as their mother-tongue languages (see Chapters 1 and 2).

Cases of gradual language death have also been reported in Kenya, where the Yaaku-speakers, who were mainly hunter-gatherers, were swallowed by the Maasai, who are pastoralists and whom the Yaaku considered to be politically and militarily better organized, and economically more prosperous and stable (Dimmendaal 1992). The El Molo, a fishing community around Lake Turkana in northern Kenya, likewise seem to have been assimilated by the Samburu, abandoning their language in the process, so that there remains no known living speaker of the language (Heine 1982). There are, however, traces of the original El Molo language in the lexicon of the Samburu dialect they speak today, especially in the nomenclature of fishing (Dimmendaal 1992).

In recent years, the use of one's cultural language has become a human rights issue, so that a national legal system that encourages the suppression of a minority language and imposes the use of a majority language is considered to be promoting **linguistic hegemony**.[2] As this involves expanding the scope of one language at the expense of another, it is also sometimes called **linguistic expansionism**. When this leads to the loss of the minority language, then we say that **linguicide** has been committed. This means that one language is responsible for the death of another. Linguistic hegemony can also lead to discrimination (as shown in Chapter 1), and, when this happens, those discriminated against are said to have been subjected to **linguicism**, which is the linguistic equivalent of racism or tribalism. For example, the proscription of Kurdish by the Turkish government is said to be a form of linguicism; and if the Kurdish people eventually lose their mother tongue because their children have been forced to learn Turkish at school, we will have witnessed a case of linguicide.

Similarly, the Sri Lankan government's imposition of Sinhala (as the language of education and government administration) on minority Tamil-speakers is a case of abuse of power by the majority, and an infringement on the linguistic rights of the minority community. Translated into a cultural context, these forms of injustice can be classed as forms of cultural or ethnic violence and likened to physical torture and massacre. (Given the prevalence of ethnic or inter-group violence in the world today, such cultural violations need to be taken extremely seriously, as they all too often act as a vanguard for overt violence and 'ethnic cleansing'.) Both national and international bodies thus need to consider developing appropriate systems of redress to help victims of cultural violence and to deal with those responsible, in the same way that the International Court of Justice at the Hague deals with cases of crimes against humanity.

To return to our story of the two Kenyan boys, it is important to note that there are always 'strong' languages (for which read strong people) and 'weak' languages. This means that, in spite of the initial assumption by policy-makers that languages can coexist peacefully, this doesn't necessarily happen in multilingual societies. Instead, what often happens is a process of attrition that generally goes as follows:[3] the economically and politically weaker (language) community becomes bilingual; in situations of language choice, there is an increasing preference for the stronger language, so that the weaker one is used for fewer functions and in fewer domains; and, inevitably, the weaker language acquires a negative social meaning and becomes stigmatized. Once this happens, those who speak it as a first language lose faith in it, often regarding it as worthless and no good for significant functions such as learning or finding employment. Eventually they conclude that it is pointless spending time and energy on the language. The language itself is thus used less and less, fading first from public situations and then even from private and primary domains. Once these developments have taken place, the language becomes functionally and stylistically reduced, begins to lose vocabulary (especially technical terminology), and can even become structurally reduced, losing, for example, morphological and syntactic structures. This stage is known as (advanced) **language attrition**. What then follows is that children born into these communities don't readily acquire their parents' language, with the result that inefficient **intergenerational transfer** or **transmission** of the language occurs (Sasse 1992). The next stage is **language obsolescence** – the language exists, but is used rarely or not at all. Once a language has reached this stage, its native speakers generally speak it only with hesitance, and tend to use a simplified form of it, as some of its rules have been lost. This language can now be classed as an **endangered language**, which means that unless something drastic is done to revitalize it, it is likely to die out altogether.

Returning once again to our anecdote, the developments described above can be clearly seen in the development of the boys' linguistic repertoire, in particular the demise of Dholuo and the rise of English. In fact, many African languages are equally apt examples, especially in terms of their relationships with English, French, or Portuguese. Here you might like to turn back to Chapter 1, in particular the discussion of the restrictions on schoolchildren's access to knowledge and skills. In South Africa, as we pointed out in Chapter 1, English has acquired such prestige that people are often regarded as civilized, developed, and successful only if they know some English, regardless of the real degree of their literacy and numeracy. The criterion of esteem is based not on their abilities and talents, but on whether they know English. This is most unfortunate, given that English may actually be a barrier to the development of someone's potential, for the simple reason that if they cannot understand the language being used for learning and teaching, they cannot learn or be taught.

A vital point mentioned earlier must be stressed once again: the issue here is not the protection or promotion of languages as such. Our concern is for those who speak and use languages. Language is an issue only to the extent that it facilitates or obstructs the well-being of people. It is likely that many parents of schoolchildren will argue that they want their children to be taught in English (or French or Portuguese) precisely because it is in the interests of their children that this should happen. They feel that a school-leaver who is proficient in an 'international' language is far better prepared for life (particularly the economic or professional domains) than one who is not. This is of course true, provided that the child has indeed been able to develop cognitively and emo-tionally to his or her full capacity. But this is only possible if the child has in the first place been able to understand the language of instruction. Furthermore, research has also shown that optimal first-language education provides a rich cognitive preparation for the acquisition of a second language. This means that the literacy skills already acquired in the first language provide an easier transi-tion to the second-language-medium education and thus enhance academic achievement (Cummins 1984).

One question concerning the position of African languages is whether the governments of the African states are responsible for the linguistic phenomena described above. Clearly, they play a major role; our two Kenyan boys have English as their strongest language because it is supported by the legal and political structures of the country. Kiswahili is also a popular choice for infor-mal communication, but it is much less prestigious than English. Dholuo, however, is being eroded by the official languages, as it has been allocated only limited communicative space in public life by government policy.

Sometimes it happens that politicians can use language policy explicitly for their own political objectives. The case of Suba in Kenya is a fascinating case in point. At present, pockets of active users of Suba still exist, and the language is thus still alive. In many areas of Subaland, however, the language is obsolete, as only a few elders speak it fluently. Many of the younger generation can under-stand Suba, but formulate their replies in Dholuo. Furthermore, all Suba-speakers are bilingual. Given this scenario, we would imagine that the chances for the survival of the Suba language are not good.

However, for purely political reasons, the ruling politicians created an administrative district named Suba in 1994 as a ploy to encourage the Suba people to identify themselves as Suba rather than Luos, thereby creating an eth-nic and political rift between the two communities. (These were people who for all practical purposes had regarded themselves as members of the Luo com-munity; now, however, they have been awakened to the fact that they have dif-ferent origins.) To underline the serious intent of the ruling party to placate the indigenous Suba community, the following measures were immediately insti-tuted:

1   A slot for the Suba language was provided on the national radio.
2   A panel was established at the Kenya Institute of Education to design a Suba syllabus and produce teaching materials to be used in primary schools.
3   A special quota was created for candidates from the Suba district for entrance to teacher-training colleges.

Besides these efforts by the government, the Bible Translation and Literacy Society, a Christian organization, had meanwhile embarked on a Suba transla-tion of the Bible and the writing of Suba primers, a project which has received a great deal of official support since 1994. The immediate result of these moves has been the sensitization of the Suba people to their 'difference' from the Luo community. This has paid political dividends, with the ruling party gaining approbation, but whether the result will be the revitalization of the Suba language remains to be seen. Two primers have been provided to some schools on a trial basis, but so far the response has been ambivalent, not least because most teachers do not speak the language; even the few who do were trained in Dholuo and English, and therefore have only a shaky knowledge of Suba, much less the ability to teach it.

Apart from institutional support, language revitalization requires strong and positive **attitudinal orientation**. In other words, people must want to use their language as a symbol of their ethnic or cultural identity, and take pride in it. It is not yet clear how strongly the Suba people support the reinstating of Suba as the primary language of the home and local public domain. (See Ambrose, Read, and Webb (1998) for a discussion of the role of African languages in public life.)

Questions

1   Are you aware of any languages in your community that seem to have a special meaning for their speakers? Have you ever heard someone say (or write) that he or she loves his or her language? If so, how was/is this manifested? What were the consequences, if any?

2   What does it mean to say that a particular language is a symbol of ethnic identity?

3   Language shift is a very technical topic, and it is sometimes difficult to determine whether a language has undergone or is undergoing a shift. However, sometimes laypeople are aware of languages losing ground, for example, being used for fewer public functions. If you know of such cases:
   (a) What are the signs of ongoing shift?
   (b) How does this take place?
   (c) What processes are involved?
   (d) What factors are causing it?

Language attitudes in multilingual communities

While the contrary reasons were used when English was given the pride of place in official transactions way back at the dawn of independence, it is now not too late for the country to admit that the language is exclusive, and indeed, one infringing on the rights – specifically on the liberty – of a large section of Kenyans. (Mugo Theuri, *The People*, 24 December–1 January 1998)

The official status of English in Kenya has made it the most visible language in most Kenyan public institutions and official dealings. The fact that it is the most important medium of learning has guaranteed its availability to all Kenyan schoolchildren, and, because it is the language of the workplace in the more prestigious occupations, it is regarded as the most important language for those who would like to embrace modernity and compete in a technological society.

However, after thirty-five years of independence, do Kenyans still have the reverence they had for English in colonial times, when it was given pride of place by the legal system? It seems that many Kenyans who have acquired English are now beginning to question its worth, especially in the administration of justice, education, cultural development, and politics. There seems to be a growing feeling among some Kenyans that English is alienating them from other citizens and excluding them from the mainstream activities of the country.

The conventional theory has been that most of the speakers of a minority language will want to learn the majority language because of the socio-economic benefits associated with it. In this case, English is the majority language, as it is functionally the most powerful language in the public domain, whereas the other Kenyan languages, including Kiswahili, are used mostly in informal and private domains. However, recent research in Kenya suggests that young educated Kenyans are gradually becoming more negative towards English (Kembo-Sure 1991). This is consistent with the findings of Holmes et al. (1993) regarding attitudes to English among immigrants in New Zealand. These researchers suggest that speakers of minority languages who have invested time and effort acquiring English in the hope of bettering themselves nevertheless find themselves without jobs or social influence. The resulting disillusionment leads to the rejection of English and to what Fishman et al. (1985) call **ethnic revival** (often ironically spearheaded by the educated elite who are the supposed beneficiaries of the English-medium education). As Theuri goes on to argue,

> Indeed, the English language as a medium of daily communication seems to be getting out of vogue. It is as though, while literary critics berated Ngugi Wa Thiong'o when he called for the decolonization of the African mind by instead using local languages in literature, Kenyans today are making their point by siding with Ngugi and defying his critics.

The view that European languages would promote national development is also being questioned in many other parts of Africa, as citizens begin to take stock of the actual (as opposed to the ideal) economic, educational, and social benefits of the use of European languages in public life. Most indices of development in the 1990s point to an intolerable level of poverty, increasing illiteracy, increased dependence on imported manufactured goods, and decaying infrastructure. This is true throughout the continent, including South Africa, whose superior infrastructural development is still accessible only to a tiny minority. It remains to be seen how the newly democratic South Africa is going to solve the enormous social, political, and economic problems it faces.

An appreciation of local languages seems to be increasing around the globe. This is probably partly due to the quest for recognition by cultural minorities worldwide, in a bid to obtain political and cultural space in their home countries. These are the winds of change that have reintroduced multi-party politics into Africa. Also, the view that many languages (multilingualism) present a problem whereas one language is good for national unity is increasingly being challenged. Pluralism in politics is now being matched with **plurilinguistics**, which affords all languages space to develop, to be recognized, and to be used for crucial private and public purposes.

The earlier policy of one official language as the ideal is now seen as a relic of the nineteenth-century notion of 'one language, one nation'. This is a legacy of the European concept of the nation state, according to which national integration (or national unity) can best be attained if all the citizens of a country are culturally similar (have one cultural identity, and can be described as somehow 'typical' of their nationality). Logically, such cultural homogeneity implies that only one national language is needed. In extreme cases, this view has led to attempts to suppress minority cultural groups so that only one language emerges as the nationally accepted standard. However, the survival of minority languages in Europe (Frisian in the Netherlands, Irish, Welsh, and Gaelic in Britain, Basque in Spain and France, Breton in France, and Sami in Sweden) and elsewhere suggests that minority cultures and languages are resilient. These events have led to the demise of the concept of the nation state, and the realization that it is not a viable model for Africa. It has also led to the recognition that cultural and linguistic plurality is a reality.

A positive attitude towards indigenous languages also seems to be growing among ordinary citizens. For example, at the recent presidential swearing-in ceremony in Nairobi (in January 1998), Presidents Yoweri Museveni of Uganda, Daniel arap Moi of Kenya, and Benjamin Mkapa of Tanzania all addressed the gathering in Kiswahili. The crowd was jubilant, especially at President Museveni's address, because he was not expected to use Kiswahili, even more so because his speech was unwritten. This obviously boosts the social status of Kiswahili in East Africa and abroad. The same goes for the constitutional recognition of the nine indigenous South African languages.

In spite of this evidence of positive attitudes to local languages, African governments still seem to hold that European languages are more effective instruments for public life. The Organization of African Unity, for example, has yet to adopt an official indigenous African language, in spite of numerous recommendations that an African language like Kiswahili should be considered. Perhaps governing bodies should pay more attention to the views and attitudes of voters, and perhaps voters should insist that their governments intervene to promote and develop local languages. If governments were to undertake such interventions, they would play a useful role in changing language attitudes.

Language attitudes[4] are generally associated with two human desires: the desire for personal gain, and the desire to be accepted by others. The wish to use a language for individual gain is called **instrumental motivation**, and the wish to use or learn a language in order to be accepted in the community of its speakers is called **integrative motivation** (Gardner and Lambert 1972). This model has been used to describe language attitudes, language use patterns, and language acquisition among bilingual immigrants in the USA, Canada, and Australia; the general agreement is that speakers of minority languages:

- tend to want to acquire a majority language because they would like to be accepted as members of the majority group;
- tend to learn the majority language faster and better when they are motivated by the desire to integrate; and
- tend to learn and maintain their minority languages in order to ensure cohesion and emotional security for members of the minority group (however, this is said to last for only two generations, after which minority languages begin to decline and are eventually lost).

The impression that speakers of a minority language stand to gain by learning the majority language is embedded in the notion of **assimilation**, in which there is a strong desire on the part of immigrants to adopt the characteristics of the majority culture so that they, and later their children, can enjoy the benefits of membership of this new society. Language is seen as the most important cultural characteristic that can provide easy entry into the new culture.

However, the linguistic and socio-political situation in most African countries is very different to the situation in the USA, Canada, or Australia, where those learning the majority language (English) were immigrant communities. The numbers of those who speak European languages as first languages are negligible in most African countries (excepting South Africa, which has three million people who are native speakers of English). This being the case, there is no urgent need for local-language speakers to integrate into the culture of the speakers of English, French, or Portuguese. The major motivation for learning these languages is therefore not integrative, but instrumental. In other words, European languages are learnt in order to gain access to education and, thereafter, good jobs. (In fact, any attempt by an African to behave or speak like a European is generally resented and viewed as a case of cultural deviance.)

European languages, however, are used as link languages, especially by the educated elite, as effective means of communication across linguistic and international borders. In this regard, they have become important instruments of access to knowledge and privilege, and of trade on the African continent, a fact that must be acknowledged and utilized.

As can be expected, European languages have undergone various changes in Africa,[5] and several Africanized varieties of these languages have evolved. For example, there are a number of Englishes in Africa. These varieties are often resisted, especially by teachers and other gatekeepers (those who act as guardians of linguistic properties), who argue that the British or so-called international standard should be the norm for use in public domains. Other varieties, they say, are deviations, and their users must be penalized, as they might imperil communication with the international world. However, there is now a strong move towards accepting these indigenized varieties of European languages (such as Nigerian, South African, Ugandan, and Kenyan English), and giving them official recognition both as national standards and as varieties that can be identified with unique local ideas, practices, and institutions.[6]

The acceptance of indigenous varieties of European languages implies that they need to be standardized. As described in Chapter 4, this means that a particular national variety has to be selected, its norms determined (that is, the vocabulary, spelling, and pronunciation appropriate for formal situations must be described), and these decisions implemented; in other words, their use must be generalized across the nation. The acceptance of African Englishes implies an obligation to popularize them through the mass media, the education system, the publishing houses, and in government administration. Once this has been done, these varieties can be said to have been **institutionalized**. This also means producing dictionaries and style manuals for these local varieties and printing textbooks that propagate them. All these processes are important because they determine people's responses to the new variety. A standardized variety is respected more, and is therefore sought after by learners. It is a way of nurturing a positive attitude towards the national variety by giving it official recognition and popularizing its use.

The standardization and popularization of the local varieties of European languages should not mean that indigenous languages are once more relegated to inferior positions. On the contrary, the acceptance and recognition of European varieties require a parallel recognition and popularization of the local languages, so that they too can gain respectability. They must be assigned more important roles in the public institutions, including the mass media, schools, and churches. They must also be used in the provision of government services. This way, people will develop more positive attitudes to them, and their vitality can be enhanced.

Language and identity

In this section, we discuss the issue of language and identity, as this relates directly to the main theme of this chapter, namely languages in competition. As pointed out in Chapter 1, one of the social functions of language is to symbolize its speakers' social and cultural identity. In fact, language is the most potent of all cultural symbols, and people are often identified culturally primarily (and even solely) on the basis of the language they speak. This is probably why, in Western practice, communities are named after the names of their languages; for example, Suba is spoken by the Suba, English by the English, Somali by the Somalis, and so on.

The link between language and culture (or cultural identity)[7] is sometimes perceived to be very direct. Some speakers of Afrikaans in South Africa, for instance, feel so strongly about this that they regard any changes to their language as a threat to their cultural identity. One also often hears the view that using a foreign language (such as English or French in most of Africa) poses a threat to a person or a group's cultural identity, and even that acquiring such a language (at school, for example) may lead to cultural alienation. Clearly, therefore, languages in contact and conflict often also imply cultures in contact and conflict.

In Africa, multilingualism is the norm; as children grow up hearing more than one language spoken around them, they soon gain mastery in two or more of these. We thus have individual multilingualism. Societal multilingualism is also the norm, with almost all African countries accommodating many languages. For example, Nigeria has about 400 languages in a population of 100 million, and Kenya, with a population of 24 million, has forty languages. (See the Appendix at the end of this book.) The interplay between languages, multilingualism, and cultural identity is thus a vital topic in the African context.

In this section, we intend to investigate the following questions

1   In the African 'Tower of Babel', how do people signal their identities without offending one another, or constantly being in conflict?
2   How do Africans feel about the link between language and culture?
3   Are the European languages a threat to African culture? (Can a foreign language be used for learning and teaching in primary and secondary schools without the culture associated with that language also being transmitted?)

Before tackling these questions, we must look more closely at the interrelationship between language and culture. This has been debated ever since the ground-breaking work done by one of the most important linguists of modern times, Edward Sapir, and his student Benjamin Lee Whorf. In spite of their important research, there is still no clarity on the matter.

Simplistically put, one can distinguish four views about the direction and the extent of this interrelationship or link:

- that language determines thought and perception (and thus people's culture, their views of the world) in a causal way, so that any changes in the structures, functions, or social meaning of a language impacts upon the cultural character of its speakers;
- that language determines thought and perception (and thus people's culture, their views of the world), but in a constitutive, not causal, way; for example, acquiring a 'racist' language as a first language will promote a racist perception of the world;
- that culture stands in a causal and deterministic relationship to language, so that cultural changes automatically lead to linguistic changes, even, possibly, to language shift, attrition, and loss; and
- that cultural changes impact upon language, but not in a causal way, thus leading to linguistic adaptation and change, but not necessarily to shift, attrition, and loss.

Given that it has not yet become possible to observe cultural and linguistic processes systematically and in depth, anthropologists and linguists have not been able to provide enough information and insights to allow us to choose decisively between these models. However, most sociolinguists accept some version of the second and fourth scenarios above (thus accepting the mutual influence of language and culture, but rejecting the causal possibilities). In so doing, they accept the following:

- that languages reflect the world in which people live, in their vocabularies, the lexical meanings of many of their words, and even in the socio-cultural meanings of the sounds, structures, and varieties of a language;
- that our use of a language also reflects the world in which we live, in the ways that people from different cultures greet one another, and in the rules that govern who may talk to whom, when, and about what (see Chapters 10 and 11);
- that languages can develop into symbols of their associated cultural worlds and identities; and
- that cultural changes lead to language change (for example, technological changes have brought about the addition of new terms and words, as happened when computers became a feature of modern societies); this includes changes in the meaning of words, as in the case of words such as *nation, tribe, people, democracy*, and so on.

1 In the African 'Tower of Babel', how do people signal their identities without offending each other?

On 24 December 1997, the first author's wife (JK) and he went to the Department of Income and Excise to present papers for the clearance of her personal effects, which had been shipped to Kenya from Britain. They were directed to Long Room No. 1. As they walked in, they noticed that the place was packed with clearing agents, all anxiously waiting either to lodge their papers or to hear their names being called to collect their processed papers. They could hear people speaking English, Kiswahili, Dholuo, and Kikuyu. These four languages were used in conversations between those waiting for service, as well as for conducting business with the officials at the counter. The author and his wife eventually lodged their papers with an official named Kariuki, whose mother tongue they were sure was Kikuyu. The author's wife spoke to the official in English and the transaction went smoothly. Next, they were asked to wait.

After about twenty minutes, her name was called out and she was directed to see a Deputy Commissioner to seek special exemption for her consignment. At the Deputy Commissioner's office, she addressed both the secretary and the officer in English. She was directed back to Long Room No. 1, where she gave the papers to another official, not the Mr Kariuki who received them upon her arrival. The man looked at the papers, read her name, and the following conversation ensued:

OFFICER:	*Bwakire.* ('How are you?')
JK:	Fine.
OFFICER:	You don't speak Ekegusi?
JK:	I understand a little, but I don't speak it.
OFFICER:	Where do you come from?
JK:	Just a Kenyan.

(Ekegusi is a Bantu language with more than a million speakers, making it one of the major Kenyan languages.)

Guessing from the name Kembo, the officer took the risk of speaking a mother tongue in the hope of striking up a special relationship. In a situation where speaking a non-official language carries particular significance, he was signalling his identity and inviting her to assert hers, hoping that they had a shared identity. This is a fairly common experience for the couple, as they have a relatively neutral last name (Kembo) which is not easily identifiable as belonging to any of the Kenyan ethnolinguistic communities.

The point here is that Kenyans, like members of other linguistic communities, signal their identities through their languages. They will use their mother tongues to signal ethnic association, and use Kiswahili or English to do business. As they code-switch, they also switch identities, as the nature of a discourse may call for a change of identity. In a multilingual society, the ideal Kenyan has a full repertoire of identities, and part of his or her linguistic competence is the ability to put forward the appropriate identity in order to ensure effective communication.

2 How do Africans feel about the link between language and culture?

The interplay between language and cultural identity is seldom straightforward or simple, and this is true for Africa. For example, as part of ongoing research into the revival of Suba identity, the first author of this chapter recently spoke to a young university-trained teacher from the Suba district, who told him emphatically that he could not 'stomach the stupid idea of reviving a dead cultural group'. As far as he was concerned, he was a Luo and 'that was it'. On the other hand, the researcher has also spoken to many educated young people who are categorical about their Suba identity, even though they do not speak a word of the language. Among the latter, there are two categories: those who want to signal their dissociation from the Luo in order to find favour with the government, and those who see Suba identity as a means of re-establishing a strong, reinvigorated cultural home for their community. Even among the older people, who are frequent users of the language, there is no unanimity over the issue.

Language is neither a sufficient nor a necessary symbol of cultural identity. People can identify themselves with a cultural group without speaking its language (or even being able to speak it); they can also dissociate themselves from those who speak the same language as they do. Similarly, people who lose their language and adopt a new one do not necessarily lose their cultural identity, or adopt the identity of those whose language they now speak.

3 Are the European languages a threat to African culture?

Given these views on the interrelationship between language and culture, we now return to the issue of the potential cultural conflict between the indigenous languages of Africa and the European languages used on the African continent.

Should the European languages be regarded as a threat to the cultural integrity[8] of African communities? Can they be used for learning and teaching in primary and secondary schools without automatically leading to the acquisition of the associated foreign cultures and loss of one's own? Is it possible to psychically accommodate more than one language?

It is true that the introduction of European languages into Africa has led to serious problems (see Chapter 1). It is also true that there are Africans who, having been educated through the medium of foreign languages, shun their mother tongues and behave like Europeans. There is an old joke in Kenya, for instance, that Kenyan girls who attended the former European schools toss their heads back every now and then, as if to throw back the hair hanging over their faces; in fact, they are simply imitating their (white) European teachers and forgetting that their hair does not flop around in that way.

But it is equally true that European languages also brought with them enormous advantages, such as access to the knowledge, creativity, and entertainment of the entire Western world, as well as participation in global trade and commerce. European languages have become an integral part of the lives of the African people, and are indeed resources to be nurtured and developed.

The learning of European languages (or any second language) by schoolchildren need not involve embracing new cultural identities. In fact, these languages can be adapted (as has happened in many cases) to give expression to the cultural yearnings, beliefs, and intellectual peculiarities of the African world. Kachru (1982) describes how new cultural elements can be fed into a language structure so that the new language becomes part of the new cultural environment. One way of doing this, he suggests, is to recognize the African versions of these languages, and not to treat them as deviations from some mythical norm. The development of local varieties of English in India, Nigeria, Uganda, and South Africa should be allowed to take a natural course, without enforced adherence to untenable foreign standards and norms by language teachers. Krio has developed into the most important lingua franca in Sierra Leone, Creole in Hawaii is part of the Hawaiian national identity, and so is Pidgin English in Nigeria and Cameroon.

Research on attitudes towards English among students (Kembo-Sure 1992) shows that young Kenyans do not regard English as foreign. They reject, for example, suggestions that English makes Africans European-minded, and that it is not suitable for the African mentality. They seem to regard English as just one of the languages they need to learn in their multilingual surroundings.

The preference for a language is in any case not about the inherent nature of the language concerned. It stems from attitudes fashioned by the social and historical experiences of individual people. If the speakers of a language are a dominated group, they may want to escape their servitude by adopting the language of the powerful group and abandoning their own. This happens in all circumstances of language competition in which the speech communities are unevenly matched, whether numerically, militarily, economically, or technologically.

In conclusion, we would like to emphasize that these views on the consequences of the interaction between (foreign) languages and (local) cultural identities should not be seen as insensitive towards the position of African languages. On the contrary, we believe that government intervention on behalf of the 'weaker' languages of Africa is necessary, that these languages should be protected, and that the resources they need should be developed. Furthermore, we believe that schoolchildren should be made aware of the threat of language shift, attrition, and death, as well as the possible consequences of such process-es. They should also be trained in cross-cultural communication (Chapter 11), and their tolerance for other languages, as well as their respect for the right of people to be different, should be developed. The roles of the ex-colonial lan-guages and the indigenous languages are complementary, not oppositional.

The promotion of African languages: a case study

It is clear that a chapter that deals with languages in competition, recognizes the fact that languages are embedded in the power relations in a country or community, and realizes that African languages are generally marginalized on the continent that is their home, should discuss the promotion of minority languages.

In most African countries (such as Kenya, Nigeria, and Uganda), a European language is the language of parliament, government administration, trade and industry, and most of the mass media. In most education systems, African languages are recognized and used as the medium of instruction during the first few years of primary school. However, this recognition is often merely symbol-ic. In Kenya, for example, mother-tongue education is allowed for the first three years of schooling, but in some schools this does not happen, and English is introduced during this period. The result of this is that English dominates the education system, with little or no attention given to the development of pupils' cognitive, affective, and social skills in their first language, or to their ability to use their primary languages in technological and intellectual discourse.

Recently, the Ethiopian government decided to recognize all ethnic groups as autonomous political and cultural entities, and to make them primary units of government development planning. Thus all Ethiopian languages have been recognized as official, which means that each region uses its language in the provision of government services, and as a medium of instruction in schools. Although the estimated number of languages spoken in the country is seventy (Bender et al. 1976), the country is divided into fourteen linguistic regions in terms of mother-tongue or ethnic group affiliation (McNab 1989: 54).[9]

The measures taken by the Ethiopian government to manage the potential for conflict between the various ethnolinguistic groups have great political significance in a country that has witnessed the ruthless domination of local languages by Amharic, a government-sponsored language imposed during the rule of Haile Selassie. In terms of language planning, it represents a notable effort to ensure the survival of all Ethiopian languages. These languages will be used in schools and in government offices; this will provide them with the necessary functional prestige, which in turn will increase the demand for them among the residents of the various regions. So far, the outcome of this initiative cannot yet be determined. However, we do have the success story of Kiswahili in Tanzania, where institutional support was given to the promotion of Kiswahili, thereby contributing to its vitality and prestige. The declaration of Kiswahili as the official and national language of the Republic of Tanzania in 1967 gave it a prestige that at first surpassed that of English. Today, it is used in the courts, parliament, educational institutions, and in all the important public spheres.

Institutional support has also been successful in Kenya. The 1987 constitutional amendment in Kenya, which made Kiswahili a parliamentary language, enhanced its status nationally and gave the less-educated members a sense of worth, as they can now participate in parliamentary debates in a language they know well. And because Kiswahili is now a compulsory school subject up till the end of secondary education, it has become more respectable, as more people are now willing to learn it and use it in various public functions.

Educational issues in multilingual societies

In multilingual societies in which languages are frequently in competition, there are also educational consequences. For instance (as seen in Chapter 1 and above), in communities characterized by asymmetric power relations, parents and school authorities often select an ex-colonial language as the language of learning and teaching, very often to the detriment of the pupils themselves (as has been discussed before).

One of the more frequent consequences of multilingualism in societies, and one that often leads to heated debate, is a high incidence of **bilingual education**. We would like to look more closely at this issue in this section.

The intuitive or gut response to the use of two languages in education seems to be that this will lead to inferior or inadequate educational achievement. This reaction was lent weight by early research findings, which also viewed bilingualism in a negative light. The main objections to bilingualism were based on the following beliefs:

- that it creates more tasks for the brain than is necessary;
- that it leads to mental confusion, as the child does not know when to use which language in communication;
- that it slows down or hinders proper acquisition of the second language;
- that it leads to a split personality; and

- that it creates cultural and political divisions when there are many vernacular languages alongside a second language.

The fears regarding bilingualism are very real, and greatly influence parents' choice of schools for their children, as well as teachers' choice of school language policy, even in cases where central planning supposedly determines the official medium of education (as in Kenya, Uganda, South Africa, and so on). These fears can be summarized in the following statement by a Cambridge University professor as early as the nineteenth century:

> If it were possible for a child to live in two languages at once equally well, so much the worse. His intellectual and spiritual growth would not thereby be doubled, but halved. Unity of mind and character would have great difficulty in asserting itself in such circumstances. (Laurie 1890, cited in Baker 1996: 116)

However, research in recent years has shown that bilingualism is not detrimental to a child's mental and personal development or educational progress, as long as it occurs in a positive environment. Peal and Lambert (1962), in their study of bilingual education in Canada, concluded that bilinguals often perform better in tests of intelligence (IQ tests) than monolinguals. They also found that bilinguals have greater mental flexibility and are superior in abstract thinking and concept formation (that is, they are less dependent on words to find meaning). Most importantly, the research showed that bilingualism actually stimulates further IQ development.

Other research has shown that, contrary to the popular belief that using a first language in elementary grades makes later transition to a second language difficult and counter-productive, the opposite is true. Cummins (1984), for instance, has shown that optimal first-language education provides a rich cognitive foundation that prepares for the acquisition of a second language. In other words, the literacy and cognitive skills already acquired in the first language provide easy transition to second-language-medium education, and thus enhance academic achievement.

Finally, research has also shown that maximum educational benefit from bilingualism is possible only when children are trained to a level where they are **stable bilinguals**, i.e. where competence in the first language is comparable to that in the second language. This is what Cummins (1977) calls the **threshold level**. This means that if their competence in the first language is inadequate, there will be no advantage when the second language is introduced; in fact, there will be difficulty in mastering second-language skills, thereby leading to educational failure. Moreover, if the first language eventually becomes weaker than the second language as a result of neglect in education, the chances are that it will be weakened further by the switch to the second language, which means that language shift may eventually occur.

What are the implications of these research findings for African educational planning and language planning in education? Firstly, there must be a greater and swifter move towards strengthening mother-tongue education in order to provide a solid literacy base for later education in European languages. This means that the current three- or four-year mother-tongue education policy is not sufficient and must be reviewed, if maximum benefit is to be expected from education. This is made even more imperative by the prevailing economic crisis on the African continent, which forces a great many African children to terminate their education after only seven or eight years, before the second-language-medium education can take firm root. Besides, longer mother-tongue training is eventually both cheaper and more rewarding.

Secondly, teachers must be provided with solid bilingual training to prepare them for the challenges of bilingual education. Most African countries today do not really offer bilingual education, as the teaching of mother-tongue languages is taken for granted. This means that teachers are not specifically trained to teach the African languages, as these are considered to carry little or no serious educational value.

Thirdly, governments and educational planning agencies must decide which subjects should be taught in European languages, and which in African languages. The latter cannot be strengthened without first assigning them greater functional status. If they are used in the teaching of school subjects and in examinations beyond the elementary level, they will gain prestige, thus increasing the demand to study them seriously.

Fourthly, greater use of African languages will lead to the growth of more balanced citizens, both culturally and educationally. Those trained in their mother tongues seem to have a more positive self-image and greater respect for other languages and their speakers. Bilinguals are also more culturally flexible, as they are socially more balanced and accommodating. There will thus be fewer chances of political and cultural polarity if people are exposed to more languages than if they are putting up barriers against certain languages.

Lastly, the very cultural and linguistic plurality of African societies provides a *raison d'être* for bilingual education and the teaching of indigenous languages in schools. The harnessing of linguistic resources is a move towards greater cultural and political harmony and economic development, not the contrary. This issue, of language in education, is discussed more fully in Chapter 12.

Endnotes

1   *Native language* is used here to refer to the language associated with a community's historical origins; it is thus not necessarily the language actively used as their main in-group language.

2   Technically, *hegemony* means leadership and dominance. Given that linguistic dominance often carries negative consequences, the term has acquired negative connotations.

3   Our knowledge of the sociological fate of languages is uncertain, and it is therefore not possible to predict what will happen to a particular language, even knowing all the relevant facts. The most we can do is indicate what might possibly happen.

4   It is necessary to keep in mind that attitudes are deep-seated emotional entities, and they must not be confused with opinions or views, which are generally far more superficial.

5   These adaptations are also examples of language conflict, as their appearance is the result of competition between two (or more) linguistic elements (sounds or words), namely the international variant and the African variant, with the latter coming out on top. Consider, for example, the pronunciation of the vowels in words like *cat*, *work*, and

bid by African speakers of English (see also Chapter 6).

6   For more details on the debate about norms for English in Africa, see Webb (compiler), 1996.

7   The term *culture/cultural identity* refers to a person or community's beliefs about the world, perceptions, attitudes, aspirations, norms, and values. Culture therefore includes religion, morality, and the value people attach to ethical and spiritual principles.

8   *Cultural integrity* refers to the intactness of the essential and distinctive features of cultural identity. Retaining cultural integrity implies loyal adherence to its values and norms in everyday behaviour; recognizing the cultural integrity of a group involves allowing that community to be who they want to be. This notion thus stands in opposition to that of cultural hegemony.

9   A similar move is being made in neighbouring Eritrea, where nine nationality languages (as they prefer to call them) have been recognized and designated as national languages of the country, with parents being given a choice as to what language they want their children to be taught in (Tocrurai 1996).

Bibliography

AMBROSE, MARGUERITE, JULIA READ, and VIC WEBB (compilers). 1998. *The role of the African Languages in Democratic South Africa.* Unpublished CentRePoL Workshop Report. University of Pretoria.

BAKER, C. 1996. *Foundations of Bilingual Education and Bilingualism.* Clevedon: Multiligual Matters.

BENDER, M.L., J.D. BOWEN, R.L. COOPER, and C.A FERGUSON (eds.) 1976. *Language in Ethiopia.* Oxford: Oxford University Press.

CUMMINS, J. 1984. *Bilingualism and Special Education: Issues in Assessment and Pedagogy.* San Diego: College-Hill Press.

———— 1977. 'Cognitive factors associated with

the attainment of intermediate levels of bilingual skills.' *Modern Language Journal*, 61, 3–12.

DIMMENDAAL, G. 1992. 'Reduction in Kore recognized.' In M. Brenzinger (ed.), *Language Death: Factual and Theoretical Explorations with Special Reference to E. Africa.* Berlin: Mouton de Gruyter.

FARDON, R., and FURNISS, G. (eds.) 1994. *African Languages: Development and the State.* London and New York: Routledge.

FISHMAN, J., M.H GERTNER, E.G LOWY, and W.G. MILAN. 1985. *The Rise and Fall of Ethnic Revival.* Berlin: Mouton de Gruyter.

HOLMES, J., M. ROBERTS, M. VERIVAKI, and

A. AIPOLO. 1993. 'Language maintenance and shift in three New Zealand Speech Communities.' *Applied Linguistics* 14(1), 1–23.

KACHRU, B. (ed.) 1982. *The Other Tongue.* Urbana: University of Illinois Press.

KEMBO-SURE, E. 1992. 'Falling Standards of English in Kenya.' *English Today* Vol 8.

——— 1991. 'Language Functions and Language Attitudes in Kenya.' *English World-Wide* 12:2, 245–260.

MAZRUI, A., and A. MAZRUI. 1993. 'Dominant Languages in a Plural Society: English and Kiswahili in post-colonial East Africa.' *International Political Science Review*, Vol. 14, 3, 275–292.

MCNAB, C. 1989. *Language Policy and Language Practice.* Stockholm: University of Stockholm.

PARKIN, D.J. 1974. 'Language Switching in Nairobi.' In W. Whiteley (ed.), *Language in Kenya.* Nairobi: Oxford University Press.

PEAL, E., and W.E. LAMBERT. 1962. 'The relationship between bilingualism and intelligence.' *Psychological Monographs.* 76 (27), 1–23.

SAPIR, EDWARD. 1921. *Language.* New York: Harcourt, Brace & Co.

SASSE, H. 1992. 'Language Decay and Contact-induced change: Similarities and Differences.' In M. Brenzinger (ed.), *Language Death: Factual and Theoretical Explorations with Special Reference to E. Africa.* Berlin: Mouton de Gruyter.

WEBB, VIC (compiler). 1996. *Appropriate English for a Democratic South Africa.* Unpublished CentRePoL Workshop Report, University of Pretoria.

WHORF, BENJAMIN LEE. 1956. In J.B. Carrol (ed.) *Language, Thought and Reality. Selected writings of Benjamin Lee Whorf.* Cambridge, Mass.: MIT.

6 The sounds of Africa: their phonetic characteristics

Herman Batibo

Expected outcomes

At the end of this chapter you should be able to:

1 Explain what the terms *phone*, *phonetics*, and *phonetic characterization* mean.
2 Describe the bases for the description of vowels and consonants.
3 Provide accurate descriptions of individual speech sounds.
4 Provide examples of uniquely African speech sounds (such as the clicks of the Khoisan languages).
5 Discuss the orthographic representation of some African languages.
6 Explain to teachers and prospective employers why they should not underestimate the knowledge and skills of people on the basis of the way they pronounce the sounds of English, French, or Portuguese.

Introduction

When people in Africa and elsewhere communicate with each other, they use what we commonly call words. Each of the words we use is made up of sounds that enable us to hear and decode the meanings of utterances when people speak. However, have you ever asked yourself how these sounds are produced in our mouths, how many sounds are used in each of our languages, how these sounds differ from each other, or how they are organized in different languages? This chapter will discuss the sounds found in human languages, particularly the African languages and other languages spoken in Africa. It will have the following objectives:

- to familiarize you with the various sounds found in the languages of Africa;
- to introduce you to the mechanisms involved in producing them; and
- to develop your ability to describe them.

As well as the above, two related issues will be discussed, namely the orthographic representation of the sounds of the African languages, and the social evaluation of speech sounds. Both these aspects of the 'sounds of Africa' can be quite problematic.

The study of speech sounds is called **phonetics**. Phonetics deals with the physical aspects of sounds; that is, it studies their physical features. In some senses, it is not a linguistic discipline, as it doesn't pay direct attention to these sounds as elements in the systems of languages. That particular aspect of the study of speech sounds is called **phonology**. The **phonological characteristics** of speech sounds – the way in which these sounds are organized into linguistic systems – will be discussed in Chapter 7.

Most animals are capable of producing noises: dogs bark, monkeys screech, and birds 'sing'. These noises are made with organs known as the **vocal organs**, which are situated inside the upper front side of the neck in the area we commonly call the Adam's apple in humans. Animals use these noises to express emotions such as pain, loneliness, the desire to mate, hunger, or other specific emotions. We are all familiar with the types of noise made by domestic animals such as dogs, cats, cows, donkeys, and even wild animals such as lions, hyenas, or wolves. Although these noises are often intended to express emotions or to signal certain kinds of information to fellow animals, they are not elaborate enough to enable animals to transmit the same kinds of messages that humans are able to convey to each other.

Humans also use noises in their speech. These are produced through a complex combination of actions of different body parts, such as the lungs, the ribs, the Adam's apple, and so on. Humans have advantages over animals in producing sounds because of their upright posture, the complex muscles of their lips, their soft and flexible tongue, their level teeth structure, as well as a special facility in the structure of their brains, which controls speech. The sounds produced by humans that can be used in speech are known as **speech sounds**.

Every language has its own selection of speech sounds, which may differ in type, number, and organization from those of any other language. A collection of speech sounds in a language is called a **speech sound inventory**.

An important part of any description of a language is the description of its speech sounds. For this, a descriptive framework is needed. This must allow us to identify the speech sounds of a language, to label them, and to classify them. We therefore need to know what the possible speech sounds of human languages are, and what descriptive terms we can use. This chapter will provide the descriptive framework required for characterizing the speech sounds of a human language.

Before we embark on a discussion of the descriptive framework, we need to mention a convention followed internationally in phonetics: indicating speech sounds by placing them between square brackets. The speech sounds in the English word *bat*, for instance, are [b], [æ], and [t].

Phonetics: the production of sounds

Approaches to the analysis of speech sounds

The sounds that are used in human languages, such as the ones found in African languages, can be studied from three points of view. Firstly, the way in which they are produced can be studied. This involves describing the various organs and mechanisms used in producing sounds. This approach, which deals with human body functions and structure (physiology and anatomy), is known as **articulatory phonetics**. Speech sounds can also be studied in terms of their physical properties, that is, their features as disturbances of the air around us. This kind of study thus deals with the nature of the sound waves that are transmitted from the speaker to the hearer, and normally includes the study of sound waves in terms of how loud they are, how long they last, and so forth; in technical terms, the frequency of the waves, their amplitude, their intensity, and their duration. This approach is known as **acoustic phonetics**. The third way of studying speech sounds involves describing how the ear perceives them, and the factors that determine their interpretation by the hearer. This approach is known as **auditory phonetics**.

As acoustic phonetics depends heavily on complex physical analyses of sound properties, and the use of sophisticated equipment (not easily available in most of our institutions), and given that auditory phonetics is in the early stages of development, and also requires special instruments for speech synthesis, we shall limit ourselves, at this introductory level, to articulatory phonetics.

The organs of speech

The sounds we use to form words in human languages are produced by what are generally known as the **speech organs**. These are organs that we normally use for sucking, tasting, chewing, swallowing, smelling, breathing, crying, and shouting; in other words, the lips, the teeth, the tongue, the nose, and the inside of the Adam's apple. How do we 'know' how to use these organs to speak? Speech came into existence through physical development in the brain, body posture, and changes in the mouth cavity, triggered by the interactive development of humans.

The organs of speech constitute a list of more than a dozen parts of the body which are in one way or other connected with speech production. These organs are numbered in the diagram below.

FIGURE 6.1 The human organs of speech

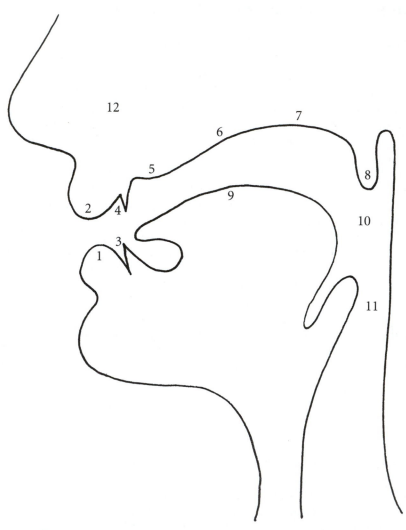

1 lower lip	7 soft palate or velum
2 upper lip	8 uvula
3 lower teeth	9 tongue
4 upper teeth	10 pharynx
5 alveolar ridge	11 larynx
6 hard palate	12 nasal cavity

The area between the larynx (11) and the lips is called the vocal tract, and it is here that most human speech sounds are produced. The space between the soft palate (7) and the lips is referred to as the mouth cavity (or oral cavity). As some sounds are also produced with the aid of air moving out through the nose, we also speak of the nasal cavity.

Other parts of the body are also used in the production of speech sounds. These are the stomach, the diaphragm, the lungs, the trachea (the windpipe), and the jaws, all of which are indirectly involved in the movement of the speech organs.

The production of speech sounds

Most speech sounds are produced by blocking or narrowing (constricting) the passage through which air moves through and out the mouth. Normally, the constriction of the airflow is caused by two of the speech organs moving closer together, or even touching each other. One of these organs is referred to as the **active articulator** (generally one of the organs situated in the lower part of the mouth, and which can easily be moved: the lower lip, the lower teeth, the tongue, and the velum), and the other is the **passive articulator** (generally the organs situated in the upper part of the mouth, and which can't be easily moved: the upper lip, the upper teeth, the alveolar ridge, the hard palate, and the soft palate). The vocal cords, which can also be moved, are also said to be active articulators.

Most of the sounds used in human speech come from air which is pushed out of the lungs. We call this airflow being exhaled from the lungs the **pulmonic airstream**. There are also other airstream mechanisms that are used as sources of energy in the production of human speech sounds, and these will be discussed later.

Pulmonic airstream mechanism

This is the most common mechanism used in the production of speech sounds. Air being expelled from the lungs is the source of energy. Usually, the muscles of the stomach contract, causing a set of muscles in one's lower chest under the lungs (the diaphragm) to rise, thereby compressing the air in the lungs, which then flows out through the trachea (a wide air-pipe) up into the larynx (or Adam's apple). Here, it may or may not be hindered by the vocal cords, which are a pair of membranes (or muscles) that can open or close. These vocal cords can be pulled away from one other, thus allowing the air to move through them unhindered, or they can each be pulled tight (tensed) and moved close together, thus hindering or even blocking the airflow. The space between the vocal cords is called the glottis. When the vocal cords are tightly closed, the air forcing itself through them will cause them to vibrate, thus producing voiced sounds. Such a process is called **voicing**. Some speech sounds are associated with voicing, while others are not. Those that are produced with the airflow moving freely through the glottis are called voiceless.

We suggest the following practical exercise. Pronounce the English sounds [f] and [v] (as in *feel* and *veal*), and try to describe the phonetic difference between them. You will find that the difference has to do with the tenseness of your vocal cords; as you say *feel*, your vocal cords are relaxed, allowing the air to move freely through them. The [f] is thus voiceless. As you say *veal*, however, your vocal cords tighten, thus causing them to vibrate as the air from your lungs moves through them. This vibration changes the free-flowing air into sound, called voice, so that we describe the [v] as a voiced sound.

From the larynx, the air passes through the pharynx into the mouth cavity, where the air or voice will be further altered to form different sounds. This takes place through changes in the positions of the speech organs (the tongue, the lower teeth, and the lower lip). What happens in the mouth cavity is that these organs (called the active articulators) change position, moving closer to or coming into contact with the passive articulators. Through these movements, different types of cavities are created in the vocal tract, so that different speech sounds are heard. Speech sounds formed in this way are called oral speech sounds. It can also happen that the air or voice moving up through the pharynx can be blocked off (wholly or just partially) from the mouth cavity, and moved through the nose. This happens when the velum is lowered, closing the passage to the mouth cavity, and diverting the air behind it through the nose. Sounds produced in this way are called nasal sounds, and have a nasal quality.

It must be noted that the different types of cavities listed above, which cause the differences in the quality of speech sounds, are in fact differences in the resonance tract. Changes in the resonance tract lead to the air in it vibrating differently, causing differences in the sound frequencies as the configuration alters. You can check this by filling two identical containers with water up to different levels, and then dropping two identical pebbles into each; the sounds made by the pebbles as they splash into the water will be different, because of the differences in spaces for resonance.

The speech sounds produced in the ways described above can broadly be classified into two main categories of sound: consonants and vowels. These are the basic elements in the formation of any units of meaning (or words). Consonants are those sounds produced when the flow of air is considerably interfered with, from being squeezed through narrow openings to being blocked off altogether. Vowels are speech sounds produced when the airflow is minimally disturbed, without friction or blockage occurring.

The production of vowels

Vowels are a class of speech sounds that are central to the building up of words in all languages. They are normally produced by the vigorous vibration of the vocal cords, but with no major stricture in the mouth cavity. The vowels used in most languages are produced through the pulmonic airstream mechanism; that is, with air movement issuing from the lungs.

The production of vowels involves mainly the tongue and the lips. The tongue can move backwards and forwards (horizontally), or upwards and downwards (vertically). If the tongue moves forward, front vowels are formed. If it moves backwards, back vowels are formed. If the tongue moves neither horizontally nor vertically, but stays in a neutral position, central or neutral vowels are formed. As regards the vertical movement of the tongue, we can distinguish between high vowels (or close vowels); high-mid vowels (or half-close vowels); low-mid vowels (or half-open vowels); and low vowels (or open vowels). The lips, meanwhile, can be either spread or rounded.

If we now combine these three dimensions, we can begin to describe how vowels are formed, by referring to the part of the tongue involved (front or back), the height of the tongue position in relation to the hard palate (high, mid, low), and the shape of the lips (rounded or unrounded). Given this framework, the vowel [i], for example, can be described as an unrounded, high, front vowel.

The normal Latin alphabet has five symbols representing vowels, namely *a*, *e*, *i*, *o*, and *u*. However, these are not enough to cover all the vowel sounds found in human languages. So an International Phonetic Alphabet (generally called the IPA) has been devised to provide other symbols to distinguish between various vowels. In this book, we will use the IPA symbols (or notations) to represent vowels and consonants.

Vowels do not all function at the same level, and we distinguish between cardinal vowels, secondary cardinal vowels, and other vowels. These three levels are not typically found in any specific language. Rather, they are abstractions, idealizations, and should be thought of as fixed points in terms of which the vowels of a particular language can be described.

The cardinal vowels

The cardinal vowels are those that can be produced with the organs of speech, particularly the lips, in their most 'natural' positions. The vowels that correspond with these positions are the ones most commonly found in the languages of the world. There are normally four front vowels [i, e, ɛ, a], produced with spread lips, and four back vowels [u, o, ɔ, ɑ], produced with rounded lips. Another vowel [ə] (schwa) is pronounced centrally with the lips in a neutral position. The position of the tongue in the mouth cavity during the articulation of the cardinal vowels can be represented diagrammatically in the form of a trapezium, which is a two-dimensional figure showing the articulatory positions of vowels in terms of tongue height (close, half-close, half-open, or open) and horizontal localization (front, central, or back).

Two points that must be noted:

- the positions given for the cardinal vowels are 'geometrically' determined; in other words, they are precisely equally far from one another (as mentioned above, the cardinal vowels are 'imaginary' vowels, serving only as reference points for the description of natural vowels);
- the use of a trapezium should not be taken as a representation of the physical character of the vowel space in a person's mouth – the vowel space does not literally have the form of a trapezium.

FIGURE 6.2   The cardinal vowels

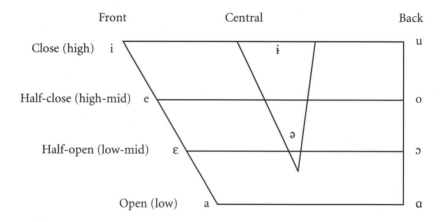

The three most common vowels in the African languages approximate the cardinal vowels [a], [i], and [u]. However, most Bantu languages (i.e. the majority of the languages spoken in eastern, central, and southern Africa) use five vowels, corresponding with the cardinal vowels. For example, languages such as Kiswahili, Chishona, isiZulu, isiXhosa, siSwati, and ChiChewa have a five-vowel system [a, e, i, o, and u]. Several others, such as Luganda, Lingala, Kikuyu, Sukuma, Efik, Birom, and Maba, have a seven-vowel system [a, ε, e, i, ɔ, o, u].

The secondary cardinal vowels

As we have seen, the front cardinal vowels are articulated with the lips spread wide, and the back cardinal vowels with the lips well rounded. Although this is normally considered the natural way of articulating these vowels, it is possible to reverse the lip mechanism so that the front vowels are articulated with the lips closely rounded, and the back vowels with the lips spread out. When this happens, the resultant vowels are known as secondary cardinal vowels. The following trapezium shows the main secondary vowels.

FIGURE 6.3   The secondary vowels

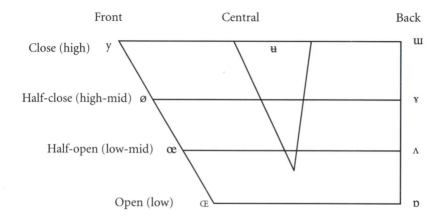

The secondary vowels are not common in the languages of the world because of their articulatory complexity. The sounds [y], [ø], and [œ] are found in the French words *tu* ('you'), *deux* ('two'), and *soeur* ('sister') respectively. Afrikaans (spoken in South Africa) also contains these vowels, as in *vuur* ('fire'), *deur* ('through'), and *put* ('water-well'). The sound [ʌ] is found in the English word *but*. Secondary vowels are uncommon in African languages. The only known African language with a considerable number of secondary vowels is Ngwe (spoken in Cameroon), which has the sounds [y], [ɒ], [ʌ], [ɤ], and [ɯ] in the words [aty] ('stick'), [mbɒ] ('tadpoles'), [ntsʌ] ('water'), [mbɤ] ('brass gong'), and [mbɯ] ('dog') respectively.

Other vowel articulations in African languages

Apart from the cardinal and secondary vowels, a number of other vowels are also found in the African languages. These are described below.

The lax vowels [ɪ] and [ʊ]

In standard British English, the vowels in the word pairs *bit* and *beat* and *foot* and *food* are quite different; in the pronunciation of the vowels in the first words of each pair, the muscles of the tongue in particular, the cheek, and the throat are relatively relaxed, whereas they are tensed in the case of the vowels in the second words of each pair. Phonetically, the vowels are [ɪ] and [iy], and [ʊ] and [uy] respectively. These vowels are described as **lax** vowels and **tense** vowels respectively.

Speakers of African languages often have difficulty in keeping their pronunciation of the vowels in these two pairs apart, because the distinction is not common in these languages.

The high lax vowels [ɪ] and [ʊ] are, however, very common in African languages. The vowel [ɪ] is sometimes transcribed as [ɪ], and the vowel [ʊ] as [ʋ] or [Ɒ]. As indicated, the two vowels differ from [i] and [u] because they are articulated with the muscles of the tongue relaxed, while the latter are articulated with the muscles of the tongue tightened. Lax high vowels are found in many African languages, such as Setswana, Sesotho, Sepedi, Sukuma, Kikuyu, Kpelle, Dyola, Masaai, Ik, Akan, Lugbara, and a number of other languages whose vowel system is of the following type.

The tense/lax vowel distinction is sometimes referred to as advanced tongue root (ATR), because the muscles of the root of the tongue move forward during the articulation of the tense vowels and are relaxed during the articulation of the lax vowels. This characterization is especially true of some West African languages, such as Ewe or Kpelle.

The vowel [æ]

The vowel [æ] is articulated between [ɛ] and [a], as in the English word *cat*. It is rare in African languages. The only known African language in which it is found is Ngwe.

Additional vowel features

There are several phonetic processes that are often used in African languages to produce additional vowels. These are as follows.

Nasalization

Most vowels are oral, that is, pronounced in such a way that the voiced air moves only through the mouth. However, sometimes voice is channelled through the nose. When this happens, the sounds are said to be nasalized, or to have undergone the process of nasalization. Therefore, we need to distinguish between nasalized and oral (non-nasalized) vowels. Nasalized vowels are usually produced with a lowered velum, thereby allowing part of the voice to pass through the nose. The tilde symbol [˜] is placed above nasalized vowels to indicate nasality. Thus, in Desano, we can distinguish between [wai] ('name') and [waĩ] ('fish'). The African languages with distinctive nasalized vowels include Bariba, Senadi, Ewe, Igbo, Akan, Ga, Lelemi, Gbeya, Songhai, Lugbara, and Sara (Maddison 1984).

Pharyngealization

Thus far, vowels have been said to be oral – produced in the mouth. However, it sometimes happens that vowels are formed in the pharynx (see Figure 6.1, which shows the pharynx behind the root of the tongue, just above the larynx). When vowels are formed in this way, they are said to have been pharyngealized: formed in the pharynx, and articulated with an active retraction of the tongue root. A number of the African languages use the process of pharyngealization, and we therefore have to distinguish between pharyngealized and non-pharyngealized vowels. Pharyngealized vowels are also known as epiglottalized, spincteric, or strident vowels (Ladefoged and Maddison 1996: 306). Such vowels are commonly found in Khoisan languages, particularly with back vowels, represented phonetically as [ɑˤ] and [oˤ]. There are, in fact, many types of pharyngealized vowels, some of which involve the simultaneous use of breathiness.

Vowel lengthening

In many African languages, vowels can be short or long. A colon (:) or doubling of the vowel is used to indicate vowel length, for instance as in [seba] ('boil') compared with [se:ba] ('excavate' in Kisukuma). Languages with long vowels include Degbani, Fur, Arabic, Tigre, Wolof, Tuareg, Iraqw, Hausa, and Ngizim (Maddison 1984).

Diphthongs

Diphthongs are vowels that end differently from the way in which they begin. For example, in the English word *buy*, the vowel begins with an [a] and ends with an [ɪ]; in other words, it has two articulatory qualities. The same happens in the English word *day* [deɪ]. However, in both cases, the two vowels are treated as one articulatory unit.

Diphthongs are rare in African languages. The known African languages with diphthongs include Hausa, Matengo, Degbani, Toro, and Nyoro. Some languages (like Kiswahili) have acquired diphthongs from adopted foreign words. In many African languages, words with diphthongs are nativized by treating the diphthongs as vowels belonging to two separate syllables. Afrikaans is also characterized by the presence of a number of diphthongs, as in *leeu* ('lion'), *huis* ('house'), *rooi* ('red'), *koei* ('cow'), *koud* ('cold'), and *laai* ('load').

The production of consonants

Consonants are formed when the free flow of air is 'radically' disturbed (i.e. markedly more than when vowels are formed) as it passes through the vocal tract. To put it technically, consonants are normally considered those speech sounds whose production involves stricture at one or several points in the vocal tract, usually between active and passive articulators.

Consonants are described with reference to three aspects of speech sound production: the presence or absence of voicing, manner of articulation, and place of articulation. Each of these three variables is discussed separately.

Presence or absence of voicing

Whereas all vowels are voiced – that is, they are associated with the vibration of the vocal cords in the larynx – not all consonants are. Some are voiced, while others are voiceless. An [f], as in *feel*, and a [v], as in *veal*, for example, are identical except for one feature: as demonstrated above, the [f] is voiceless, while the [v] is voiced. It is possible to feel the difference between voiced and voiceless consonants; touch your Adam's apple lightly when pronouncing these two sounds. You will feel your vocal cords vibrating when you produce the [v].

Point of articulation

The type or quality of a consonant is also determined by the point or place in the vocal tract where it is formed, that is, where the maximum stricture takes place. This is known as the point of articulation – another name is place of articulation). So consonants may be bilabial (if pronounced with both lips – [p]); labio-dental (if pronounced with the lower lip against the upper teeth –

[v]); dental (if pronounced with the tip of the tongue against the teeth – the first sound in *think*); interdental (if pronounced with the front part of the tongue between the upper and lower teeth); alveolar (if pronounced with the tip or blade of the tongue against the alveolar ridge – [t]); retroflex (if pronounced with the front part of the tongue curved backwards towards the hard palate – the 'r' in standard English *red*); palato-alveolar (if pronounced with the blade or front part of the tongue in contact with the hind part of the alveolar ridge); alveo-palatal (if pronounced with the central part of the tongue against the hard palate towards the alveolar ridge); palatal (if pronounced with the central part of the tongue against the hard palate – the 'y' in *young*); velar (if pronounced with the back of the tongue against the soft palate or velum – [k]); uvular (if pronounced with the back of the tongue against the uvula); pharyngeal (if pronounced with the root of the tongue, at the back, against the wall of the pharyngeal cavity); and glottal (if pronounced with blockage or constriction of the vocal cords). (See Figure 6.1, as well as Table 6.1.)

Manner of articulation

The third variable in the production of consonants is the manner of articulation (also known as the mode of articulation). This refers to the way the two articulators (active and passive) come into contact. The mode of contact normally ranges from complete blockage (or closure) to mere proximity.

Consonants are categorized according to their manner of articulation. The most common categories are plosives, fricatives, affricates, laterals, trills/flaps, semivowels, and nasal consonants.

Plosives

Plosive sounds are those produced by completely blocking the flow of air, letting pressure build up behind the closure, then releasing it in a sudden burst (for example, the sounds [p] and [b] in *pin* and *bin*). The term *stop* is also often used as an alternative. Strictly speaking, however, stops include non-plosive sounds whose articulation involves blockage, such as the affricate (ch in *church*) and nasal consonants ([m] in *mother*). Plosive sounds, particularly the bilabial [p, b], alveolar [t, d], and velar [k, g], are very common in African languages and other languages of the world.

Fricatives

Fricative sounds are produced by putting the two articulators (the active and the passive) in sufficiently close contact to cause a constriction, which then causes friction when air forces its way through. Some examples are the sounds [f], [v], [s], and [z]. African languages are rich in fricative sounds, as these are sounds that can be articulated at practically all points where the articulators come into contact (see Table 6.1 below).

Affricates

Affricate sounds are consonants that resemble plosives, but which are released gradually, allowing friction to occur. This is the case in sounds that we normally spell as *ch*, *j*, or *dg* in English (such as in *church* and *judge*). Some African languages have other affricate sounds, including pf, ts, dz, kx, and qχ (see Table 6.1 below).

Laterals and lateral fricatives

Lateral sounds are generally sonorous or highly voiced, and are produced by blocking the mouth cavity at the mid-line by bringing one part of the tongue (tip, blade, or middle) into contact with the alveolar ridge or palate. An opening is then created at one or both sides of the tongue. The most common lateral sound in the African languages is [l], which is usually articulated as an alveolar sound. However, the palatal lateral [ʎ] and the retroflex [ɭ] are also sometimes found.

Although laterals are normally not associated with air friction, some African languages, particularly those of the Bantu languages spoken in southern Africa, have **lateral fricatives**. These are laterals in which air is constricted to create friction. The most common lateral fricatives are [ɬ] and [lʒ] (conventionally spelt as *hl* and *dl* respectively in the Nguni languages). In some languages, particularly those of the Sotho and Tsonga families, the lateral fricatives are associated with plosive consonants, as in [tɬ] and [tɬʰ], spelt as *tl* and *tlh* respectively. Some of these laterals, notably the *hl*, are unvoiced.

Trills and flaps

Trill sounds are those consonants whose production involves the rapid vibration of the tongue against the upper teeth, the alveolar ridge, or the uvular. These sounds are also known as vibrants or rolled sounds. The types of trills differ in terms of the number and intensity of the vibrations. This would range from the most intense [r̄], as in Kurya, through the normal trill [r] to a mere flap [ɾ], as in Chagga and Chishona. Where the vibrations are very soft, a frictionless continuant [ɹ] may result, as in the English word *very*. Occasionally, in languages like Sekgalagadi, the trill is articulated as a voiceless sound (transcribed with a zero underneath: [r̥]).

African languages differ tremendously in the type and quality of trills. Many of them use trills as variants of the lateral sound [l]. In fact, trills and laterals constitute one category known as **liquids**. Because of the many differences in their articulations, liquids are among the sounds that tend to characterize speakers of a given language.

Semivowels and approximants

The **semivowels** constitute a category of consonants whose articulation involves neither blockage nor constriction of the air from the lungs. The active and passive articulators are close enough to effect change in the configuration of the mouth cavity. Semivowels are also known as glides. The most common semivowels are y [j] and w [w]. The former has palatal characteristics, while the latter has both bilabial and velar features. In the latter case, the predominance of the bilabial or velar characteristics would depend on individual languages. For example, the former predominates in the Nguni languages and the latter in the Sotho languages.

On the other hand, **approximants** are consonants which, like semivowels, are articulated by the close approximation of the active and passive articulators at one point in the vocal tract. However, in the case of approximants, the two articulators are in much closer contact. Such sounds are sometimes known as frictionless continuants. Such sounds, especially [ɥ] and [ɹ], are common in some West African languages such as Twi and Late (Ladefoged 1964). In some descriptions, the semivowels are considered to be a sub-category of the approximants.

Nasal consonants

Nasal consonants are those whose articulation is associated with the blockage of the air in the mouth cavity, with some air, however, allowed to flow through the nose before the main stream of air is released through the mouth cavity. The most common nasal consonants in the African languages are [m], [n], [ɲ] (commonly spelt as *ny*), and [ŋ] (commonly spelt as *ng* or *ng'*).

Other consonants

Certain consonants that exist in other languages of the world are very rare in African languages. These include the bilabial trill [B], the velar lateral [L], the retroflex approximant [ɻ], and the velar approximant [ɯ].

Below is a two-dimensional chart showing most of the consonants that occur in African languages and elsewhere, against the three variables described above.

TABLE 6.1   The consonants produced by the pulmonic mechanism (using the IPA symbols based on the revised 1993 version). Where the symbols appear in pairs, the one to the right represents the voiced consonant.

		Bilabial	Labio-dental	Dental	Alveolar	Post-alveolar	Retro-flex	Palatal	Velar	Uvular	Pharyn-geal	Glottal
1	Plosives	p b		t d	t d		ʈ ɖ	c ɟ	k ɡ	q ɢ		ʔ
2	Fricatives	ɸ β	f v	θ ð	s z	ʃ ʒ	ʂ ʐ	ç ʝ	x ɣ	χ ʁ	ħ ʕ	h ɦ
3	Affricates	pf bv		tθ dð	ts dz	tʃ dʒ			kx gɣ	qχ		
4	Laterals				l		ɭ	ʎ	ʟ			
5	Lateral fricatives				ɬ	lʒ						
6	Trills	ʙ			r					ʀ		
7	Taps/Flaps				ɾ		ɽ					
8	Semi-vowels	w						j	w			
9	Approx-imants	ɥ	ʋ		ɹ		ɻ	j	ɰ			
10	Nasals	m	ɱ		n		ɳ	ɲ	ŋ	ɴ		

The secondary articulation of consonants

Many consonants are associated with secondary articulations; features or segments that accompany the primary consonant. The most common secondary articulations in the African languages are as follows.

Aspirated consonants

Some consonants, particularly the stops (plosives, affricates, and nasals) may be aspirated, in other words, produced with an audible amount of air, created by a considerable delay in the interval between the explosion or release and the closure of the vocal cords, resulting in an *h* sound accompanying the stop. In the African languages, aspiration is more common with the voiceless plosive consonants, giving [pʰ], [tʰ], [cʰ], and [kʰ]. However, some languages, such as those of the Sotho family, have aspirated affricates such as [tsʰ], [tʃʰ], and [tɬʰ]. Moreover, some languages, such as Kisukuma, Chishona, Kirundi, and Kinyarwanda have aspirated nasals, namely [mʰ], [nʰ], [ɲʰ], and [ŋʰ]. In some languages, particularly Chishona and Xitsonga, the nasal aspiration is voiced.

Prenasalized consonants

Some African languages, particularly those of Bantu origin, have prenasalized consonants. These are oral consonants, usually plosives, which are preceded by nasalization. The resulting nasals reflect the following consonant regarding its place of articulation, such as [mb], [nd], [ŋg], [mp], [nt], and [ŋk], or [ᵐb], [ⁿd], [ᵑg], [ᵐp], [ⁿt], and [ᵑk] respectively. Because of this similarity, these nasals are called homorganic bi-segments.

Geminated consonants

The production of geminated consonants involves the lengthening of the consonants (sometimes described as their repetition), often as single long units. They are found in a few distantly related African languages, such as Arabic, Peul, Luganda, and some of the Chadic languages. Geminated consonants are normally transcribed by doubling the consonant or using a colon (:) after the consonant. For example, in Arabic, we distinguish between [ila] ('but') and [illa] or [il:a] ('defect').

Palatalized consonants

Palatalized consonants are non-palatal sounds that are articulated by moving the tongue to the position of the palate, which means that they acquire palatal features. Such consonants are usually transcribed with the superscript [ʲ], as in [kʲ], [gʲ], [tʲ], or [dʲ]. When a sound becomes fully palatalized, it changes into a palatal sound such as [c], [ɟ], [tʃ], or [dʒ]. Palatalized consonants are very common in African languages.

Labialized consonants

Labialized consonants are likewise non-labial sounds whose articulation is accompanied by the involvement of the lips in the articulation process. For instance, a [kw]'s articulation is accompanied by the bilabial [w]. Such consonants are usually transcribed with the superscript [ʷ], as in [pʷ], [bʷ], [gʷ], and [kʷ]. Sometimes the superscript [°] is used, as in [p°], [b°], [k°], and [g°].

Lateralized and trilled consonants

In some languages, particularly those of the Sotho group, some consonants are lateralized. This means that their articulation is accompanied by lateralization: the air used for the formation of the sound is forced through the side of the tongue while the central part is blocked. This is the case with the [tɬ] and [tɬʰ] sounds in Setswana, written as *tl* and *tlh* respectively, as in *tla* ('come') and *ntlha* ('edge'). Tsonga (Tswa dialect) also has [kɬ] and [kɬʰ], written as *kl* and *khl* respectively. The lateral component is usually a voiceless fricative because of the preceding voiceless plosive segment. Historically, these consonants were [ɟ] and [c] in proto-Bantu.

In some languages, such as Emakhuwa, Comorian, and Rimi, some consonants are trilled, that is, accompanied by a trill articulation: [tʳ]. The trill is normally de-voiced, such as [tʳatʳu] ('three' – spelt *tratru*) in Comorian.

Labio-velar consonants

A type of consonant common in African languages, especially in West Africa, is the labio-velar consonant, whose articulation involves simultaneous bilabial and velar contacts. The most common labio-velars are the plosives [kp], [gb], and the nasal [ŋm]. Languages with labio-velars include Igbo, Yoruba, Ewe, Kpelle, Mende, Dagbani, Ovatime, Efik, Logba, and many other languages spoken in Nigeria, Benin, Togo, Ghana, Ivory Coast, and Sierra Leone. In some Bantu languages, such as Kirundi and Kinyarwanda, labialized consonants like [kʷ] and [gʷ] are changing into [kp] and [gb] respectively.

Non-pulmonic airstream mechanisms

Although most of the speech sounds are produced via the pulmonic airstream mechanism, some sounds, consonants in particular, are produced through other mechanisms. The following are the most common non-pulmonic mechanisms used in African languages.

Ingressive airstream mechanism

The ingressive airstream mechanism of speech production involves using the inhalation of air into the lungs as the source of energy. In African languages, the most common such sounds are the implosive consonants transcribed [ɓ], [ɗ], [ʃ], [ʄ], and [Ɠ]. Examples are found in the Nguni languages, such as the isiZulu word [ukuɓona] ('to see'). The implosive consonants result from the blockage of one position in the mouth cavity followed by an inward explosion, hence the term *implosive*. Implosives are also found in Chishona, Chopi, Inhambane, and Comorian, as well as some West African languages such as Kpelle, Kalabari, and Nyangi.

Glottal airstream mechanism

In this mechanism, air is compressed in the mouth or pharynx while the vocal cords are tightly closed. The most common speech sounds produced in this way are the ejective consonants, which are usually voiceless plosive consonants, checked by a sudden stop before the accompanying vowel. They are thus normally transcribed with the glottal stop [ʔ] as a superscript, as in [pˀ], [tˀ], and [kˀ]. Sometimes an apostrophe is used, as in [p'], [t'], and [k']. Ejective sounds are found in several African languages, including those of the Chadic family (such as Hausa), Khoisan (such as Ju/'hoan), those of the Bantu family (such as Sesotho, Sekgalagadi, and Setswana), and those of the Nilo-Saharan family (such as Ik and Uduk). For example, in Setswana and Sekgalagadi, we have the words [rat'a] ('love'), [rek'a] ('buy'), and [p'ula] ('rain'). However, the glottalization in Setswana is in the process of disappearing, partly because it is not marked in the official orthography.

Velaric airstream mechanism

In this mechanism, the airstream is blocked in the velaric position. The tongue is then lowered in order to create a vacuum and an explosion at a specific point in

the mouth cavity as air is sucked into the compressed area. The sounds thus produced are known as **clicks**, and an example is the sound made by a kiss. So far,
the only languages with clicks are those of the Khoisan family, used by the Khoi-
speakers and the San-speakers of South Africa, Botswana, Namibia, Tanzania,
Angola, Zambia, and Zimbabwe. Some Bantu languages such as isiZulu,
isiXhosa, siSwati, seSotho, and Shiyeyi have also adopted them. Common clicks
include the bilabial [⊙], the dental [/] (orthographically *c*), the lateral [//]
(orthographically *x*), the (post) alveolar [!] (orthographically *q*), and the pre-
palatal or palato-alveolar [≠] (orthographically *tc*). Clicks can be accompanied
by prenasalization, aspiration, or voicing. This tends to multiply their number in
the languages that include them in their inventory of speech sounds.

The representation of African words[1]

Traditionally, most African languages were used exclusively for oral communication. They were used to exchange greetings, to deliver messages, to express ideas,
to discuss community matters, to narrate past experiences, and to preserve cus-
toms and cultural practices. Except for a few languages such as Bamileke (spoken
in Cameroon) and Amharic (spoken in Ethiopia), the words in most African languages were not written down, as there were no scripts or orthographies.

On the other hand, in North Africa, the Coptic, Tuareg, and Berber languages have each had their own script for centuries. Coptic is the oldest
language in Africa in terms of having its own script, as its writing tradition goes
back to the hieroglyphics of the Pharaohs at the start of the third millennium
BC – about 5000 years ago. Throughout North Africa, the Phoenicians also
used a pre-Roman script, but this was aside from their own language.

Normally, the writing system of a language involves three areas: a system of
graphic symbols (such as an alphabet) to represent the sounds of the language;
a convention through which these graphic symbols would be related to the
respective sounds of the given language (these symbols may represent syllables,
as in Japanese, or concepts, as in Chinese); and a set of principles to be used in
dividing the units of the sentence into words.

There are two main alphabetical systems, introduced into Africa during the
first and second millennia, which subsequently became dominant on the continent. These are the Arabic and the Roman graphic systems. The Arabic system was the first to be used in Africa, following the spread of Islam in northern
and eastern Africa in the seventh century. Before the arrival of the European
colonialists and missionaries, Arabic orthography was used for writing in a
number of African languages, such as Kiswahili and a number of indigenous
languages in northern and eastern Africa. For various reasons, some languages
changed from the Arabic to the Roman system. For example, Kiswahili, which

was written in the Arabic graphic system from as early as the tenth century (Whiteley 1969),[2] has changed to the Roman system. The use of Arabic script enhanced Kiswahili's long association with Islam and the Arab world; however, the change to the Roman alphabet was made not only because of the latter's association with formal education and access to Western ways of life, but also because many common sounds are not found in the Arabic alphabet. These include [e], [o], [p], [v], [g], [ŋ], and [ɲ]. Moreover, in the case of the Bantu languages, the common pre-nasal consonants [mb], [nd], [nz], [ɲɟ], and [ŋg] cannot be properly represented.

The Roman alphabet was introduced into Africa mainly from the eighteenth century onwards, after the arrival of the European colonialists and missionaries. The three main colonial powers, the British, the French, and the Portuguese, each interpreted African sounds according to their own writing systems and traditions. Examples of these differences in representation for the sounds [u], [ɪ], [ʊ], [ʃ], [ʒ], [ɲ], [ŋ], [tʃ], [dʒ], and [s] are shown in Table 6.2 below.

TABLE 6.2 Representations of African sounds in three colonial orthographies

	[u]	[ɪ]	[ʊ]	[ʃ]	[ʒ]	[ɲ]	[ŋ]	[tʃ]	[dʒ]	[s]
British	u	i/e	u/o	sh	zh/z	ny	ny/ng	ch	j	s
French	ou	e	o	ch/tsh	g/j	ny/n/ñ	ny/ñ	tj/tch	dj	ss
Portuguese	u	i	u	sh/x	zh/xj/jh	ny/ng	ng'/ñ	c/ch	j/dj	s/c

Moreover, the different colonial experiences and traditions were reflected not only in their writing systems, but also in the pronunciation of sounds. Thus, the rolled sound [r] in Sesotho (Southern Sotho), whose orthography was designed by French missionaries, was changed to the guttural [R], as in French. The traditions introduced by colonialists and missionaries have also been responsible for creating different orthographic modes. These have, in turn, often caused gross differentiation between otherwise closely related varieties. Thus, the emergence of Setswana, Sesotho, and Sepedi in the latter part of the nineteenth century was largely the result of three separate missionary activities, each with a different heritage: the London Missionary Society (for Western Sotho, which became Setswana), the Catholic missionaries (for Southern Sotho, which became Sesotho), and the Lutheran missionaries (for Northern Sotho, which became Sepedi). As a result, words with identical pronunciations were now spelt differently in the three varieties, for example, *kwena* (Setswana)/*koena* (Sesotho) for 'crocodile', and *podi* (Setswana)/*poli* (Sesotho) for 'goat'.

The colonial method of allocating **graphemes** (the technical term for graphic symbols) to sounds did not often consider economy. Thus, three graphemes (*ng'*) were used to represent a single sound [ŋ] in a language like Kiswahili; similarly, the graphemes *tch* represent a single sound [tʃ] in Monokotuba (spoken in the Democratic Republic of Congo). This is in spite of the principle that one graphic symbol should correspond to one sound.

The presence of Afrikaans in southern Africa has also had an influence. The symbol *g*, which is usually used to represent [x] in Afrikaans, has been adopted in a number of languages, including Setswana, Sepedi, Sekgalagadi, Sebirwa, and Setswapong, to represent a similar sound.

An important issue in the representation of African words has been the question of how to divide the sentence into its constituent units (words), which in the written mode are separated by spaces. Two systems have emerged, the **disjunctive** system and the **conjunctive** system.[3] An example of each is given below:

> Conjunctivism in isiZulu: *Ngiyabathanda* ('I like them').
> Disjunctivism in Sepedi: *Ke a ba rata* ('I like them').

In South Africa, the Sotho languages write disjunctively, and the Nguni languages (as well as Tshivenda) write conjunctively. Most of the eastern African languages use the conjunctive system, while most of the languages in central Africa use the disjunctive convention.

The disjunctive system is partly based on the principle that words should be determined on the basis of the units of meaning, roughly following the English and French word-division systems, such as *je ne te vois pas* (French), *I do not see you* (English), and *ga ke go bone* (Setswana). The conjunctive system, however, is partly based on the principle that since the Bantu languages are fundamentally agglutinative (where the units of meaning are attached to each other), the meaningful units should form prefixes and suffixes (see Chapters 8 and 9) under one root, thus constituting a single word, such as *hatutakupelekea* (*ha-tu-ta-ku-pelek-e-a*) 'we shall not send (it) to you' (Kiswahili). In this example, the elements *ha-* (negative), *-tu-* (we), *-ta-* (future), *-ku-* (you), *-e-* (applicative suffix), and *-a* (final vowel) are considered prefixes and suffixes and are therefore attached to the verb root *-pelek-* (send).

A second consideration concerns the phonological system of languages. Sepedi vowels are in many cases syllabic, which means that a conjunctive method of writing could cause confusion, as illustrated by the following example:

Gaaaapee	vs.	Ga	a	a	apee
		Not	they	it	boil
		neg	s.c	o.v	verb stem

'They do not boil them (eggs)'

If phrases such as these were written conjunctively, they would be incomprehensible. However, the phonological systems of other Bantu languages are more suited to a conjunctive way of writing. A case in point is isiZulu, a Nguni language. Phonological processes such as vowel elision, vowel coalescence, and consonantalization, which abound in this language, make a disjunctive method of writing totally impractical, as illustrated by the following example:

W a ye s' e zo fika ekhaya
'He would still have arrived at home'.

A disadvantage of the disjunctive method of writing is that it requires many rules to regulate word division. In Sepedi, for example, fourteen rules on word division have had to be formulated. The conjunctive method of writing in isiZulu, however, requires only two rules for word division.

The existence of two methods of writing presents a serious problem in countries where the languages are written according to both traditions, including South Africa, Mozambique, Zambia, Botswana, Namibia, and the Democratic Republic of Congo.

The orthographic imperfections in the ex-colonial languages have also been exported to the African continent. In English, for example, there is not a one-to-one relationship between the sounds of the language and the corresponding graphemes. So, for example, the sound [k] in English is represented by the graphemes *k*, *ck*, *ch*, *q*, and *c*, as in *kin*, *kick*, *choir*, *quick*, and *cow*. Meanwhile, the grapheme *th* can stand for two sounds, namely [θ] as in *thin* and [ð] as in *this*. Graphemes in African languages often stand for more than one distinct sound. This is especially true of vowels, where the Roman vowel system *a*, *e*, *i*, *o*, and *u* does not cover the wide range of vowels in the African languages. Many African languages have between seven and ten vowels; Ingwe in Nigeria has twenty-four. Therefore, finding a convenient system to represent the vowel phonemes has not been easy. Meanwhile, the complex nature of some of the African consonants (such as the clicks, the pre-nasals, the affricates, and the labio-velars), has made it difficult to find unitary symbols to represent them as well.

The role of pronunciation in African social evaluation

So far in this chapter, we have discussed the technical aspects of speech sounds and their orthographic representation. This is generally what phonetics is all about. However, given the orientation of this book, and its concern with the role of language in the educational, economic, political, and social problems of Africa, it is appropriate to consider some social aspects of pronunciation.

We know that linguistic heterogeneity is a basic feature of all languages, and that language users build words and sentences in different ways and also pronounce the sounds of a language in diverse ways. This is the case with first-language speakers (dialectal and stylistic variation), as well as many second- or foreign-language speakers (who may not yet have acquired their target languages adequately[4]). In the latter case, think of the way that Africans generally pronounce English, French, and Portuguese sounds; for instance, the vowels in the English words *bit*, *beat*, and *word*.

We also know that the variants of a sound (or a word or a sentence construction) are socially embedded, and thus acquire different social meanings. In other words, they can serve to signal a person's social status and cultural identity. These social meanings can be either positive (highly esteemed) or negative (stigmatized).

In both cases, but particularly in the latter case, the social meanings of speech sounds can have serious consequences, as they can disqualify otherwise perfectly able people from particular jobs, and can lead to the loss of self-esteem among schoolchildren, leading to their educational failure.

It is therefore important to challenge the validity of these views, and linguists (and trainee linguists) should be able to debate these issues from a linguistic perspective. The first point a linguist is likely to make is that all languages are equal. As we have shown elsewhere in this book, all languages, all varieties of a language, and all variants of a linguistic unit (word or sound) are equally grammatically complex and allow their users full expressive capacity. So if a Sengwato-speaker (a northern variety of Setswana) pronounces *tlala* ('hunger') as *tala*, or a Kimvita-speaker (a northern variety of Kiswahili) pronounces *mchanga* ('sand') as *mtanga*, this should never be grounds for embarrassment or teasing.

Secondly, a linguist would point out that linguistic differences are not the result of differences in people's intelligence or differences in their speech organs (such as their lips or nasal cavities).

Thirdly, a linguist would demonstrate that the social meanings of speech sounds, idioms, and so forth are highly subjective. They arise because a particular way of speaking becomes associated in the community with certain types of people. In industrialized countries in Europe, for example, the way that urban working-class people speak is often stigmatized as being ugly and uncultured, while the way that people from rural areas speak is often regarded as quaint and pretty. The same happens in Africa, but in reverse; rural speech is often considered to be conservative, traditional, and even backward, while the speech of the urban youth is seen as progressive, modern, and 'with-it'. Similarly, the social meanings of the second- or foreign-language varieties of a language (used by second- or foreign-language speakers) depend on the social identities of the speakers; Europeans sometimes look down on Africans who speak English, French, or Portuguese 'with an accent', regarding this as evidence of cognitive and cultural 'backwardness'.

To check the truth of this claim – that the differing social evaluations of linguistic elements are subjective – monitor people's reactions to the second-language speech of various individuals or groups. Isn't it true that an African who speaks English with an 'African accent' is often regarded as uneducated, perhaps even a bit backward, while a German industrialist or a French politician who speaks English with a German or a French accent is considered to be pleasing to listen to? (In South Africa, we see the same thing happen when an Afrikaans-speaking person speaks English with an Afrikaans accent; he or she is often considered to be backward and uncultured, but when a Dutch person speaks English with a Dutch accent, no negative attitudes are triggered.) It is thus all a question of people's attitudes to others, of the relationships between different communities.

Fourthly, it can be pointed out that pronunciation differences in the case of second- or foreign-language speakers are often due to influences from their own languages (often called linguistic interference, or negative transfer – speaking a foreign language on the basis of the grammar of one's first language). This explains why many Africans find it difficult to pronounce the sounds of foreign languages like the native speakers of these languages. Such influences usually arise for the following reasons:

1 Several of the sounds in the foreign languages do not exist in the local languages. The foreign-language speakers thus tend to substitute these sounds with the closest sounds in their mother tongues. This is the case with the English vowels /ɜ/, /ə/, /ʌ/, and /æ/, which do not exist in most of the Bantu languages. These sounds are often pronounced as [ɛ], [a], [ɑ], and [ɒ] (or [ɛ]) respectively. Many French-speaking Africans tend to replace the sounds /y/, /ø/, and /œ/ in French with the sounds [u], [o], and [ɔ] respectively, thus 'confusing' them with the back vowels.

2 Even where the same sounds do exist, there are often differences in the variations thereof. For example, although both Chishona and English have the sound [p], in standard British English the sound is always aspirated in word-initial position (pronounced [pʰ]), whereas this is not the case in Chishona. So, when a Chishona-speaker speaks English she or he will probably not aspirate the [p] in word-initial positions. Other good examples are the liquids [l] and [r], whose pronunciations differ from language to language. For example, in Afrikaans and Sesotho, [r] is trilled, so that when speakers of these languages speak English they ('incorrectly') produce trilled [r]'s. Likewise, the phoneme /l/ in English is often pronounced as a fricative by Setswana- and Sesotho-speakers when preceded by a voiceless consonant, as in *class*, *atlas*, or *play*.

3   The placement and realization of features such as stress, tone, and intonation (called prosodic features) differ from language to language. For example, while stress is placed on the penultimate syllable in most Bantu languages, it appears on the final syllable in French, and is variably organized in English. Also, stress is realized by intensity or force in English, by pitch in Kiswahili and French, and by length in Setswana, Sesotho, isiZulu, and isiXhosa. Tone and intonation patterns also vary from language to language.

These phonetic differences tend to 'stand in the way' when the speaker of an African language sets out to learn a language like English, French, or Portuguese.

Finally, an informed linguist will accept that social perceptions and evaluations, attitudes, and beliefs are realities (in spite of their subjective nature), and recognize that they need to be taken seriously. However, they would point out the subjective nature of these social evaluations, and attempt to persuade both employers and teachers not to base their judgements about people's abilities, knowledge, and skills simply on the way they pronounce speech sounds. Although heavily influenced pronunciations may not correspond to the privileged norms, they should not be regarded as defective. After all, even in Britain, the speakers of English from Scotland, Wales, and Yorkshire pronounce the sounds of English with distinctive regional accents, and yet they are accepted as part of British society.

Endnotes

1   The author wishes to express his gratitude to D. Nurse and A. Ngunga for providing him with useful information on the graphic history and notation in African languages.

2   Some scholars, including D. Nurse, believe that Arabic graphic symbols were used in writing Kiswahili as early as the seventh century (personal communication).

3   The authors of Chapter 9 originally wrote parts of this discussion of conjunctivism and disjunctivism in the Bantu writing systems.

4   The notion of 'adequate acquisition' of a foreign language is problematic, as this implies a fixed, 'correct', or even 'superior' form of the target language, to which all learners should aspire. Many sociolinguists would argue against such an implication, as it is in conflict with the principle of linguistic equity and the legitimacy of linguistic diversity (see Webb, comp., 1996).

Bibliography

LADEFOGED, PETER. 1964. *A Phonetic Study of West African Languages: An Auditory Instrumental Survey* (1st edition). Cambridge: Cambridge University Press.

LADEFOGED, PETER, and IAN MADDISON.

1996. *The Sounds of the World's Languages.* Oxford: Blackwell.

MADDISON, IAN. 1984. *Patterns of Sounds.* Cambridge: Cambridge University Press.

WEBB, VIC. (compiler). 1996. *Appropriate*

English for Democratic South Africa.
Unpublished CentRePoL Workshop Report,
University of Pretoria.

WHITELEY, W.H. 1969. *Swahili: The Rise of a
National Language.* London: Methuen & Co.

7 System in the sounds of Africa

Herman Batibo

Expected outcomes

At the end of this chapter you should be able to:
1 Explain what is meant by the concept of a sound system and the organization of speech sounds.
2 Describe the organization of the speech sounds of your language of study, as well as their features and the ways in which these sounds vary.
3 Explain what is meant by phonological processes and be able to construct, describe, and formulate phonological rules.
4 Compare and contrast the vowel systems of an ex-colonial language of Africa and an indigenous one.
5 Compare and contrast the consonant systems of an ex-colonial language of Africa and an indigenous one.

Introduction

We saw in Chapter 6 what mechanisms the languages of the world use in the production of speech sounds, and that each language uses these mechanisms to produce the speech sounds it needs to build up its words. In most African languages, the number of vowels ranges from five to ten, with twenty to forty consonants. However, some languages (such as Arabic) have as few as three vowels, and others (such as Ngwe) have sixteen vowels. Likewise, some languages have consonant inventories of only about ten units, such as Efik and Sebei (Maddison 1984), while others have nearly 100 units. This is the case with the Khoi languages !Xóõ and Ju/'hoan, for example.

The speech sounds discussed in Chapter 6 are called **phones**, and they exist primarily as physical entities, making it possible for us to recognize the words a speaker uses. However, if we look closely at some speech sounds, we notice that, although they are physically different (and are therefore different phones), they don't distinguish different words. For instance, if we look at the example quoted from Kimvita, a northern variety of Kiswahili, at the end of Chapter 6, we see that *mchanga* ('sand') is pronounced *mtanga*. This shows that, although the *ch* and the *t* are quite different physically, they don't identify different words in this case. From the perspective of word identification, they are the same entity. A similar example from British English: the vowel of the word *bath* is sometimes pronounced as [a] and sometimes as [æ], without a new word being signalled. Thus, although these two vowels are physically different, they are not functionally different in this case. We can also study the sounds of a language from the perspective of their function in signalling word identity. We are then looking at speech sounds from a different perspective. The entities described from this perspective are called **phonemes**.

The difference between phones and phonemes (or between phonetics, which studies phones, and phonology, which studies phonemes) can also be explained from the perspective of the concept of system, which was discussed at the beginning of Chapter 3. There the term *system* was used to refer to 'a collection of entities organized into a whole'. When a speech sound is studied from the point of view of its place and role in a linguistic system, it is studied as a phoneme.

Vowels and consonants in each language are thus organized into systems. The study of the way they are organized is known as **phonology** or **phonemics**.

The phoneme

The phoneme is the smallest distinctive unit of sound in a given language, distinguishing words from each other at the level of speech sounds. Thus the vowels *a, e, i, o,* and *u* are phonemes in Kiswahili because they are capable of signalling the existence of different words,[1] as in *panda* ('climb'), *penda* ('love'), *pinda* ('bend'), *ponda* ('throw at'), and *punda* ('ass'). Likewise, the consonants *l* and *g* are phonemes in Lulogoli, as they distinguish between the words *guga* ('grandfather') and *gula* ('buy'). Two other terms often used in defining phonemes are opposition and contrast; when two phonemes are in opposition to each other, they are signalling different words, and when they are in contrast, they are also signalling different words. Phonemes are transcribed between slanting lines, for example /a/ and /p/.

Additional functions of phonemes

Although the primary function of phonemes is to form words as well as distinguish between them, they can play other roles too. One of these is to provide expressive or aesthetic values to word meanings. This is often seen in African languages, where ideophones, onomatopoeia, and interjections are common. Many African languages associate certain sounds with specific meanings, or combine sounds to provide certain expressive values. This phenomenon is put to use in literary works such as poetry, drama, or narratives. Moreover, many proverbs, sayings, and riddles contain such sounds or sound sequences. For example, in Kisukuma, the different vowel qualities in [i], [u], and [a] can have different expressive values, as in *piligina* (struggle to be free as a small animal), *puluguna* (struggle to be free as a feathered animal, e.g. bird), and *palagana* (struggle to be free as a large animal). Likewise, the consonants [t] and [p] would have acute and grave impressions, as in *talaluka* (explode like explosives) and *palaluka* (explode like thunder).

Phonemes can also be used as indicators of word or syllable boundaries. For example, the phoneme /h/ in English usually signals the beginning of a syllable or word, and the phoneme /ŋ/ the end of a syllable or word.

Distinctive features

As mentioned above, phonemes can be said to be in an oppositional or contrastive relationship. They 'oppose' each other or stand in contrast to each other on the basis of a single phonetic difference. This can consist of any feature, such as point of articulation, manner of articulation, or voicing in the case of consonants, and vertical and horizontal tongue position and lip-form in the case of vowels. The different characteristics responsible for the distinction of phonemes are known as **distinctive features**. Thus /p/ and /b/ differ because one is voiceless and the other is voiced. Likewise, /n/ and /d/ are different because one is nasal and the other is plosive/oral.

In the structuralist approach (generally followed in this textbook), distinctive features are selected from a list of several articulatory features (see Chapter 6). In the case of consonants, these features result from one of the three articulatory parameters, namely the point of articulation, the manner of articulation, and voicing.

Point of articulation

bilabial	palato-alveolar	uvular
labio-dental	alveo-palatal	pharyngeal
dental	palatal	glottal
alveolar	velar	

Manner of articulation

plosive	trill
fricative	semivowel
affricate	approximant
lateral	nasal

Voicing

voiceless	voiced

Thus, from one perspective, phonemes could be regarded as units that are made up of distinctive features, or, in the words of the Russian linguist Nikolai Trubetskoy (1939), one of the founders of phonology, 'bundles of distinctive features.' In this way, the phonemes /p/, /v/, /l/, /m/, /i/, and /a/ in Chishona can be described as being characterized by the following features:

/p/	/v/	/l/	/m/	/i/	/a/
$\begin{bmatrix} \text{bilabial} \\ \text{plosive} \\ \text{voiceless} \end{bmatrix}$	$\begin{bmatrix} \text{labio-dental} \\ \text{fricative} \\ \text{voiced} \end{bmatrix}$	$\begin{bmatrix} \text{lateral} \end{bmatrix}$	$\begin{bmatrix} \text{bilabial} \\ \text{nasal} \end{bmatrix}$	$\begin{bmatrix} \text{front} \\ \text{close} \end{bmatrix}$	$\begin{bmatrix} \text{open} \end{bmatrix}$

Redundant features

The features characterizing the speech sounds that we use in our languages are not all distinctive, which means that not all of them have a phonological function. Some of them are **redundant**; in other words, they do not play any distinctive role.

Redundant features have a direct implication for the phonological characterization of phonemes. Because of them, a phonological description need not refer to all the features of a phoneme. For instance, some features are implied by the presence of others, and do not have to be mentioned in the phonological description. For example, we know that laterals, trills, and nasals are by nature voiced. It is thus sufficient to describe /m/ in a language like Chishona merely as bilabial and nasal. Redundancy may also be due to the non-existence of other sounds sharing the same feature in a given language. This is the case of the lateral phoneme /l/ in Chishona, where there are no other laterals. It thus becomes unnecessary to specify the point of articulation (alveolar, in this case).

Redundant features therefore do not play any distinctive role; rather, they specify the proper phonetic qualities of a phoneme and also indicate the characteristics of the varieties of phonemes. For language learners, mastery of the distinctive features of each phoneme makes it possible for them to be understood when they speak; however, mastery of the redundant features in a given language means that a learner has acquired mother-tongue proficiency in that language.

Allophonic variation

It should be clear from this discussion that a phoneme is an abstract entity, a theoretical construction that in itself cannot be observed (heard), but that underlies the speech sounds we actually hear. When a phoneme is given concrete form, we say it has been phonically realized.

Phonemes are frequently realized in different phonetic forms (called variants). For example, the English phoneme /p/ can be realized as a [ph], a [pʰ], or a [p]. These three realizations together form the phoneme /p/. We can thus say that the /p/ is a 'family' of sounds. The variants of a phoneme often do not occur in the same position in a word. For instance, the English [ph] occurs word-initially, the [pʰ] syllable-initially, and the [p] at the end of a word (word-finally). When the different forms of a phoneme systematically occur in different positions in a word, we say that they occur in complementary distribution, that is, in mutually exclusive phonetic environments.

The variants of phonemes are known as **allophones**, and there are two types. The first is the one in which the allophones occur in different phonetic environment; that is, they are in complementary distribution. One example is the phoneme /l/ in Setswana, which has two allophones, [l] and [d] (note that allophones are transcribed between square brackets, as they are phonetic realizations). The allophone [d] occurs before the close tense vowels /i/ (*motsadi* 'parent') and /u/ (*-bodu* 'rotten'); while [l] occurs before all the other vowels, for example *-tsala* ('give birth') and *selelo* ('crying'). In this case, the allophones [l/d] are phonetically similar (both of them are voiced alveolar consonants differing only in the manner of articulation) and are therefore in complementary distribution.

Another example is the phoneme /l/ in Luganda, which has two allophones, [l] and [r]. The allophone [r] occurs after the high front vowel /i/ (*buulira* 'tell' and o*muliro* 'fire'); while [l] occurs elsewhere, for example, *olulimi* ('tongue'). The two allophones (which are phonetically similar as they are both liquids) are in complementary distribution, as they occur in different or mutually exclusive phonetic (or phonic) environments.

The second type of allophone occurs in free variation; this means they can appear interchangeably in the same phonetic environments. This is the case with many African languages that have the five-vowel system /a, e, i, o, u/. The middle vowels /e/ and /o/ can occur either as [e] and [o], or as [ɛ] and [ɔ]. The choice between the two variants is seldom conditioned by phonetic environment. Instead, this choice is usually determined by non-linguistic factors such as individual habits, geographical location, stylistic context, or social environment. This is the case in Kiswahili, where the words *penda* ('love') and *ponda* ('throw') can be pronounced with the variants [e/ɛ] and [o/ɔ] respectively.

Distribution of phonemes

As the main function of phonemes is to build word forms, each phoneme of a language is expected to occur in all positions in words or syllables, namely initially, medially, and finally. However, in reality, some phonemes may occur only in certain positions in words or syllables. For example, as we have seen, in English, /ŋ/ cannot occur in word-initial position, and /h/ cannot occur in word-final position. This also happens in several African languages. It can also happen that the distinction between two phonemes can be neutralized in certain word positions. This phenomenon is called neutralization. For example, in American English, /d/ and /t/ are distinct phonemes in initial and final positions as in *ten*, *den*, *bet*, and *bed*. But they are neutralized between vowels, as *betting* and *bedding* are both pronounced as [bɛɾɪŋ]. When this happens, a 'super-phoneme' is often recognized, representing both the phonemes in that position. This is then referred to as an **archi-phoneme**, and represented by the capital letter /R/ in the American case.

There are also often restrictions in the way phonemes follow each other. In most Bantu languages, for example, the only permissible consonant sequences are the ones between nasals and their homorganic (formed in the same place) oral counterparts, such as [mp], [mb], [nt], [nd], [ŋk], and [ŋg]; or consonants followed by semivowels, such as [bw], [bj], [tw], [tj], [kw], and [gw]. However, even sequences such as these may be restricted. For example, Sesotho allows the sequences [tw], [kw], and [jw], but does not allow the sequences [bw], [bj], or [kj]. And while some languages allow vowel sequences such as [ai], [ea], or [ua], others do not. Each language has its own pattern of phoneme combination.

In the study of phonology, the frequency of occurrence of phonemes also has to be determined. Some phonemes occur more frequently than others do. For example, in African languages, the vowel [a] is more frequently used than [e] or [o]. Likewise, the alveolar (or dental) consonants, such as [n], [l], [s], and [t], are usually more frequently used than the palatal and velar consonants, such as [c], [j], [k], [g], and [x].

The study of the frequency of occurrence is often linked to the study of frequency of the opposition between phonemes; that is, the frequency of cases where the substitution of one phoneme by the other would result in a different word. This is known as functional load. Phonemes that characterize many words have a high functional load, whereas phonemes that contrast only a few words have a low functional load. Determining the functional load of phonemes is important when designing an orthographic system for a language. Two distinct writing symbols (or **graphemes**) would be needed for phonemes with high functional loads, but distinct graphemes may not be as necessary if the functional load is low. Thus, in present-day Setswana, the grapheme *tsh* is used by many writers to represent /tʃ/, /tʃʰ/, and /tsʰ/ without causing serious communication problems, because the functional load between them is low.

Generative phonology

As this is an introductory textbook, we shall touch only briefly on the basic concepts of generative phonology. (See Chapter 3 for an explanation of the concept 'generative'.) This is a more recent approach to the study of phonology than the structuralist approach. It is based on the concept that human language is made up of abstract sound segments that are organized in each language to form meaningful units, including words. Each of these segments (in a way, identical to phonemes in the structuralist approach) is made up of distinctive features. These are represented in terms of their presence or absence, namely [+F] and [−F]. Thus /m/ would be [+nasal], while /b/ would be [−nasal]. Similarly, /p/ would be [−voiced], while /b/ would be [+voiced]. We can use these distinctive features to characterize all the sounds in a language. Thus we can show the phonological distinction between the seven Sesotho vowels (if we consider Sesotho as having seven vowel phonemes) by using the distinctive features shown in Table 7.1 below.

TABLE 7.1 The Sesotho vowel system and its respective distinctive features

				Segments			
Distinctive features	i	ɪ	ɛ	a	ɔ	ʊ	u
High (high tongue position)	+	+	−	−	−	+	+
Low (low tongue position)	−	−	−	+	−	−	−
Back (back tongue position)	−	−	−	−	+	+	+
Tense (tenseness of the muscles of the tongue)	+	−	−	−	−	−	+

In fact, some of the features in Table 7.1 can be said to be redundant. For example, it is enough to describe /a/ simply as [+low], as the other features are not essential in distinguishing it from the other segments. Likewise, /ɛ/ and /ɔ/ need not be specified as [−tense], as they do not have any [+tense] counterparts.

The distinctive features of ten of the thirty-six isiZulu consonants are given in Table 7.2 below.

TABLE 7.2 Some of the isiZulu consonants and their respective distinctive features

	Segments									
Distinctive features	pʰ	t	dʒ	f	ɓ	z	lʒ	l	m	//
Labial (involving lips)	+	−	−	+	+	−	−	−	+	−
Coronal (involving alveolar ridge)	−	+	+	−	−	+	+	+	−	+
Continuant (continued airstream)	−	−	−	+	−	+	+	+	−	−
Sonorant (highly sonorous)	−	−	−	−	−	−	−	+	+	−
Lateral (production at the side of tongue)	−	−	−	−	−	−	+	+	−	+
Nasal (articulated with nasal cavity involvement)	−	−	−	−	−	−	−	−	+	−
Delayed release (affricate articulation)	−	−	+	−	−	−	−	−	−	−
Ingressive (inward airstream)	−	−	−	−	+	−	−	−	−	−
Velaric (air compression through velaric closure)	−	−	−	−	−	−	−	−	−	+
Tense (aspirated)	+	−	−	−	−	−	−	−	−	−
Voiced (with vibration of vocal cords)	−	−	+	−	+	+	+	+	+	−

Once again, many of the consonants in Table 7.2 could be specified by fewer features, as some are either implied or unnecessary, as they do not distinguish the given sound from other consonants in isiZulu. For example, /ɓ/ could simply be described as [+ingressive], as it is the only ingressive segment in isiZulu. The other features are useful only in characterizing it phonetically.

Apart from the distinctive features used to distinguish the vowels and consonant segments in Tables 7.1 and 7.2, there are other features that could be used to distinguish between segments in languages. These include:

- Consonantal: distinguishes consonants from vowels (the latter are usually nuclear units of syllables).
- Syllabic: distinguishes segments that are centres of syllables (vowels and syllabic consonants) from segments in peripheral positions.
- Round: distinguishes sounds (particularly rounded vowels and labialized consonants) in which lips are rounded from those sounds in which lips are spread.
- Palatal: distinguishes sounds with palatal characteristics from those without.
- ATR: distinguishes sounds, particularly vowels, articulated with advanced tongue root from those without.
- Strident: distinguishes noisy sounds, particularly among fricatives and affricates such as [f], [s], [z], and [ts] from non-noisy ones such as [ɸ], [β], [θ], and [ð]. The latter are more rare in human languages because they are audibly softer.
- Place: indicates the relationships involving places or points of articulation between consonants.
- Fortis: indicates the degree of strength of sounds (for example, [tʰ] would be described as [+fortis], while [r] would be described as [−fortis].
- Mid: sometimes used to distinguish middle vowels such as [e] and [o] from non-mid vowels such as [a], [i], and [u].

Some of the features used to distinguish vowels such as [high], [low], and [back] can also be used to distinguish consonants. The feature [high] distinguishes palatal and velar consonants (articulated with the tongue at its highest point) from other consonants. The feature [low] distinguishes pharyngeal and glottal consonants from the rest, while the feature [back] distinguishes velar and uvular consonants from the rest.

Phonological processes in African languages

In every language, there are constraints on the way phonemes may co-occur in sequences. Some sequences may be allowed in one language but not in another.

Thus, although the Nguni languages generally allow the sequences [bw],[pw], or [pj], the Sotho languages do not permit them. There are processes in each language that change or replace one phoneme or variant/allophone of a phoneme with another in specific environments in order to comply with permitted phoneme sequences. These are known as **phonological processes**. These processes, also known as morphophonological or morphonological processes (because they concern phonemes frequently found at the boundaries of meaningful units, or morphemes), are described below.

Assimilation

The assimilation process involves changing one phoneme into another phoneme or allophone so that it is more like a neighbouring phoneme. This takes place in order to facilitate pronunciation, as it is difficult to pronounce two very different sounds in succession. It usually involves the change of a feature value. One common assimilation process is the one found in most Bantu languages, in which the nasal sound that normally represents noun classes 9 and 10 (i.e. *n-*), is assimilated to the point of articulation of the first consonant of the stem, as demonstrated in the Kisukuma example below:

1	n - buli	>	mbuli	'goat'
	n - dama	>	ndama	'calf'
	n - jeemu	>	ɲɟeemu	'marijuana'
	n - guzu	>	ŋguzu	'strength', 'energy'

There are different types of assimilation processes in the African languages. The most common are the following.

Vowel harmony

One of the most common assimilation processes is **vowel harmony**. This occurs if two or more vowels in successive syllables of a word or part of a word share certain common features. In some of the languages of the Kwa, Voltaic, and even some Nilotic groups, vowels tend to exist in the same word or part of a word, depending on whether they belong to [+ATR] (i.e. i, e, a, o, u) or to [−ATR] (i.e. ɪ, ɛ, ə, ɔ, and ʊ). Thus, in Igbo, for example, we have a distinction between [ózòrò] ('he did') and [ɔ́zɔ̀rɔ̀] ('he pulled').

In most Bantu languages, vowel harmony occurs where the derivational suffixes, such as the applicative and the neutral forms, display two forms (-il-/-el- and -ik-/-ek-). The use of one or the other form depends on whether the vowels of the root are [a, i, u] or [e, o], as demonstrated in the following Kiswahili examples:

2 (a) *Applicative*   (b) *Neutral*

pand - i - a	('climb for')	pand - ik - a	('be climbable')
pend - e - a	('love for')	pend - ek - a	('be lovable')
pind - i - a	('bend for')	pind - ik - a	('be easily bent')
pond - e - a	('smash for')	pond - ek - a	('be smashable')
ruk - i - a	('jump for')	ruk - ik - a	('be easily bypassed')

Palatalization

Palatalization involves moving the point of articulation of a sound towards the palatal area. It happens when a velar, dental, alveolar, or any other sound either becomes a palatal sound or acquires palatal characteristics through the influence of a neighbouring palatal sound. The most common source of environmental influence is the vowel [i], which is articulated with the tongue in the proximity of the palatal area.

Thus, in some languages, the sequence *ki/ti* and *gi/di* would trigger a palatalization process to [ci], [tʃi], or [kʲi] respectively. For example, Jita-speakers tend to pronounce the Kiswahili word *kiazi* ('potato') as [tʃiazi].

Nasalization

Nasalization occurs when an oral sound is assimilated either to become a nasal sound or to acquire nasal characteristics through the influence of a nasal sound in the neighbourhood. Vowels that appear between nasal consonants often tend to be nasalized, as in the Nyamwezi example *ngombe* (cow), which is realized as [ŋɔ̃mbɛ]. The tilde [˜] is used to indicate a nasalized sound.

Strengthening

Strengthening or hardening occurs when a sound (usually a consonant) changes in order to become stronger. In fact, we can categorize the consonants in terms of their degree of strength. The following types of consonants are stronger than others:

- voiceless consonants are stronger than voiced ones;
- aspirated consonants are stronger than non-aspirated ones;
- stops (plosives, affricates, nasals) are the strongest consonants;
- fricatives are the next strongest consonants; and
- liquids (trills and laterals) are among the weakest consonants.

Some of the African languages, particularly those of southern Africa, are sensitive to the strengthening process, with the nasals and high vowels acting as the strengthening elements. This is illustrated in the Setswana example below:

3	fa	'give'	>	mpho	'gift'	(f > ph)
	ruta	'teach'	>	ithuta	'learn'	(r > th)
	rata	'love'	>	nthate	'love me'	(r > th)
	tsala	'give birth'	>	motsadi	'parent'	(l > d)
	bola	'rot'	>	bodu	'rotter'	(l > d)

Assimilation may be progressive, regressive, or reciprocal. It is **progressive** if one phoneme influences the following phoneme, as seen in the examples in 2 above. It is **regressive** if a phoneme influences a preceding phoneme, as in the examples in 1. It is **reciprocal** if two phonemes influence each other, as in the Kisukuma form *m-lomo* ('mouth'), pronounced [nnomo]. In this case, [m] changes to [n] to assimilate to the point of articulation of [l] (i.e. alveolar), but [l] changes to [n] to assimilate to the manner of articulation of [m] (i.e. nasal).

Dissimilation

Dissimilation is the process in which two contiguous (or neighbouring) sounds become less like each other, normally because of an increase in one or more feature differences. One common dissimilation process in certain Bantu languages is known as Dahl's Law; here, whenever two voiceless plosives (sometimes also affricates and fricatives) occur in successive syllables, one of them must become voiced. This is shown in the following Kirundi example for the infinitive-marker *uku-*:

4	uku - raaba	'to look at'
	uku - bona	'to see'
	uku - mala	'to finish'

but

	ugu - kora	'to do', 'perform'
	ugu - tema	'to cut'
	ugu - fa	'to die'

Another case of dissimilation includes glide formation or a-syllabification, in which the first vowel in a sequence of two vowels changes to a semivowel, as seen in the change from [u] to [w] in Kinyarwanda, for example from *uku - ambara* to *ukwambara* ('to put on').

In a number of African languages, particularly those of Bantu origin, there exists a dissimilation rule in which, when there is a sequence of two stops (a

nasal and a plosive), the plosive turns into a fricative, as in the case of the
Kisukuma example *m + pela* > *mhela* ('rhinoceros').

Metathesis

Metathesis is the process in which two adjacent sounds exchange positions. This
is often done in order to facilitate ease of articulation. The historical examples of
this process include the exchange of the consonants [k] and [s] in the English
word *dusk*, which was initially [doks] (from *dox*), apparently to allow a succession of the two alveolar consonants [d] and [s]. Metathesis, which often starts as
a slip of the tongue, is common in African languages, as shown in 5 below:

5   le (l)obu   >   lebodu   'chameleon' (Setswana)
    ʃibiliti   >   ʃilibiti   'box of matches' (Kisukuma)
    bahaʃa   >   habaʃa   'envelope' (Nyamwezi)

The process of metathesis shows us that any speech sounds or organization of
speech sounds will tend to change so as to ease pronunciation in terms of voicing, point of articulation, or manner of articulation. Another reason is to
bring about maximum clarity in communication.

Coalescence

Coalescence involves the merging of two sounds, usually vowels, to form one
unit with intermediate quality. The common coalescence cases involve the
merging of [a] with [i] or [u] to form [e] or [o] respectively, as shown below:

6   ma + ino   > meno   'teeth' cl. 6 (Sesotho)
    ma + ingi   > me:ngi   'many' cl. 6 (Kiswahili)
    wa + umuntu   > womuntu   'of the person' cl. 1 (isiZulu)
    wa + imithi   > wemithi   'of the trees' cl. 4 (isiXhosa)
    wa + umukadzi > womukadzi   'of the woman' cl. 1 Chishona)
    sa + ihuku   > sehuku   'like a fowl' cl. 9 (Chishona)

In languages where long vowels exist, coalescence may result in long vowels.

Phoneme deletion

Phoneme deletion occurs in a particular phonetic environment where the
presence of the phoneme is not compatible with the other sounds in the

neighbourhood. The most common deletion process in African languages is known as vowel elision, in which a vowel (usually the low vowel [a]) is deleted before another vowel. This is demonstrated in the following examples:

7 nabona omuti   >   nabon'omuti   'I see a tree' (Nyambo)
   ɓonke aɓantu   >   ɓonk'aɓantu   'everybody' (isiZulu)
   na ʊmunhʊ   >   n'ʊmunhʊ   'with the person' (Nilyamba)

Another common vowel deletion arises where non-tense vowels, particularly [ɪ] and [ʊ], are found in certain phonetic environments, as in Setswana [mʊlɪlɔ] > [mʊlɪlɔ] ('fire') and [mʊɓɪlɪ] > [mmɪlɪ] ('body'), spelt *mollo* and *mmele* respectively.

The consonants which are easily deleted are the ones described as weak on the consonant strength scale, namely the trills and laterals. They are frequently deleted in certain phonetic contexts in many African languages, as are the lax vowels [ɪ] and [ʊ]. Moreover, they are also the sounds most easily lost in a language.

Phoneme addition

Another common phonological process involves the addition of a phoneme, usually a vowel. An example of this process is found in a number of Bantu languages where a vowel, usually the high vowel *i*, is added to the nasal prefix of classes 9 and 10 in monosyllabic stems. This process is meant to meet the dissyllabic requirement of word formation. This is found in the following examples:

8 n-zi > inzi   'housefly' (Kiswahili)
   n-gwe > ingwe   'leopard' (Hangaza)

Likewise, in some languages the vowel [i] or [e] is added to a monosyllabic verb stem in order to make the form disyllabic, as shown in the following examples:

9 -dla 'eat' (stem), idla 'eat!' (isiZulu), but
   ɓona 'see' (stem), ɓona 'see!' (isiZulu)
   -ja 'eat' (stem), eja or jaa 'eat!' (Sesotho), but
   bona 'see' (stem), bona 'see' (Sesotho)

The other cases of vowel addition are found in the processes of nativization of loan words into languages where clusters are not allowed. This is the case in most Bantu languages (which do not normally allow consonant clusters), as shown below:

10 terekere   <   [træktə]   'tractor' (Setswana)
    sukulu   <   [skul]   'school' (Chichewa)
    giligita   <   [træktə]   'tractor' (Kisukuma)
    peteroli   <   [petrl]   'petrol' (Luganda)
    isikolo   <   [skul]   'school' (isiZulu)
    basikeli   <   [baisɪkl]   'bicycle' (Nyamwezi)

Phonological rules

In generative phonology, the processes discussed in the section above are often **formalized**, that is, formulated in a technical way, using a particular formalism. One of the reasons for this is that the essential nature of a process becomes clearer if the process is formulated in explicit terms.

The basic logic behind the formulation of these rules is that phonological processes are predictable. The rules follow this form: if A, then B, given C. For instance, the assimilation process discussed above is a prediction that an /n/ will be pronounced as an [m] before a following /b/, that it will be pronounced as an [n] before a following /d/, that it will be pronounced as an [ŋ] before a following /g/, and so on.

Particular features of the phonological rules are that they are formulated in terms of distinctive features (not sound segments), and that they make use of specific rule-writing conventions. For instance, 'becomes' (or 'is pronounced as') is represented by an arrow; the phonetic context in which the process occurs is specified by a front slash (/), and the specific environment in which the process occurs is indicated by a horizontal bar (underscoring). Schematically, a phonological rule has the following form:

$$A \rightarrow B/ \_\_\_ C$$

We will not provide more detailed attention to the concept of formalized phonological rules. This is because, in order to do justice to this important facet of phonology, a far more detailed knowledge of generative phonology (in particular, of the distinctive features, the underlying principles, the ways in which generalizations are made, and the rule-writing conventions) is necessary. Students who would like to learn more about these aspects of the 'systems' in the sounds of Africa are advised to study one of the introductory textbooks on generative phonology.

However, we would like to give one example of a generative phonological rule, based on the discussion of the assimilation rule above. The rule is first given in an informal formulation, and then in more formal notation.

Assimilation rule (based on 1 above):

Informal

$$
n \rightarrow \begin{bmatrix} m \\ n \\ \textrm{ɲ} \\ \textrm{ŋ} \end{bmatrix} \Big/ - \begin{bmatrix} b \\ d \\ \textrm{ɟ} \\ g \end{bmatrix}
$$

Formal

$$
\begin{bmatrix} -\text{syllabic} \\ +\text{nasal} \end{bmatrix} \rightarrow [\alpha \text{ place}]/ \_\_ [\alpha \text{ place}]
$$

Note that α is a variable sign that links features in one part of the rule to features with the same value in another.

Non-segmental sound features in the African languages

Most of the discussion above has involved the description of segmental units (the consonants and vowels) that we use in our various languages. In all languages, the consonants and vowels are normally organized into larger units known as syllables. In the following section, we shall describe the structure of the syllable, and then look at other units that characterize not only syllables, but also words and even sentences. These include tone, stress, juncture, and intonation. The study of these units is known as **prosody**.

The syllable

The **syllable** can be defined as the unit in the word that is capable of receiving stress or tone. Phonetically, a syllable can be generally described as a complete segment of an utterance in the chain of speech, or as stretches of puffs of air from the lungs. A syllable is normally characterized by a sonorous central part, the core, which is its nucleus. This may be a vowel or a sonorous consonant such as a nasal or liquid. The peripheral part of the syllable is known as the onset. It is usually made up of a consonant or a cluster of consonants.

There are two types of syllables, the open syllable (which ends in a vowel) and the closed syllable (which ends in a consonant). The syllable is usually symbolized by a sigma (σ).

(a)   Open syllable   (b)   Closed syllable

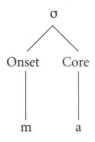

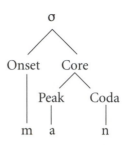

Another common distinction involves the division between long and short syllables. Long syllables are normally those made up of two (or more) moras; short syllables are those made up of one mora. (A mora is a unit of length associated with syllabic quantity.)

(a)   Short syllable   (b)   Long syllable

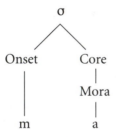

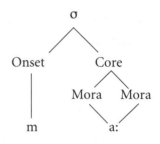

In a number of Bantu languages, syllabic length (indicated by the colon (:) after the vowel of the respective long syllable, or by the doubling of the vowel) may be distinctive, as in the Kiswahili examples of [wake] ('wives') and [wa:ke] ('theirs') (cl. 2). In some languages, such as Arabic, long syllables may be composed of short vowels followed by a succession of consonants.

Although syllables are normally made up of a consonant (or consonants) and a vowel, or just a single vowel, some sonorous sounds, such as nasals, trills, and laterals may also constitute syllables. In these cases, a small vertical line is used to indicate their syllabicity (for example, m̩, n̩, ɲ̩, ŋ̩, r̩, l̩). These are known as syllabic consonants.

Stress

Stress is any prominence given to a particular syllable in a word or phrase. This may be expressed in terms of pitch, length, intensity, or force. Some languages, such as Kiswahili, use pitch, while others like Setswana, Sesotho, and Peul use length. English, on the other hand, uses intensity or force. Stressed syllables are marked by the use of an apostrophe ('), as in [mʊsi' maːnɛ] (Sesotho).

Stressed syllables are usually called strong syllables, and the unstressed ones weak syllables. A foot is usually made up of one strong and one weak syllable. As a rule, there is only one stressed syllable in each word in a stress language. However, where long words or phrases are involved, there may be a hierarchy of stressed syllables. Some languages, such as English, have such hierarchies. However, most stressed Bantu languages have no such hierarchies, as can be seen in the following examples from English and isiZulu:

(a)   English   (b)   isiZulu

(hierarchical)   (non-hierarchical)

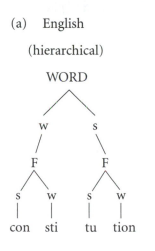

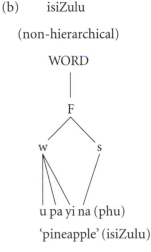

'pineapple' (isiZulu)

s = strong syllable (or foot)
w = weak syllable (or foot)
F = foot

The stress patterns displayed in the example above can be shown differently by using grids, as shown below:

(a)   (b)

		X		Word level						Foot/word level
X		X		Foot level				X		Foot/word level
X	X	X	X	Syllabic level	X	X	X	X	Syllabic level	
Con	sti	tu	tion		u	pa	yi	na (phu)		

While the word *constitution* in English can be said to have two stresses (the primary stress on *tu* and the secondary stress on *con*), the isiZulu word *uphayinaphu* has only one stress on *na*, with the final syllable *phu* being **extrametrical**, that is, outside the metrical structure of the foot. This type of description has given rise to **metrical phonology**, an approach that focuses on studying stress structure and syllabic weight in languages.

When stress always appears in only one position in the word, whether in the initial, final, or penultimate (last but one) syllable, the language is said to have **fixed stress**. But if the stress position is unpredictable, the language is known to have **non-fixed stress**. Most Bantu languages that have developed stress systems have penultimate stress that is usually expressed by length or pitch.

Tone

A **tone language** is one in which pitch can be used to distinguish between words or grammatical functions. Traditionally, there are two tone types: level tones and contour tones.

Level tones are those whose pitch quality remains the same throughout their realization. This can be illustrated in the Ngbaka language, which has three levels of distinctive tones:

High	só	'animal'
Mid	sō	'hunt'
Low	sò	'tail'

High tones (produced by a relatively high frequency of vibration of the vocal cords) are usually marked by an acute accent on the vowel of the respective syllable (´). A **mid tone** (produced by a relatively normal frequency of vibration of the vocal cords) is marked by a level accent (¯) or the absence of a mark, and a **low tone** (produced by a relatively low frequency of vibration of the vocal cords) by a grave accent (`). If a language has only a two-level distinction, this is indicated in terms of high/low. The low tone, in this case, will not be marked, as in the following Lingala example:

kokóma	'to arrive'
kokoma	'to write'
mbóto	'seed', 'grain'
mboto	'a kind of tree'

Contour tones, on the other hand, are those tones whose pitch quality changes during the articulation. In this case, the vibrations of the vocal cords may increase in frequency, giving a rising tone, or may decrease in frequency, giving a falling tone. The most common contour tones among African languages are the falling tones, marked (ˆ) on the respective vowel, and the rising tones, marked (ˇ), as in the following Lingala example:

    mbôngo 'money'
    nyŏnso   'all', 'everything'

Although distinctive tones are usually lexical, in that they can be used to distin-guish between two otherwise identical items of vocabulary, they can also have grammatical functions. For example, in Kisukuma, a phrase or word can have several grammatical significations depending on tone, as in the following:

    waasolá 'he has just picked up'
    waasolà 'he picked up long ago'
    waásola 'you picked up long ago'
    waasóla 'you have just picked up'

With the exception of the Afro-Asiatic family, all the language families and sub-families of Africa have tonal systems. Some of the languages, however, have lost their tonal distinctiveness. This is true of Kiswahili, Peul, Nyakyusa, Zaramo, Makua, Ndali, Tumbuka, Toro, Nyoro, and a number of other lan-guages. Moreover, some languages are only partly tonal, as they have lost most of their tone distinctions. In many of these languages, it is possible to design an orthography without marking the tones, as the functional load of the tones is low, so very few cases of ambiguity would occur.

In the earlier linguistic descriptions, based mostly on the structuralist approach and early generative approaches, tone was regarded as part of the syl-lable or even the vowel with which it was associated. In more recent approaches (especially those considering Bantu languages), tone has been considered as an autonomous unit capable of deleting, displacing, or spreading out from the syllable with which it is associated at the underlying level. The currently most dominant approach to tone analysis is the **autosegmental approach**, which is based on the concept that tone should be regarded as a segment on its own, with its own organizational rules, and that it is associated, in a multi-linear form, with other segments in the chain of speech. This approach, which was conceived within the generative phonological rule-based orientation, distin-guishes between toned syllables (those which are associated with tones, usually H [high] tones) and non-toned syllables (those without any marked tones). Special tone rules are then used to change the position of the tones from underlying representation (UR) to surface representation (SR), as demonstrat-ed in the following examples:

UR		SR	
(a) kubóna sagala	>	kubona sagála	'to see clumsily' (Kisukuma)
(b) kubóna badugú	>	kuboná baduguú	'to see relatives' (Nyamwezi)
(c) kubóna omutí	>	kubon'ómúti	'to see the tree' (Haya)
(d) símolola	>	símólóla	'to start' (Setswana)

The tone displacement and spread displayed above could also be captured by the autosegmental approach, as shown below:

Tone displacement rule in Kisukuma: H tone moves to the second next syllable of the same or next word.

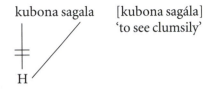

Tone displacement rule in Nyamwezi: H tone moves to the next syllable. However, if it happens to be in the final position, the syllable is lengthened and associates with the second mora.

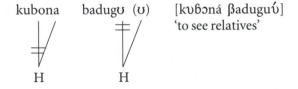

Tone displacement rule in Haya: H tone moves to the next syllable. However, any H tone in the final position is moved to the penultimate position.

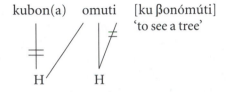

Tone spread rule in Setswana: H tone spreads to all the following toneless (non-toned) syllables, except the last one before a pause or before another H tone-associated syllable.

(i)   simololelana # [símʊ́lʊ́lelana]
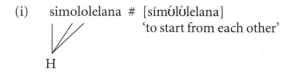
'to start from each other'

(ii)   go reka kgomo # [xʊrɛ́ká qhʊmʊ]
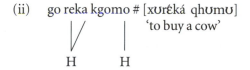
'to buy a cow'

In the autosegmental approach, the segmental units (syllables) are separated from the tones. The two are linked by association lines. Each language has its own set of tone rules that may alter the pattern of the association lines at the surface representation. Where the initial association is altered, the sign (=), cutting through the association line, is used to show delinkage of the tone to the respective syllable. Once the tone rules (which may involve deletion, spreading, or displacement of the high tone) have been applied, the low tone default rule is used to assign low tones to any syllables that may not be associated with any tones at the surface representation level.

Intonation

Intonation may be described as a pitch contour that characterizes entire utterances by giving them additional grammatical, expressive, emotional, or emphatic content. While stress and tone characterize syllables and words, intonation affects the whole sentence.

The intonation pitch contour usually depends on the type of utterance or sentence. This may be an assertion (declarative), an exclamation (interjective), a question (interrogative), an order (imperative), or a summons (vocative). However, the structure of the intonational contour may be influenced by the grammatical structure of the sentence, the nature of the constituent elements, the emphasis placed on some of these elements, the expressive intentions of the speaker, the emotional disposition of the speaker, the style of discourse involved, the speed with which the speaker is uttering, the syllabic quantities of the constituent words, the pattern of tone and stress in the respective words, as well as the idiolectal (individual) peculiarities of the speaker.

As can be seen, it is difficult to make a comprehensive or detailed description of intonation because of the many variables involved. However, there are major intonational patterns in each language. Some of these patterns may be said to be universal, as they are found in all languages.

Juncture

Juncture is a pause between segments in the articulation of words, phrases, or sentences. Such a pause may serve to distinguish between two utterances with different meanings, as in the English phrases *a name* [ə-neɪm] and *an aim* [ən-eɪm]. In Kiswahili, juncture appears in utterances such as *ana pamba* (two words) ('he has cotton'), as opposed to *ana-pamba* (one word) ('he is decorating'). Juncture is indicated in most languages by spaces or punctuation marks in the writing or word-division systems.

Phonological description of an African language

The basic task of any phonologist is to discover and then describe the phonological system of the language on which he or she is working. Once extensive fieldwork has been completed and all the speech sounds (phones) of the language of study have been collected and recorded (on tape or by other means), the important question is, which of these phones are phonemes? Or, to ask this another way, how are these phones interrelated? How do they form phonemes within the phonological system of the language? How are they organized into this phonological system? (The latter is usually presented in the form of a chart showing the opposition, relationship, and mode of distinction between the individual phonemes.)

Phonemic description

Once data has been collected and properly transcribed, the next task is to analyse it as systematically and as comprehensively as possible. The following are the steps normally taken in order to work out the phonemic system of a language.

Phonic inventory

The first step is to identify all the raw distinct speech sounds that have been collected. As explained earlier, such speech sounds are known as phones. They are considered 'raw' because we do not yet know where they belong in terms of family, as they have not yet been phonemically analysed. (Bear in mind that a phone may be a phoneme in one language, and a variant of a phoneme in another.)

If the transcription is sufficiently precise, the phonic inventory will consist of a great many phones. It is customary to distinguish the vowels from the consonants. The following is a list of words extracted from Kiswahili to illustrate the point:

love   [penda] [pɛ.nda]   duck [baːta]
climb   [pa.nda]   rope [ka.mba]
bow   [pi.nda]   read [soma]
throw   [po.nda] [pɔ.nda]   soda [soːɗa]
ass   [pu.nda]   get   [pata]

So we have:

Consonants [p, b, n, d, ɗ, t, m, s, ɓ, z, k]
Vowels   [e., ɛ., a., a, i., o., u, aː, o, oː, ɔ]

Identification of phoneme families

Once the consonant and vowel inventories have been completed, the next step is to decide how these various phones enter into different phoneme families. We need to remember that one of the definitions of a phoneme is that it is a family of sounds whose members are phonetically similar and in complementary distribution. Our task is thus to see whether any phonetically similar phones are in complementary contribution.

The best way to determine the similarity of phones is to put them onto a phonetic chart and then encircle any phones that differ by only one feature.

If we take the above Kiswahili example in a modified form, we would have the following phonetic chart.

TABLE 7.3 Phonetic chart of Kiswahili consonants

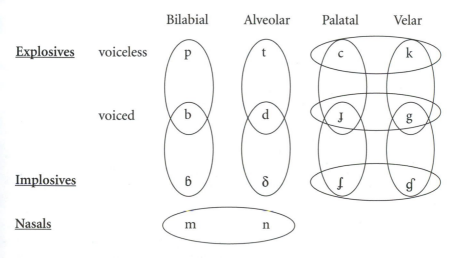

In the above chart, we have encircled all the pairs of those plosives that differ by only one feature. Note that we do not have to encircle bilabial and dental or dental and palatal, because there is a significant articulatory difference between them. However, we have to encircle palatals/velars because their points of artic-ulation are very close. The encircled pairs are as follows:

(a)	Voiced/voiceless:	b/p,	d/t,	ʃ/c,	g/k
(b)	Implosives/explosives:	ɓ/b,	ɗ, ɠ		ɲ/g
(c)	Orals/nasals:	b/m,	d/ɳ,	ɟ/ɲ,	g/ŋ
(d)	Velars/palatals:	k/c,	g/ɟ	ɲ/ŋ	

Likewise, vowels that differ by just one feature could be encircled as follows:

TABLE 7.4 Phonetic chart of vowels

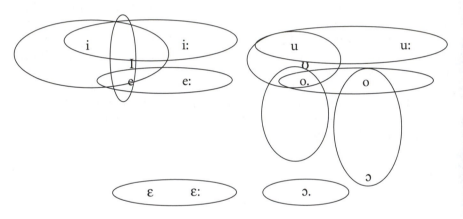

In the above chart, we have encircled the vowel phones as follows:

(a)   tense/lax: i/ɪ, u/ʊ, e/ɛ, e./ɛ., o/ɔ, o./ɔ:
(b)   short/long: i/i:, u/u:, e/e., o/o., ɔ/ɔ., ɛ/ɛ.
(c)   High lax/mid tense: ɪ/e, ʊ/o

The next step is to decide whether the pairs of phonetically similar phones belong to one family or not. The following are the principles that have to be followed.

Principle 1

If the phones in a given pair occur in the same phonic environment without any change in meaning, then they are free variants of the same phoneme. For example, the [e.] and [ɛ.] in the above example are free variants of the /e/ phoneme in Kiswahili, as shown in the words [pe.nda] and [pɛ.nda] ('love'). This is because the occurrence of one or the other does not produce a different word or render the word meaningless. The best way to apply this principle is to look for minimal pairs (pairs of different words that differ in only one sound).

Principle 2

If the phones in a given pair occur in different phonic environments of the utterance and together fill all the possible environments, then they are allophones of one phoneme in complementary distribution. This is the case with [ɓ] and [b] in the Kiswahili dialect shown above, as [b] occurs only after [m], and [ɓ] occurs elsewhere. Similarly, in Kihaya, [b] occurs after [m] and [β] elsewhere. Thus in Kiswahili, [b] and [ɓ] are allophones of /b/ in complementary distribution; equally, in Kihaya, [b] and [β] are allophones of /b/, also in complementary distribution.

Principle 3

If the phones in a given pair can occur in the same environment, and so cause different words or lack of meaning, then they do not belong to one phoneme family. In other words, they are not allophones of one phoneme, but represent different phonemes. For example, in Kiswahili, the vowels [a.], [e.], [i.], [o.], and [u.] are not allophones of the same phoneme because they can be in exactly the same position and signal different meanings, as in [pa.nda] ('climb'), [pe.nda] ('love'), [pi.nda] ('bend'), [po.nda] ('throw at'), and [pu.nda] ('ass'). Moreover, in Kiswahili, voiced consonants can never be in the same phoneme family as the respective voiceless consonants, as they are capable of differentiating between different meanings such as [paa]/[baa] ('roof', 'bar'), [saa]/[zaa] ('watch', 'give birth'), and [faa]/[vaa] ('suffice', 'put on').

   After applying these principles, it becomes possible to determine the different phoneme families to which all the phones identified by the study belong.

Notation of phonemes

Having regrouped all the phones into their respective classes or families of phoneme, the next step is to decide how to represent each family. Normally there should be only one sign or symbol to represent each family.

   The following are some of the criteria used to determine the sign or symbol to be used. Such a symbol should be:

- similar to the phones, or, more correctly, to the allophones that constitute the phoneme;
- general and simple;

- commonly used in normal orthography;
- easily printed;
- representative of the allophone with the highest frequency of occurrence/distribution;
- congruent with the other phonemes in the same series.

Some of these criteria may be in conflict. It is up to the researcher to choose the symbol he or she thinks would best represent a given phoneme. In the case of our Kiswahili example above, the symbols chosen could be as follows:

/b/ to represent [b] and [ɓ]
/d/ to represent [d] and [ð]
/g/ to represent [g] and [ɠ]
/a/ to represent [a] and [a.]
/e/ to represent [e], [ɛ], [e.], and [ɛ.]

Classification

Once all the phonemes and their notations have been determined, the next step is to classify them. This is done according to the features they have in common. Consonants are classed on two axes. The vertical axis is for ordering the consonants according to their place of articulation, namely:

bilabial: p, b, m, w
alveolar: t, d, n, l
posterior: k, g, ŋ, h

The horizontal axis arranges the phonemes in series, according to their manner of articulation, namely:

plosives, orals, voiceless: p, t, k,
plosives, orals, voiced: b, d, g
plosives, nasals: m, n, ŋ
continuants: w, l, h

Note that in the phonemic description it is possible to collapse different points and manners of articulation, as long as the system allows this. In our case, it has been possible to collapse the velar and glottal columns into one column, which has been given a more general name: posterior. Likewise, the liquids and semivowels have been collapsed into one general series: continuants. This is because there is no overlap, and therefore it can be argued that the differences between velar and glottal columns, on the one hand, and the liquid and semivowel series on the other, are only phonetic manifestations, and not phonemic, as they are not opposed to each other.

The vowels are classed along two main axes: localization and height of the tongue. Sometimes a third axis is necessary to indicate the rounding of the lips. The following is an example:

Localization of the tongue:
front: i, e
back: u, o
neutral (unclassified): a

Height of the tongue:
high: i, u
mid: e, o
low: a

The phonological table

The phonological table combines both axes (order and series) as follows:

TABLE 7.5 Phonological table of consonants

	Bilabial	Alveolar	Posterior
Oral plosives			
voiceless	p	t	k
voiced	b	d	g
Nasals	m	n	ŋ
Continuants	w	l	h

The phonological table for the vowels would be as follows:

TABLE 7.6 A phonological table of vowels

	Front	Back
High	i	u
Mid	e	o
Low	a	

As the above tables illustrate, a phonemic system is well knit. As Trubetzkoy once said, *tous les éléments se tiennent* – all the elements hold together. A good system should have as few phoneme gaps as possible.

Definition of the phonemes

Once the phonological tables for the consonant and vowel phonemes have been determined, the final step is to define each phoneme so as to demonstrate its distinctiveness and its relationship with the other phonemes.

The following is an example:

/b/ = bilabial (as opposed to /d/ and /g/)
    = plosive (as opposed to /w/)
    = oral (as opposed to /m/)
    = voiced (as opposed to /p/)

/o/ = back (as opposed to /e/)
    = mid (as opposed to /u/ and /a/)

It should be noted that, in some phonemic descriptions, it might be preferable to define the phonemes before classifying them.

Other important phonological facts

Depending on the objectives of the phonemic description, there are other important phonological facts that need to be investigated in order to complete the project. These are as follows:

(i) Realization of the phonemes

It is important for the researcher to know exactly how the phonemes are realized, as well as to understand the various phonic environments which condition the different allophones.

(ii) Other functions of the phonemes

The researcher may want to find out whether some of the phonemes have other roles in the language, such as demarcative or expressive functions.

(iii) Distribution of the phonemes

It is important to know whether the phonemes occur in all positions or not. If some of them are not found in certain positions (initial or final, for example), it is necessary to investigate whether they are neutralized into some other phoneme, or are simply absent in those positions (as in the case of the English phoneme /ŋ/, which never occur initially, and /h/, which never occurs finally).

(iv) Frequency of occurrence

The researcher should know which phonemes occur more frequently than others in the language. This will help in determining the functional load or distinctive role of each phoneme. For example, in most languages, /a/ is the most frequent phoneme among the vowels, and alveolar sounds such as /t/, /n/, and /l/ are very frequent. On the other hand, sounds like /ŋ/ and /ɣ/ are more rare. It is advisable when determining the frequency of phonemes to check not only the word lists, but also the texts, as the results are often different.

(v) Combinatory properties

It is also important to know how the various phonemes combine to constitute larger units. The canonical syllabic structure could be CV or CVC. However, other combinations might be possible. These could involve two or more consonants or vowels. Some languages do not accept certain sequences. For example, English does not accept the following sequences in the same syllable: [sd], [sb], [sg], [dl], [tl], or [nl]. Similarly, languages such as Kinyamwezi, Kiha, Kirundi, Kinyarwanda, Kihangaza, and Kikuyu do not accept the sequence of two voiceless plosives in subsequent syllables. It can be seen that some sequence constraints are natural, while others are language-specific.

Description of prosodic elements

After the phonemic analysis has been completed, and the consonants and vowels described, the researcher should then investigate the prosodic or supra-segmental elements. As stated above, these elements characterize larger units such as the syllable, the word, and the sentence, and include stress, tone, intonation, length, and juncture. As we have already seen, these are manifested by pitch, quantity, intensity, and energy in the vocal apparatus. The researcher should therefore find out:

- whether such elements exist in the language;
- how they are manifested phonetically;
- the role that they play in the language;
- the different variants; and
- the conditioning factors or environments of these variants.

Phonological systems of selected languages in Africa

To demonstrate how phonological systems can be described, the phonological tables of English, French, Kiswahili, isiZulu, and Ju/'hoan are presented below. As will be seen, there are various ways of presenting the phonological system of a language, depending on the methods and criteria used. What is given here should therefore be seen as one out of many possibilities.

English

TABLE 7.7 The consonant chart of English

	Labial	Dental	Alveolar	Palatal	Posterior (velar/glottal)
Stops					
voiceless	p	t	tʃ		k
voiced	b	d	dʒ		g
Fricatives					
voiceless	f	θ	s		h
voiced	v	ð	z		
Nasals	m		n		ŋ
Semivowels/					
continuants	w		r	j	
Lateral			l		

TABLE 7.8 The pure vowels of English

	Front	Central Rounded/unrounded		Back
High				
tense	i			u
lax	ɪ			ʊ
Mid				
tense	e	ee		o
lax	æ	ə	ʌ	ɔ
Low				ɑ

TABLE 7.9 The centring diphthongs of English

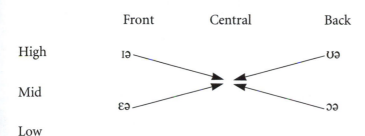

TABLE 7.10 The closing diphthongs of English

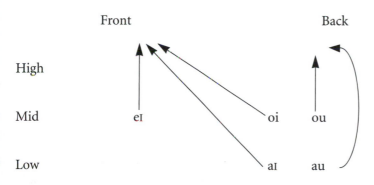

As can be seen, this is just one way of presenting the phonemic system of English. There are many others. The important thing is that the method should be followed systematically, and that the system (rather than the individual realizations) should count. In this case, we can say that English has twenty-four consonant phonemes and twenty-one vowel phonemes, of which twelve are pure, four are centring diphthongs, and five are closing diphthongs.

French

TABLE 7.11 The consonant chart of French

	Labial	Alveolar	Posterior (palatal/velar)
Plosives			
voiceless	p	t	k
voiced	b	d	g

Fricatives

voiceless	f	s	ʃ
voiced	v	z	ʒ
Nasals	m	n	ŋ
Continuants	w	l	j
Vibrant		r	

TABLE 7.12 The vowel chart of French

	Front Unrounded/rounded		Central	Back
Close	i	y		u
Half-close	e	ø		o
Half open – oral	ɛ	œ	ə	ɔ
Nasal				
Open – nasal	ɛ̃	œ̃		ɔ̃ ɑ̃
Oral	a			ɑ

Once again, it is important to note that the phonemic system of French presented here is just one of many possible systems. This one is the most economical, but also the most abstract, as many of the phonemes are defined somewhat differently from the way in which they are pronounced in current European French. However, as stated earlier, we should distinguish between the phonemic presentation of a language and a pure phonetic description. According to this description, there are nineteen consonant phonemes and sixteen vowel phonemes in French.

Kiswahili

TABLE 7.13 The consonant chart of Kiswahili

	Labial	Dental	Alveolar	Palatal	Posterior (velar/glottal)
Stops					
voiceless	p		t	tʃ	k
voiced	b		d	dʒ	g
Fricatives					
voiceless	f	θ	s	ʃ	h
voiced	v	ð	z		ɣ
Nasals	m		n	ɲ	ŋ
Continuants	w		l	j	
Vibrant			r		

TABLE 7.14 The vowel chart of Kiswahili

	Front	Back
High	i	u
Mid	e	o
Low	a	

The phonemic system presented here is the most simple, as it leaves out all the sounds that are still being debated, including dialectal sounds such as the aspirated voiceless plosives [pʰ], [tʰ], [cʰ], and [kʰ], foreign sounds that have not yet been integrated into the language, such as [h], [ʔ], [x], [ç], [ɑu], and [ɑi], as well as the complex sounds such as [mb], [nd], [nj], [ng], and so on. According to this description, there are twenty-five consonant phonemes and five vowel phonemes in Kiswahili.

isiZulu

TABLE 7.15 The consonant chart of isiZulu

	Labial	Alveolar	Lateral	(pre) Palatal	Posterior
Stops					
voiceless					
aspirated	ph	th			kh
non-aspirated	p	t		t	k
voiced	b	d		d	g
implosive	ɓ				
Fricatives					
voiceless	f	s	ɬ		h
voiced	v	z	lʒ		
Continuants	w		l	j	
Nasals	m	n		ɲ	ŋ
Clicks					
voiceless					
aspirated		/h	//h	!h	
non-aspirated		/	//	!	
voiced		g/	g//	g!	

TABLE 7.16 The vowel chart of isiZulu

	Front	Back
High	i	u
Mid	e	o
Low	a	

According to this phonological table, isiZulu has thirty-five consonants and five vowels. Nine of the thirty-five consonants are clicks. (As in Setswana, it is proper to consider the lateral or lateralized consonants under place of articulation, as they involve not only the continuant (sonorant) /l/, but also certain fricatives and clicks.) As is evident, the vowel systems in the two Bantu languages Kiswahili and isiZulu (and in most other Bantu languages) are simpler and better balanced when compared with the ones in English and French. However, the corresponding consonant systems are much more complex.

Ju/'hoan (a northern Khoisan language)

TABLE 7.17 Non-click consonants in Ju/'hoan

	Labial	Alveolar	Palatal	Velar	Glottal
Plosives					
voiceless					
aspirated	p^h	t^h/dt^h		k^h	
non-aspirated	p	t		k	ʔ
voiced	b	d		g	
velarized (ejective)		tx		kx'	
Affricates					
voiceless					
aspirated		ts^h/dts^h			
non-aspirated		ts	tʃ		
voiced		dz	dʒ		
velarized					
voiceless		tsx	tʃx		
voiced		dzx	dʒx		
ejective					
voiced		ts'			
Fricatives					
voiceless	f	s	ʃ	x	h
voiced		z	ʒ		
Nasals	m				
Semivowels			j		

TABLE 7.18 Click consonants in Ju/'hoan

Clicks:	Dental	Alveolar	Lateral	Palatal
Plain voiceless	/	≠	//	!
Fully nasalized	n/	n≠	n//	n!
Prevoiced	g/	g≠	n//	n!
Aspirated	/h	≠ʰ	//ʰ	!ʰ
Voiced aspirated	g/ʰ	g≠ʰ	g//ʰ	g!h
Velar ejection	/k	≠k	//k	!k
Nasal aspirated	n/ʰ	n≠ʰ	n//ʰ	n!ʰ
Affricated	/x	≠x	//x	!x
Voiceless nasal				
Aspirated	n/ʰ	n≠ʰ	n//ʰ	n!ʰ
Glottal release	/'	≠'	//'	!'
Prevoiced				
Affricated	g/ˣ	g≠ˣ	g//ˣ	g!ˣ

TABLE 7.19 The vowel chart of Ju/'hoan

	Front	Back
High	i	u
Mid	e	o
Low	a	

As can be seen from the above, Ju/'hoan has seventy-seven consonants and five vowels. Of the consonants, forty-four are clicks. There are four basic clicks that can be accompanied by other features. The phonemic inventory of Ju/'hoan, which is spoken in north-eastern Namibia and north-western Botswana, is among the richest, but also the most complex, in the world.

Endnotes

1 In some linguistics textbooks, phonemes are said to change the meaning of words. This formulation, though fairly common, is technically not quite correct, as phonemes do not in themselves have meaning. What does happen is that changing a phoneme in a word produces a different word, which obviously has a different meaning.

Bibliography

BATIBO, HERMAN M. 1976 [1985]. *Le Kisukuma: Phonologie et Morphologie.* Thèse de 3eme Cycle, Paris. Edition Recherche sur Les Civilizations, Paris.

——— 1984. *An Introduction to the Study and Application of Linguistics.* Unpublished.

——— 1986. 'Autosegmental Phonology and the Bantu Tone Systems.' *Journal of Linguistics and Language in Education* 2: 34–47.

——— 1996. 'Loanword Clusters Nativization Rules in Setswana and Kiswahili: A Comparative Study.' *South African Journal of African Languages* 16.2:33–41.

BROSNAHAM L.F., and BERTIL MALMBERG. 1971. *Introduction to Phonetics.* Cambridge: Cambridge University Press.

CRYSTAL, DAVID. 1980. *A First Dictionary of Linguistics and Phonetics.* London: Andre Deutsch.

DOKE, CLEMENT, M. 1967. *The Southern Bantu Languages.* London: Dawsons of Pall Mall. Published for the International African Institute.

GOLDSMITH, JOHN A. 1991. *Autosegmental and Metrical Phonology.* Oxford: Basil Blackwell.

GUTHRIE, MALCOLM. 1967. *The Classification of the Bantu Languages.* Dawsons of Pall Mall. Published for the International African Institute.

HYMAN, LARRY. 1975. *Phonology: Theory and Analysis.* New York: Holt, Rinehart & Winston.

KENSTOWICS, MICHAEL, and CHARLES KISSEBERTH. 1979. *Generative Phonology: Description and Theory.* New York: Academic Press.

8 Building techniques in African languages

D. Okoth Okombo

Expected outcomes

At the end of this chapter you should be able to:

1. Identify the grammatical constituents of different types of linguistic construction and label them linguistically.
2. Analyse linguistic constructions.
3. Provide examples of prefixes, roots, stems, suffixes, noun phrases, verb phrases, and so on.
4. Distinguish universal building techniques from language-specific ones.
5. Explain the difference between word-building and sentence-building in African languages, and define what is meant by generative grammar and transformational grammar.
6. Appreciate the uniqueness of languages in terms of how they build their words and sentences.

Introduction

In a book written for foreigners working in Malawi, Price has the following words for the learners of Cinyanja (Cingoni/Chichewa):

> ... a great deal of Nyanja is constructed in ways which are quite unfamiliar to Europeans. The constructions are identified only by comparison of sentences heard or read, and do not exist so much as separate words or phrases as in the form of affixes, single or in groups. To deal with these, one must try to adopt a new outlook and unaccustomed devices. (Price 1966: xiii)

As language scientists or linguists, we find the view expressed by Price interesting for a number of reasons, some of which are particularly relevant to our concerns in this chapter. What he says suggests the following about language and language users:

- that ordinarily we tend to use a language we already know as a model for trying to understand the nature of an unfamiliar language;
- that a language has units that are used to build larger units known as constructions;
- that the building of linguistic constructions and the units used are not always readily obvious to the observer; we often need to make some effort to identify them;
- that languages are different not only in the techniques they use for building constructions, but also in the kind of elemental units they use to build them; and
- that we can choose to look at a language in a way that is different from what we are accustomed to.

Our tendency to think of an unfamiliar language in terms of a language we already know is justifiable. By knowing one language, we already know many of the properties of human language in general. For example, we know that a language spoken by humans has rules for putting words together to form longer expressions, and that these words can be realized in different shapes in different contexts, for example when they change from singular to plural. However, although in general terms this kind of knowledge prepares us for learning another language, we will run into problems if we expect a new language to operate exactly like a language we already know. Languages are the same in terms of broad general principles, but they differ in the specific ways in which these principles are applied. Moreover, these general principles are not necessarily obvious to speakers of the various human languages. It usually takes specific and systematic investigation to discover them. It is the business of linguists to conduct such investigations. When we study linguistics, we learn the principles that such investigations have revealed. It is safer to use these broad principles as a means of discovering more about an unfamiliar language than to use the properties of a specific language that we already know. So, in trying to understand the building techniques used in African languages, we will use general linguistic principles and concepts.

Most of the concepts we will use have to do with the units of language, usually referred to as **units of linguistic analysis** or simply as linguistic units. These range from the abstract sound units known as phonemes to the larger constructions called sentences. Between the phoneme and the sentence, there are four other linguistic units, giving us a total of six linguistic units. These occur in a hierarchical relationship, which can be diagrammatically represented as follows:

Sentence
Clause
Phrase
Word
Morpheme
Phoneme

The rules that govern how one linguistic unit is formed by using lower units are conventionally referred to as the **grammar** of a language. In the strict sense of this term, these rules do not govern the occurrence of phonemes in morphemes. For this reason, a phoneme is not regarded as a grammatical unit (a unit of grammatical analysis). A phoneme is thus simply a phonological unit (a unit of sound used in speech). The remaining five units (morpheme, word, phrase, clause, and sentence) are the grammatical units of language.

The above diagram shows that the morpheme is the smallest unit of grammatical analysis, whereas the sentence is the largest. This means that a morpheme is the smallest linguistic unit to which we can apply the rules of grammar, and a sentence is the largest unit within which these rules apply. The study of the properties of linguistic units that are larger than a sentence falls outside the scope of grammar. Such a study falls within the domain of discourse analysis, sometimes called text linguistics (see Chapter 10).

This chapter concerns grammar, in other words, the relations between linguistic units that range from the morpheme to the sentence. Such units, as we have shown, occur in hierarchically ranked levels. The relationship between the units at any two consecutive levels (for example morphemes and words, or phrases and clauses) can be seen either in terms of composition (the lower units are used to compose the higher units) or decomposition (higher units are broken down into lower units). Any unit obtained by composition (by putting two or more lower-level units together) is called a **construction**, whereas any unit obtained by decomposition (by breaking a higher-level unit into smaller grammatical units) is called a **constituent**. These are basic concepts in grammatical analysis. Moreover, they are mutually defining terms in the sense that a linguistic element is a constituent simply because it is part of a construction; similarly, a linguistic element becomes a construction only when it has two or more constituents. We can now think of the study of grammar as the study of the rules governing how constructions are formed (or built) either in a specific language or, more abstractly, in human language in general. When we talk about the constituents of a given construction and the relations between those constituents, we are discussing the structure of the construction.

This chapter is about the structure of constructions in African language; in other words, how grammatical constructions are formed (or built) in African languages. Although there are many types of construction, the two main constructions studied in linguistics are the word and the sentence. Phrases and clauses are generally studied in relation to sentences.

This leads us to the major branches of grammar: **morphology** (the study of the structure of words) and **syntax** (the study of the structure of sentences). As we shall see in the next two sections, the boundary between morphology and syntax is not always clearly defined, especially in Bantu languages.

Syntax begins with words that are already formed (according to the rules of morphology) and ends with the formation of sentences. We will follow this assumption, unless it becomes problematic, in which case we will say so. Although our frequent use of the term 'building' suggests a compositional approach, most of what we will be doing in this chapter will involve decomposition (or analysis). Understanding the structure of a construction necessarily involves identifying its constituents. When we identify the constituents of words and sentences and discover how they are put together, we establish how those words and sentences are built. We have, technically speaking, discovered the grammar of the language whose words and sentences we have analysed.

Exercise

Study the following constructions from Afrikaans (South Africa). Try to 'decompose' them and to identify their morphological and/or syntactic constituents.

boek	boeke	boekie	tafel	tafels	tafeltjie
('book'	'books'	'little book')	('table'	'tables'	'little table')

lees	het gelees	sal lees	praat	het gepraat	sal praat
('read'	'read'	'will read')	('talk'	'talked'	'will talk')

Jan speel sokker en Piet
speel rugby.
Speel Jan sokker en Piet rugby?

('Jan plays soccer and Piet
plays rugby.')
('Plays Jan soccer and Piet rugby?')
['Does Jan play soccer and Piet rugby?']

Word-building in African languages

Consider the English word *good*. We find it in expressions such as *a good person, a good book, a good day*, and so on. Items 1 to 3 below are the equivalent expressions in Kiswahili:

1 mtu mzuri ('person good')
2 kitabu kizuri ('book good')
3 siku nzuri ('day good')

Even if we ignore a glaring syntactic property of these Kiswahili expressions (the order of the words – see the next section), there is still a fairly obvious difference between the Kiswahili expressions and their English equivalents. In each case where English has the plain form *good*, Kiswahili has a word form that differs from place to place, even as it represents the same meaning. Thus in 1 to 3, the English word *good* is represented by the Kiswahili words *mzuri*, *kizuri*, and *nzuri*. In all these Kiswahili words, there is a recurring element (*-zuri*), which is called the **root**, as opposed to the **affixes** (*m-, ki,* and *n-*), which change according to the context. We will ignore the context for now, as it concerns the syntactic rules governing the formation of noun phrases, which will be investigated in the next section. However, what must be noted here is that Kiswahili words (like the words of other Bantu languages) typically consist of roots and affixes. Now consider the word *goodness* and its Kiswahili equivalent *uzuri*. This shows that *good*, like *-zuri*, is also a root, with *-ness* being the affix in the word *goodness*.

The important point to note here is that, whereas the English root *good* can occur in isolation, the Kiswahili root *-zuri* never occurs in isolation. It is always found with an affix (as in *uzuri, kizuri, mzuri*, and so on). The difference between *good* and *-zuri* as roots is that *good* is a **free root** (one that can occur in isolation) whereas *-zuri* is a **bound root** (one that never occurs in isolation). Being bound is a typical property of Bantu roots. English also has some bound roots, such as *-ceive* in the words *receive, deceive, conceive,* and *perceive*. This is nevertheless not a typical property of English. However, all affixes in all languages are bound by their very nature. Roots and affixes, such as the ones we have seen above, are the **minimal units of grammatical analysis** that can be used to form words. They themselves cannot be broken down into smaller grammatical units. If we do break them down (decompose the unit), the result is units of sound (consonants and vowels) or phonological units, which fall outside the domain of grammar, as explained above. (See chapters 6 and 7 for further details.) So roots and affixes are minimal units of grammatical analysis found in the structure of words; technically, they are known as **morphemes**.

As in the cases of roots such as -*zuri* and -*ceive*, and affixes, morphemes can be bound. Or, like *good*, they can be free. Thus, any given morpheme can be categorized as free (if it can occur in isolation) or bound (if it never occurs in isolation). Languages differ in their preference for these two types of morphemes. Bantu languages typically prefer bound morphemes (and have few free morphemes), whereas languages such as English and French prefer free morphemes (and have few bound morphemes).

It is important to observe at this stage that, as both affixes and roots can be bound, the distinction between bound and free morphemes is not the same as the distinction between affixes and roots. For example, although all affixes are bound morphemes, not all bound morphemes are affixes.

Let us look at the word *kitabu* ('book') in 2 above. Its plural form is *vitabu*, and when we qualify it with -*zuri* as in the other cases, we get *vitabu vizuri* ('good books'). By comparing the forms *kitabu* and *vitabu*, and considering what gets affixed to -*zuri*, we can say that the root of the noun is -*tabu*. The prefixes *ki*- and *vi*- represent a common property of Bantu nouns, the occurrence of **class-markers**. In Kiswahili, as in other Bantu languages, every noun belongs to a class (called a 'noun class'), which is usually marked by a prefix placed before the root of the noun (typically a bound root). As we have seen in 1 and 2 above, the class-marker also appears on an adjective. With this information in mind, consider 4 and 5 below:

4 kitambaa kizuri
   cloth   good   ('a good [piece of] cloth')
5 kitambaa changu
   cloth   mine   ('my cloth')

Here we see that the *ki*- in *kizuri* and the *ch*- in *changu* both represent the class prefix *ki*- in *kitambaa*. This demonstrates that a morpheme is actually an abstract unit, which can be physically realized in different forms. We can now distinguish between a morpheme as an abstract grammatical unit and a **morph** as the physical realization of a morpheme. Some morphemes, such as the class prefix in *kizuri*, have more than one physical realization. Each of these realizations of a morpheme is called an **allomorph**. So we can define an allomorph as one of two or more realizations of the same morpheme. The occurrence of allomorphs is prevalent in all African languages, but is not unique to them. For example, the prefixes in the following English words are different realizations of the same negative morpheme.

6 intolerable
7 impossible

The occurrence of the allomorphs that we have seen so far can be explained in terms of their phonological environment; in other words, they are influenced by the sounds around them. The negative morpheme *in-* ends with a sound formed at the same place in the mouth that the following morpheme (*toler-*) begins. Similarly, the *m* of *im-* and the *p* of *possible* agree in terms of their place of formation. Such allomorphs are said to be **phonologically conditioned**. But not all allomorphs are of this type. Consider the English word *fox* and its plural *foxes*. Given this case, why is the plural form of *ox oxen* and not *oxes*? The realization of the English plural morpheme as *-en* in *oxen* is not based on any sound requirements of English; it is simply a grammatical property of *ox* as a morpheme. So we say that *-en* is a **morphologically conditioned** allomorph – one that occurs when the morpheme to which the plural morpheme is affixed selects the form of the latter. This is so even if there are known historical reasons for the irregular behaviour of the morphemes in question. The point is that speakers learn only the grammar of a language in its current form; they do not learn a language according to its history.

We are now in a position to revisit the Kiswahili expression *siku nzuri* ('good day') found in 3 above. Note that the *n-* in the adjective *nzuri* is the class-marker of the noun *siku*, yet it does not appear as a prefix on the noun itself. Remember also that if *siku* did not have a class-marker, it would not be copied (by syntactic rules) onto the adjective root *-zuri*. So we must conclude that the class-marker is realized as a **zero morph** (a morph with no sound properties) on the noun *siku*. There is no phonological reason why this should be so; the zero morph in the class-marker position of *siku* is also a morphologically conditioned allomorph (of the class-marker for *siku*), just as *-en* in *oxen* is for the English plural morpheme.

The word-building technique or morphological process we have been discussing so far is that of **affixation**: the use of affixes to modify word forms. So far, however, our discussion of affixation has been limited because we have also been introducing some basic morphological concepts such as morph, allomorph, zero morph, and the conditions governing the occurrence of allomorphs. We are now ready to look further into affixation, as well as other morphological concepts and processes.

So far, most of the affixes that we have seen have been **prefixes** – affixes that are placed before the root (or base) of a word. To consider another type of affix, let us look at the Kiswahili expressions in 8 to 10 below (the various morphemes are separated by hyphens):

8 kupika (ku-pik-a)   ('to cook')
   ku   pik   a
   infinitive   root   word-final affix

9 kupikia (ku-pik-i-a) ('to cook for [someone]')
ku   pik   i   a
infinitive root   applicative affix   word-final affix

10 kupikiwa (ku-pik-i-w-a) ('to be cooked for/by someone')
ku   pik   i   wa   a
infinitive root   applicative affix   passive affix word-final affix

The root morpheme that gives the sense of 'cook' is *-pik-*. In front of it is the infinitive prefix *ku-*, as seen in 8. The root is followed by the word-final affix *-a*. This word-final affix, which comes after the root, belongs to the category of affixes called **suffixes**. Examples 9 and 10 show more affixes that can be placed after the root, although even in these cases the word-final affix must come last. Thus, in 10, there are three suffixes after the root.

Prefixation and suffixation are the most common affixation processes in Kiswahili and other Bantu languages. In general, Bantu languages use more prefixation than Germanic languages, particularly English.

Infixation (placing an affix inside the root) also occurs in Kiswahili and other African languages, although to a much smaller extent. Consider the following items taken from Kiswahili:

11 abdi   ('God's messenger' – singular)
12 abidi   ('God's messengers' – plural form of 11)

The plural form seen in 12 is formed by inserting *-i-* into the root of the singular noun seen in 11. This grammatical behaviour is rare in Kiswahili and other Bantu languages. Words such as 11 are usually borrowings from Semitic languages, particularly Arabic. In general, infixation is a characteristic feature of Afro-Asiatic languages and is usually found in the African languages that belong to that family (Arabic, Amharic, Somali, and so on).

Affixes (prefixes, suffixes, and infixes) can also be categorized in terms of the consequences of adding them to a **stem** (what exists before an affix is added; it can consist of a bare root, or a root plus an affix added at an earlier stage). The question is whether this leads to the formation of another word, or merely modifies the grammatical form of the input word as contained in the stem. Consider, for example, the forms of *-zuri* ('good') obtained by prefixing to it the different class-markers seen in 1 to 3 (*mzuri, kizuri,* and *nzuri*). All these are different forms of the same word (i.e. word forms), representing the word *good* in different grammatical contexts. Such affixes are called **inflectional affixes**, or, when treated as morphemes, **inflectional morphemes**. By contrast, affixes such as *u-* in *uzuri* ('goodness') give us a different word rather than a different word form. In other words, while *kizuri* and *mzuri* are two forms of the same word (created by adding inflectional affixes), *kizuri* and *uzuri* are different words altogether. Affixes such as *u-* in *uzuri* are known as **derivational affixes**. As in the case of inflectional affixes, when derivational affixes are treated as morphemes, they are referred to as **derivational morphemes**. For some more examples, consider the following Kiswahili expressions:

13 imba   ('to sing')
14 imb-i-a   ('to sing for')
15 imb-i-w-a   ('to be sung for')
16 imb-i-a-n-a   ('to sing for each other')

The word-final *-a* and the passive *-w-* in 15 are inflectional affixes, while the applicative *-i-* in 14 to 16 and the reciprocal affix *-n-* in 16 are derivational affixes. The same difference can be seen in the following English words:

17 walk
18 walking
19 walker
20 walkers

The *-ing* in 18 and the plural affix *-s* in 20 are inflectional affixes, as opposed to the nominalizing affix *-er* in 19, which is a derivational affix.

Apart from affixation, there are other morphological processes found in African languages, as well as other languages of the world. The most widely reported of these are base-modification, suppletion, compounding, and reduplication.

Base-modification is the morphological process in which the root (base) of a word is modified (with or without some affixation) to reflect or accommodate a grammatical idea. A few examples of base-modification can be found in Bantu languages, but some of the best examples are found in Nilotic languages (Maasai, Dholuo, and others in East Africa). Consider, for example, the formation of plural nouns in Maa (Maasai) as reproduced from Mol (1994: 40) in 21 to 26 below:

21 en-karai   pl. in-kera   ('child')
22 ol-payian   pl. il-payiani   ('elder')
23 ol-ayioni   pl. il-ayiok   ('boy')
24 en-tito   pl. in-toyie   ('girl', 'daughter')
25 en-kitok   pl. in-kitusak   ('woman', 'wife')
26 ol-murrani   pl. il-murran   ('warrior')

It is clear from these examples that in the Maasai language nouns are formed by unpredictably modifying the base (root) in addition to replacing the singular prefix *en-/ol-* with the plural prefix *in-/il-*. (The Maasai number (plural or singular) prefixes also show gender categories in terms of feminine (*en-*) and masculine (*il-*).) Such a morphological classification of nouns is well known in Indo-European languages such as French and German. The division into feminine and masculine (with or without neuter) gives us what is called **natural gender** (gender based on sex distinctions, although not necessarily on the sex of the named object). A more elaborate system of this kind, which is not modelled on sex categories, and which is found in Bantu languages, is called **class gender**. In both cases, nouns are placed into groups that are grammatically significant.

The next morphological process we want to mention is **suppletion**, in which some grammatical information is coded by replacing one root with what looks like a totally different root (base), as can be seen in the following words from Dholuo:

27 dhako (singular)   mon (plural)   ('woman')
28 dhano (singular)   ji (plural)   ('person'/'human being')
29 nyako (singular)   nyiri (plural)   ('girl')
30 pacho (singular)   mier (plural)   ('homestead')

The distinction between suppletion and base-modification is not always clear, as we can see from 29 above. For this reason, linguists often treat both as cases of suppletion.

Compounding, however, is much clearer as a morphological process. It involves putting together two different roots (with some of their affixes if necessary) to give expression to a unique meaning. The Kiswahili word *mwana* ('child'), for example, appears in many compound words, where it has the meaning of 'one who does something' or 'one who is a member of something', as in 31 to 34 below:

31 mwanachama   child-party association   ('member')
32 mwanajeshi   child-army   ('soldier')
33 mwanasoka   child-soccer   ('soccer player')
34 mwanahewa   child-air   ('airforce man/woman')

A process that is close to compounding is **reduplication**, where the same root (with some affixes where necessary) is repeated to give it a nuance of meaning it would not normally have. Thus in Kiswahili, for example, *kulia* means 'to cry', but *kulialia* means 'to cry all the time without good cause'. Similarly, *kucheza* means 'to play', but *kuchezacheza* means 'to play about when one could be doing something better'. Here are some more examples from Kiswahili:

35	kucheka	to laugh
	kuchekacheka	to laugh without good cause
36	nyekundu	red (as of a house)
	nyekundunyekundu	reddish
37	wakubwa	big (as of people)
	wakubwakubwa	(people) of some importance

Languages are sometimes classified into types according to their preferred morphological behaviour. So languages such as Kiswahili, which make plentiful use of affixes to express many ideas, are called **agglutinating** languages. Those such as Maasai, which employ a considerable amount of base-modification, are referred to as **inflectional** languages. Both agglutinating and inflexional languages are **synthetic** languages if compared with those that tend to express every idea in isolation by using appositions (pre-positions and post-positions). The latter are called **isolating** or **analytic** languages. The difference between an analytic language and an agglutinating language can clearly be seen if we compare the English expression in 38 with its Kiswahili equivalent in 39:

38 He cooked for me.
39 Alinipikia.

a	li	ni	pik	i	a
3person sg subj	past	1person sg obj	root	applicative	word-final affix

However, it is important to remember that no language is a pure type. In a synthetic language one can sometimes encounter analytic behaviour and vice versa. Most languages have mixed systems. Calling a language synthetic or analytic is to talk about its dominant, not exclusive, behaviour.

Exercise

1 Identify the different types of morphemes in the following words from Afrikaans.

skryf	het geskryf	nes	neste
('write')	('wrote')	('nest')	('nests')
eet	het geëet	bees	beeste
('eat')	('ate')	('ox'/'cow')	('oxen'/'cows')
kan	kon	wa	waens
('can')	('could')	('wagon')	('wagons')

2 What are the morphological processes involved in the formation of these words?

Sentence-building techniques

Some key concepts and orientations

At the beginning of this chapter, we pointed out that the most basic concepts in the study of grammar are **construction** and **constituent**. Our building metaphor is based on our central concern with how linguistic constructions are formed. However, as we mentioned in the previous section, we understand the structure of constructions by identifying how their constituents are related to one another. To repeat what was said earlier, the study of grammar conventionally refers to **morphology** (the study of the structure of words) and **syntax** (the study of the structure of sentences). Later, we will discuss a radically different conception of grammar.

Sentences are essentially constructions, although in speech we sometimes come across imperative sentences (such as *Go!*) that have only one constituent. Despite having only one constituent, they are still regarded as constructions (what occurs in speech thus does not always reveal the whole constructional nature of a sentence). All sentences are indeed constructions, as we shall demonstrate later on.

The main constituents in the structure of a sentence exist at the level of phrases, as clauses are essentially sentential structures. (For a discussion of why traditional grammarians thought it necessary to use the term *clause*, see Lyons 1968: 170–208.) In sentence 1 below, there are two main constituents: a noun phrase (NP) and a verb phrase (VP):

1 [My friend] [took my share].

Note that *my friend* and *took my share* are also constructions, with their own constituents. Consider the NP *my friend*. Its constituents are the possessive adjective *my* (called a determiner, together with articles, demonstratives, possessive forms of nouns, and so on) and the noun *friend*. Let us represent this information (and a bit more) on a tree diagram[1] or phrase-marker, as in 2 below.

The diagram shows us a number of important things. Firstly, it shows that structure is hierarchical, which means that, for example, the subject NP (in this case NP[1]) occurs at a higher level of structure than the object NP (here NP[2]). Generally, constituents of a sentence do not occur at the same level of structure. This is something we cannot easily pick up simply by looking at the string of words that make up a sentence. Following on from this, we can categorize the constituents of a sentence accordingly: constituents on the first level of structure, those represented by nodes directly dominated by S (for example NP and VP), are known as immediate constituents, whereas constituents on the last level

2

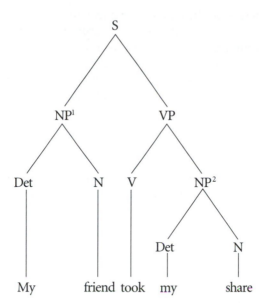

(for example Det, N, and V) are known as ultimate constituents of the sentence. Any constituents that might occur between the immediate and the ultimate constituents are known as intermediate constituents. In terms of the actual words (lexical items) of the sentence, only *my friend* (NP¹) and *took my share* (VP) are immediate constituents. The single words *my, friend, took, my,* and *share* are the ultimate constituents of the sentence, while the combination of words *my share* (NP²) is an intermediate constituent. Another thing we can see by looking at diagram 2 is that the constituents belong to groups of words, the largest of which is the sentence (S) itself. For this reason, S is known as the initial (top or highest) node of the tree diagram. It dominates all other nodes. Other groups of words constitute phrasal categories, such as NP (noun phrase) and VP (verb phrase). Single words belong to specific lexical categories (traditionally called parts of speech) such as N(oun), V(erb), and Det(erminer). These (the lexical categories) constitute the non-branching or terminal nodes. They dominate (without branching) the actual words of the sentence that together constitute what is referred to as the terminal string of the phrase-marker. The nodes are related to each other in terms of dominance and/or precedence, i.e. vertically or horizontally (or both). Vertically, one node dominates or is dominated by another, with the initial node dominating all the others. Horizontally, one node precedes or is preceded by another on a left-to-right reading. Thus, in diagram 2, NP¹ precedes NP². Nodes which are immediately dominated by the same node (NP¹ and VP, for example) are called sister nodes. Thus, under the VP node, V and NP² are sisters, but V and Det are not.

When we analyse a sentence by showing its constituents, the kind of grammar we write is known as a **constituent-structure grammar**. Such an analysis can be done without indicating the phrasal and lexical categories to which the groups of words and single words in the sentences belong. The technical term for this approach to a constituent-structure grammar is **unlabelled bracketing**. This is what we would be doing if we identified the constituents of sentence 1 as in 3 below:

3   [My friend] [took my share].

We do such bracketing by comparing the sentence to one whose immediate constituents are obvious, for example, *Juma laughed*, which we can represent like this:

4   [Juma] [laughed].

In terms of structural patterns, *my friend* can be said to be an expansion (but syntactic equivalent) of *Juma*, while *took my share* is an expansion of *laughed*. Such comparisons can be done repeatedly at various levels of structure to establish the immediate constituents of different constructions, until the ultimate constituents of a sentence are established. However, there are many syntactic questions that cannot be answered through unlabelled bracketing, especially questions concerning structural ambiguity. To illustrate this, let us consider sentences 5 and 6:

5   She likes Egyptian cotton dresses.
6   She hates visiting relatives.

Both 5 and 6 are structurally ambiguous; in other words, each has more than one possible meaning depending on how it is structurally analysed. (However, they are not lexically ambiguous, as the different possible meanings are not based on words with more than one meaning.) In the case of 5, the question is whether *Egyptian* qualifies *cotton dresses* (i.e. cotton dresses that are Egyptian) or whether *Egyptian cotton* as a unit qualifies *dresses* (i.e. dresses made of Egyptian cotton). We can show the two structural meanings of the sentence by means of bracketing, as in 7a and 7b:

7a She likes [Egyptian] [cotton dresses].
7b She likes [Egyptian cotton] [dresses].

However, in the case of 6, the structural ambiguity does not depend on how the bracketing is done, but on whether we treat *visiting* as a verb (going to visit relatives) or as an adjective (relatives who visit). Thus, in cases such as 6, we cannot account for structural ambiguity without using syntactic labels show-ing the lexical and phrasal categories of the constituents of the sentence. Evidence of this kind has led linguists to believe that syntactic structures should be represented in labelled brackets, usually in the form of phrase-mark-ers such as 2 above. (The advantage of phrase-markers over ordinary brackets is that they are easy to read and, as we have observed above, show the hierarchi-cal nature of structure.)

When we use labelled brackets, the kind of grammar we write is called a **phrase-structure (PS) grammar**. The phrase-markers (PMs) that we draw in a PS grammar are based on rules of structure known as phrase-structure rules. Technically, PS rules are re-write rules; they involve a set of instructions con-sisting of arrows with symbols on either side of each arrow, as shown in 8:

8 $X \rightarrow Y\ Z$

According to these rules, the symbol on the left-hand side should be replaced with the string of symbols on the right-hand side. Also, there can be only one symbol on the left-hand side. Thus, the phrase-marker (PM) in 2 above can be set out according to these rules as in 9 below:

9
S	→	NP VP
VP	→	V NP
NP	→	Det N
Det	→	my
N	→	friend, share
V	→	took

Such rules can generate (explicitly account for the structure of) many different sentences which use the same words in the combinations allowed by the rules. Every PM based on such rules (e.g. 2) represents the constituent structure of each generated sentence.

Any grammar, such as a PS grammar, that explicitly accounts for sentence structure is called a **generative grammar**. (This is the radically different con-cept of grammar we alluded to earlier on.) When we say that a grammar explic-itly accounts for sentence structure, we mean that its rules say everything that is needed for the formation of the sentence(s), leaving nothing unclear or ambiguous. The ability of a grammar to generate sentences in this sense is called its **generative capacity** – which may be too weak, if it does not generate all the target sentences, or too strong, if it generates all the target sentences plus others that are outside the set of target sentences, some of which may be ill-formed (not formed according to the grammar of the language in question). A grammar whose generative capacity is too weak needs to be made stronger; one whose generative capacity is too strong needs to be constrained so that it does not generate unwanted sentences.

PS grammars do well in capturing the constituent structures of sentences. However, they have shortcomings based on their inability to reflect everything that we know about our languages. For example, PS grammars cannot show structural relations among sentences that speakers of a language treat as systematically related sentences; see, for example, 10a and 10b:

10a   Juma made a mistake.   (Active construction)
10b   A mistake was made by Juma. (Passive construction)

In this case, we know that those who speak English can give a sentence of type 10a if they are first given one of type 10b.

Moreover, in the area of structural ambiguity, PS grammars cannot account for cases of ambiguity based on unsaid but understood elements in the structure of a sentence; see, for example 11:

11   Juma loves Maria more than Sue.

This could mean either 12a or 12b:

12a   Juma loves Maria more than Juma loves Sue.
12b   Juma loves Maria more than Sue loves Maria.

What these problems of PS grammars point to is the need for a generative grammar that can relate one kind of structure to another kind of structure; in other words, a grammar that has not only rules of formation, but also rules of transformation. Such a grammar was proposed in the mid-1950s by the American linguist Noam Chomsky, who called it a **Transformational-Generative Grammar** (or simply transformational grammar). Since it was first proposed, the idea has been revised and developed by Chomsky (and his followers) to become the most dominant theory in linguistics to date. It has various models, but what we need to first familiarize ourselves with is the **Standard Theory**, which treats grammar as a model of language competence (Chomsky 1965). According to this, a grammar is a system of rules and other elements (for example, vocabulary) that fully accounts for what speakers of a language know about its sound system, its sentence-formation procedures, and the meanings of the sentences. This is a much broader conception of grammar than the conventional one that includes only syntax and morphology. However, for our purposes, sentence-formation and transformation rules are found only in the syntactic component of this grammar.

We cannot cover the details of such a grammar in an introductory textbook, but we do need to know that this grammar works on the assumption that there are two levels of structure, known as **deep structure** (the abstract level) and **surface structure** (the level close but not identical to what is actually said in speech). At the deep-structure level, every constituent remains where we logically expect it to be, and everything necessary for meaning is still in the sentence. The two levels of structure are related by rules called transformations. These can perform a number of syntactic operations, including moving a constituent from its deep-structure position to another position. Thus, in 13a, *my friend* is in its deep-structure position, whereas in 13b its position changes because of the application of a movement rule:

13a   I didn't see my friend.
13b   My friend I didn't see.

The actual deep-structure sentence would be more abstract than 13a, but whatever happens to other elements in the deep structure, *my friend* remains in position as the object of the verb *see*. We need to know this if we are to understand 13b, in which *my friend* comes at the beginning of the sentence.

These rules are also responsible for the deletion of all sorts of sentential elements, which are understood (as in 11), but not clearly spelt out (as in 12a and 12b). They can also insert a non-deep-structure element. For example, a sentence such as 14a is often expressed as 14b:

14a   A man is at the door.
14b   There is a man at the door.

The occurrence of *there* in 14b is believed to be the result of applying a transformational rule. Thus, according to the Standard Theory, transformations can perform a number of operations, including movement, deletion, insertion, and (as we shall see a little later) copying.

In general, the theory is organized as follows. Grammar, in the broad sense mentioned above, consists of three components. These are the syntactic component, which represents our knowledge of how sentences are formed; the semantic component, which represents our knowledge of how sentences are interpreted (assigned meaning); and the phonological component, which represents our knowledge of how sentences are pronounced in speech. Other forms of knowledge, such as our knowledge of contextual considerations (for example, when to be polite), are not considered part of grammar, even in this broad definition.

Of the three components of grammar, only the syntactic component is generative (as far as sentence formation is concerned). The semantic component and the phonological component are both interpretive, the former interpreting the deep structures generated by the syntactic component in terms of meaning, while the latter interprets the surface structures generated by the syntactic component in terms of pronunciation. In syntax, we study only the design and operations of the syntactic component.

The syntactic component itself has two major sub-components: the base component and the transformational component. The base component in turn consists of what is called the categorial sub-component (which has phrase-structure rules and the necessary symbols) and the lexicon – the dictionary part of the grammar. The presence of the categorial sub-component, together with PS rules, shows that Chomsky did not do away with PS rules; he simply added another set of rules (transformational rules), but then named his theory after this new set of rules. It is the base component that generates deep structures by applying PS rules, as well as rules that take items from the lexicon and insert them into the right places in phrase-markers (PMs) generated by the application of the PS rules. One important point to note here is that in this theory (as opposed to what happens in a phrase-structure grammar), PS rules do not introduce lexical items as they did in example 9. Their work ends with the introduction of lexical categories (N, V, Det, and so on), leading to what are called pre-lexical phrase-markers (i.e. syntactic structures without lexical items). When words/morphemes from the lexicon are already inserted into the phrase-marker (the work of lexical-insertion rules), we have a deep-structure phrase-marker such as 15 below, which shows the deep structure for the sentence *I didn't see my friend* given in 13a.

15

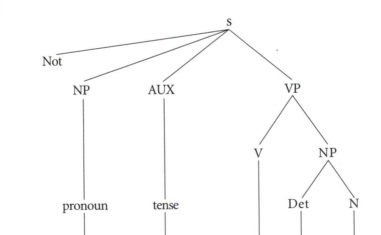

Note that this deep-structure PM is very different from the target sentence 13a. In particular, note that the word *not* is there without its surface bearer, *do*. Since *do* is not semantically significant, and does not have to be there in all sentences, it is introduced later by a transformational rule to perform the syntactic function of supporting *not*, which, in English, cannot be borne by a main verb, such as *see*. *Not* will also need to be placed in its right position by a rule responsible for placing negative morphemes. Note also the independence of auxiliary elements such as tense in the deep structure. In example 15, the tense affix ends up being attached to *do* (which the phonological rules will then interpret as *did*). If there were no auxiliary tense-bearer (such as *do*), the affix would end up attached to the verb *see* (as in *I saw my friend*). So there is quite a bit of work that needs to be done by the transformational component in relating the deep structure to the surface structure. Normally, there is no sentence that can be derived from the deep structure into the surface structure without the application of at least one obligatory transformation, which, at the very least, will place deep-structure affixes in the correct surface-structure positions where they can be interpreted by phonological rules (which will indicate how they should sound in speech). The application of each transformational rule leads to a new (modified) PM that is different from the one before it. The last PM produced by the application of transformational rules is the surface-structure phrase-marker. It forms the input to the phonological component. As mentioned earlier, it is the deep-structure PM that is fed into the semantic component. According to the Standard Theory, transformations do not change meaning (the Katz–Postal hypothesis), so all linguistic elements necessary for the meaning of a sentence must be represented in the deep structure.

Implications for African languages (other than English)

The general theoretical strategies that we have outlined above are capable of giving us fairly satisfactory accounts of sentence structures in African languages outside the Indo-European family. However, certain issues require special attention.

One of these is the deep-structure positions of various affixes, especially in Bantu languages. Consider, for example, the Kiswahili noun phrases (NPs) in 16 and 17 below:

16 Mtu mzuri   ('a good person')
   M-   tu   m-   zuri
   CM   person   CM   good

17 Watu wazuri   ('good people')
    Wa-   tu   wa-   zuri
    CM(pl)-   person   CM(pl)-   good

The class-marking prefixes are properties of the nouns, whose bound roots never occur in speech without prefixes. However, the adjective *mzuri/wazuri* appears with different prefixes depending on the noun it modifies. Thus, in the deep-structure PMs, adjectives and other noun modifiers within an NP will initially appear without the class-marking (or other forms of concordial or agreement) affixes. Such affixes will be acquired by the modifiers through the operation of copying (transformational) rules.

A similar position is adopted for the appearance of class-markers and other elements indicating the subject and object of a sentence around the verb, as in 18:

18 Wageni wanampenda mtoto.   ('The visitors like the child.')
    Wa-geni   wa   na   m   penda   mtoto
    Visitors   CM   tense   CM   like   child

Here the affixes *wa-* and *-m-* represent the subject and object NPs in that order. Such elements cannot be present at the deep-structure level before they are copied from the respective NPs.

A related issue that is also illustrated by 18 is the fact that, given the appropriate context, the verb and its copied affixes can occur in isolation as a complete sentence. Thus, a speaker could simply say, as in 19:

19 Wanampenda.   ('They love him/her.')

One strategy that could be adopted to handle such cases is to assume that such sentences begin in the deep structure with NP positions (subject and/or object) occupied by appropriate lexical items, on whose class and number properties the copying rules are based. We further assume that, after the copying rules have applied to equip the verb with the necessary affixes, the NPs are deleted by a transformational (deletion) rule that applies after the copying rules. The problem with this strategy is that, given that NPs can be very specific in cases such as 18, if such NPs are deleted, they would not be recoverable. This creates problems in terms of accounting for the hearer's perception of the sentence. Generally, there should be a condition that deleted elements in the structure of a sentence should be recoverable without considering the context outside the sentence itself.

This means that we need a different strategy to account for the occurrence of constructions such as the one seen in 19. One less problematic possibility is to assume that the NP positions in the deep structures of such sentences are occupied by non-specific pronominal elements that have all the required grammatical features, but no phonological properties. It is these grammatical features that are copied onto the verb when the copying rules apply. As the NPs are phonologically void, they do not appear in speech. Such an NP would look like 20, for example:

20 NP
$$\begin{bmatrix} + \text{ pronoun} \\ + \text{ class I} \\ + \text{ plural} \end{bmatrix}$$
(etc.)

In addition to the considerations mentioned above, there would be other language-specific problems to be sorted out on a language-to-language basis. However, one general problem we should mention here is the fact that in most African languages, both Bantu and non-Bantu, question words for object NPs are realized (in the surface-structure PMs) in their deep-structure positions. In other words, they are realized *in situ*. Compare, for example, the English sentence in 21a and its Kiswahili equivalent in 21b (the question words are italicized):

21a   *Who(m)* does Yohana like?
21b   Yohana anapenda *nani*?

Note that in 21a, *who(m)* represents the object of *like* and should therefore appear in the object position in the deep structure. Its occurrence in the left position is based on the application of a movement rule. On the other hand, such a movement rule does not apply in the Kiswahili sentence, where *nani* appears exactly where we expect it to be in the deep structure, as the object of *-penda*.

The lesson to be learnt from this example is that when trying to identify the transformations that apply in a given African language, we should not expect them to be exactly the same as those that have been identified in thoroughly studied languages such as English.

The general transformational operations (movement, deletion, insertion, and copying) will apply to varying extents in all human languages, but the specific structural elements affected by their application must be discovered for each language.

Exercise

1   Study the following sentences from Afrikaans, and, using the information supplied, determine the syntactic constituents and their syntactic labels and functions. Also draw a tree diagram in which the structure of sentence (a) is described.
    (a) *Die student lees 'n boek oor linguistiek.* ('The student reads a book about linguistics.')
    (b) *Lees die student 'n boek oor linguistiek?* ('Is the student reading a book about linguistics?')
    (c) *'n Boek oor linguistiek word gelees deur die student.* ('A book about linguistics is being read by the student.')
    (d) *Oor linguistiek lees die student 'n boek.* ('About linguistics the student is reading a book.')

2   Afrikaans and English differ syntactically. Can you identify and describe any of the differences shown in question 1?
3   The field of linguistics includes a discipline known as comparative grammar. Given the information supplied in this chapter, suggest some of the issues that such an area of study would encompass.
4   The Germanic languages (English and Afrikaans, for example) differ from the Bantu languages in a number of ways, some of which are described in this chapter (for example, the absence of noun classes in the Germanic languages, and the absence of rules that copy the class prefixes of nouns onto verbs). Other differences include the absence of lexically distinct articles (*a, the*) in the Bantu languages, the very low frequency of lexically distinct prepositions (*on, under*), and differences in the order of words/syntactic constituents. Do these differences mean that (for example) indefiniteness and definiteness, or the relationship between objects, cannot be expressed in the Bantu languages? Explain your answer.

Endnotes

1   A tree diagram (or phrase marker) is a diagrammatic representation of the structure (see also Chapter 3) of a grammatical construction (a complex word or sentence). It usually specifies the constituents of the construction, the grammatical relationship between them, and their grammatical identity (what they are; determiners, nouns, verbs, and so on).

Bibliography

BACH, EMMON. 1974. *Syntactic Theory.* New York: Holt, Rinehart & Winston, Inc. (Chapters 1–6 in particular).

CHOMSKY, NOAM. 1965. *Aspects of the Theory of Syntax.* Cambridge, Mass.: MIT Press

GLEASON, H.A. 1955, 1961. *An Introduction to Descriptive Linguistics.* New York: Holt, Rinehart & Winston (Chapters 5–14 in particular).

LANGACKER, R.W. 1967, 1968. *Language and its Structure: Some Fundamental Linguistic Concepts.* New York: Harcourt, Brace & New World, Inc. (Chapters 4–5 in particular).

LYONS, JOHN. 1968. *Introduction to Theoretical Linguistics.* Cambridge: Cambridge University Press (Chapters 4–6 in particular).

MOL, FRANS. 1997. *Lessons in Maa: a Grammar of Maasai Language.* Kenya: Maasai Centre Lemek.

PRICE, T. 1966. *The Elements of Nyanja (For English-speaking Students).* Blantyre: The Synod Bookshop.

9 The lexicons of Africa

Danie Prinsloo, Albina R. Chuwa,
and Elsabé Taljard

Expected outcomes

At the end of this chapter you should be able to:

1 Explain what a lexicologist, a lexicographer, and a terminographer are.
2 Argue for and against the view that the lexicons of the Bantu languages reflect the cultural character of their speakers.
3 State the case for the proposition that Bantu languages are not inferior to Western languages with regard to technical terminology.
4 Write a dictionary entry for a nominal and a verbal element from the Bantu languages.
5 Persuade a friend that one can teach nuclear physics in any Bantu language.
6 Defend the usefulness of dictionaries and the work done by lexicographers.
7 Indicate how a dictionary can contribute to the standardization of a language.
8 Provide a critical overview of the available dictionaries in the main language of your interest.

Introduction

The aim of this chapter is to introduce various aspects of the notion of the lexicon. It stands to reason that it is not possible to discuss these aspects in detail within a single chapter, but we will nevertheless attempt to touch upon the most relevant issues, such as the history, nature, and structure of the lexicon, orthographic traditions, dictionary compilation, word creation and borrowing, and so on.

The term **lexicon** refers to the vocabulary of a specific language or person, or it can simply mean a dictionary. When we talk about dictionaries, several terms come to mind that require a brief explanation, namely lexicology, lexicography, and terminography.

Lexicology has as its aim the study of the lexicon. This includes a great variety of linguistic aspects. A lexicologist studies the theoretical aspects of the vocabulary of a language.

Lexicography is often defined as the art, craft, or science of compiling dictionaries. Compared to lexicology, we could thus say that, while the latter deals with the more theoretical aspects of the lexicon, the aim of lexicography and its practitioner, the lexicographer, is to compile actual dictionaries.

Terminography is the study of technical terms, or terms used in a particular field of study (such as linguistics, which has terms such as *noun*, *verb*, and *adjective*) or a trade, such as a carpentry or masonry.

Task and question

1 Make a list of published dictionaries that deal with your language.
2 Is there any official committee working on technical terminology in the country in which you live? If so, find out the details.

The structure of the lexicon

A question often asked by linguists is whether the lexicon of a language is structured in one particular way or another. In principle, it seems that the answer to this question is 'no'. A lexicon is not structured in the same way as words and sentences, which display an internal structure. Any structure that is ascribed to a lexicon is to a large extent arbitrary, and depends on the point of view from which that lexicon is studied. If the lexicon is studied from a linguistic point of view, it could be argued that lexical items should be categorized into linguistic categories, such as nouns, verbs, adjectives, and so forth. (See the discussion on the classification of nouns and verbs in Sepedi and Kiswahili below.)

If the emphasis is on the study of vocabulary, lexical items can be classified in a number of ways, for example into items with a high frequency of use or a low frequency of use, or as items that belong to the core vocabulary or to the peripheral vocabulary. Lexical items can also be thematically categorized, for example into groups of words referring to deities, the universe, humanity, and so on. And if the lexicon is studied from an etymological point of view, items can then be classified in terms of their origin: whether they represent borrowings from other languages, whether they have been inherited from a parent language, or whether they represent creations within the language itself.

Questions

1 Using any dictionary as an example, determine its organizing principle. How are the entries (words) arranged in the dictionary? Is a linguistic principle used? Give reasons for your answer.
2 What is a thesaurus? How does it differ from a dictionary?
3 Dictionaries of antonyms and synonyms have also been published. What do these tell us about the linguistic character of a language?
4 How can the frequency of use of the words of a language be determined?
5 What linguistic basis for a distinction between core and peripheral vocabulary items could be used?
6 Make a list of ten words that your language has borrowed from another language; ten that were created afresh (called neologisms); and ten that were inherited from previous generations of speakers of the language. Study these three sets of words carefully, and try to find the linguistic logic behind these three origins of the lexicon of the language.

A brief history of the lexicons of the Bantu languages

When compared with the ex-colonial languages, any study of the history of the lexicons of the Bantu languages is at a disadvantage. Linguists who wish to investigate the history of these languages do not have adequate historical texts, in which earlier forms of these languages were recorded, at their disposal. Another strategy therefore needs to be found, and the one often used is historical reconstruction. As the structural similarities of the Bantu languages clearly presuppose a common ancestor language, the linguist can make a hypothetical reconstruction of such a language. This can be done by making a synchronic[1] comparison of existing Bantu languages.

The two most important reconstructions of the proto-language (or ancestor language) of the Bantu languages are those of Carl Meinhof and Malcolm Guthrie. Meinhof produced what is called *Ur-Bantu*, and Guthrie what is called *Proto-Bantu*. These two 'proto-languages' are not languages in the literal sense of the word; instead, they represent a reconstruction of the most common features of the Bantu languages. The basic premise is that every Bantu language developed from the ancestor language by means of regular sound shifts. Very little information is available concerning the nature of the lexicon of the ancestor language, as both reconstructions are of a mostly phonological nature. The only way in which lexical items can be reconstructed is by making use of the phenomenon of sound shift. Compare the following lexical items that were listed by Meinhof (1932: 223, 221) with their equivalents in some modern Bantu languages:

Ur-Bantu		tatu ('three')	ma-ta ('saliva')
Modern Bantu:	Sepedi	-raro	ma-re
	Kiswahili	-tatu	ma-te
	Konde	-thathu	ama-tha
	isiZulu	-thathu	ama-the
	Otjiherero	-tatu	ma-nte

We shall return to the issue of historical change below when we look at the categorization of nouns in the Bantu languages.

Cultural characterization of lexicons

The cultural heritage of the Bantu-speaking people of South Africa is reflected in their lexicon. For example, it is characterized by a large number of terms connected to animal husbandry. An extended system of colour terms is used to refer to the colour of cattle. A few Sepedi examples are the following (Mönnig 1978: 169):

Bulls and oxen	Cows	English
khulong	nakhulwana	red
ntsho	naswana	black
nala	nalana	red with a few white marks
hlaba	nahlabana	red with brown spots
tšumu	natšungwana	red with white mark on face

There are also various names for differences in the build of the animals and particularly for different shapes of horns.

The importance of the extended family is also reflected in the system of kinship terms. Kinship terms are highly specific – each term refers to a particular individual. Consider these examples from Sepedi:

malome	('maternal uncle')
rakgadi	('father's elder sister')
rangwane	('father's younger brother')
rakgolo	('father's elder brother')
mmane	('father's younger sister')

Traditional religion has also contributed many distinctive items to the lexicon. Ancestor worship formed a central part of traditional religion, so many specialized terms are associated with ancestral worship and divination. The terms *ngaka*, *lephala*, and *sedupe* all refer to persons involved in divination, but each has a specialized function. The *ngaka* is the traditional doctor who specializes in healing and protection. He or she is the only one who uses *ditaola* or *dikgagara* ('divining bones'). *Lephala* is a prophet who divines through direct spiritual contact with the ancestral spirits, whereas *sedupe* usually refers to a soothsayer or sorcerer.

Rites of passage are also an important part of the social structure of the Bantu-speaking people. Initiation schools are still very much part of African rural life, and the culture of Sotho-speaking people (among others) living in rural areas. Lexical items connected with these rituals have specialized meanings, and their usage is restricted to circumstances connected to these rituals. As young boys go through the different stages of the initiation process, different terms are used to indicate their status. Young boys are known in Sepedi as *bašemane* ('boys'), but as soon as the elders are of the opinion that they are ready to enter the initiation school, they are called *mašoboro* ('uninitiated boys'). After circumcision, the initiates are called *badikana*. When the initiation session is drawing to a close, the ones having survived are called *dialogane* ('survivors'). After having been received by the men in the *kgoro*, the initiated boys are known as *banna* ('men').

Continued urbanization is causing many of these culturally related terms to fall into disuse. It is interesting to note that many of these so-called traditional terms are used to refer to modern concepts. One example is that of *dialoga(ne)*, a term now used to refer those who have graduated from a university.

Questions

1 Ritual language is found in all communities, and even Western urban communities have their rites of passage (rituals that mark transitions such as the passage into adulthood, marriage, birth, death, and so on). Does this type of language play any role in the linguistic lives of the communities that use them?

2 Can you give examples of words that are typically used by rural members of your linguistic community, but not by urban members? Why did they get lost?

3 What about the converse – words typical of urban centres, but not of rural contexts? Also, think of words used in both contexts, but with differences of meaning or association. Supply examples and then analyse them.

4 What does it mean when the vocabulary of a community changes? Is it a good thing, or a sign of degeneration? Is it a sign that people are losing their culture? If so, is losing one's culture a bad thing?

Structuring of lexicons in terms of dialects

Lexicons can also be structured in terms of dialectal variation. Differences between dialects can be found at any level of the grammar, including the lexical level. Continued standardization of languages such as Sepedi (which has twenty-three dialects) is diminishing lexical variation in languages, with the lexical terms of the standard variety becoming dominant, while those of the dialects are marginalized (used less than before). As indicated in earlier chapters, the standard variety of a language has great power.

When dialectal forms are entered into a dictionary, they are labelled as dialectal or non-standard. It is only since the work of the American sociolinguist William Labov, and his colleagues, that linguists are acknowledging that, in spite of their non-standard label, dialect forms are not inferior to standard forms. A few examples of lexical variation in Sepedi dialects are as follows:

Standard Sepedi		*Dialectal form*
bolela	('speak')	apa
lehono	('today')	nase
dula	('sit down')	nna
šikara	('carry on shoulders')	atha

Questions

1 Can you give similar examples from the languages that you know?
2 There are many labels used in dictionary entries (such as dialectal and non-standard). Page through any dictionary and make a list of at least five such labels.
3 It is clear that dictionaries have significant linguistic power; they can influence readers' attitudes to their languages, making them negative about certain ways of speaking and positive about others. Is this a good or a bad thing?
4 Is it important to protect linguistic diversity? (See Chapters 1, 2, and 3.)

Structuring of lexicons in terms of social groups

Marked differences seem to exist between the lexicons of social groups within a specific speech community. In the case of Sepedi, a clear distinction can be made between the lexicons of speakers living in a more traditional rural environment and those living in urban areas. These differences probably result from contact with speakers of other languages in the urban areas, as well as extensive contact with Western culture and concepts. According to mother-tongue speakers, the differences in the lexicons of these two language varieties are already influencing mutual intelligibility. Due to the pressure to communicate effectively in a culturally and linguistically diverse urban community, speakers of Sepedi have developed a type of lingua franca known as Setoropo (which translates as 'language of the town[ship]'). This language is based on Sepedi and Setswana, but has been heavily influenced by English and (to a lesser extent) Afrikaans. Setoropo (also known as Pretoria Sotho) is characterized by extensive borrowing and adaptation of lexical items from other languages. In many cases, these borrowings are not used to refer to new concepts, but are used to replace the standard item. Here are some examples:

Standard term	Pretoria Sotho	
-bina ('dance')	-dans	(<Afr/Eng dans/dance)
serapa ('garden')	khadene	(<Eng garden)
bjalwa ('beer')	piri	(<Afr/Eng bier/beer)
tsela ('road')	pata	(<Afr pad)

Another variety spoken in the townships in South Africa is Tsotsitaal/Setsotsi ('tsotsi' language), generally used by youths in the townships. The lexical differences between standard Sepedi and Setsotsi are so marked that a person who is not a member of the latter social group is automatically excluded from conversations between members.

Questions

1   Debate the following statement: 'the way that city people speak a language is really degenerate.' (See Chapters 2, 3, and 7.)
2   Is it true that urban varieties are difficult to understand by rural members of the same linguistic community? If so, why? Is this problem linguistic in nature (in other words, caused by differences in words, pronunciation, and grammar)? Or is it social (and subjective) by nature? To what extent does it reflect an attitude? (Remember that the English spoken by communities in Britain and the USA differs quite significantly, and yet their speakers can understand one another.)

Categorization of nouns and verbs in the Bantu languages

In this section, the sub-categorization of the nouns and verbs of the Bantu languages will be discussed. This topic is actually more central to morphology and syntax (Chapter 8, see p. 202), but is nevertheless discussed here because it sheds light on the history of Bantu lexicons, and because it has direct relevance to lexicography, as will be demonstrated later.

One of the most notable characteristics of the lexicons of the Bantu languages is the classification or subdivision of nouns into different classes. Noun class systems of the various Bantu languages can easily be compared, as they reveal a remarkable similarity. The same holds true for verbs. Compare, for example, Sepedi and Kiswahili in the section below.

The noun class system

Nouns are subdivided into different classes, each with its own class prefix.

Sepedi

Class no.	Class prefix	Examples
1	mo-	monna ('man') mosadi ('woman') motho ('human being') morutiši ('teacher')
2	ba-	banna ('men')
3	mo-	monwana ('finger')
4	me-	menwana ('fingers')
5	le-	lesogana ('young man') leoto ('foot') lerato ('love') leihlo ('eye')
6	ma-	masogana ('young men')
7	se-	selepe ('axe')
8	di-	dilepe ('axes')
9	n-	nku ('sheep') kgoši ('king') tafola ('table')
10	di-	dinku ('sheep')
14	bo-	bogobe ('porridge')
15	go	go sepela ('to walk')
16	fa-	fase ('below')
17	go-	godimo ('above')
18	mo-	morago ('behind')

Kiswahili

Class no.	Class prefix	Examples
1	m-	mwanaume ('man') mwanamke ('woman') mtu ('human being')
2	wa-	wanaume ('men') wanawake ('women') watu ('human beings')
3	m-	mti ('tree') mhogo ('cassava') mkono ('arm'/'hand')
4	mi-	miti ('trees') mihogo ('cassava' pl.) mikono ('arms'/'hands')
5	ji/-	jicho ('eye') jambo ('matter') shamba ('farm')
6	ma-	macho ('eyes') mambo ('matters') mashamba ('farms')
7	ki-/ch-	kitu ('thing') kiti ('chair') chakula ('food')
8	vi-/vy-	vitu ('things') viti ('chairs') vyakula ('foods')
9	n-/-	ngoma ('drum') nyoka ('snake') meza ('table')
10	n-/-	ngoma ('drums') nyoka ('snakes') meza ('tables')
11/14	u-	ukuta ('wall') uji ('porridge') ushanga ('bead')
10	n-/-	kuta ('walls') uji ('porridge') shanga ('beads')
15	ku-	kucheza ('to play') kutembea ('to walk') kula ('to eat')
16	pa-	pale ('there')
17	ku-	kule ('over there')
18	m(u)	m(u)le ('inside there')

Historical changes in the noun class system

From the examples above, it is clear that classes 1 and 2 in Sepedi contain human beings only. We could call this a one-to-one relation between class and semantic content. However, most of the other noun classes contain words with unrelated meanings (for example, class 9, which contains human beings, animals, and objects). The linguist Talmy Givon hypothesized that all noun classes originally showed a one-to-one correlation between class and meaning:

class 3/4	plants
class 5/6	fruits
class 6	liquids
class 7/8	inanimates
class 9/10	animals
class 11/10	elongated objects
class 12/13	small objects
class 14	masses

class 15   infinite nominalizations
class 15 /6   paired body parts
(Givon 1971: 33)

According to Givon's hypothesis, there was no separate class for human beings. He grouped human beings and animals together in what is today numbered as class 9 for Sepedi.

Different grammarians have classified Kiswahili noun classes in different ways. Some have used morphological criteria (based on the noun prefix), while others have used syntactic criteria (classifying them according to either adjectival or pronominal prefixes). Those who use morphological criteria also differ; some identify the nouns by numbers, others refer to them by their nominal prefixes, and still others use both numbers and prefixes. Those who use numbers also differ. Some recognize only eight classes (by grouping the singular and the plural forms together as belonging to one class). Others separate the singular from the plural forms, thus ending up with eighteen classes. The classification presented above has followed the eighteen number system, plus the noun prefixes often found in the more user-friendly grammar books.

The description of the Kiswahili noun classes is based on Ashton (1944), Steere (1955), Kapinga (1983), Safari (1980), Mbaabu (1992), Mgullu (1990), and Kihore (1995).[2] They all agree as to what falls in the first two and the last two classes. The order of the middle classes, however, is still a controversial issue, which is why we refer to them by their noun prefixes. The M-/Wa- class contains nouns of living things (human beings, animals, birds, insects, and snakes). Nouns belonging to this class are also found in other noun classes, although syntactically they will have similar pronominal and adjectival prefixes. The M-/Mi- class contains nouns of plants and trees, non-living things, some parts of the body, and some nominalized verbs. An example of a human noun found in this class is mtume/mitume ('prophet/s'). The Ji-/Ma- class covers names of parts of the body that come in pairs or in sets, parts of trees, and nouns showing the state of things. Human nouns found in this class include examples such as jambazi/majambazi ('armed robber/s'). Some nouns in this class appear only in the plural form, such as maji ('water') and maziwa ('milk'). The Ki-/Vi- class also features nouns with Ch-/Vy- prefixes. This class includes nouns of non-living things, but also nouns of individuals suffering disability, such as kipofu/vipofu ('blind person/s'), and people with certain titles, such as kiongozi/viongozi ('leader/s'). The N- class, although designated by this sound, also contains nouns beginning with other consonants. The main characteristic of this class is that there is no difference between the singular and the plural forms of the nouns. It features nouns of common objects, some animals, and many of the borrowed nouns. Most of the kinship terms are also found in this class (baba 'father/s', dada 'sister/s'). The U- class contains mostly abstract nouns, or nouns of single items or particles of the whole mass. The *Ku-* class contains nouns created from verbs that use the prefix indicating the infinitive marker to express the act of doing, becoming, or the state of being. The last class is the *MAHALI* (*place*) class. It has three different prefixes: *Pa-* (referring to an exact place), *Ku-* (indicating a general place), and *M(u)-* (indicating 'inside something').

Verbs

Two aspects of verbs will be emphasized here: (a) the complex system of verbal derivation; and (b) the categorization of verbs into different moods.

Verbs are derived by adding a suffix or a combination of suffixes to a verb root, thus rendering numerous derivations from a single verb (see Chapter 8). These suffixes are often described by means of very specific terms, such as causative (the action is caused by somebody), reciprocal (the action is mutual), applicative (the action is done for somebody), and so on.

Consider a few examples from Sepedi in this regard:

aga	build		
agiša	**cause** to build	(-ag-+-iš-)	(causative suffix)
agela	build **for/on behalf of**	(-ag-+-el-)	(applicative suffix)
agile	**built**	(-ag-+-il-)	(perfect)
agilwe	**is/was built**	(-ag-+-il-+-w-)	(perfect + passive)

The same holds true for Kiswahili. The Kiswahili verbal derivational system is made up of a verb root plus five derivational suffixes and one prefix *ji-* (self). The five suffixes represent the applicative (*-ia/-ea*), the reciprocal (*-ana*), the stative and potential (*-ka*), the causative (*-isha/za*), and the passive (*-wa*). From one root, we get the primary and the secondary derivation; the latter is a second derivation based on the verbs already derived.

Nouns can also be created either from the root or from the derived verbs. Some of the derivations create words with different meanings (marked with the sign +) from those reflected in the original root, as can be seen in the examples below:

piga ('hit'/'strike')
pigia , +pigilia ('pound into'), pigiana, +pigilisha, pigiwa (+ applicative)
pigana, pigania, piganika, piganisha, piganwa (+ reciprocal)
pigisha, pigishia, pigishana, pigishika, pigishwa (+ causative)

Verbs are also categorized into different moods; compare Sepedi and Kiswahili once more.

Moods

Mood	Tense	Example
1 Indicative	Imperfect	**mosadi ga a šome (Sepedi)** *mwanamke hafanyi kazi (Kiswahili)* the woman does not work
2 Situative	Imperfect	**[ge] monna a sa rate mpša** *[je] kama mwanamume hampendi mbwa huyo* if the man does not like the dog
3 Relative	Imperfect	**monna yo a sa ratego mpša** *mwanamume asiyempenda mbwa huyo* the man who does not like the dog
4 Subjunctive		**[gore] monna a ratê mpša** (positive) *[ili] mwanamume ampende mbwa huyo* so that the man will like the dog **[gore] monna a se ratê mpša** *[ili] mwanamume asimpende mbwa huyo* so that the man will not like the dog
5 Consecutive		**monna a se ratê mpša** *na kisha mwanamume hakumpenda mbwa huyo* and then the man did not like the dog
6 Infinitive		**go se bolêlê Sesotho** *sio kusema Kisotho* not to speak Sesotho
7 Imperative		**mo thušê!** (positive) *msaidie!* help him! **se thušê mosadi!** *usimsaidie mwanamke huyo* do not help the woman!

8   Habitual

monna a bolêle Sesotho
kwa kawaida mwanamume huyo
huzungumza Kisotho
the man usually speaks Sesotho
monna a se bolêle Sesotho
kwa kawaida mwanamume huyo
hazungumzi Kisotho
the man does not usually speak Sesotho.

Words, word creation, and borrowing

The lexicons of Bantu languages contain and are expanded by means of a substantial number of derivations, borrowings, and coinages (creation of new words – neologisms). The areas most affected are trade, commerce, and modern technology. Efforts to create terminology for the Bantu languages vary from one linguistic community to the next, as well as according to the specific needs these communities have for such vocabulary expansions. Obviously, the Bantu languages are in no sense of the word inferior to other languages (including the ex-colonial ones) in terms of high-function usage, and have the same potential for expressing even very technical concepts.

The Bantu languages, firstly, contain many words that are regarded as original or non-derived forms. See, for example:

Sepedi
mosadi ('woman'); monna ('man'); leru ('cloud')
Kiswahili
mtu ('person'); mwanamke ('woman'); mwanamume ('man'); wingu ('cloud')

Secondly, they contain words (usually nouns) derived from verbs. See, for example:

Sepedi
moagi ('builder' – from aga 'to build')
Kiswahili
mjenzi ('builder' – from jenga 'to build'); msemaji ('speaker' – from sema 'to speak'); mkulima ('farmer' – from lima 'to farm'); mpishi ('cook' – from pika 'to cook')

Thirdly, they contain borrowed words. See, for example:

Sepedi
radio ('radio'); Aids ('Aids')
Kiswahili
data ('data')

The above are examples of words borrowed from English without any changes. In most cases, however, borrowed words are adapted to the morphological structure of the language by adding, among others, a noun class prefix and changing the syllable structure to the typical CV-syllable (consonant + vowel), with the final syllable ending on a vowel. See, for example:

Sepedi
moprofesa (from 'professor'); Matshe (from 'March'); Desemere (from 'December'); keramafomo (from 'gramophone'); pene (from 'pen')
Kiswahili
pini (from 'pin'); shati (from 'shirt'); supu (from 'soup'); sosi (from 'sauce'); silinda (from 'cylinder'); zoni (from 'zone'); saksafoni (from 'saxophone')

Fourthly, they contain coined words and compounds. See, for example:

Sepedi
molongwana ('a little mouth' for 'nozzle')
bekepedi ('weeks-two' for 'fortnight')
modulasetulo ('one who sits in the chair' for 'chairman')
Kiswahili
mwenyekiti (mwenye = who has + kiti = chair, for 'chairman')
kionjamchuzi (ki+onja = that tastes + mchuzi = stew, for 'chin beard')

Finally, they contain multiple-word expressions. See, for example:

Sepedi
jago tsohle ('that eats everything' for 'omnivorous')
kgwele ya diatla ('game of the hands' for 'netball')
Kiswahili
mteka nyara (m+teka = one who captures + nyara = loot, for 'kidnapper')
(n) zana za mvuvi (zana = equipment + za = of + mvuvi = fisherman, for 'tackle')

Questions

1 Many languages borrow technical terms from other languages without any concern for the integrity of their language. English, for example, borrowed freely from Greek and Latin. Other linguistic communities are opposed to such borrowings, arguing that the 'purity' of their languages (and indeed the future of their languages) is threatened by such borrowings. The (white) speakers of Afrikaans in South Africa were often unwilling to borrow any words from English, even though they were less concerned about borrowings from German or French. And the French are today strongly opposed to borrowings from English. Why is this? Can borrowings really undermine the future of a language? Was English ever under threat?

2 What do you think about your language importing words for technical purposes (such as *jazz, rock music, computer, screen, keyboard,* and *printer*) from English?

3 Have you encountered the following statement? 'Mother-tongue speakers of the African languages do not have the will to fully develop their languages in the technical fields, but prefer to use the terminology of languages such as English or French.' What is your opinion?

(Lexical) Semantics

An important topic in dealing with the lexicon of a language is the question of meaning. The study of meaning is called **semantics**.

One of the first tasks in semantics is to define the meaning of lexical items. A **lexical item** is a linguistic symbol that is used to refer to some entity in the real world via an intermediary mental concept. In semantics, it has become common practice to explain the relationship between the notions lexical item, mental concept, and the real world entity by means of a triangle:

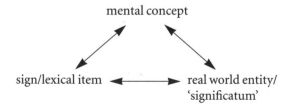

mental concept

sign/lexical item ⟷ real world entity/ 'significatum'

Different types of meaning can be distinguished, each of which has to be separately defined. Two main types are conceptual meaning and associative meaning.

Conceptual meaning refers to the basic or core meaning of a lexical item. Componential analysis is used to define the conceptual meaning of lexical items. According to this method, the meaning of a word is broken down into its smallest semantic components (see below). The presence of a particular component is indicated by a plus (+) sign, whereas its absence is marked by a minus (–) sign. The aim of componential analysis is to provide a componential definition of a lexical item in such a way as to distinguish it from all other lexical items in the lexicon. Compare the following examples:

woman: [+human], [+adult], [–male]
girl: [+human], [–adult], [–male]

Whereas conceptual meaning is defined without any reference to the attitude of the speaker towards the utterance, **associative meaning** 'refers to all those associations and connotations which each individual speaker calls to mind when he or she hears a word. These associations are said to be subjective, as they are determined by each language user's personal background and real life experiences' (Louwrens 1994: 15). It is therefore often said that associative meaning is open-ended, as it varies from individual to individual. The Sepedi lexical term *lephodisa* has a basic meaning that can be defined as 'a member of a government department responsible for maintaining public order by enforcing the laws of the country' (or more briefly, 'police'). However, different speakers may attach different connotations to this word over and above its basic meaning, some of which might be negative or positive, depending on the speaker's real-life experience.

Semantic relations between lexical items

The lexicon of a language forms an integrated system in which lexical items are semantically related to one another in a variety of ways. (See also the discussion at the beginning of this chapter.) These relationships between words are generally referred to as 'sense relations'.

Synonymy

Synonymy as a sense relation is usually defined as 'lexical items having the same meaning'. Linguists such as Palmer (1976: 89) question the existence of true synonyms, stating that no two words can have exactly the same meaning.

When pairs of lexical items that are superficially judged to be synonymous are investigated, it is often found that these words are not really synonymous after all. According to Palmer, there are at least five ways in which possible synonyms can differ. Four of these are given below.

Differences between dialects

It often happens that lexical items seem to have the same meaning, but that the reason for this apparent sameness of meaning is that they belong to different dialects. In standard Sepedi, the lexical item *lehono* means 'today', but in the Tlokwa dialect, this item appears as *nase*. The reason for the synonymy is that the two lexical items belong to different dialects and can thus not be regarded as representing synonymy in the true sense of the word.

Differences in styles or speech registers

According to Louwrens (1991: 162), a speaker may use different synonymous lexical items, depending on his or her style of communication. For example, a Sepedi-speaker may use any of the following lexical items (all having the meaning 'to pay'), *lefa, patela, putsa,* and *ntšha tšhelete,* depending on the style of communication which they are using. However, it is not always possible to decide whether the different lexical items are style-related or whether they belong to different dialects. Louwrens furthermore points out that speech registers play an important role in the Bantu languages. Examples of speech registers are the 'hlonipha' language (a language of respect used by isiZulu- and isiXhosa-speakers), 'tsotsi' languages (used by teenagers living in urban areas), and the languages used in initiation schools. Examples from the language used in Sepedi initiation schools are *dithamaga* (in standard Sepedi, *dipudi* 'goats') and *kgeetla* (in standard Sepedi, *meetse* 'water'). These examples can be regarded as stylistic synonyms.

Differences in emotive value

Members of pairs of lexical items may have the same basic meaning but differ in their emotive meaning or content. In Sepedi, the pairs *bjalwa : bodilana* ('beer') and *kgarebe : tshehlana* ('young girl') do not represent true synonyms, due to the difference in their emotive meaning.

Differences in collocational restrictions

Palmer (1976: 91) points out that some words are collocationally restricted; this means that they occur only in combination with specific words. In Sepedi, the verbs *-apara, -tšwara,* and *-rwala* all refer to the wearing of clothes, but *-apara* refers to the wearing of clothes on the upper body only, *-tšwara* refers to the wearing of clothes on the lower body, and -*rwala* refers to the wearing of a hat or shoes.

True synonymy therefore does not seem to exist, and the term **approximate synonym** may be a more appropriate way to describe the lexical pairs listed above (Louwrens 1991: 163).

Antonymy

A second sense relation is that of **antonymy**. This is generally defined as opposition in meaning between lexical items, although many linguists consider this an oversimplification, as words may oppose each other in many different ways. In order to qualify as antonyms, lexical pairs must in fact have a great deal in common as far as their semantic content is concerned. This explains why the lexical pair *dog : computer* cannot be regarded as antonyms. Different kinds of antonymous relationships have been distinguished. Here we have space only to mention two types.

Ungradable versus gradable antonyms

In the case of ungradable antonyms, the opposition between two lexical items is absolute, with no continuous scale running between the two polar extremes. As Louwrens (1991: 158) points out, the Sepedi items -*phela* ('live') and -*hwile* ('be dead') should be regarded as ungradable antonyms, as no degrees of being dead or being alive can be distinguished. The items -*golo* ('big') and -*nyane* ('small'), however, are regarded as gradable, as it is possible to distinguish different degrees of bigness or smallness.

Morphologically related versus morphologically unrelated antonyms

When one member of a lexical pair is morphologically derived from the other member, the two lexical items are said to be morphologically related. Sepedi examples are: -*tšhela* ('pour in') : -*tšholla* ('pour out'), -*reka* ('buy') : -*rekiša* ('sell'), *kgoši* ('chief') : *kgošigadi* ('female chief'). In all these cases, the second member of the pair has been morphologically derived from the first member. In other cases, no morphological relationship exists between members of the lexical pair; see, for example, *letšatši* ('day') : *bošego* ('night'), *fase* ('underneath'): *godimo* ('on top').

Polysemy

Polysemy is a third type of sense relation. It can be defined as one lexical item that has two or more related meanings. The Sepedi item *letlakala* can refer to a leaf or a page, *hlogo* has the meaning 'head (body part)', 'principal of a school', or 'locomotive of a train'. These meanings are all related to one another. Polysemy is regarded as the broadening or expansion of the basic meaning of a lexical item in order to name new or foreign objects. Compare the following examples: *lebala* ('open plain') : *lebala* ('sports field'), *letlapa* ('stone') : *letlapa* ('blackboard').

Homonymy

Polysemy as a sense relation is often linked to **homonymy**, which refers to two or more lexical items with identical forms, but unrelated meanings. Examples from Sepedi are *pela* ('rock rabbit', 'dassie'), *pela* ('xylophone'), and *pela* ('quickly'). Even though the definitions of polysemy and homonymy given here seem to be quite clear, it is often difficult to decide whether the relation between forms is one of polysemy or homonymy. In the case of polysemy, the criterion usually applied is that of relatedness of meaning. However, linguists such as Lyons (1977) are doubtful as to whether this criterion is reliable enough to identify all instances of polysemy. According to Lyons, 'related meanings which were originally associated with the same form can drift so far apart during the course of time that it later becomes impossible to determine whether they have developed from the same core meaning or not' (Louwrens 1991: 164).

From the above, it is clear that the lexicon of a language forms an intricate system in which all the lexical items are interconnected. It is only by scrutinizing this semantic interconnectedness that sense relations such as synonymy, antonymy, and polysemy can be distinguished.

The role and function of dictionaries

> A dictionary is probably the single most important reference book that a student can buy. (Introduction, *New Student's Dictionary*)

The classification or categorization of dictionaries in general is a complex issue and lies beyond the scope of this chapter. Refer to Gouws (1989: 55) for a more detailed analysis of the different approaches to the classification of dictionaries. We will present a greatly simplified view here. To begin with, a primary distinction can be made between monolingual and bilingual dictionaries. In monolingual dictionaries, the meaning of a word is explained by means of a definition and examples. See, for example, the extract below, taken from the *New Student's Dictionary:*

> **die...** When people, animals or plants **die**, they stop living. *My mother died of cancer.*

In a bilingual dictionary, words are not explained. Instead, one or more translation equivalents in the other language are supplied. See, for example, this extract from the *New Sepedi Dictionary*:

Die   *hwa, hlokafala.*

In modern lexicography, the emphasis is on the compilation of user-friendly dictionaries. Increasingly, dictionaries are being judged on how easy or hard it is for the user to find the meaning of a word. Lexicographers increasingly strive to anticipate and supply the information most likely to be looked for by their target users. This is especially the case in learners' dictionaries. Such dictionaries are designed for specifically defined target users, such as primary-school pupils, secondary-school pupils, or students, and are very much in demand.

> One of the primary purposes of a learner's dictionary is to provide information about those words that the user already 'knows', as well as to provide information that the user does not know. Many words have several uses and meanings, and we do not really 'know' a word until we are familiar with its full range of meaning and grammatical behaviour. (Introduction, *New Student's Dictionary*)

In general, dictionaries are also becoming more descriptive (in other words, they describe the actual usage of the language) rather than being prescriptive (prescribing how words should be used). For languages that are not yet standardized, or that do not have an established lexicographic tradition, a more prescriptive or normative approach is required. This is the case for many African languages.

Although dictionaries are readily available for many African languages, lexicographers agree that they often lack proper lexicographical planning:

> the majority of dictionaries for African languages are the products of limited efforts not reflecting a high standard of lexicographical achievement ... with a few exceptions these dictionaries offer only restricted translating equivalents and reflect a complete lack of lexicographical planning. (Gouws 1990: 55)

Mbogho (1985: 152) adds that certain technical procedures should be followed by future lexicographers, using phrases such as the following:

> bilingual lexicography seems to be developing without any basic theory ...
> the inefficiency of Bantu bilingual lexicography ...
> the basic methodological principles for compiling bilingual dictionaries were largely unknown or overlooked ...

African bilingual lexicography is still in its infancy ...
one way of promoting African languages is to apply several methodological principles that are tailored to the needs of the users of bilingual dictionaries involving Bantu languages ...

Lexicographic work in Africa has been criticized for its so-called 'Euro-centred' or Eurocentric approach:

Until recently most lexicographical publications have been 'Euro-centred' in the sense that they have been primarily intended for use by Europeans who wish to learn the African languages ... (Awak 1990: 15)

... these dictionaries are less informative for the African language speakers ... (Busane 1990: 20)

This criticism is often directed specifically at bilingual dictionaries, with the implication that these dictionaries are produced solely for the benefit of the *learners* of African languages, thus stigmatizing these dictionaries. However, like monolingual dictionaries, they also serve the interests of mother-tongue speakers of the African languages.

Complexity

The complexity of the nominal and verbal systems of the African languages has been demonstrated in earlier sections. Linguistic analyses of verbs and nouns are indispensable for the dictionary compiler. For the lexicographer, however, linguistic analysis is not an end, but a beginning. For example, linguists can tell us that nouns are subdivided or sub-grouped into more or less fifteen classes (in Sepedi, for instance) on the basis of commonly shared class prefixes (such as *mo-, ba-, se-, di-*, and so on). They can also tell us that nouns in classes 1, 3, 5, 7, and 9 are singular, that those in 2, 4, 6, 8, and 10 are plural, and that there are exceptions or irregular forms (such as *meno* and *meetse*, which actually belong to class 6 and not class 4). They will also point out the different sound changes that occur. This is their main task. However, here is where the lexicographer's work begins. Apart from having to note the analyses of the noun class system, he or she has to design strategies for entering nouns into a dictionary. The lexicographer asks questions such as, 'Am I going to **lemmatize** (write a dictionary entry) for singular and plural forms or only for singular forms?' 'What about the irregular forms?' If they follow one strategy, their dictionary may be reader-friendly, but contain too much information (thus becoming too unwieldy and expensive), whereas another strategy might result in a slimmer and cheaper, but less user-friendly, dictionary.

The same holds true for all the verbal derivations illustrated for Sepedi and Kiswahili above. Linguists meticulously analyse the complex system of verbal derivations, but this important work is once again merely the departure point for the lexicographer. Linguists describe the modifications that verbs can undergo. For instance, Kiswahili can have at least seven: the root, the applicative form, the reciprocal form, the stative/potential form, the causative form, the passive form, and the reflexive form. In a Kiswahili dictionary entry for a verb, the last item of that lemma will be the derivational suffixes, which are usually entered in the form ~ia, ~ana, ~ika, ~isha, and ~wa. Any derivational form with an extra meaning, or a meaning deviating from that of the basic verbal form, is entered again as an independent lemma, possibly featuring the derivational suffixes that apply to it.

Lexicographers have tried various approaches to handling these complex systems. Their efforts can be broadly classified into the following three methods.

Traditional method

The most basic and frequently used method is the one in which lexicographers enter words into their dictionaries as they encounter them. One disadvantage of this method is that important words are left out, simply because the compiler (as one honestly admitted) did not come across them. The other side of this coin is that words that might not be of use to a target user are nonetheless added to a dictionary. The kind of dictionary that results is often no more than a glorified list of translated words.

The 'enter-them-all' syndrome

This approach is manifested in one of two ways. In the first instance, lexicographers try to enter all the derivations of verbs in the dictionary. This is achieved by lemmatizing the stem and adding all the derivations. Such compilers often concentrate so hard on the inclusion of all the nominal or verbal forms that they do not define their meanings adequately or give adequate translation equivalents in another language. Alternatively, they try the 'enter-them-all' approach by entering only the stem with a definition or with translation equivalents. A complex list of all the derivations and their many rules is then given in the guidelines to the dictionary. The user who wants to find the meaning of a word containing a suffix or combinations of suffixes is forced to first disentangle these derived forms in order to isolate the stem, and so to find the meaning of the word.

The frequency-of-use approach

The selection of words to be included or omitted can also be based on frequency of use. This method has great advantages, especially when difficult decisions have to be made about which words should be entered and which left out. Today, frequency-of-use methods usually rely on the aid of computers.

The computer and dictionary compilation

Computers are very useful instruments in lexicographical work, and can be used in a number of ways. Here we list three examples of their use in the compilation of dictionaries.

1 Computers are helpful as instruments for the calculation of word frequency and the distribution of the words of a language in different types of texts. Being able to determine which words have the greatest frequency will help African lexicographers solve one of their major problems, namely, what to include and what to exclude as the main words (the head-words) in the dictionaries they wish to compile.

2 Computers are also useful as instruments with which we can collect examples of particular words from extended texts. For example, a computer program was used to find all the uses of the Sepedi word *bula* ('open') in a published text, and also to provide the immediate linguistic context in which the word was used. An example of the result obtained is as follows:

Go fihleng ga gagwe o ile a	**bula**	lebati a itahlela ka gare, mme gwa kwala modumo wa …
Kgarebe ya batho ya godiša mahlo, ya	**bula**	molomo ya ba ya o tswalela …
Ge a	**bula**	faporiki ye semmušo ka Dibatsela 1978, Dr. Phatudi, o itše:
… ntše, ke phusotše nnete, hle lehono nneele.	**Bula**	dikgoro Yo maatla, lešoko ke la tatago ngwana, Jonna!
a le lentšu la go fihlela godimo. La tsena la	**bula**	hlogo le tša lerato. Ka molodi wa ona o ntšha matshwenyego
Moruti o ile a	**bula**	lengwalo la …

With information such as this, a lexicographer is better able to write definitions and to decide on translation equivalents.

3   There are also computer programs that can be used for the actual compilation of dictionaries themselves. These programs use a special 'language'
known as a mark-up language; for example, there is one called the
Standardized General Mark-up Language (SGML). SGML can be used to
annotate texts (entire books, for instance) in such a way that all the information required for producing dictionary entries can be extracted from the
marked-up text. Of course, an ordinary word-processing program can also
be used to extract information from a text and organize it into dictionary
format. This method, however, is less than satisfactory, as it depends too
heavily on the efforts made by the user.

Projects and initiatives

In spite of a variety of difficulties relating to dictionary compilation in Africa,
quite a few significant and promising initiatives exist, such as the work of the
Institute of Kiswahili Research in Dar es Salaam, Tanzania, the Summer Institute
of Linguistics (SIL), which has many branches throughout Africa, and a number
of dictionary projects in South Africa (supported by the South African government, particularly in the case of the African languages).

An equally important initiative is the work undertaken by the African
Association for Lexicography, called AFRILEX. More information about their
work can be found on the internet at the following address: www.up.ac.za/aca-
demic/libarts/afrilang/homelex.html

Endnotes

1   The term *synchronic* refers to a description of
linguistic phenomena that exist at the same
point in time. *Synchronic* stands in opposition to *diachronic*, which refers to a

description over time – a historical description.

2   The classifications of Kapinga, Mbaabu, and
Mgulla were based on syntactic criteria.

Bibliography

ASHTON, E.O. 1944/1982. *Swahili Grammar,
Including Intonation*. London: Longman.

AWAK, M.K. 1990. 'Historical Background with
Special Reference to Western Africa.' In
R.R.K. Hartmann (ed.), *Lexicography in
Africa*, vol. 15. Exeter Linguistic Studies:
University of Exeter Press.

BUSANE, M. 1990. 'Lexicography in Central

Africa: the User Perspective with Special
Reference to Egypt.' In R.R.K. Hartmann
(ed.), *Lexicography in Africa*, vol. 15. Exeter
Linguistic Studies: University of Exeter Press.

GIVON, T. 1971. 'Some Historical Changes in the
Noun-Class System of Bantu, their Possible
Causes and Wider Implications.' *Papers in
African Linguistics*, 3, pp. 33–45.

GOUWS, R.H. 1989. *Leksikografie*. Pretoria: Academica.

——— 1990. 'Information Categories in Dictionaries, with Special Reference to Southern Africa.' In R.R.K. Hartmann (ed.), *Lexicography in Africa*, vol. 15. Exeter Linguistic Studies: University of Exeter Press.

KIHORE, Y. 1995. *Kiswahili for Beginners*. Dar es Salaam: University Press.

KAPINGA, M.C. 1983. *Sarufi ya Maumbo ya Kiswahili Sanifu*. Institute of Kiswahili Research, Dar es Salaam.

LOUWRENS, L.J. 1991. *Aspects of Sepedi Grammar*. Pretoria: Via Afrika.

——— 1994. *Dictionary of Sepedi linguistic terms*. Pretoria: Via Afrika.

MBAABU, I. 1992. *Sarufi ya Kiswahili*. Nairobi: Longman Kenya.

MBOGHO, K. 1985. 'Observations on Bilingual Lexicography Involving Bantu and Indo-European Languages.' *Babel* 31, 3: 152–62.

MEINHOF, C. 1932. *An Introduction to the Phonology of the Bantu Languages*. Berlin: Dietrich Reimer.

MGULLU, R. 1990. 'Uainishaji wa Kimofolojia wa Ngeli za nomino za Kiswahili.' In *Mulika* 22. Institute of Kiswahili Research, Dar es Salaam

MÖNNIG, H.O. 1978. *The Pedi*. Pretoria: J.L. van Schaik.

PALMER, F.R. 1976. *Semantics: a new outline*. Cambridge: Cambridge University Press.

SAFARI, J.F. 1980. *Swahili Made Easy*. Dar es Salaam: Tanzania Publishing House.

STEERE, E. 1955. *A Handbook of the Swahili Language*. London: Sheldon Press.

WILKES, A. 1985. 'Word and word division: A study of some of the orthographical problems in the writing systems of the Nguni and Sotho languages.' *Southern African Journal of African Languages* 5, 3: 148–53.

Dictionaries cited

PRINSLOO, D.J., AND B. SATHEKGE. 1996. *New Sepedi Dictionary*. Pietermaritzburg: Shuter & Shooter.

SINCLAIR, J. 1997. *Collins Cobuild New Student's Dictionary*. London: HarperCollins.

10 Discourse: language in context

Hilton Hubbard

Expected outcomes

At the end of this chapter you should be able to:
1 Distinguish between linguistic competence and discourse competence and explain why this distinction is important.
2 Identify the concepts in terms of which the appropriateness, purposefulness, and coherence of discourse can be analysed.
3 Collect and analyse examples of spoken and written discourse in terms of these concepts.
4 Compare and contrast different types of discourse.

Introduction

'What is it that speakers of a language know that enables them to use their language?' This is one of the most important questions that linguists have to deal with, and now that you have read Chapters 6 to 9 you already know part of the answer to this question. As speakers of a language, we know, in a mostly subconscious and automatic way, the sounds of our language, how those sounds may be put together to form meaningful units (morphemes and words), and how the words in the lexicon of the language can in turn be joined to form sentences. This underlying knowledge of the sound system, the lexicon, and the grammatical system of the language is known as **linguistic competence**.

As we saw in Chapter 3, however, linguistic competence is only part of what underlies a speaker's use of language. If we examine discourse (the use of language in real contexts), it becomes clear that speakers know a lot more than just how to build words and sentences.

Firstly, we know how to use language appropriately. We would not, for example, say *Hi guys!* as we walk into a room to be interviewed for a job, because that kind of language is far too informal for such a situation.

Secondly, we know how to use language purposefully. We know what kinds of things we can do with different language structures. Think about the different ways in which the following sentences are used:

1   You can stay in at breaktime and tidy the classroom. [said by a teacher to a naughty pupil]
2   I can stay in at breaktime and tidy the classroom. [said by a pupil to a teacher]

The two sentences have very similar structures and both seem to say something about the pupil's ability (through the word *can*). However, we know that while 1 is ordering something, 2 is offering something.

Thirdly, we know how to use language coherently, in stretches that are usually much longer than single sentences. We might say, for example (as in this letter to a magazine):

3   Many people are dying as a result of cigarettes and alcohol. I appreciate that the government has raised the price on these items because it wants people to quit or consume less than they usually do. But will they? Unfortunately I drink alcohol, but I'm aware that the stuff is destroying my life. There are so many orphans today because their parents have died as a result of smoking or alcohol. People should not take their lives for granted.

Here the sentences are connected coherently to one another. But we would be most unlikely to say:

4   Many people are dying as a result of cigarettes and alcohol. It's a forged licence and the bookcase is falling apart. There's still a lot of copper being mined in Zambia. Cook them with four cups of brown rice.

These sentences do not form a coherent whole, even though the syntax of each sentence is perfectly correct, and the words are all from the lexicon of English.

So we see that discourse, that is, language use in real contexts, is usually appropriate, purposeful, and coherent. We call our ability to use language in this way our **discourse competence**. This discourse competence, together with our linguistic competence (the phonological, lexical, and grammatical abilities), makes up our overall **communicative competence** – our ability to communicate in language.

The study of discourse and discourse competence is known as **discourse analysis**, and in this chapter we aim to introduce you to this fascinating branch of linguistics and to help you develop new insights about how language is used in context. The next three sections of the chapter deal with each of the characteristics of discourse that we have identified: appropriateness, purposefulness, and coherence. The final section then focuses specifically on a text type that university students usually find very relevant: academic writing.

The appropriateness of discourse

Both sociolinguists and discourse analysts are interested in the appropriateness of discourse. When the American sociolinguist Dell Hymes developed the idea of communicative competence, he was concerned mostly with appropriateness:

> We have then to account for the fact that a normal child acquires knowledge of sentences, not only as grammatical, but also as appropriate. He or she acquires competence as to when to speak, when not, and as to what to talk about with whom, when, where, in what manner. (Hymes 1972a: 277)

Communicatively competent speakers of a language thus know how to use language that is appropriate to the context. But as discourse analysts we have to ask the question, 'What do speakers know about context that enables them to use appropriate forms of language to express appropriate meanings?'

For an answer to this question, we need to turn again to Hymes, who provides us with a framework for analysing context. Central to this framework is the concept of the **speech event**, defined as 'activities, or aspects of activities, that are directly governed by rules or norms for the use of speech' (Hymes 1972b). Possible examples of speech events are: a conversation between friends; a wage negotiation between employer and trade union representatives; a religious ritual, such as a church service; a university lecture; a court case; and a joke.

Hymes identifies various contextual variables that can have an effect on the language used in a speech event. These are listed as follows:

Setting
Participants
Ends
Acts
Key
Instrumentality
Norms
Genre
Topic

As can be seen from the list, we can use the acronym SPEAKING+T to help us remember these contextual variables. Let us look briefly at each in turn.

Setting

The setting relates to the physical circumstances of the speech event, such as time and place. When people go into a church, for example, they will tend to speak quietly and won't argue, shout, or swear. They will feel constrained to speak this way even if there is no church service going on at the time and they are just visiting the building. Here the setting alone affects the language used.

Some other aspects of the setting include the size of the venue and the arrangement of the furniture. Consider the difference in setting between a lecture and a small class-tutorial at university. Lectures tend to be more formal than tutorials, and this is partly because, as a general rule, the larger the venue, the more formal the language. Tutorials are usually more intimate, taking place in smaller rooms, and interaction between speakers can be further encouraged if everyone sits in a semi-circle or around a large table so that they can see one another. This is very different from a lecture, where students sit in rows at quite a distance from the lecturer, who is the only person standing (usually on a raised platform or behind a lectern).

Participants

Here we are interested in who takes part in the speech event and what the role relationships between the participants are. Examples of role relationships are:
- lecturer–student
- friend–friend
- customer–shop assistant
- adult–child
- judge–witness.

How would you change your language in these different role relationships? Consider, for example, what kind of greetings would be appropriate for each of the above role relationships in your language, and also what forms of address would be used. (In English, for instance, the same person might be addressed as *Mr Masango*, *Elias*, *Elly*, or *Teacher*, depending on how he and other participants relate to one another).

Ends

The ends are the general goals and the individual aims of the speech event. Thus, in a tutorial, the general goal would be to deepen understanding of the relevant topic. As they work towards this goal, the aims of individual students will most likely be to raise questions, discuss examples, criticize, clarify issues, and so on.

Acts

The individual aims just mentioned are realized by way of particular speech acts – forms of language that perform particular functions. Thus, in a tutorial, the participants might question, criticize, and clarify, but they will not usually insult or threaten one another. (We shall discuss speech acts in more detail in the next section, where we focus on the purposefulness of discourse.)

Key

The key, which is similar to the concept of register (see Chapter 2), relates to the tone, manner, or spirit of the speech event or speech act. It may be friendly or hostile, cautious or incautious, humorous or serious, and so on. The key in a courtroom trial, for example, is expected to be formal and respectful, so that when a prosecuting lawyer refers to the defence he might say something like:

My lord, my learned friend for the defence is incorrect

but not

Look, my man, that idiot on the other side is talking nonsense!

Instrumentality

This relates to the medium and the channel used by the participants. The medium can be speaking or writing. Compare, for example, the language used during a tutorial discussion about an assignment and the language considered appropriate when a student writes the assignment. If we analyse the medium further, we see that the written medium uses one channel, namely print, but the spoken medium can be associated with various channels, such as face-to-face, radio, film, and the telephone. A friend who was a diplomat describes the following little speech event that took place in a country foreign to her. When she opened the door to a man who was delivering a parcel to her, his greeting was:

Hello. This is Abdul speaking.

What he had done was to use in a face-to-face channel language that was appropriate to the telephone.

Norms

The norms of a speech event relate to behaviour that accompanies language, such as how loudly one should speak, how speaking turns are organized (for example, whether one is allowed to interrupt or not, and how long pauses should be). Some norms may vary not just from one speech event to another but from one culture to another. Thus, for example, isiZulu-speakers will in general expect slightly longer pauses during a conversation than English-speakers will. As a result, an English-speaker talking to an isiZulu-speaker will sometimes think that the latter has come to the end of a speaking turn when this is not yet so, and when the English-speaker then takes a turn, this might seem like an interruption to the isiZulu-speaker.

Genre

Language can also be appropriate to a certain genre, that is, a category of language use that has clearly identifiable typical features. Examples are sermons, riddles, praise poems, and the like. Often the speech event and the genre will coincide, as when the speech event 'sermon' follows the features of the genre 'sermon'. Sometimes, however, speech event and genre are not the same. For example, a comedian might make fun of a politician by pretending to give a political speech, using all its typical genre features, but, although the genre here would be 'political speech', the speech event would be 'satire'.

Topic

The topic is of course what is being spoken about. It will be obvious that the topic of a speech event will affect the language used, particularly with regard to vocabulary.

We began this section with the question: what do speakers know about context that enables them to use appropriate forms of language to express appropriate meanings? As a way of answering, we have discussed Hymes' nine contextual variables. These do not cover all the contextual factors that influence language use in all cultures, but they probably represent most of the important ones. Note that not all the contextual variables will always be relevant when we analyse the language of a particular speech event, and they are often interdependent. For example, setting can affect key, and topic can affect ends.

We have thus seen that it is possible to analyse the context of language use, and that this is necessary if we want to understand how speakers can be both communicatively and grammatically competent in a language. They are able to be both grammatically correct and appropriate when they use language because they are sensitive to the sort of contextual variables we have discussed.

The purposefulness of discourse

We now turn to the second characteristic of discourse, or language in use: the fact that it is purposeful. Consider the following sentence:

5   My son is a big, strong boy.

What does this sentence mean? This question can be answered in at least two different ways, depending on what we understand by 'meaning'.

The first kind of meaning, which we looked at in Chapter 9, can be called the **semantic meaning**. This is the basic meaning of the words and the sentence, independent of any context. If we can paraphrase the sentence (for example, by saying that it means 'the male child of the speaker is large, physically powerful, and not yet an adult'), or if we can translate the sentence accurately into another language, we can show our understanding of the semantic meaning of the sentence. This ability, or **semantic competence**, is part of our grammatical competence as a speaker.

However, sentences are seldom used independently of a context, and when we study what they can mean in real contexts, we deal with a second kind of meaning, called **pragmatic meaning** or **discourse meaning**. Let us consider three contexts in which sentence 5 could be uttered.

During a conversation between two friends who have not seen one another for many years, the one says, *Okay, so tell me a bit about this child of yours.* The other answers:

5   My son is a big, strong boy.

In this context, the speaker simply means to inform the hearer, and so 5 functions here as a statement.

In another context, a man who has just bought two dozen beers from a bottle store says, *I'll need someone to help me carry them to my car.* The owner of the bottle store replies:

5   My son is a big, strong boy.

He then calls his son. In this context, the speaker means to offer help to the hearer, and so 5 functions here as an offer.

In a third context, a woman waiting outside a shop is being bothered by two teenagers who want her to give them money. As her son comes out of the shop, she points at him and says to them:

5   My son is a big, strong boy.

In this context, the speaker means to warn the hearers, and so 5 functions here as a warning.

So now we can see that while a sentence has a certain form and semantic meaning, when it is actually used as an utterance in different contexts, its pragmatic or discourse meaning – its function – can differ. Sentence 5 can thus function as a statement, an offer, or a warning.

Speech acts

The theory that so far offers the best explanation of how language forms and functions are linked is **speech act theory**. This was first set out in the book *How to do things with words* (Austin 1962). In this book, J.L. Austin argued that whenever we say something, we perform a speech act, and that this has three aspects.

Firstly, we utter something that has sound structure, grammatical structure, and semantic meaning. This is called a **locution**. So, if the teacher in our earlier example says

1   You can stay in at breaktime and tidy the classroom

she is using English sounds and grammatical structures that have the literal, semantic meaning of 'you are able to stay in at breaktime and tidy the class-room'.

Secondly, when we utter something, we intend our utterance to have a communicative function, such as promising, offering, assuring, informing, or warning. This is called an **illocution**. We can see that the illocution relates to pragmatic or discourse meaning. In 1 above, the illocution is that of an order. In the context of a teacher speaking to a pupil who has been disobedient, 1 has the same meaning as

6   I order you to stay in at breaktime and tidy the classroom

where the speaker starts the sentence by explicitly naming the illocution that she intends. Such sentences are called **performative sentences**, because they name the act being performed when the sentence is uttered.

Thirdly, our utterance has the potential to affect the hearer. It might anger, dismay, amuse, or puzzle, and it might lead to certain activities, such as tidying a classroom. These effects are called the **perlocutions** of the utterance.

However, our main concern in discourse analysis is to try to explain how speakers and hearers (and also readers and writers) understand one another's illocutions – in other words, how they connect the locution (form and semantic meaning) of an utterance with its illocution (function or discourse meaning). The child who hears the teacher's utterance in 1 knows that she doesn't mean 'you are able to stay in at breaktime and tidy the classroom' but 'I order you to stay in at breaktime and tidy the classroom', even though there is no explicit mention of ordering. How does the child know this?

In terms of speech act theory, hearers can interpret speakers' illocutions because they know what contextual conditions are needed in order for an utterance to have a certain illocution. Contextual conditions can be better understood if we look at some examples of utterances that don't meet the relevant contextual conditions. Why don't 7 and 8 succeed as orders?

7 Explain the political effects of changes in the World Bank's lending policy in Africa since 1990. [said by a bank manager to her four-year-old grandson]

8 Stand up! [said by a shell-shocked officer to a soldier who is wounded in both legs]

These utterances don't succeed because one of the contextual conditions of ordering is that the hearer should be able to perform the relevant act, and this is clearly not the case here. It is also partly because of their (subconscious) knowledge of this condition of ability that hearers can interpret utterances such as

1 You can stay in at breaktime and tidy the classroom

as orders. It seems that, in English, one speech act rule is that we can order someone to do something by asserting one of the contextual conditions for ordering – that the hearer must be able to carry out the order.

In a similar way, we understand

2 I can stay in at breaktime and tidy the classroom

as an offer, because a contextual condition for offering is that the speaker must be able to carry out the act mentioned. Another speech act rule for English is thus that a speaker can offer to do something by asserting his or her ability to do it.

Of course, the illocution can be more directly expressed by using a performative sentence, as we saw in

6   I order you to stay in at breaktime and tidy the classroom.

Or, for ordering, an imperative structure could be used, as in

9   Stay in at breaktime and tidy the classroom!

We don't need to explain our understanding of such direct speech acts in terms of contextual conditions and speech act rules. It is utterances such as 1 and 2, where the connection between form and function (between locution and illocution) is indirect, that need to be explained with the help of these conditions and rules. We don't have the space to explore more examples here, but, as you can imagine, for each of the more indirect speech acts, there are a number of contextual conditions and a number of rules for linking its illocution with its locution – its function with its form.

Part of our communicative competence comes from being able to make such links, and one of the difficulties that even advanced learners of a language often have is that, although they understand the words of an utterance they hear (the locution), they don't understand the speaker's purpose in saying these particular words (the illocution). Speech act theory provides us with a fairly systematic account of how forms and functions can be connected, and applied linguists have made use of research on speech acts to produce language learning materials that focus on language functions instead of just on forms.

Sometimes the connection between form and function is a lot more indirect and unsystematic than the examples just discussed, and so they are difficult to analyse in terms of contextual conditions and speech act rules alone. In the next section, we look at an approach that has been developed to help us to understand further how speakers understand one another, particularly in ordinary conversation.

Conversational principles: co-operation and politeness

Look at the following conversation (A and B have been talking about soccer):

10 A: What are you doing on Sunday?
   B: Man, I'm supposed to be doing a few jobs around the house.
   A: Couldn't you come with us to the match?

B: I'm afraid that if I don't paint the bedrooms this Sunday, Nonhlanhla's going to murder me.

A: Okay.

There is a lot of indirectness here, but A and B clearly understand one another. This is partly because of the knowledge they share about one another, the topic, and so on, but also partly because each assumes that the other is co-operating towards a conversational goal. This, as described by Grice (1975), is the **co-operative principle**, and he suggests that when we co-operate in a conversation, we usually follow four rules or co-operative maxims. These maxims concern the quantity, quality, relation, and manner of our utterances:

- **quantity:** give just the right amount of information – neither too much nor too little;
- **quality:** do not say anything for which you lack evidence or which you know to be false;
- **relation:** make your contribution relevant to the conversational goal; and
- **manner:** be clear – avoid obscurity and ambiguity.

In reality, conversational partners seldom follow these maxims strictly, even when they try to follow the co-operative principle. Consider our sample conversation, 10. A's conversational goal is to see whether B can go with him to the soccer match. Why, then, doesn't he just say *Come to the match with us*, instead of first asking B what he is doing and then asking him if he couldn't go to the match? B's goal is to let A know that he can't make it, so why doesn't he just say *No*? Why do they seem to ignore the maxims of quantity and manner?

The answer, of course, is that A is being polite. This **politeness principle** ('be polite') has also been suggested for conversation, together with politeness maxims such as don't impose on your hearer; give your hearer options; and make your hearer feel good. These maxims help ensure that speakers and hearers don't lose face, or self-esteem, and avoid embarrassment. It should be clear that politeness maxims could often clash with co-operative maxims (for example, because the truth can hurt, we will sometimes lie to people, or be ambiguous or obscure in an attempt to be tactful).

In 10 above, A doesn't want to impose on B, so, instead of inviting him directly, he first asks him what he will be doing on the relevant day. However, because he is not being as clear as possible, we could say that here he breaks the manner maxim. (On the other hand, in English, this is a common way of preparing the hearer for an invitation, so there is a good chance that B will understand this question in the way it was intended.) After B's reply, A realizes that B might not be able to accept the invitation, so he doesn't bluntly say *Come to the match with us*, but gives B an easy yes/no option by using the polite formula *Couldn't you ...?* Here again we see a clash between a politeness maxim and the manner maxim.

B's reply (*I'm afraid that if I don't paint the bedrooms this Sunday, Nonhlanhla's going to murder me*) avoids hurting A's feelings by avoiding a flat *No*, but it seems to ignore both the quantity and manner maxims as a result. But B is nevertheless being co-operative. He knows that A will understand his answer, because they share knowledge about where they are in the conversation (it is time for acceptance or refusal of the invitation), and because they also share knowledge about how long it takes to paint several bedrooms and the impossibility of simultaneously painting bedrooms and attending a soccer match. Thus B doesn't say no directly, but implicates it (communicates indirectly by relying on A's knowledge). So we see here how, by violating maxims (in this case, quantity and manner), B implicates the answer *No*. This kind of implication is known as an **implicature** (consider also the 'offer' and 'warning' implicatures of *My son is a big, strong boy* in 5 above).

Implicatures can also be signalled by violations of other maxims, such as quality and relation. Consider a situation where A gets B to listen to a piece of music by a new jazz band, and then asks

So, how do you like the Zebo Four?

B answers

Nice beer you've got me.

Does B like the music? Clearly not, but instead of saying so directly, he implicates this by changing the subject – thus violating the relation maxim and saying something that seems to be irrelevant to A's question. However, if he believes that A knows that changing the subject is often a way of signalling a negative answer, he is still being co-operative.

B could also have answered

Pity that the man on bass hasn't got a thumb.

Here he would break the quality maxim, as both speakers know that the musician isn't missing a thumb, but, by saying that he is, A implicates that the double bass player is not very good. Here we see an example of a speaker who violates a maxim not because he wants to be polite, but because he wants to make his point in a creative, amusing manner.

This was also partly the case in B's reply in 10 (*I'm afraid that if I don't paint the bedrooms this Sunday, Nonhlanhla's going to murder me*). We saw that this reply violated both the quantity maxim (it gives more information than necessary) and the manner maxim (it doesn't simply and clearly state *No, I can't*). Doesn't it also deliberately violate another maxim? This is of course the quality maxim, because the speaker isn't really afraid that he will be murdered!

In spite of this, A understands that B is exaggerating, and that his meaning should not be taken literally. If he had used a metaphor or irony, the same would apply, but once again, because A and B assume that they are co-operating, they understand one another in spite of the violations of the maxims.

In this section, we have seen that discourse – language use in context – is not only appropriate but also purposeful, with speakers using the different forms of language to perform various functions. Sometimes the links between form and function are indirect, and we have seen that speech act theory, with its distinction between locutions and illocutions and its use of the concept of contextual conditions, helps to explain how some of these links work. Conversational partners also interpret one another's utterances on the understanding that they are co-operating with one another towards a goal. This means that, even when the co-operative maxims are ignored, speakers try to work out one another's implicatures, using all the relevant knowledge they have. We have also seen that one of the main reasons for the violation of co-operative maxims is the clash between these maxims and maxims of politeness. Another reason is simply that conversational participants like to use language creatively – to exaggerate, to speak metaphorically, and so on. As long as they recognize one another's violations of maxims and the reasons for them, and don't try to interpret one another literally, they will generally achieve their communicative goals.

With the help of speech act theory and the co-operative and politeness principles and their maxims, discourse analysts have made progress in explaining the connection between the forms of language and the purposeful utterances of speakers. Now we need to look at the third, related characteristic of discourse – its coherence.

The coherence of discourse

Discourse is also coherent; in other words, it forms a unified, meaningful whole. In the previous section, we saw that discourse is purposeful, and part of the coherence of discourse derives from the fact that speakers can interpret each other's utterances because they understand one another's purposes. In this section, however, our focus will be on other sources of coherence, particularly on two concepts that help us to describe connections between clauses and sentences in a discourse: **cohesion** and **relational coherence**.

Cohesion

Let us look once more at 3 (the letter written to a popular magazine) and 4, repeated here:

3 Many people are dying as a result of cigarettes and alcohol. I appreciate that the government has raised the price on these items because it wants people to quit or consume less than they usually do. But will they? Unfortunately I drink alcohol, but I'm aware that the stuff is destroying my life. There are so many orphans today because their parents have died as a result of smoking or alcohol. People should not take their lives for granted.

4 Many people are dying as a result of cigarettes and alcohol. It's a forged license and the bookcase is falling apart. There's still a lot of copper being mined in Zambia. Cook them with four cups of brown rice.

Both 3 and 4 are grammatical, but only 3 is coherent. Why? Partly because 3 has cohesion, a property that has been defined as follows:

> Cohesion occurs when the interpretation of some element in the discourse is dependent on that of another. The one PRESUPPOSES the other. (Halliday and Hasan 1976: 4)

This definition will become clearer if we look more closely at the clauses and sentences that make up 3. Here we will find examples of all the five main types of cohesion: reference, substitution, ellipsis, conjunction, and lexical cohesion.

Reference

Consider the sentence

> I appreciate that the government has raised the price on these items because it wants people to quit or consume less than they usually do.

In discourse 3, what does *it* in the clause *because it wants* refer to? *The government*, of course, mentioned in the previous clause. Thus *it* presupposes an element in an earlier clause of the discourse, and so we can call the pronoun *it* a cohesion element. The connection between *it* and *the government* is one of reference (both words refer to the same thing), so, more specifically, *it* is a reference cohesion element and the connection itself is known as a reference cohesion tie.

There is a similar tie between *people* in the second sentence and *they* in a later clause of the sentence. This connects once again with *they* in the next sentence (*But will they?*), so that there is a chain of two reference cohesion elements that both presuppose *people*.

In English, the main reference cohesion elements are:
- the personal pronouns (*I, me, we, us, you, he, she, it,* and *they*);
- the possessive pronouns (*my, our, your, his, hers, its,* and *their*);

- the definite article and determiners (*the, this, these, that,* and *those*); and
- the demonstrative adverbs (*here, there,* and *then*).

It is important to note that these categories of words are not always used cohesively. For example, let's look at the three occurrences of the determiner *the* in 3. In *the stuff*, it is cohesive because it confirms that the noun it determines (*stuff*), refers to the same thing as another expression in the discourse, namely *alcohol*. The *the* in *the government*, however, is not cohesive because it doesn't link with another expression that actually appears in the discourse. Rather, it presupposes a definite concept in the context of which the reader is expected to be aware (i.e. the reader should know which government is meant).

In *the price on these items, the* is also not cohesive, because it does not presuppose or link with another expression that appears in a different clause or sentence. We see, then, that just because an expression such as a pronoun or a determiner can function as a cohesion element, this does not mean that it always does so.

Substitution

In reference cohesion, the presupposing and the presupposed expressions both refer to the same thing. In substitution cohesion, the two expressions don't refer to the same thing, but they do have the same meaning, as in the last clause of the second sentence of 3:

... than they usually do.

Here *do* substitutes for, and has the same meaning as, *consume* in the previous clause, and is equivalent to *less than they usually consume*. The word *do*, as it is used here, is thus a substitution cohesion element, and the connection it makes with *consume* is a substitution cohesion tie.

In English, the verb *do* can substitute for verbs and verb phrases, whereas *one* is the cohesion element that can substitute for nouns and noun phrases, as in:

The president was wearing a beautiful afroprint shirt. I wish I had one.

Note that, in using *one*, the speaker is not referring to exactly the same shirt that the president was wearing (in which case the reference element *it* would have been used). What he wants is another, similar shirt that can be described in exactly the same words.

Ellipsis cohesion

This is very similar to substitution cohesion, the difference being that in ellipsis there is no word such as *one* or *do* to mark the repetition of meaning. This repetition is understood from the context, as in the third sentence of our sample discourse 3:

> But will they?

Here, what is understood and what could thus be added to this phrase is *quit or consume less than they usually do*.

Lexical cohesion

This is the cohesion that results from the fact that discourses tend to contain words that relate to one another in meaning or associate with one another in a more general way. There are, as we already know, a number of possible meaning relations between words, including synonymy, antonymy, and hyponymy (see Chapter 9). In our sample discourse, 3, there are no synonyms or antonyms, but *cigarettes* and *alcohol* are hyponyms of *items*, *alcohol* is also a hyponym of *stuff*, and *drink* is a hyponym of *consume*. Another type of lexical cohesion is repetition of the same word or expression (in this sample, *alcohol* and *people*) and near-repetition (*dying* and *died*).

The last type of lexical cohesion that we will mention is collocation, a term that includes words that (unlike synonymy, antonymy, and hyponymy) are not in a systematic semantic relation, but that nevertheless tend to associate with one another and occur together in discourse. In 3, for example, *cigarettes* and *smoking* collocate with one another, as do *dying*, *died*, and *lives*, and *orphans* and *parents*.

Conjunction

This is the only type of cohesion that consistently links the meanings of clauses and sentences as wholes, expressing 'the way in which what is to follow is systematically connected to what has gone before' (Halliday and Hasan 1976: 227). In 3, there is one example of a conjunctive that joins whole sentences, namely *but* in

> But will they?

There are also two examples of conjunctives joining clauses rather than sentences; in both cases, the conjunctive is *because*. Conjunctives can be divided into four main groups, depending on their meanings:

- **additive** (connected by some kind of addition): *and, furthermore, namely, for example, similarly*;
- **adversative** (connected by an 'against expectations' relation): *but, yet, however, although, rather, on the other hand, instead, in spite of*;
- **causal:** *therefore, thus, as a result, for this reason, because, if ... then*; and
- **temporal** (connected by time): *then, later, after that, before, previously, while, meanwhile, finally*.

To sum up, we can now see that one of the reasons why 3 is coherent and can therefore be considered a piece of discourse is because, unlike the non-discourse 4, it contains many elements of cohesion.

Task

Review your understanding of cohesion by identifying and classifying all the ties in 3. The discourse is repeated below, with words that have reference, substitution, conjunction, or lexical cohesion ties given in bold print; ellipsis is marked by a gap (___).

Many people are dying **as a result of** cigarettes and alcohol. I appreciate that the government has raised the price on **these items because it** wants **people** to quit or consume less than **they** usually **do. But** will **they** ___? Unfortunately **I drink alcohol, but** I'm aware that **the stuff** is destroying **my** life. **There** are so many orphans today **because their** parents have **died as a result of smoking or alcohol. People** should not take **their** lives for granted.

Relational coherence

The examples of conjunctive cohesion identified above also signal four basic kinds of relation between clauses or sentences: additive, adversative, causal, and temporal (these can be called the *and, but, so,* and *then* relations). This type of relation is known as a **clause relation** (whether it applies to clauses or sentences). Much of the coherence we perceive, particularly in written text, derives from our awareness of clause relations in the discourse. Consider, for example, the following paragraph from a text about acid rain (clauses and sentences are numbered and separated by slashes, and conjunctives are in bold print):

(1) Power stations, factories, and traffic spew out smoke and exhaust fumes. / (2) **As a result**, clouds in urban areas can become very acidic. / (3) They can

then travel long distances / (4) **and** drop their load of rain. / (5) Much harm can be done to trees, crops, rivers, and lakes. / (6) On the highveld, for example, giant power stations supply vital electricity, / (7) **but** in the process huge quantities of gas are released into the air / (8) **and so** acid rain **now** falls in an important farming and timber area.

Although most of the clause relations are here signalled by conjunctives, we can usually infer a clause relation even when there is no conjunctive, or when the conjunctive has a very general or vague meaning, as in the case of *and*. Consider the relation between (3) and (4) in the sample text above. The conjunctive *and* mostly signals an additive relation, but it can also signal a temporal or causal relation. From our knowledge of how the world works and our understanding of the text, it seems most likely that the clause relation here is a temporal one (first the clouds travel long distances and then they drop their load of rain). What about the clause relation between (4) and (5)? Once again, because of our knowledge of the world and because the text has been coherent so far, we can infer that it is the rain mentioned in (4) that causes the harm referred to in (5), and so the clause relation between (4) and (5) is a causal one.

The clause relational structure of this paragraph can thus be summarized as follows:

(1) so (2), then (3), then (4), so (5) and (6), but (7), so (8).

When the clause relational structure is relatively clear, as it is here, we can say that the discourse has relatively high relational coherence. We can also see that here the predominant relation is a causal one. In the next section, we shall see that different discourses can be distinguished partly in terms of their different clause relational structures, and that relational coherence is a useful concept for distinguishing good from poor writing.

Discourse analysis and academic literacy

We now know that language users expect, and aim to produce, discourse that is appropriate, purposeful, and coherent. We have looked at some of the more important concepts that help to explain how this comes about (contextual variables of the speech event; speech acts and contextual conditions; the co-operative and politeness principles; implicature; and cohesion and relational coherence). In other words, these concepts have helped us to throw light on some of the ingredients that go into making up the language user's discourse competence.

Perfect discourse competence, however, is an ideal. In reality, users don't always succeed in producing discourse that is sufficiently appropriate, purposeful, and coherent. This is partly because there are many different discourse types, and the skill that individuals possess in using them varies (for example, think of the different abilities of people you know – including yourself – with regard to the following types of discourse: a joke; a bedtime story; a wedding speech; a lecture; and an argument). If we are using a language that is not our primary tongue, it is even more difficult to produce discourse that is fully appropriate, purposeful, and coherent.

In this final section, we shall focus briefly on one type of discourse that has to be developed as part of tertiary-level academic literacy: student academic writing. This is the kind of writing expected of university students in assignments and examinations in their chosen subjects. Student academic writing varies, of course, depending on the task and the subject, but our focus will be on essay-type assignments and examination answers in the human sciences. We will consider some features of this discourse type and also look at some of the problems students have in trying to produce academic writing that is appropriate, purposeful, and coherent. As we do so, we will be able to see how some of the concepts explored above can be applied to this kind of discourse.

Academic writing: appropriateness

The appropriateness of student academic writing can be discussed in terms of Hymes' contextual variables (remember SPEAKING+T?). Unlike speaking, writing is usually part of a split speech event, where the writer and reader are separated by space and time. Here, our primary concern is with the writer.

Settings, in writing as opposed to speaking, will usually be different for the writer and reader. Because tackling an assignment or essay is a more difficult business than writing a short letter to a friend, for example, assignment writers will try to find quiet settings where they can concentrate most easily. An inappropriate setting (one with too much noise, or too many interruptions) will make it more difficult for the writer to produce a piece of discourse that is appropriate to the standards required. In an examination, the setting will be essentially the same for all writers. On the other hand, the fact that the exam writer has much less time and cannot usually consult sources will make an exam answer rather different to an assignment, even if the topic is essentially the same.

Participants in the assignment and examination context are in the role relationship of student–lecturer. Think about how this variable alone will determine some characteristics of the language used, particularly the key or register.

Ends or aims will include those of displaying the writer's knowledge and ability to focus on the question concerned. This also relates to the contextual variable of topic. We will consider these aspects in a little more detail when we discuss the purposefulness of academic writing in the next section.

Acts such as stating, comparing, contrasting, and evaluating will be determined by the question that is set. In the section below, we will look more closely at how the wording of examination and essay questions is analysed.

Key would tend to be serious, impersonal, and fairly formal. Think about how the key or register in an assignment differs from that of a letter to a friend or a loved one.

Instrumentality in this case is written medium and print channel (written marks on paper, whether typed or handwritten). Think about some of the differences between the way that language is used in a written examination and an oral one.

Norms of behaviour applying to student academic writing would include, for example, the fact that even though students usually know who will be reading their assignment or exam answer, they should not address these readers explicitly by name, or even in the second person ('you'). This links with the impersonal key that is appropriate to this kind of writing.

Genre relates to the combination of features that distinguish one type of discourse from another. The features we have identified above all help to define student academic writing as a particular genre of discourse – one that must be developed if a student is to write appropriately.

Tasks

1 Exchange written assignments with a friend in your class and identify examples from these of each of the contextual variables discussed in this section.
2 Tape-record a friend's conversation (with his or her permission, of course!) and then compare this conversation with a text written in academic style. List (and explain, if you can) the differences.

Academic writing: purposefulness

The main purposes of assignments and examinations are to test students' knowledge of a topic, their ability to select relevant information on this topic from the literature, and their ability to organize and express the selected knowledge in the required manner. In an assignment or examination question, the topic is usually clearly labelled, and the way it has to be dealt with is given by a verb, as in

Explain and exemplify Grice's co-operative maxims.

In order to write a good, purposeful answer, students must first carefully examine the topic keywords (*Grice's co-operative maxims*) and what we can call the speech act keywords (*explain* and *exemplify*). These speech act keywords (examples of others are *evaluate, discuss, list, define, compare, outline,* and *distinguish*) indicate what the most important speech acts in the response should be, and students often fail to answer a question properly because they ignore the aim of the question as expressed in these keywords.

In student academic writing, then, the speech act keywords in particular show students what their purposes should be in answering assignment and examination questions. These purposes are very different from those of many other kinds of texts, such as adverts, praise poems, and jokes, for example (compare the aims of advertisement creators, praise singers, and joke tellers). Thus we see here that different texts can also be distinguished in terms of their different aims or purposes.

Academic writing: coherence

When we discussed coherence in general in an earlier section, we focused on two aspects, namely cohesion and relational coherence. Here we will do the same in examining coherence in student academic writing.

One question often asked is: if one piece of writing has more cohesion elements in it than another, will it also tend to be more coherent? Quite a few researchers have applied this question to student academic writing, but the results vary. There does not seem to be a strong connection between the frequency of cohesion elements in such writing and teachers' or lecturers' evaluations of its coherence.

What is important, however, is to try to avoid cohesion errors in one's writing. The most frequent cohesion errors in student academic writing are reference and conjunction errors, and we shall look at a few examples, taken from examination answers.

Three of the most common types of reference cohesion error can be described as number, gender, and ambiguity errors. A number error is found in

We can say Simon was a prophet because he used to see things before it could happen.

Here the presupposed element, *things*, is plural, so the reference cohesion element should have been the pronoun *they*, and not *it*.

A gender error is found in

John was one of the twins. She was small and very frightened of the beast.

Here the correct cohesion element would obviously have been the pronoun *he*. An ambiguity error is found in

Stereotyping goes hand in hand with a negative attitude. When one is learning a new language, this will develop.

Here it is not clear whether *stereotyping* or *negative attitude* is the element presupposed by *this*.

The most common type of conjunctive cohesion error occurs when the relationship between two clauses or sentences that the conjunctive is supposed to signal does not exist, as in

Children pronounce the sounds of a second language more correctly than adults. Therefore, they learn it more quickly.

The conjunctive *therefore* usually signals a relationship between sentences, in that one sentence provides evidence and the other makes a conclusion based on that evidence. However, the evidence in this extract does not justify the conclusion in the second sentence.

It should be clear that the conjunctive cohesion error in this example is part of a larger relational coherence problem: there is no proper coherence relation between the two sentences. Poor student academic writing often reveals this kind of weakness. Another feature of poor writing is a tendency to list ideas or facts in a rather unstructured or unconnected way instead of building up a clear argument. The main type of clause relation in such cases is the relatively vague additive ('and') relation. Thus we might get the clauses of a paragraph structured as

(1) and (2) and (3) and (4)

instead of, for example,

(1) but (2) and (3) so (4).

Good student academic writing tends to contain fewer additive relations and more adversative ('but') and causal ('so') relations than weaker writing. (Obviously, much depends on the nature of the relevant assignment or examination question.)

More generally, different text types can often be distinguished in terms of the kinds of clause relations that they prefer. Thus, in novels and jokes that involve a story or narrative, there will be a high frequency of temporal ('then') relations; in evaluations, such as a newspaper review of some of the latest musical releases, there will be many adversative relations as the writer weighs up positive and negative aspects; while in the argument of a newspaper editorial, there will generally be a relatively high number of causal relations.

In this section, we have seen how text types can be distinguished from one another partly in terms of the key features of discourse: appropriateness, purposefulness, and coherence. We have looked most closely at one type of text, student academic writing, and we hope that this has not only helped to deepen your insights into discourse, but also that it will be useful to you in making your own writing all the more appropriate, purposeful, and coherent.

Bibliography

AUSTIN, J.L. 1962. *How to do things with words.* Oxford: Oxford University Press.

GRICE, H.P. 1975. 'Logic and conversation.' In P. Cole and J.L. Morgan (eds.), *Speech Acts.* New York: Academic Press: 41–58.

HALLIDAY, M.A.K., and R. HASAN 1976. *Cohesion in English.* London: Longman.

HYMES, D. 1972a. 'On communicative competence.' In J.B. Pride and J. Holmes (eds.), *Sociolinguistics.* Harmondsworth: Penguin: 269–293.

———— 1972b. 'Models of the interaction of language and social life'. In J.J. Gumperz and D. Hymes (eds.), *Directions in Sociolinguistics.* New York: Holt, Rinehart & Winston: 35–71.

11 Cross-cultural communication in Africa

Oswald K. Ndoleriire

Expected outcomes

At the end of this chapter you should be able to:
1 Explain why cross-cultural communication is not always successful.
2 Explain the cultural context of the verbal communication process.
3 Distinguish clearly between the concepts of language and culture, and describe their interrelationship.
4 Explain some of the factors relevant to cross-cultural communication and relate them to situations with which you are acquainted.
5 Suggest possible strategies for resolving cross-cultural communicative failures.
6 Argue for or against the protection of cultural diversity.

Introduction

In daily life, communicating efficiently is not always an easy matter. Many of the misunderstandings in families arise because of a lack of proper communication between parents and children, and between children themselves. Communication between groups, communities, and nations can, as in person-to-person communication, be a difficult process, with social, cultural, economic, and other factors playing an important role. Ineffective communication is often a contributing factor in conflicts between groups and nations.

Understanding cross-cultural communication is an important task, especially if a country is in the process of national integration and nation-building. In this chapter, we would like to discuss a number of issues that underlie cross-cultural communication. The topics to be covered are: the nature of the verbal communication process; the interrelationship between language and culture; the factors that contribute to miscommunication across cultures; and strategies for the management of cross-cultural communication.

The communication process

The communication process can be represented in a simple chart, which indicates the sender (speaker), the channel (that through which the message is sent), the receiver (hearer), and the 'noise' factor present in the process. The chart, in its simplest form, is as follows:

$$\text{Sender} \quad \rightarrow \quad \text{Channel} \quad \rightarrow \quad \text{Receiver}$$

$$\textit{Noise}$$

In this chart, the message originates from the sender. On its way, it has to go through a channel, through which the message is sent. The message can take the form of a letter, an e-mail, speech sounds, and so on, and the medium can be written or oral. The 'noise' factor is any obstacle that might hinder the smooth transmission of the message. The message then reaches its destination, the receiver.

It is, of course, possible to construct a far more complex model of the communication process, using concepts such as encoding the message, decoding the message, interpreting the message, and feedback. This kind of model involves an idea, feeling, or wish that a sender wants to transmit, to which he or she gives visual or aural form by 'translating' it into a 'code' (encoding it, in other words). This can be Morse code (used in sending telegraphic messages), semaphore (used to control the running of trains), drum language, and so on. It can also be the grammar of a particular language. On receipt, a hearer (or reader) decodes the message, using the same code as was used to encode the message. As we all know from our experiences of misunderstanding each other, the ideas, wishes, or feelings that senders want to convey are not always fully contained in the message itself, and hearers (or readers) sometimes have to interpret the message and try to understand the sender's intentions with the help of, for example, background knowledge. However, they don't necessarily succeed at first, and need further messages from the sender, which are supplied in the form of feedback.

In the remainder of this section, we wish to focus on the noise factor, as it plays a vital role in miscommunication.

The noise factor

Specialists in communication work with the concept of **noise** to explain the various obstacles that hamper efficient communication. These obstacles include real physical noise during the communication interaction, but could also include lack of attention on the part of the hearer, disorganized sentences or ideas, poor articulation, and distorted information given by the speaker.

Physical noise refers to real noise, such as other people talking or singing at the time of the message transfer, so that the hearer receives only part of it, the rest having been obstructed by the physical noise. It may also happen that, at the moment the message is being sent, some other event takes place in the immediate environment of the speaker and hearer, for example the arrival of a visitor, a bird flying by, a sudden unfamiliar smell, or a mosquito biting the hearer. Such events can also affect the transmission and reception of the message, and therefore constitute noise.

The sender can also contribute to the presence of noise, especially through the way he or she transfers the message. Among such aspects of noise are the poor articulation of words and phrases, inadequate co-ordination and ordering of ideas, unintended ambiguity, false or distorted information, and information whose technical character makes it impossible to grasp the message fully. Many such examples of noise can be cited. In Uganda, for instance, political leaders and other opinion-makers continually preach that Uganda is a fertile land, and that people should take advantage of the fertility of the soil by getting involved in productive agriculture, the backbone of the economy. Agricultural scientists, however, tell us that Ugandan soil has been undergoing degradation at a very fast rate. This is due, among other things, to rapid population growth, deforestation, anachronistic land tenure systems, unsatisfactory land policies, and insufficient attention given to the agricultural sector. A politician who extols the fertility of the Ugandan soils is either himself misinformed, or he wants to misinform the public. If he does not mention the need for fertilizers (organic or otherwise), better methods for soil conservation, the need to fight against land fragmentation, and so on, then the message he is sending to his audience is partly noise. In the language of discourse analysis (see Chapter 10), the politician is flouting the maxim of quantity, as he is not giving adequate information to his audience.

In the same way, the receiver can also contribute to noise. Sometimes he or she is not attentive enough. This is seen, for example, when in the middle of a sentence the hearer interrupts the speaker with an utterance on a completely different topic, a clear manifestation that the hearer was not paying attention to the speaker's words.

Sometimes, those hearing are not psychologically ready to receive the message. They may not like the arguments of the speaker; they might have their own convictions that they are unwilling to change; or they may be eager to put forward their own opinions. As mentioned above, such conversations or dialogues are often characterized by interruptions from the hearer.

In other circumstances, a hearer may 'over-interpret' what the speaker is saying, very often to suit his or her own needs and feelings. For example, in the case of fanaticism (whether political or religious) over-zealous or self-important individuals might sometimes add 'more salt' to the message given by their church or party, to meet their own wishes for power or self-aggrandizement.

It is also obvious that cultural beliefs and practices can also constitute noise in the communication process. For instance, noise can be caused by the dialectal variations of the same language. An example can be found in Runyakitara, a group of mutually intelligible dialects in western Uganda, eastern Congo, and northern Tanzania. In the Runyoro/Rutooro dialect, the word *kuswera* means 'to marry'. In Rukiga, however, the same word *kushwera* means either 'to marry' or 'to make love'. (We can imagine the scandalous misunderstandings and broken heads that might arise from confusing these two meanings!)

A similar type of noise can be found among Uganda's Baganda, who inhabit the central region, and who speak Luganda, the most standardized of all the Ugandan languages. The Baganda often expect other groups to speak Luganda, and do not make much effort to learn or to understand other languages. As a consequence, whereas a non-Muganda will generally be disposed to try to understand what a Muganda is saying, a Muganda often makes no effort to understand what, for instance, a Mugwere is saying. In some cases, even when a language or dialect is very close to Luganda, a Muganda may not be psychologically disposed to understand what is being said in that language or dialect. The attitude of a member of a language community towards another language or dialect and its speakers could therefore in itself contribute noise to the communication process, especially if the languages or dialects involved are, to some extent, mutually intelligible.

Socio-cultural practices and biases could also constitute noise. For instance, in some ethnic groups in many African countries, women speak more softly than men. In others, women avoid making direct eye-contact with their menfolk during communication interactions. And in certain communities (for example, the Batooro and Baganda of Uganda), children are not supposed to address their elders when standing, especially if the latter are sitting. Instead, they should first kneel or sit down. In an interaction involving other ethnic groups in which such practices do not exist, part of the message could be lost because of reactions and confusion arising from different modes of encounter and interaction.

Task

The issue of noise (particularly from the point of view of the sender and how it can affect communication), is indirectly covered in Grice's conversational principles, specifically the co-operative principle (explained in Chapter 10). Consult the discussion in Chapter 10 and then indicate how noise in the communication process can be reformulated in terms of the maxims of quantity, quality, and manner.

Language and culture

The second major issue to bear in mind in any discussion of cross-cultural communication is the interrelationship between language and culture.

The concept of language knowledge was discussed in Chapter 3; here, we wish only to remind you that language knowledge involves more than a knowledge of the grammatical system of a language. As we already know, a knowledge of how language is used in order to communicate with others (including textual competence, pragmatic competence, and strategic competence) is also part of language knowledge. A discussion of the interrelationship between language and culture must therefore take into account all these facets of language knowledge.

The concept of culture was discussed in Chapter 5, and you might like to turn back to that chapter to look over the relevant issues and views. Here, we would simply like to add some comments.

Some scholars have argued that language is part of culture, while others view culture and language as two different phenomena. The latter group point out, for instance, that the people of Western Europe and North America increasingly share the same culture (the so-called modern or Western culture), even though both communities house a multiplicity of languages, many not even mutually intelligible. In the same manner, the Luhya and the Dholuo languages of Kenya belong to two very different language families (Bantu and Nilotic respectively), yet the Baluhya and the Luo are neighbours, some even sharing the same villages. This has meant that, in terms of culture, the two have much in common (apart from male circumcision, which is not traditionally practised by the Luo). The Baluhya are culturally closer to the Luo than they are to fellow Bantus such as the Gikuyu and Kamba.

A view that seems to be generally accepted is that language can be considered as a cultural practice, and that language is both an instrument and a product of culture. This would mean that the diverse languages spoken by Western Europeans are not simply products of a given culture, but are also used to express cultural norms and practices that are increasingly similar in the different European countries. Similarly, the Baluhya and Luo of Kenya use languages that are historically products of distinct cultures, but which are increasingly used to express the same cultural reality. This has been the result of extensive interaction that has caused cultural convergence between linguistically different groups.

In exploring language and culture, it is helpful to take note of the views of Ali Mazrui (1990) and Alessandro Duranti (1997). Mazrui argues that culture performs seven functions: it provides people with lenses of perception and cognition, motives for behaviour, criteria of evaluation, a basis of identity, a mode of communication, a basis of stratification, and a system of production and consumption.

As we can see, according to Mazrui, culture entails far more than communication, which is only one of its seven functions. The other function that can be fairly closely linked to language is the provision of lenses of perception and cognition. This is because perception and cognition are often expressed in human language. The function of identity is also fundamental. The Baluhya of Kenya are Luhyas firstly because of their language, and only secondly because of their culture, which to some extent they share with the Luo and other ethnic groups in Kenya.

Duranti (1997) also identifies seven views relating to culture. He argues that culture is distinct from nature, that it is knowledge, communication, a system of mediation, a system of practices, a system of participation, and acts of predicting and interpreting.

If we compare the functions proposed by Mazrui and the theories discussed by Duranti, we notice some similarities:

- where Mazrui speaks of lenses of perception and cognition, Duranti speaks of knowledge;
- where Mazrui speaks of human behaviour, Duranti speaks of culture being distinct from nature (by which he means that culture is learnt through human interaction and linguistic communication);
- Mazrui's evaluation function can be equated with Duranti's acts of predicting and interpreting;
- Duranti's mediation function, whereby cultural tools help us to transform the environment (mediate between humans and nature), can be equated with Mazrui's production and consumption function;
- Mazrui's identity can probably be likened to Duranti's participation, as, in most cases, identifying with a given group or community means participating in what that community or group does;
- Mazrui's stratification function (hierarchy and social classes/groups) can be equated (if rather tentatively) with the practices theory of Duranti, as membership of a social class is often based on what one does or says; and
- finally, both Mazrui and Duranti agree that communication, and thus also language, is one of the principle functions or 'theories' of culture.

To sum up, the interrelationship between language and culture is demonstrated by the following:
- individual people learn the values, norms, beliefs, views, and behavioural patterns (in other words, the culture) of the group or groups of which they are members through linguistic interaction;
- groups give expression to their cultural identities, and practise their cultural life, not only through music, art, dancing, and dress, but also through language; and
- language reflects the cultural character of people both in their vocabulary (see Chapter 9) and in their discourse conventions[1] and ways of speaking (see Chapter 10).

Language transmits, sustains, and reflects culture

For the purposes of linguistics, we need to be a little more precise about the ways in which culture is embedded in language. The cultural context of a community is reflected in the following ways:
- the socio-cultural meanings of linguistic units (such as speech sounds) and of linguistic varieties (such as Pidgin English in Nigeria, Sheng in Kenya, and Fanagalo in South Africa);
- the internal structure of the vocabulary of a language or a language variety (compare the vocabulary items of remote rural communities with those of industrialized, urban communities);
- the meanings of lexical items (for example, compare the way that Europeans and Africans use words such as *colonialism, European, African,* and *American*); and
- discourse conventions (such as greetings, expressions of thanks and praise), as illustrated below.

In addition to these linguistic reflexes of the cultural context of language and language use, there are also paralinguistic and non-linguistic reflexes. Paralinguistic reflexes refer to features that co-occur with linguistic features, but which are not grammatical by nature, such as the tempo and loudness of speech and tone of voice. Non-linguistic reflexes of culture refer to aspects such as gestures, facial expressions, eye-contact, and the proximity between discourse participants, which are clearly not linguistic aspects, but which are nevertheless crucial for meaningful communication.

Furthermore, the interpretative schemata that people use, as well as their knowledge of contextualization cues, also play a role. The term *interpretative schemata* refers to peoples' knowledge of how the world works. For example, in order to interpret a story about a Hindu wedding, we would have to know what takes place in such a ceremony, otherwise our understanding of the story will be incomplete or distorted.

The term *contextualization cue* refers to signals that speakers automatically use to signal their understanding of the context of a discourse to other participants. For example, when a minister of religion uses certain words, a certain tone of voice, and certain gestures, church-goers will be able to interpret these and thus tell whether he or she is delivering a sermon or reading out the notices. In other words, speakers (indirectly) inform their hearers about the specific context of communications, so that the hearers can understand what the speakers' communicative intentions are.

Finally, people invariably work with stereotypes. This means that they often rely on oversimplified characterizations of the participants in a particular discourse. This usually happens when people do not yet know each other. For example, if we are introduced to a university professor, but we don't yet know what kind of person he or she is, our interpretation of what he or she says is likely to be shaped by our expectations of what a professor is like.

All these discourse features (paralinguistic and non-linguistic features, interpretative schemata, contextualization cues, and stereotypes) are culturally determined. This means that if people from different cultural worlds communicate, they may misunderstand one another, especially if their cultures differ with respect to these features. It is worth noting that cross-cultural miscommunication is a phenomenon that affects not only 'culturally opposite' groups (such as remote rural communities as opposed to highly industrialized urban communities), racial groupings, or ethnic divisions. It can also apply to communication between different age groups and different gender groups, as these too can differ culturally.

Three factors at work in cross-cultural communication

Communication between people who differ culturally often breaks down, as their differences function as noise (in the sense discussed above). In this section, we will discuss and illustrate three factors that often cause conversational derailment: non-verbal factors, paralinguistic factors, and discourse conventions.

Non-verbal factors

Non-verbal factors at work in intercultural communication are obviously those that are not expressed in linguistic form. One example is the physical proximity or distance between the participants in a communication inter-action.

In some African societies, physical distance is determined by rank, or social hierarchy or differentiation. It may not be appropriate for a child to be too close to an adult in a discussion, for a subordinate to be too close to a chief, or for a pupil to be too close to a teacher, unless they are authorized to come closer. In the same manner, depending on interpersonal relationships, it may not be wise for a man to stand too close to a woman in a communication inter-action. If this were to happen, it could lead to misunderstanding that could hamper the smooth running of the conversation.

Recently, a woman came to my office seeking information. While talking, she stood very close to me. After her departure, another woman in the office remarked that this visitor had no doubt spent a long time in Europe or the USA, or had just arrived from there, because, according to her, no African woman would stand that close to a man during a normal communication process!

There is also the issue of posture during communication. As we said earlier, in some ethnic groups in Uganda, children are expected to kneel when address-ing elders. Daughters and sons, in particular, must kneel when greeting their parental relatives (their fathers, mothers, grandparents, aunts, uncles, and so on). Such groups include the Batooro, the Baganda, and the Basoga. Among the Baganda, women are also expected to kneel before their menfolk during a greeting interaction.

In certain other cases, a speaker may not stand up straight when addressing a person of a higher rank. Out of respect, they should adopt a slightly hunched posture, with drooping shoulders.

With the advance of 'modernity', however, some of these practices are no longer strictly adhered to. Nevertheless, situations remain where these prac-tices must be respected if one wants to ensure a proper conversational exchange. An interesting incident took place when President Nelson Mandela of South Africa visited Uganda at the beginning of 1998. The vice-president of Uganda, Dr Speciosa Wandera-Kazibwe (a woman), was asked to interpret for the South African president during one of his public appearances. In order to show her respect, Dr Kazibwe knelt before Mr Mandela while interpreting.

Physical contact and eye-contact are other significant non-verbal factors. Among the Banyoro and the Batoro of Uganda, one may not touch (or shake hands with) one's father-in-law or mother-in-law of the opposite sex. This is a kind of taboo; the belief is that if one touches them, one will be struck by a dis-ease known as *entengera*, a disorder that makes one tremble and quake all the time. Among the Baganda, the situation is even more grave: one may not stay under the same roof as one's parents-in-law.

As regards eye-contact, in many African societies a woman may not look directly at the face of a man, particularly one she is not very familiar with. If she does so, he may totally misinterpret her intentions. Similarly, a child may not look an adult in the face. If this interactional norm is transgressed, an adult may shout at the offending child, ordering him or her not to stare him in the face. If reprimanded in this way, a child should immediately look down.

In many African societies, people do not kiss in public. In Uganda, women may kiss young children, especially babies. By contrast, it is natural for the French to kiss those with whom they are familiar on the cheeks, regardless of gender, although this interaction is most common between a man and a woman, or a woman and another woman. This is done during the greeting interaction, or while saying good-bye. Many educated French-speaking Africans from the former French colonies have also adopted this habit of social kissing, an interaction that is simply unheard of in most African societies.

The closest thing to this practice found in the East African region is the embracing practice of the Banyarwanda and the Barundi. In these two groups, men may embrace women, men may embrace men, and women may embrace other women during greetings among people who are familiar with each other.

Dress is another non-verbal factor in communication that is of considerable significance in many societies. It is clear that we will dress to fit the occasion when going for an interview, to class, to the office, or to the farm. These dress 'codes' are also determined by culture. In the case of funerals, for example, while Europeans usually wear dark, sombre clothing, women in Uganda tend to wear *busuti* (traditional ceremonial attire for women). Women who do not wear *busuti* will usually cover the lower part of their dresses from the hips downwards with a piece of cloth normally known as *lesu* in East Africa (what West Africans call a *wrapper*). They will also usually cover their heads with a piece of cloth to hide their hair. Whereas men in Europe will commonly wear black suits, Ugandan men usually dress casually, and avoid putting on suits and neckties. If an elegantly dressed man came to address a funeral gathering, part of his message might be lost, as he would be regarded as being inappropriately dressed.

Paralinguistic factors

Among the paralinguistic factors, we can mention the pitch of the voice. In many Ugandan ethnic groups, particularly among the Bantu-speakers, the voice of the speaker tends to become higher (i.e. the pitch tends to rise) when they wish to be kind, especially towards persons of equal or lower rank, or towards children. In the case of the Baganda, the pitch becomes higher and higher as one moves towards the end of a greeting interaction. In this particular case, a greeting exchange does not end with words. After having thanked each other for the work that has been done, and after having enquired about the health of the family members and so on, the speakers end with

ee... ee... ee... ee...

with the pitch rising on each repetition, until it cannot go any higher.

In some societies, loudness or softness of the voice can also signal different messages in various circumstances. In one culture, loudness could mean joy, in another anger, while in a third it could signal fear or respect.

The speed or tempo at which the speaker conducts the communication interaction can also carry different meanings. For instance, among the Banyarwanda and the Barundi, as well as the Banyoro, Batoro, and Banyankole of Uganda, recitals are one of the genres of oral literature. These are known as *Engabu* in Runyoro-Rutooro or as *Ebyevugo* in Runyankore-Rukiga. These recitals are usually performed at a very high speed. The faster the recital, the more the reciter is admired, as their speed is proof that they have mastered the language and its articulation. To the audience, the pace at which the recital is made does not affect the transmission of the message; it only adds to its beauty.

In other settings, such as public speaking, casual conversation, and greetings, speed has to be controlled if we are to communicate efficiently.

All the factors described above are generally interpreted according to the cultural background of the hearer. Clearly, this can sometimes bring about serious misunderstandings in a conversation in which different meanings are attached to similar discourse features. For example, a Frenchman might be taken aback if a Muganda woman knelt down on the grass beside the road to greet him. He might even think that the woman had mistaken him for a deity! On the other hand, the Muganda woman might get the greatest shock of her life if the Frenchman decides to kiss her on the cheeks as a form of greeting.

Discourse conventions

Our discussion of discourse conventions will be limited to greetings and forms of address.

In many African societies, a feature of greetings is that they tend to be long. This is probably due to the African concept of time, which does not necessarily correspond with the European notion of time. Another reason may be that many Africans are village dwellers, and the tempo of life in a village or rural locality is generally very different from that found in towns and cities. For instance, when a Musoga of Uganda greets someone, he will usually enquire not only after all the humans related to his interlocutor, but about the goats, chickens, cows, and sorghum at that interlocutor's homestead.

One interesting form of address connected with greetings is found among the Banyoro and Batooro of western Uganda and the Bahema of the Democratic Republic of Congo. This form is known as *empaako*, and it is a kind of pet name, an extra name that is given to each individual at birth. *Empaako* in themselves have no meaning to the speakers who use them (i.e. in the Runyoro-Rutooro or Ruhema language communities). It is agreed, however, that *empaako* have their origin in Lwo language communities, most likely Acholi. In Acholi, for instance, every *empaako* has a meaning.

There are only twelve *empaako* from which names can be selected. These are the following:

- For men and women: *Amooti, Abwoli, Atwoki, Ateenyi, Akiiki, Abbooki,* and *Adyeri.*
- For men only: *Acaali, Araali, Apuuli,* and *Bbala.*
- For the king only: *Okaali*

As regards the king, *Okaali* is more of a praise name, and it is given to every king. In addition, each king is given a further personal pet name or *empaako*, chosen from among the remaining eleven.

The *empaako* convention also has consequences in the naming of children. Since the coming of Islam and Christianity, every child is given a surname and a Christian or Muslim name. In addition, the child must also be given one of the eleven *empaako*.

The *empaako* is extremely important in daily life. It is used in speech situations such as greetings, leave-takings, and thanks.

Greetings

You generally cannot greet someone if you do not know their *empaako*. If they are a stranger, you first have to ask them:

Empaako yaawe niiwe oha? ('What is your empaako?')

They will then tell you their *empaako* and will in turn ask for yours. It is only then that you may greet each other. The greeting then goes like this:

A: Oraire ota Amooti? ('How have you slept, Amooti?')
B: Oraire ota Atwoki? ('How have you slept, Atwoki?')
A: Muliyo muta? ('How are you people there?')
B: Tuliyo kurungi. ('We are alright.')
etc.

As it is difficult in a village to know whether a visitor belongs to a particular ethnic group or not (it is worse in towns, but then there is usually some lingua franca), one sometimes comes across some interesting exchanges when a Mutooro meets a Mugisu (from eastern Uganda) and asks *Empaako yaawe niiwe oha?* ('What is your empaako?') The response is often confusion or a bewildered smile, as the hearer may not even understand what the notion of *empaako* involves, even if he or she understands some Rutooro.

Leave-taking

In western Ugandan culture, using *empaako* is also strictly required during leave-taking. When bidding someone farewell, the correct formula is:

A: Ogoroobe Ateenyi. ('Goodbye, Ateenyi.')
B: Ogoorobe Adyeri. ('Goodbye, Adyeri.')
A: Aboomuka obaramukye. ('Greet the people at home.')
B: Ndaabaramukya. ('I'll greet them.')

Thanks

Once again among western Ugandans, thanking someone involves more than simply saying 'thank you'. The *empaako* must be added:

A: Weebale muno Apuuli. ('Thank you very much, Apuuli.')
B: Ego Araali. ('You are welcome, Araali.')

In all the above situations that involve greeting, the *empaako* is essential. Failure to use it would be interpreted as a sign of rudeness, disrespect, or disregard. *Empaako* is thus what is sometimes called a politeness formula. When someone in this culture wants to show politeness, respect, affection, love, praise, or pity for an individual, regardless of age and rank, the *empaako* has to be used. Let us look at the two dialogues below:

A: Abwoli ninkusaba onyikirize ngende. ('I am asking you for permission to leave, Abwoli.')
B: Kale, genda. ('You may go.')
A: Weebale muno Abwoli. ('Thank you very much, Abwoli.')
B: Ego Abbooki. ('You are welcome, Abbooki.')

A: Akiiki weebale kwija. ('Thank you for coming, Akiiki'; or 'Welcome, Akiiki.')
B: Ego Acaali. ('Yes, Acaali'; or 'Thank you, Acaali.')
A: Kootubuzireho, Akiiki ('Why have you been lost to us, Akiiki?' or 'You have been scarce, Akiiki.')

B: Bizibu, Acaali. ('It's because of problems, Acaali.')

A: Hati Akiiki, ija kunu enyuma oramukye Omugurusi. ('Now Akiiki, come behind this way and greet the old man.')

B: Kale Acaali. ('OK, Acaali.')

The first dialogue demonstrates respect, especially on the part of A. In the second dialogue, both A and B show mutual affection coupled with politeness. (Obviously, other paralinguistic factors, such as intonation and softness of the voice, also play a role in these leave-takings.)

Another form of address worth mentioning is what could be called introductory formulas at the beginning of a speech. In Africa, this is common during political campaigns, political addresses, and the like. These are 'performed' to capture the attention of the audience and to create a sense of solidarity with them.

Another example comes from a different context; at Makerere University in Kampala, one cannot address a group of students during a social gathering unless one first 'tests'. This means starting one's speech as follows:

A: Makerere Oyee!

B (students): Oyee!

A: Lumumba (Hall) Oyee!

B: Oyee!

Now the speaker is free to go ahead with the speech. If the speaker is obstinate or unaware of this custom, and does not 'test', the students may interrupt him or her by shouting 'testing' until he or she performs the 'testing' greeting!

A similar situation is found among the Igbo of eastern Nigeria. In this community, before any social gathering can be addressed, certain opening phrases must be used. These are as follows:

A: Umuaka kwe nu! ('Children agree!')

B: Hee!

A: Umuaka rye nu! ('Children, let's eat!')

B: Hee!

A: Umuaka ngwa nu! ('Children, let's drink!')

B: Hee!

The orator can now proceed with the speech. The term *umuaka* ('children') can be replaced by the name of a village, community, school, party, or social club. Other variations can also be used in place of 'eating' or 'drinking'. For example, in the town of Abakaliki, the greeting might sound like this:

A: Abakaliki kwe nu! ('Abakaliki, agree!')

B: Hee!

A: Abakaliki, mua nu! ('Abakaliki, give birth!')
B: Hee!
A: Abakaliki zu nu! ('Abakaliki, bring up the children!')
B: Hee!

The function of these opening phrases is to obtain the co-operation of the audience. In the first example, the orator gets their attention and then solicits their consent and support by asking them first to be with him or her (to agree) and then to eat and drink with him or her. In the second formula, the orator prays for the fertility of the community, so that they may get children to raise. So, in both formulas, the orator wishes the audience happiness and prosperity. It is also worth noting that after such a formula the orator is free to address the gathering in Igbo, or even in English.

Such formulas and forms of address exist in various forms in most, if not all, African societies. They are of vital importance in ensuring that a communication process fulfils its objectives.

Strategies for the management of cross-cultural miscommunication

Given that cultural differences between people have the potential to cause miscommunication and possibly even conflict, it is important to ask how these problems can be avoided. Obviously, we can provide only a brief overview of this complex issue.

Logically, it seems that there are two possible approaches to this problem. One involves the development of a lingua franca that can be used for inter-group communication; another solution is to promote national multilingualism, so that all citizens of a country share at least one medium of communication.

If we choose the option of a single lingua franca, the most pressing question is which language should be selected for this purpose. One obvious choice is the ex-colonial language of a state. In general, these languages are already official languages, are the main media of economic activity, are established educational languages, and have the required status.

However, the track record of teaching and learning these languages is not very encouraging. In many African countries where these languages are used for teaching and learning purposes, the examination performance of children, especially in rural schools, is dismal. After almost a century of continuous teaching of English and French (several centuries in the case of Portuguese), there is hardly any country in Africa where these languages are adequately spoken by a significant proportion of its inhabitants.[2] The use of ex-colonial languages as languages of instruction has in fact led to a decline in the quality of education in the rural areas. While the majority of good schools in Uganda are today found in Kampala, there used to be many excellent schools in rural areas in pre-colonial days and in the early 1960s. These schools competed very favourably with the urban schools, in spite of using the vernacular languages during the first years of their school programmes.

A second negative consequence of developing (or promoting) the ex-colonial languages as lingua francas is that they may lead to the demise of the indigenous languages of Africa (see Chapter 1).

Thirdly, language policies that support the ex-colonial languages have also had the unfortunate consequence of favouring a relatively small elite, who are comfortable with the colonial language. The majority of the people, however, experience difficulty in communicating in the 'official' languages, or are totally incapable of doing so, thus leading to the problems mentioned in Chapter 1.

An African language or an Africanized variety of an ex-colonial language (for instance, Kiswahili in East Africa or Pidgin English in Nigeria) could also be used as an alternative lingua franca. The advantages and disadvantages of such a course of action have already been discussed elsewhere in this book.

The multilingualism option, on the other hand, implies that all the citizens of a (highly multilingual) state will need to learn at least three languages, and that these languages will also become the languages of official use. If this approach is followed, one result will be that African languages will be used in public life (probably together with an ex-colonial language). However, any decision to use African languages for official and public functions generates its own problems. One of the most important obstacles is likely to be the reluctance of politicians and government officials to provide their full support.

Africa does not have an impressive record in this domain. Even those countries where serious attempts have been made to promote indigenous languages, these efforts have had shortcomings. Tanzania, for example, opted for an aggressive policy of promoting Kiswahili, but, in so doing, suffocated the other indigenous languages. Kenya has also given Kiswahili considerable support, but has remained hesitant about other local languages. Similarly, Uganda, in spite of recommendations that mother tongues be taught, has done very little to promote the use of African languages. Nigeria meanwhile declared Igbo, Hausa, and Yoruba to be national languages way back in the 1970s, a decision that remained on paper. In practice, English and Pidgin have become the cross-cultural languages of Nigeria. In monolingual countries such as Rwanda, Burundi, and Madagascar, the ex-colonial languages still receive far more attention than the national languages. In Rwanda, a new reality has emerged, whereby English has become as much an official language as French, in spite of Kinyarwanda being the locally spoken language.

Whichever of these options is accepted as policy, it is vital that school syllabuses (not just the language syllabuses) be directed at promoting knowledge of the cultural diversity of a country, as well as tolerance and respect for the right of people to differ socio-culturally. Moreover, formal education should explicitly focus on the development of pupils' skills in handling the various obstacles to cross-cultural communication.

Conclusion

We would like to conclude this chapter with a question: if cross-cultural communication is a problem, as we have demonstrated here, and if it does indeed contain the potential for conflict, why should cultural diversity be protected? Why not opt for a strenuous policy of cultural assimilation, one that replaces cultural diversity with a single cultural character?

This issue was first raised in Chapter 1, and you might like to refresh your memory by turning back to the relevant section. At this stage, we would merely like to make a few comments that we believe are pertinent to this debate:

- the possession of a distinctive socio-cultural identity is possibly a non-negotiable and basic human need, with members of a particular group both unwilling and unable to relinquish their identity and to vanish into universal inconspicuousness;
- socio-cultural diversity is an essential component of creativity, as exposure to societies whose members think and behave differently compels communities to question the validity of their own views, beliefs, attitudes, values, and norms, as well as to explore the views of others; and
- the history of group relations throughout the globe, particularly in Africa (and Eastern Europe, in its present state of crisis), underlines the need to recognize and respect the realities of socio-cultural identity.

We in Africa would do well to ponder these matters.

Endnotes

1   Note, for instance, the praise poem as genre in many African communities.

2   A corollary of the decision to use an ex-colonial language in public life is that an Africanized version of the ex-colonial language be accepted as standard, and that decision-makers, educational authorities, and the intellectual leadership of the country give their full support to the use of this localized variety.

Bibliography

AUSTIN, J.L. 1961. *Philosophical Papers*. Oxford: Oxford University Press.

BOAS, FRANZ. 1911. 'Introduction.' In F. Boas (ed.), *Handbook of American Indian Languages* (vol. BAE-B40, 1). Washington D.C.: Smithsonian Institute.

BOURDIEU, PIERRE. 1977. *Outline of a Theory of Practice*, trans. Richard Nice. Cambridge: Cambridge University Press.

DE CLEENE, N. 1957. *Introduction a l'Ethnographie du Congo Belge et du Rwanda-Burundi*. Antwerp, Editions de Sikkel, S.A.

DURANTI, ALESSANDRO. 1997. *Linguistic Anthropology*. Cambridge: Cambridge University Press.

ERVIN-TRIPP, SUSAN. 1972. 'On Sociolinguistic Rules: Alternative and Co-occurrence.' In J.J. Gumperz and D. Hymes (eds.), *Directions in Sociolinguistics: the Ethnography of Communication*. New York: Holt.

GEERTZ, CLIFFORD. 1973. *The Interpretation of Cultures*. New York: Basic Books.

GRICE, H.P. 1971. 'Meaning.' In J.F. Rosenberg and C. Travis (eds.), *Readings in the Philosophy of Language*. Englewood Cliffs, N.J.: Prentice-Hall.

GUMPERZ, JOHN J. 1964. 'Linguistic and Social Interaction in Two Communities.' *American Anthropologist*, 66 (6): 137–53.

IRVINE, JUDITH. 1974. 'Strategies in Status Manipulation in Wolof Greetings.' In R. Bauman and J. Sherzer (eds.), *Explorations in the Ethnography of Speaking*. Cambridge: Cambridge University Press.

JAKOBSON, ROMAN. 1968. 'Poetry of Grammar and Grammar of Poetry.' *Lingua*, 21: 597–609.

LABOV, WILLIAM. 1972. *Sociolinguistic Patterns*. Philadelphia: University of Pennsylvania Press.

LEECH, GEOFFREY. 1983. *Principles of Pragmatics*. London and New York: Longman.

LEVI-STRAUSS, CLAUDE. 1963. *Structural Anthropology*. New York: Basic Books.

MALINOWSKI, B. 1930. 'The Problem of Meaning in Primitive Languages.' In C.K. Ogden and I.A. Richards, *The Meaning of Meaning*, London: Routledge.

MAZRUI, ALI. 1990. *Cultural Forces in World Politics*. London: James Currey.

MUKAMA, RUTH. 1989. 'The Linguistic Dimension of Ethnic Conflict.' In Rupesinghe Kaman (ed.), *Conflict Resolution in Uganda*. Oslo: Oslo Research Institute.

NDOLERIIRE, O.K. 1996. 'Towards Language Homogeneity or Heterogeneity? The Vexing National Language Issue in Uganda.' In M. Muranga et al. (eds.), *Makerere Papers in Languages and Linguistics*. Kampala.

PIKE, KENNETH L. 1966. 'Etic and Emic Standpoints for the Description of Behaviour.' In A.G. Smith (ed.), *Communication and Culture: Readings in the Codes of Human Interaction*. New York: Holt, Rinehart & Winston.

SAPIR, EDWARD. 1924. 'Culture, Genuine and Spurious.' *Journal of Sociology* 29: 401–29.

SCHLEGOFF, EMMANUEL A.1972. 'Sequencing in conversational openings.' In J.J. Gumperz and D. Hymes (eds.), *Directions in Sociolinguistics: the Ethnography of Communication*. New York: Holt, Rinehart & Winston.

SEARLE, JOHN R. 1969. *Speech Acts: an Essay on the Philosophy of Language*. Cambridge: Cambridge University Press.

SILVERSTEIN, MICHAEL. 1977. 'Cultural Prerequisites to Linguistic Awareness.' In M. Saville-Troike (ed.), *Linguistics and Anthropology*. Georgetown University Round Table on Languages and Linguistics. Washington D.C.: Georgetown University Press.

WEBB, V.N. (ed.) 1995. *Language in South Africa. An input into Language Planning for Post-apartheid South Africa*. The LiCCA Research and Development Programme, University of Pretoria.

WHORF, BENJAMIN LEE. 1956. 'Linguistics as an Exact Science.' In J.B. Carrol (ed.), *Language, Thought and Reality: Selected Writings of Benjamin Lee Whorf*. Cambridge, Mass: MIT Press.

12 Language in education and language learning in Africa

Jane Kembo

Expected outcomes

At the end of this chapter you should be able to:
1 Explain the role of language in educational development.
2 Distinguish between first-language learning, second-language learning, and foreign-language learning.
3 Debate the statement that serious study of the first language is fundamental to cognitive, affective, and social development.
4 Discuss the levels of proficiency in the ex-colonial languages in Africa.
5 Identify and describe factors that affect second-language learning.
6 Identify and describe sources of error in second-language learning.
7 Give a critical overview of language teaching methods and practices.

Introduction

It is generally accepted that the decisive factor for a possible future renaissance in Africa is formal education. This continent will not reduce its deficit in economic and technical performance until the required knowledge and skills of its (future) citizens have been developed through effective formal education. In this regard, *language* is a vital factor, as has been emphasized throughout this book. If the people of Africa want to give themselves a realistic opportunity to develop to their full potential educationally, economically, and politically, and to contribute to the resolution of their many problems, the issue of language in education must be addressed. This concerns matters such as the role of the indigenous languages and proficiency in the ex-colonial languages. Before tackling these issues, however, we provide a brief reminder of the socio-linguistic background.

As described in Chapter 2, African states (especially south of the Sahara) are characterized by linguistic complexity: large numbers of languages and dialects, indigenous languages that are underdeveloped in terms of function and prestige, the presence throughout the continent of dominant European languages, a generally inadequate proficiency in these ex-colonial languages, and a number of indigenous languages of wider communication (Wolof and Pidgin English in West Africa, Kiswahili in East Africa, and the Nguni languages in southern Africa). In addition, Africans are usually highly multilingual. People who live in linguistic border areas find it necessary to learn more than one language in order to communicate with their neighbours. Similarly, those who live in urban areas inevitably have to learn more than one language for inter-ethnic communication.

Many of these speakers will 'pick up' the languages of wider communication, such as Kiswahili in Kenya and Tanzania, for example. These languages of wider communication are learnt informally through interaction with people who need to relate to one another in trade or jobs, socially as neighbours or friends, and so on.

Many Africans also have a first language (mother tongue) that is different from the official languages of their countries. However, the official languages are often also the languages of education and power, as well as instruments of social mobility. English, for example, is not just a language of power within individual nations; it has become internationally dominant. The fact that many African countries now strive to give their citizens some proficiency in English has to do with the need to gain a stake in international communications and trade, and to keep abreast of technological advancements. It is clear that language teaching in Africa must take note of this intricate web of linguistic complexity.

The high value placed on the ex-colonial languages and the low status of indigenous languages have had at least three serious consequences for educational development:

- the indigenous languages have not been taken seriously as subjects of study, which means that the cognitive, affective, and social development of young people, which must necessarily occur through a language that is well known, cannot take place effectively;
- proficiency in the ex-colonial languages is so highly sought after that parents and educational authorities argue that learners should be exposed to them at the very first opportunity (sometimes even from day one of the school programme), notwithstanding the fact that educational development cannot take place in a language one does not know; and
- proficiency in the ex-colonial languages remains inadequate, partly because the necessary cognitive skills needed for effective learning have not been developed.

The result of these three situations has generally been that inadequate educational development has taken place and hence that there has been an inadequate level of general achievement.

There are, of course, a number of ways in which something can be done about these matters. The role of language in education in Africa needs urgent and thorough attention, particularly with reference to policies concerning the languages of learning and teaching, the significant development of pupils' linguistic skills through the study of their first languages, and the learning of English, French, and Portuguese.

Using indigenous languages as languages of learning and teaching

Generally speaking, African states follow a policy of using the ex-colonial language as the main language of learning and teaching, restricting the indigenous languages to subjects of study. The reason behind this policy seems to be the belief that proficiency in the ex-colonial language can only really be ensured if it is also used as the language of learning and teaching. In Kenya, for example, the language policy is that the language of the catchment area is to be used for instruction for the first three years of primary school, during which time English and Kiswahili are to be taught as subjects. English, the official language of the country, becomes the language of instruction from the fourth year of primary school onwards. The language of the catchment area may be one of the over forty ethnic languages of Kenya. If this is a language other than Kiswahili, the national language, it is supposed to be phased out after the third year of primary schooling. In other words, there is no provision for mother tongues, the child's first language of identity, in the syllabus after the first three years of primary education. In spite of the strong policy support for Kiswahili and especially English, many children in Kenya have been observed to be fluent in neither language (Kimani wa Njoroge 1985).

In Zambia, which has a policy very similar to that in Kenya, Williams (1994) observes that there is lack of proficiency in English, the language of instruction, among Zambian primary-school children. This in turn prevents them from learning effectively. It has also been observed that many teachers still use the various mother tongues for teaching, give notes in English (Obura 1984), and expect pupils to write examinations in English. In Tanzania, Kiswahili is the language of instruction in primary school, with English only taught as a subject. However, learners who complete primary school are expected to have adequately mastered English and to be able to cope with it as a medium of instruction throughout secondary school. As Roy-Campbell and Quorro (1987) point out, most students have difficulty learning in English and perform poorly in all subjects taught in it.

It seems obvious that the use of an ex-colonial language as language of learning and teaching needs serious re-evaluation, and that the use of indigenous languages for this purpose should be considered. The use of indigenous languages as languages of learning and teaching has been adequately discussed elsewhere in this book (see particularly Chapter 5), and we therefore want only to summarize the main arguments. Firstly, cognitive and affective development occurs more effectively in a language learners know very well. This usually means using a first language.[1] Secondly, learning – in general, but including second-language and foreign-language learning – occurs more effectively if the required cognitive development has already occurred through the use of a first language as a language of learning. Cummins (1984) shows that 'optimal first language education provides a rich cognitive preparation for the acquisition of a second language', and that 'the literacy skills already acquired in the first language (and, of course, the cognitive skills) provide easy transition to the second-language medium education'.

Questions

One of the major tasks of formal education is to develop pupils' cognitive abilities; that is, their memory, their ability to generalize, to grasp relationships such as cause and effect, to predict the consequences of events, to grasp the essential message of a speech or a book, and to evaluate situations. The school must also develop its pupils' affective skills; that is, it must help them to develop positive attitudes to work and study, loyalty to their country, and tolerance for people who may differ from them. Finally, the school must develop its pupils' social skills; that is, their ability to work together with other people, to communicate with them, and to support those who need assistance. To develop all these skills requires a great deal of understanding, and, in our opinion, they can be developed only in a language that both the pupils and their teachers know very well, which is generally the mother tongue.

1 In your experience, did pupils and teachers at your school know English, French, Portuguese, or another official language well enough to be able to develop these skills?

2 What was the official language of learning and teaching in the school you attended? Was this policy always strictly applied? If not, what was the actual practice in your classes?

3   Some have argued that a world language must be used as a language of learning so that Africans can have access to the international world. Is this a valid argument? How many of your friends are likely to make use of such access? Is it necessary to use such a language as a language of learning in order to get to know it? What do the Japanese do in this regard? And the Chinese?

First-language study

A remark often heard about the teaching of indigenous African languages as first languages is that there is no need to study them, as pupils 'already know them'. This is, of course, a serious misconception, as can be seen from the absence of similar views about the study of English, French, and Portuguese as first languages in communities where they are the mother tongues.

This misconception is based on a number of factors that include the low status of the African languages as instruments of educational and economic activity, the high value placed on the ex-colonial languages, and uncertainty about the content of study programmes in these languages as subjects of study.

Linguists and language teachers can do very little about the first two of these factors; changes to these depend on the political and economic leadership of a country. Linguists and language teachers can, however, provide some guidance on the third factor.

Space does not allow for a full discussion of the goals of first-language study in African languages, and we therefore provide only a list of some of the possible goals. These include:

* the development of pupils' skills in performing advanced language-based cognitive tasks, such as reasoning, understanding, and explaining abstract concepts; more specifically, listening, reading, speaking, and writing skills need to be fully developed, and school-leavers should have the ability to comprehend complex texts, to produce such texts themselves, and to interpret and evaluate them;
* the development of linguistic skills in the standardized variety of the language (in other words, the acquisition of the ability to operate effectively in formal contexts and public life in the first language);
* understanding the linguistic character of pupils' first languages;
* understanding the ways in which language is used in social and public life;
* understanding and appreciating the products of the first-language community, including its literary products;
* the development of pupils' ability to discover information (language as a heuristic tool), to explore their own inner world, and to develop their

creativity (something that can only really occur in a language that is known extremely well); and
- understanding the role of language in cultural life, including the development of an attitude of tolerance towards communities with different languages.

Intensive attention to the first language as a school subject is of fundamental importance to the development of the individual and the society, and is arguably vital to the success of pupils in their other subjects.

Learning the ex-colonial languages

While the use of indigenous languages in schools and the upgrading of first-language study are vital for educational development in Africa, the levels of proficiency in languages such as English, French, and Portuguese must also be addressed. When a speaker of an indigenous African language learns other languages, different processes of acquisition are involved. Here we must distinguish between first-language learning, second-language learning, and foreign-language learning.
- First-language learning takes place spontaneously, with very little formal instruction (besides the guidance given by parents). The language the child acquires is the language she or he is exposed to during early childhood.
- Second-language learning usually takes place in situations of formal instruction, such as schools, and learners acquire the rules and units of the target language through guided instruction by a teacher.[2] A characteristic feature of this type of language learning situation is that learners are exposed to the target language in informal situations, as it is heard on the radio and television, in shops, and in public places. An example of second-language learning in Africa would be the learning of English, French, or Portuguese in certain urban areas.
- Foreign-language learning also takes place in formal learning situations with guidance from teachers. However, the target language is not usually part of the everyday experience of the learners, and therefore does not play a meaningful role in their lives. An example of foreign-language learning in Africa would be the study of German or Spanish, or the learning of English, French, or Portuguese in rural Africa.

Second-language learning and foreign-language learning obviously have the same goal: to enable learners to gain a competence in the target language that is as close to mother-tongue use as possible. However, they are separate process-es, with different assumptions and different methods.

In debates about teaching and learning an ex-colonial language in Africa, the subject of the debate is usually said to be English as a Second Language – ESL (or French as SL, or Portuguese as SL). In the rest of this chapter the focus of attention will be mainly on learning and teaching English, French, or Portuguese as second languages. Part of it, however, may be applicable to foreign-language learning.

It is generally accepted that many Africans have inadequate language proficiency in the ex-colonial languages. Consider, for example, the following examples of writing by two Kenyan pupils finishing their primary school, who were responding to a task set in the exam (*KCPE Newsletter* 1991: 12, 14):

Task:
The following is the beginning of a farewell speech to Standard 8 pupils by the head-teacher. Write down the rest of the speech.

This is both a happy and a sad occasion. We are happy because you have worked hard and completed your primary education. It is sad because you are leaving us and we shall miss you.

Answer 1
I am go finish my primary school I will infor my mother that I will worked hard and go to a scondary and I will be happy be if if I finish my scondary school and formation my people what I will wroked to do my best so that Ica be abe the worked for myself and half my money and my children.

Answer 2
I can remeber very well the day you came to my school, that was in 1987 when you came for enrolment for class five. You did the inteview and passed very well, allowed you in my school because you passed very well.

The first example is written by a very weak student; besides the fact that she or he is not even writing on the topic, she or he can hardly communicate in the language. There are numerous spelling and grammar mistakes. The second student can communicate, but his or her writing is repetitive and the composition is rather uninteresting. These are the kind of results we can expect unless the teaching of second/foreign-language writing is radically overhauled. If we consider the amount of money, time, and energy invested in the teaching of these languages,[3] it is clearly necessary to investigate the reasons for this state of affairs.

In the rest of this chapter, four factors affecting language learning and teaching will be explored. These are:
• the realities of teaching languages such as English, French, or Portuguese in Africa, most notably the unsupportive learning conditions;

- factors affecting language learning, such as age, motivation, and cognitive and affective factors;
- the influence of other languages that the learner already speaks, known as the sub-strate influence on language learning; and
- the use of Western and other inappropriate language teaching methods and practices.

The realities of language teaching in Africa

A major reason for the unsatisfactory level of proficiency in languages such as English, French, and Portuguese is that the realities of teaching these languages in Africa do not allow for their adequate acquisition. These languages often play no meaningful part in the lives of the communities from which pupils come. The pupils have commonly had almost no exposure to these languages, either in real life, on the radio, or on television – they are thus heard only in school class-rooms. In addition, the teachers who of necessity function as role models for the pupils very often have only a limited proficiency in these languages.

Another feature of the language learning reality is that the learning condi-tions in African schools are often extremely unsupportive. There are a number of factors which negatively affect all formal education, including language teaching. First of all, there is the condition of the physical facilities in many African schools, such as the shortage of desks, insufficient space, and poor lighting, all of which make education extremely difficult.

Secondly, there is the general size of classes. In Kenya, teachers handle groups as large as fifty pupils. This means that pupils may often not get a chance to say anything other than to repeat (usually in chorus fashion) the structures being 'taught'. Large classes also mean that, even if teachers want to use a communicative method to teach, they will find that their classes are prob-ably too large to engage in meaningful communication. If they organize their classes into pairs for practice purposes, the noise generated may prevent pupils from concentrating, and may end up distracting other classes. To get round this, teachers may decide to use the lecture approach, in which they outline a topic, give examples, and elicit a few more examples from pupils before giving them work to do.

Thirdly, there is the problem of textbooks. In many parts of Africa, as many as eight learners may share a textbook. Sometimes, particularly in Malawi and Zambia, the teacher may be the only one with a textbook. This obviously has far-reaching consequences for pupil performance and learning. It means that learners do not have personal contact with what they are learning, other than through their teachers; homework cannot be done; and learners cannot do any reading on their own on topics dealt with in class.

Fourthly, the knowledge, skills, aptitudes, attitudes, and motivations of the teachers, and their experience and training (Brumfit 1984), are also factors, as are pupils' discipline and their level of interest and dedication (including their attitudes to the target language and their level of motivation to acquire a foreign language). Also in this category are teacher–pupil relationships, and outside interference, such as classes being interrupted for non-educational reasons (for instance, pupils being forced to attend political rallies).

Finally, the extreme formality of the language learning context in Africa probably also contributes to ineffective learning. Typically, this context involves a learner, a teacher and an institution, and a programme for teaching the rules of the target language – grammar, textbooks, sessions of practice, and continuous or summative (end-of-term) assessments to find out whether learning has taken place. In formal language learning, the teacher is usually a figure of authority. She or he determines what goes on in the classroom in terms of what is taught, how, how much and what type of practice pupils have, who gets to speak in class and for how long, and perhaps even what learners can or cannot say. In addition, formal language teaching is generally aimed at 'correctness' (rather than successful communication or appropriateness), sometimes to the detriment of communication. In this kind of context, many learners will not risk producing the wrong responses, as the teacher demands the 'correct' response (and may punish those who do not produce them) and tends to ignore incorrect answers without explaining why they are wrong. Language study is regarded in the same way as a content subject such as History, as a string of data that can be either correct or incorrect, rather than as an opportunity to develop a communicative skill.

Factors affecting language learning

There are a number of factors which affect a learner's ability to acquire a new language. These include age, cognition, motivation, and emotion, all of which act together to produce certain results in language learning. We shall examine some of these factors a little more closely.

Age

According to Brown (1987), age results in differences that are mental, physical, and affective, which impact on how we think, how our bodies function, and how we feel. Neurological research shows that, as the body matures, different functions are assigned to different parts of the brain, with control of language assigned to the left side. The 'division of labour' between the right and left sides of the brain is believed to be completed by the time we are sixteen. It is thought that this is why learners do not easily attain native-like control of a new language, especially where pronunciation is concerned, after the age of puberty. One reason for this could be that, as people grow older, the elasticity of the many muscle groups required to produce certain sounds decreases. Or it may be that these muscle groups become so conditioned to producing the sounds in our first language that we find it difficult to retrain them to produce those sounds in the target language that differ from those of the first language.[4]

Age also affects our attitudes to other people and the languages they speak, our perceptions about ourselves, and the risks we take or choose not to take. In Africa, there are examples of children beginning school at the age of six, eight, or (in extreme circumstances) only at adolescence (after the age of twelve). It is then likely that one of the obstacles to successful second-language acquisition is the age factor.

Cognitive factors

As we already know, cognition refers to knowledge, and our ability to process and use that knowledge. Ausubel (quoted in Brown 1987) notes that most items are successfully learnt when they are related to knowledge acquired through experience. In mother-tongue learning, children use meaningful contexts to learn. They will communicate about things that are immediately important to them, and will also begin to associate results with their communication. Their mother tongue is thus an instrument for controlling the environment around them to best serve their needs. However, one difference between the mother-tongue and the target-language learner is that, while the young child may have no other language, the foreign-language learner invariably already has at least one language in which she or he is able to communicate.

Imagine a six-year-old child, who is learning English for the first time, venturing out for the first time to play with neighbouring children who only speak Sesotho or Luhya. This child has probably learnt most of the basic structures she requires in her mother tongue. In other words, she already has one language in which she can operate with ease. She may therefore not have such a strong instrumental incentive to acquire another language. However, in order to make friends, control her environment, express opinions, and make her feelings known, she will have to learn to communicate with the rest of the group. She will do this in contexts that require her to make her wishes and needs known in English and Sesotho. In doing this, she will be learning language in meaningful situations, language that is aimed at acting on the learner's environment and getting needs met. This is different from language learning in the classroom, where there is seldom any meaningful situation or reason to communicate in the target language.

Goals and motivation

Another factor related to language learning has to do with the goal for which another language is learnt. The child who is learning a new language in order to be accepted by a play-group may only be vaguely aware of her reasons for trying to acquire the language, but because her wish to play with other children is the driving force or motive, she will learn the language in question. Her learning the language of the playground may be motivated both by a need for acceptance and a desire to take part in the activities of those around her. Unlike an adult learner, she will often be so focused that she will learn the language in a very short time. The reasons for this may be the amount of time she is able to dedicate to the learning, the exposure to the new language, and the fact that at this stage she has formed very few rigid opinions about groups and other languages that might inhibit her learning of another language. A central factor is that she will be learning the new language in order to meet real needs; in other words, her learning will be goal-oriented.

Adults learning a target language might have different reasons for doing so; they may be learning a new language because they are in a job where they will need to use it. In many parts of Africa, as in other parts of the world, people are increasingly finding themselves in a country that does not necessarily make use of a language they know. These people are forced to learn the language(s) of the host country. In other words, adults seem to learn other languages for more conscious reasons, rather than spontaneously.

Adults who are learning another language are also not likely to give all their attention to this task, as they have other responsibilities. They are thus not likely to learn as quickly as a child might (although there are exceptions). Furthermore, because of their proficiency in at least one language and their intellectual development, they may tend to over-analyse the language data that they encounter, using their first language for points of comparison even where there are no similarities. Adults are more aware of the differences between their own languages and the new language, and this awareness, together with the effort involved, may discourage many from learning a foreign language. This may in turn result in slower learning, or eventual inadequate mastery of the target language. Adults may thus bring more knowledge of the world to the learning situation than a child learner, but they also have various handicaps.

Affective factors

Humans are not only 'thinking' beings, but also 'feeling' beings. There are instances in which the feeling (emotional) faculty takes over, and dominates our thought processes. The affective factors, which have to do with how we feel, may be pivotal in determining why one person learns a language more successfully than another. We have already noted that children seem to be less self-conscious and more spontaneous learners than adults. These factors seem to be more important for target-language learning than mother-tongue learning. The affective domain includes personality factors, such as our image of ourselves: are we secure and confident, or insecure and shy? Do we feel threatened? Are we outgoing or inward-looking? Inhibited? Anxious? Do we have a positive attitude, or do we have prejudices about the target language or the learning situation? Someone who has self-confidence is more likely to take the risk of making mistakes. Similarly, a friendly person is more likely to have input from friends and acquaintances, as well as more opportunities to speak the target language. While a shy person may not want to risk making errors, the extrovert's concern will be to forge relationships. A negative person might be surrounded by input in the target language, but their attitude blocks it from becoming part of their knowledge. This is an interesting area of language learning, both because of its pervasive nature and because for a long time it has not been taken seriously in language teaching and learning.

Young children believe that the world revolves round them. As they grow older, however, especially during adolescence, they become more shy; their self-doubt makes them self-protective. During adolescence, they are trying to forge a new identity. This is at least partly related to the languages to which they have been exposed. The learning of a new language might thus pose a threat to the self-image that has been formed through the first language. Willingness to make a fool of oneself is often part of the learning process, something that children usually find easy, but that is very difficult for both adolescent and adult learners. Affective factors will also determine how quickly and successfully someone will learn the target language. Motivation is crucial; we are aware of people who have lived all or most of their lives with a certain linguistic group but cannot speak that language. The reasons for this probably reflect their attitude or lack of motivation rather than their ability to learn the language.

Questions

1 What role does cultural context play in foreign-language learning? (You might like to turn back to Chapters 5 and 11.)
2 What can teachers do to overcome or minimize factors such as a negative attitude to a particular language?

The sub-strate influence on language learning

The term **sub-strate influence** refers to the role of the languages a learner already knows at the time of learning a foreign language. This factor clearly affects formal language learning. A number of aspects will be discussed below.

Interlanguage

When a learner who already knows one language (known as the 'source language') very well begins to learn a new language, he or she has already internalized certain ideas about how language is used and how language rules broadly operate to produce meaning in communication. However, this learner still begins with no knowledge of the target language, and thus has to progress gradually towards native-speaker ability. The learner's newly acquired knowledge and performance are part of an ability that changes constantly as his or her knowledge of the target language increases. Nemser (1971) captures this ability in the following diagram, the 'approximative system continuum'.

FIGURE 12.1   The approximative system continuum

Zero   Native-speaker
knowledge   competence

A_____B_____C

For many learners in foreign-language contexts, native-speaker competence is never achieved. If we look at Figure 12.1, it can be said that learners will tend to 'stop' at different points between A and C. The learner's language at any point is 'approximative', given that the target is native-like proficiency. The language that a speaker develops somewhere between, say, points A and B, may be nothing like a native speaker's language, but will perhaps reflect the learner's mother tongue. It will have some features of the mother tongue, and some of the target language, and represents the rules internalized at that point in the learner's developing knowledge of the target language. Selinker (1969, 1972) refers to these 'temporary' grammars built by the learner as the **interlanguage**.

It is important to study learner errors, because these reveal the hypotheses that a learner may be testing out, the generalizations he or she is making about certain linguistic structures or rules, and the progress that a learner may be making towards native-speaker competence. Language learning, like any other form of learning, will entail 'mistakes', as well as mistaken assumptions about data being dealt with. Ideally, the learner's errors are largely eradicated or reduced as a result of feedback and input from his or her target-language environment.

Here are some examples of learner errors:

1   *When day reach, fast in the morning we eat food.
2   *When I was see that soming I was very appearance at first.
3   *I did not despair in every corner of the dormitory, but it was in vain.
4   One of the men signalled us to settle down.
5   *After we recognized him, we felt sorry for what we had done *for* him.

(Excerpts from Primary 8 examination papers (English Paper 1, Composition). Kenya National Examinations Council 1993: 6)

Students at the university where I teach have been heard to make statements such as:

6   *May I use *this your* pen (a direct translation from Kiswahili and other Kenyan languages).
7   *You will be punished if you *repeat it again.*

There are two points to make about interlanguage that many of us will have observed. First of all, the learner's interlanguage on this continuum will most likely be neither the mother tongue nor the target language, but a combination of the two, as can be seen in sentences 1 and 2 above. Secondly, the examples above confirm that students who all begin learning a new language at the same time will progress at different rates along the continuum, depending on factors such as age, motivation, and exposure. While examples 1 and 2 make almost no sense, 5 does, even though there is a 'wrong'[5] use of the word *for*.

The learner's inadequate knowledge of the rules of the language may lead them, for example, to add *-ed* to the end of a verb such as *fly* to form the past tense in English, so that the speaker ends up with **flied*. Sentences in which *for* is used instead of *to* (as in 5 above) are also typical. Certainly, the 'misuse' of prepositions by those learning English is very common. Sentence 6 has the 'wrong' syntactical ordering, while 7 is an 'error' resulting from repetition of words that have the same meaning – *again* and *repeat*. (In other words, it contains 'unnecessary' redundancy.) It has also been noted that a speaker of Kiswahili (or a similar African language) who is used to saying *pole* when someone trips or has an accident, will usually call out *Sorry*! (in English) when witnessing similar events, a direct transfer of linguistic reaction from the first language.

According to Selinker (1972), interlanguage is the product of:
- what a learner already knows in his or her mother tongue, as in the last-mentioned illustration;
- transfer, especially in cases where language rules are learnt by rote (as is common in many second/foreign-language classrooms);

- strategies a learner uses in communicating in the new language; and
- overgeneralization of the linguistic information with which the learner comes into contact (McLaughlin 1987; Schmied 1991).

At each stage in the learner's progress towards native-speaker competence, his or her performance (production and comprehension) is governed by a system of rules. Thus, even what might be called 'mistakes' demonstrate what a learner has internalized, that is, the system of rules (grammar) she or he is using (as demonstrated in the example of *flied above).

Technically, we use the terms 'mistakes' and 'errors'. Mistakes are 'slips' that are random, as learners fail to use the knowledge they already possess 'correctly'. So a speaker might say *You did not went home yesterday*, even though they know that this is not acceptable (perhaps because they are tired or preoccupied). All speakers make mistakes in both mother-tongue and target-language situations. Thus, another feature of mistakes is that speakers are capable of self-correcting, as they already know the 'proper' form their constructions should take.

Errors, on the other hand, are deviations in the interlanguage of the learner caused by the difference between the system the learner is trying to grasp and the native language. This is how speakers produce the structures quoted in 1 to 7 above.

Examples 1 and 2 are breakdown errors. Little communication is achieved, even though we recognize the words as English. Sentence 1 has 'ignored' all rules of tense-marking. Sentence 3 meets the requirements of English syntax, and all the words are English, but the writer does not communicate at all. In other words, the writer has used the rules of word-ordering without conveying meaning. Sentences 6 and 7 communicate even though there is a 'wrong' placement of the demonstrative *this*, while in 7 (as already mentioned) there is 'unnecessary' repetition. Note that learners may not always be able to correct their errors, even when these are pointed out to them. Errors occur because learners add, omit, substitute, or order items incorrectly in the target structure. They therefore arise either from an application of the 'wrong' rules from the first language, or from wrong application and/or ignorance of the rules of the new language.

Corder (1974) identifies three stages of error: pre-systematic, systematic, and post-systematic. At the pre-systematic stage, a learner will produce both correct and incorrect forms of a target structure, for example:

Mary has my book.
*Mary is having my book.

Most likely, the learner will be unable to explain the source of the problem, or paraphrase his or her utterance.

At the systematic stage, where learners have begun to identify a system or pattern, they might still occasionally produce *Mary is having my book*, but will more consistently produce *Mary has my book*. Although they may not be able to explain what is wrong with *Mary is having my book*, they will be capable of recognizing it as an 'incorrect' form that needs amending.

The post-systematic stage is reached when learners are able to both explain the source of their errors and correct them. Errors will have become more infrequent, as the learner seems to have acquired both the new system of rules and an understanding of their use in communicating particular messages. It should be remembered that a learner can be at different stages in 'error production' with different structures and rules of the language. In other words, while they might be at the systematic stage in using stative verbs, they could also be at the post-systematic stage in using phrasal verbs. It is not always easy to determine what specific error a learner is making by observing only a few examples. Mistakes are identified from their frequency and consistency, or from the learner's inability to correct them.

Negative transfer

Negative transfer is interference of a mother tongue or other well-known language in the use of the target language. In these cases, learners effectively speak the target language while using the grammar of another language, either a mother tongue or another familiar language. Let's look more closely at how this happens. In this section we will discuss both cases of negative transfer.

When first learning a second or foreign language, speakers tend to transfer many of the characteristics of their native language into the new language. Brown (1987) calls this **interlingual transfer.** For example, Kiswahili-speakers may say **the car of John* (a direct translation of *gari la John*), instead of *John's car*. It is not only at the level of ordering words in sentences (syntax) that learners produce errors of transfer. Those whose languages either do not have certain sounds or do not differentiate between them (for example [k, g], [t, d], [l, r], and [z, θ]) may eliminate the ones that occur in the target language. So we might hear a speaker say *he slaughteret a koat for his kuests,* instead of *he slaughtered a goat for his guests; fis* instead of *fish; the rolly came down by the liver side;* or *in geongraphy, the ladscape is often an idication of the kid of ndrainange system you are likely to find.* In these cases, learners' first languages heavily influence their pronunciation.

This kind of mother-tongue influence may not necessarily arise from speakers' own mother tongues, but from other languages around them (Schmied 1991). When we learn a third language, it is possible that there will be varying degrees of interlingual interference from not only the mother tongue, but also the second language, or the language in wide usage in the community (Brown

1987). In Africa, it is more likely that this will be a lingua franca, such as French in Cameroon, Kiswahili in Kenya, and Afrikaans or English in South Africa. These languages will have an impact on both the target language and the mother tongue. For example, a Kenyan speaker of Dholuo, who uses English in his or her place of work, but who also uses Kiswahili for wider communication, will experience **interlingual influence** from all these languages. Figure 12.2 illustrates this hypothetical situation.

FIGURE 12.2: Hypothetical interaction between the three languages of a Dholuo-speaker

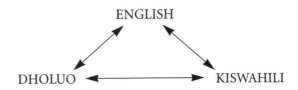

Intralingual transfer

Some errors arise because a learner has either mislearnt or overgeneralized particular rules that occur in the second or foreign language. This kind of transfer is known as **intralingual transfer**. For example, a learner may overgeneralize rules (such as adding -*ing* to stative verbs) to produce utterances such as:

1 * John is liking his school
2 * They singed in the party
3 * he reached to the city
4 * he is good man

In sentence 1, the learner exhibits errors in the use of stative verbs. In sentence 2, there is an overgeneralization of the past-tense rule that has been applied to the irregular verb *to sing*; a preposition has been incorrectly added to the verb *to reach* in sentence 3; and, in 4, the article *a* is omitted. These are examples of errors that we tend to see in writing.

The learner who acquires a language within a particular community, for example an Afrikaans settlement in South Africa, or a Luganda-speaking area in Kenya, may acquire the peculiar features of English as spoken by that particular community. Errors can occur in these circumstances because the learner has not internalized a general rule, or has isolated particular rules governing the formation of certain constructions. For example, a learner who has internalized the use of syntax in *Wh-* questions, but has not internalized the rules governing their conversion to statements, may produce sentences such as:

*I am not sure where is it.

Language teaching methods and practices

One of the root causes of the problems Africans experience in learning the ex-colonial languages is the use of inappropriate language teaching methods and practices. In the next section we will consider various methods of language teaching; then we will consider language teaching practices in African class-rooms. Finally, the importance of teacher training will be discussed.

Typical teaching methods

In this section we look briefly at key features of some typical teaching approaches or methods. (Stern, 1983, gives a more detailed account of these methods.) These are the traditional method, the direct method, the reading method, the audio-lingual method, the audio-visual method, and the communicative method.[6]

The **traditional method** emphasizes the teaching of target-language grammar, and its main feature is translation from and into the target language. Its methodology consists of brief presentations of grammatical items and substantial translation practice from one language to the other. It also features the memorizing of rules and facts that act as a frame of reference for the learning of the new language. There seems to be an overemphasis on the language as a 'mass' of rules (Stern 1983: 455). One criticism of this method points to its failure to prepare learners for actual daily use of the new language. The traditional method has also been called the grammar translation method.

The **direct method** is a kind of immersion approach, in which the target language is extensively used as the vehicle for instruction and communication in the language classroom. Although translation is used as a technique, the mother tongue is avoided for most learning purposes (Stern 1983). Activities include substitution, dictation, and narrative, as well as free composition. Emphasis is laid on pronunciation, as much of the learning is oral. The principle underlying this method is the assumption that all languages are learnt in a similar way. In other words, second or foreign languages can be learnt in the same way as the first language – mainly orally and through association.

The **reading method**, which also makes use of this approach, generally confines the objective of language learning to training in reading comprehension, with emphasis on vocabulary control in texts. It uses both intensive and extensive reading to achieve this. This trend has influenced the structure of class readers, especially at beginner levels. In many countries today, beginner readers are designed with vocabulary control in mind.

The following three methods are all variations on what is known as the **behaviourist-structuralist method**, as they assume that language learning is a process of habit formation, and that the 'habits' to be acquired consist of the rules of grammar.

The **audio-lingual method** is based on the following behaviourist assumptions:

- foreign-language learning is a mechanical process of habit formation;
- habits are strengthened through reinforcement and feedback;
- habits are formed by rewarding correct responses and punishing wrong responses; and
- language behaviour in the learner can be changed by changing behaviour.

This method emphasizes 'correctness'. Classes are characterized by drills and oral repetition, without adequate consideration of function. Dialogue is extensively used to introduce language items, and mimicry, memorization, and pattern drills are favourite strategies. In addition, language laboratories are used (where available).

However, we know that, as speakers of diverse mother tongues, we all make utterances that we have never heard anyone make before (see Chapter 3). In other words, we use language creatively because we have internalized the rules of the languages we have learnt, and thus have the ability to use them automatically in constructing sentences. Language knowledge is therefore not acquired only through habit formation.

The **audio-visual method** is similar to the audio-lingual method, but with visual stimuli as the primary teaching material. It is characterized by the use of film strips or visual images accompanied by dialogues or narratives, which the teacher amplifies by pointing, demonstrating, listening, questioning, and answering. During 'practice' sessions, learners are shown the same or similar visual images and expected to recall the dialogue and narrative, and master it through question-and-answer routines. Grammatical principles are isolated and drilled. One aspect of this method worth noting is the primacy afforded speech. Writing and reading are not altogether absent, but delayed. Remnants of this method can be seen in the use of pictures and diagrams for language teaching, and it is experiencing a resurgence now that computers and videos are extensively used in developed countries for the teaching of languages.

The **structural method** arose out of Bloomfield's structural linguistics, and is thus based on the following tenets:

- a structural analysis of the target language forms the basis for graded content;
- the organization of the material is handled by a linguist;
- the basic activities in classrooms are drilling and practice for the learner; and
- the emphasis is on speech.

Words are broken down into sounds and morphemes, and sentences are analysed in terms of the relationship of the lexical items. Many of us have had some experience of this approach, and we are thus familiar with the following kind of analysis:

John beat the drum loudly:

John	beat	the	drum	loudly
S (N, agent)	(V, active, pt)	(article, def)	O (N, patient)	Adverb (manner)

where *John* is the subject, a noun, and the agent of the sentence; *beat* is an active verb, past tense; *the* is a definite article; *drum* is object, noun, and acted upon in the sentence; and *loudly* is an adverb of manner.

This sentence could also be analysed as follows: *John* is the subject, while *beat the drum loudly* is the predicate of the sentence. Although this method is at least linguistically sound, the ability to identify how lexical items are related in a sentence is no guarantee that a learner will also internalize the rules underlying sentence formation and then be able to use the language for communication in real-life situations. (This method is the one most commonly followed in first-language teaching.)

Since the 1960s, particularly as a result of the work done by the sociolinguist Dell Hymes (see Chapter 10), an approach called the **communicative method** has been developed. It is still very popular, but does not seem to be clearly understood or effectively practised. It is organized around theories of communication, in particular the functions for which people use language. For example, we know that language can be used to conduct an argument. A learning unit on argument would deal with how one presents, defends, or challenges information. Related strategies might include seeking and gathering information, agreeing, disagreeing, and so on. The language structures covered in class would relate to the needs of argument as a language function, so expressions such as *I support, concur with, think what so and so says, I disagree*, and *on the other hand*, would be introduced and explained to learners to enable them to apply them in contexts of communication. Communicative approaches generally aim at teaching meaning, form, and use.

The communicative approach is geared towards developing situational, thematic, notional, and functional communicative competence (Brumfit 1984; see also Chapter 10) in the learner. In other words, communicative methods aim at teaching *how, when, with whom, and for what purposes* the linguistic material being learnt could be used.

One pitfall in the use of communicative syllabuses is that they can degenerate into a list of unrelated language items found in communicative situation types. Questions are still asked about how communicative content should be organized, so as to become more systematic. For possible ways of systematizing communicative content, see Halliday (1973, 1978).

It is probably a good idea to use a combination of these teaching methods, the advantage being that what one method lacks could be supplemented by another. For example, teachers could use mechanical exercises such as substitution tables and gap-filling exercises, but then have the learners try to use the same structures in specific situations, with the help of visual aids, or small-group work.

Language teaching practice in African classrooms

An important contributing factor to the general lack of proficiency in the ex-colonial languages in Africa is the use of inappropriate teaching methods. Perhaps the most significant of these is the fact that Western approaches, inappropriate to African conditions, are followed in teaching these languages. Four aspects of this will be discussed.

Firstly, the ex-colonial languages are often taught in the same way that first languages are taught (in Europe, for instance). Instead of using methods directed at developing a communicative ability in these languages, the focus in the teaching of English, French, and Portuguese seems to be on the grammars of these languages. We believe that such an approach underlies the ineffectiveness of efforts to teach the ex-colonial languages in Africa.

Secondly, the standards and norms usually set as targets for appropriate language behaviour are Western. Their relevance for Africans, or the degree to which they can be realistically achieved as targets, is not adequately considered.

Thirdly, typical African discourse conventions and patterns of communication seldom feature in language teaching approaches. Western patterns of teacher–pupil interaction (the use of questions and answers, and the method of rote-repetition) are often used, without any attempt to establish some congruence between classroom behaviour and the patterns of language behaviour and modes of communication that might be typical of local communities (see Chapter 11). It would make more sense to shift the culture of formal education closer to the culture of the local communities.

Finally, textbooks used in the training of language teachers, which are often written with North American and European conditions in mind, are used relatively unquestioningly by trainers, who seldom adapt them to African conditions. If we look at textbooks that deal with second-language acquisition in the USA, for example, we find that these are typically directed at immigrant communities (such as Italians, Poles, and South-East Asians in the USA) who have a strong need to become part of mainstream society, which, in this case, is predominantly English-speaking. These immigrants have to deal with the different stages of reculturalization (first wonder, then alienation, and finally a sense of loss), but they have strong (occupational) incentives to acquire English and to become integrated into American society. Furthermore, they are maximally exposed to English. Africans learning English (or French, or Portuguese), on the other hand, are not immigrants, experience little culture threat, are already part of the mainstream society, often have very little exposure to English (or French, or Portuguese), and have little occupational incentive to acquire it with anything like mother-tongue proficiency. It is obvious that language-teacher-training programmes and textbooks for use in African communities are in dire need of insightful adaptation.

Let's now look in more detail at how inappropriate teaching methods often are in African classrooms. It is common for teachers to use a linear approach, as illustrated by the following step-by-step lesson plan:

1   Introduce a topic: 'Today we will look at sentence connectors.'
2   Define items: 'Connectors are items we use to join different ideas in a sentence.'
3   Give examples of connectors: 'Connectors are words such as *and* and *but*.'
4   Explain the function of connectors: 'Connectors relate items to something that has been mentioned before.'
5   Give examples, which learners are then supposed to learn through drilling and choral repetition, particularly if the class is large: '*John bought a red shirt. John bought blue trousers.* We can use *and* to join these two sentences as follows: *John bought a red shirt and blue trousers.* Now repeat the sentence after me.'
6   Give a written exercise to ensure that the learners have grasped what has been taught: 'Join the following pairs of sentences using *and* or *but*:
   a *Anyango came yesterday. Anyango brought the news.*
   b *Dora can read. Dora cannot write.*
   c *Sam likes to herd goats. Sam likes to milk cows.*
   d *Boy Jim was late. The teacher did not punish Boy Jim.*'

While actual lessons may not be quite as inflexible as we have suggested here, there will be elements of greater or lesser rigidity depending on the teacher, his or her mastery of content, the level of the class, the support systems in place (such as appropriate physical surroundings), and the teacher's understanding of strategies of language teaching.

Another issue that needs some comment is the use of definitions in foreign-language teaching, as these can create a number of problems. Firstly, definitions tend to draw attention away from the basic structures of the language. Secondly, they are often phrased in language that is more difficult or convoluted than the structure itself, for example, 'The past tense is the tense that designates an action that has been completed at the time of utterance'. Thirdly, definitions and explanations do not always cover all the circumstances of the use of a structure. For instance, the explanation that the past-tense inflection is formed through the addition of -*ed* and -*d* to the end of a verb does not cover the irregular ones that do not change at all (such as *cut*) or that change in unpredictable ways (such as *rend*). It is important to remember that natural human languages are almost never entirely logically organized. Language use is in fact often rather arbitrary.

The point is that definitions and explanations should be used judiciously, only when necessary, and if they aid rather than obstruct the learning of target structures. These days, it is assumed that if learners are given enough exposure to a language, they will be able to work out its rules and principles for themselves. It must be remembered that the test of a learner's knowledge of a language is their ability to use the target structures in communication, rather than absolute accuracy in the classroom. The balance between accuracy and function is difficult to strike, but the language teacher must try to give learners opportunities to make use of structures taught on an ongoing basis, through drama, debate, dialogue, and simulation, through both pupil–pupil and teacher–pupil interaction.

Much language teaching aims primarily at 'correctness', and is not geared towards providing learners with contexts in which they can use the newly learnt structures appropriately. Instead, the bulk of language teaching seems geared towards teaching mastery of grammatical rules rather than developing communicative ability. It seems to be assumed that once a learner knows the rules of a language, they will be able to apply them in communication.

This focus on 'correctness' extends to all the language skills – reading, writing, speaking, and listening. For example, even intensive reading lessons often seem to be aimed at accuracy and exactness, which involves getting the answers to questions 'right'. Little is done to show learners ways of dealing with textual information that will enable them to adequately understand texts and respond appropriately to given questions.

The same emphasis is seen in the teaching of writing, which means that most of the efforts go towards getting organization and language correct. The problem here is that creativity and originality are neglected. This is admittedly a difficult balance to maintain, but it must be remembered that excessive concern for accuracy tends to thwart individuality in reading and writing. In speaking, the aim is often to get learners to produce the 'correct' sounds, intonations, and stress patterns. Some instructors also seem to teach listening, as if this must precede speaking, reading, and writing. This approach may be the result of the influence of the audio-lingual method.

The focus on 'correctness' makes it difficult for pupils to acquire communicative competence. Even when learners know the 'right' structures (grammar), they may have no idea of when and where they should be applied. This leads to lack of competence in discourse (see Chapter 10), as can be seen in this little anecdote: when a Kenyan was offered a drink by a family in England, he responded, *Me, I don't want a drink*. He was, of course, unaware of how rude this sounded.

This problem is compounded by the fact that for most of those learning foreign languages, the only exposure they have is in the classroom. We find that, in areas where one language is particularly dominant, students in language classes will discuss issues and tasks in their mother tongues or a lingua franca, and use the target language only to write down their answers. The problems associated with this are numerous. For one, it is obvious that if the target language is not used in the very process of instruction and learning, then pupils are likely to take longer than they need to master the language adequately; secondly, if learners do not use the rudiments of the target language that they have already learnt for immediate and meaningful communication, they are reducing their opportunities for receiving input and producing output in that language even further.

It could be argued that learners need to draw from their mother tongues in order to learn the target language, but, while this may be acceptable in primary school, learners need to be able to formulate their thoughts in the target language at least by the time they reach secondary school, particularly because in most African countries the second language is also the language of learning and examinations. Adequate mastery of the language then becomes a resource for effective learning.

The success of second- or foreign-language teaching depends on, among many other things, the quality of teacher training. Teachers are the primary facilitators of learning, even if the circumstances in which they teach are less than ideal. Therefore, they need to be equipped to deal with the many factors that undermine the learning process. In the next section, we briefly consider the needs of foreign-language teacher training in Africa.

Teacher training

Teacher training has an absolutely vital role to play in the moulding of teachers. In many parts of Africa, it is assumed that teachers at primary-school level can teach all subjects. This misconception is costly both to pupils and society. Those involved in training primary-school teachers should consider letting trainees learn to teach those subjects in which they have a special interest. Teacher training needs to be geared to developing a three-dimensional character. Its object is to produce an individual whose attitudes allow for flexibility, who has a knowledge base that is both theoretical and practical, and who possesses a skills repertoire that enables him or her to try out various approaches before deciding which one works with a particular group (Pennington 1990).

This kind of training is especially important when training primary-school teachers, as they will lay the foundations for all language development. It is imperative that only those who qualify should be trained, and that, because language is crucial for the learning of other subjects, teachers of language be given not just general training, but specific training in language teaching skills. In addition, training should attempt to build a sensitivity to real human needs. Teachers should be conscious of the feedback they get from their students, accepting them and making the necessary adjustments to facilitate learning. Language teacher training is too important to be taken for granted.

Conclusion

This chapter has been concerned with a number of education-related language matters: the role of language in educational development, the inadequacy of first-language development in formal education, and the unsatisfactory state of second- or foreign-language learning in African schools. A number of contributing factors were discussed, and a number of proposals were made for improving the situation. It is unlikely, however, that any of these suggestions and discussions can be implemented effectively in the short term. Language learning is a complex issue, and we have an insufficient understanding of how it occurs, what factors play a role in the process, and what the role of each is, especially in the African context. Extensive research into the whole field of study is necessary.

Endnotes

1   In addition to the matter of cognitive development, there is a critical psychological consideration. This is the insecurity that many children (particularly those from rural areas) must experience when entering school: their immediate family is absent, as are intimate acquaintances, and the institution they are entering is totally foreign and threatening. If the chief language of this alien world is also totally incomprehensible, it is no wonder that educational problems are experienced.

2   In reality, many Africans acquire 'second languages', 'third languages', and so on, in a spontaneous and natural way. The model above is, of course, oversimplified.

3   As was pointed out in Chapter 1, $10 billion was spent on the English language business in 1989. This fact, taken together with the further fact that English has been taught in

some African countries for close on 150 years, suggests that there is something seriously wrong with the teaching of English as a second language in Africa.

4   That many African pupils do not acquire 'native-like' pronunciation at school could also be due to the fact that the teachers (role models) from whom the second language has to be learnt are themselves seldom native speakers of the target languages.

5   As explained below, the use of terms such as correct and wrong should not be used in language learning situations, for two reasons: (a) the 'errors' are direct reflexes of the grammar a learner has already internalized (and are therefore 'grammatical'); and (b) classifying a language form as an 'error' implies the unquestioning acceptance of some fixed standard or norm and means that all forms

that differ from that standard or norm are 'deviant'. This approach awards standard languages a status that they do not necessarily deserve and cannot claim to have (given the diversity of languages and the fact that all languages are subject to change.) The use in this chapter of words such as *mistakes, wrong,*

incorrect, or *misuse* should not be seen as a deviation from the basic principles of this book, but as a recognition of the general views on second- and foreign-language learning.

6   The methods are discussed in historical sequence. They are all still in use in various institutions around the world.

Bibliography

BENITO, Y., C.L. FOLEY, C.D. LEWIS, and P. PRESCOTT. 1993. 'The effect of instruction in question-answer relationships and meta-cognition on social studies comprehension.' *Journal of Reading Research* 16, 1: 20–29.

BROWN, D. 1987. *Principles of Language Learning and Teaching.* Englewood Cliffs, NJ: Prentice Hall.

BRUMFIT, C. 1984. *Communicative Methodology in Language Teaching.* Cambridge: Cambridge University Press.

CORDER, S.P. 1974. 'The significance of learners' errors.' In *Daily Nation,* editorial, 27 October 1997.

HALLIDAY, M.A.K. 1973. *Explorations in the Functions of Language.* London: Edward Arnold.

——— 1978. *Language as Social Semiotic.* London: Edward Arnold.

JOHNSON, D.W., and R.T. JOHNSON. 1975. *Learning Together and Alone,* Englewood Cliffs, NJ.: Prentice Hall.

KIMANI WA NJOROGE. 1985. 'Multilingualism and some of its implications for language policy and practices in Kenya.' In *Language and Education in Africa.* Edinburgh Centre of African Studies. Seminar proceedings 26: 327–353.

KOS, R. 1991. 'Persistence of reading disabilities: the voices of four middle-school students.' *American Educational Research Journal,* 28: 875–895.

NEMSER, W. 1971. 'Approximative systems of foreign language learners.' *International Review of Applied Linguistics,* 9: 115–23.

MCLAUGHLIN, B. 1987. *Theories of Second Language Learning.* London: Edward Arnold.

OBURO, A.P. 1984. 'Trilingual Kenyans: Our Classrooms and Resources.' *Kenya Journal of Education,* 2 (1).

PENNINGTON, M.C. 1990. 'A professional development focus for the language teaching practicum.' In J.C. Richards and D. Nunan (eds.), *Second Language Teacher Education.* Cambridge: Cambridge University Press.

ROY-CAMBELL, Z.M., and M.P. QUORO. 1987. *Survey of Reading Competence in English of Secondary School Students in Tanzania.* Ministry of Education Report.

SCHMIED, J.J.1991. *English in Africa: an introduction.* London, New York: Longman.

SELINKER, L. 1969. 'Language transfer.' *General linguistics,* 9: 69–92.

——— 1972. 'Interlanguage.' *International Review of Applied Linguistics,* 10 (3): 181–209.

SILBERSTEIN, S. 1994. *Techniques and Resources in Teaching Reading.* New York: Oxford University Press.

STERN, H.H. 1983. *Fundamental Concepts of Language Teaching.* Oxford: Oxford University Press.

WEBB, VIC. 1999. 'Multilingualism in democratic South Africa: the overestimation of language policy.' In *International Journal of Educational Development* 19: 351–66. Elsevier Scence.

——— (in preparation). Language in South Africa: the quest for a future. The role of language in national reconstruction and development.

WILLIAMS, E. 1994. 'Reading in two languages in year five in African Primary Schools.' *Applied Linguistics,* 17 (2): 181–209.

WORKING GROUP ON EDUCATIONAL RESEARCH AND POLICY ANALYSIS. 1997. *Languages of Instruction. Policy Implications for Education in Africa.* International Development Research Centre.

Appendix: A bird's-eye view of the language character of the African states

Country	Capital	Population in millions (1990)	Number of languages
ALGERIA	Algiers	29	
ANGOLA	Luanda	11.5	11 (42)
BENIN	Porto Novo	5.5	
BOTSWANA	Gaborone	1.5	9 (26)
BURKINA FASO	Ougadougou	10.4	
BURUNDI	Bujumbura	6.3	1 (3)
CAMEROON	Yaounde	13.5	239
CAPE VERDE	Praio	0.43	
CENTRAL AFRICAN REPUBLIC	Bangui	3.4	

(NOTE: Empty cells mean that the necessary information was not available to the editors, and figures placed in brackets indicate conflicting information. In the case of the *Main languages* column, percentages of speaker numbers have been included where possible.)

Main languages (% refers to the proportion of speakers who use the language as a primary language)	Illiteracy rate % (1995)	Official languages
Arabic, French, Berber	38	Arabic
Umbundu (38%), Kimbundu (27%), Congo, Chokwe, Portuguese	58 (1990)	Portuguese
Fon, Yoruba, Bariba, Adja, Fulani, French	63	French
Setswana (90%), English	30	Setswana, English
Moore, Manding, Fulani, French	81	French
Kirundi (95%), French	65	French, Kirundi
Fang, Bamileke, Fulani, English, French	37	English, French
Portuguese-Creole, Portuguese	28	Portuguese
Sango, Banda, Baye, Zande, French	40	French

CHAD	N'djamena	6.5	
COMOROS	Moroni	0.56	3
CONGO (People's Republic of)	Brazzaville	2.7	15 (57)
COTE D'IVOIRE	Yamoussokro (Abidjan)	14.2	
DEMOCRATIC REPUBLIC OF CONGO	Kinshasa	43.5	220 (212)
DJIBOUTI	Djibouti	0.5	
EGYPT (Arab Republic of)	Cairo	57.5	
EQUATORIAL GUINEA	Malabo	0.47	
ERITREA	Asmara	3.5	
ETHIOPIA	Addis Ababa	57	
GABON	Libreville	1.2	42 (38)
GAMBIA, The	Banjul	1	
GHANA	Accra	17.3	
GUINEA	Conakry	6.5	
GUINEA-BISSAU	Bissau	1.1	

Sara, French, Arabic	52	French, Arabic
Comorian Swahili, French, Arabic	43	French, Arabic
Kongo (50%), Lingala (20%), Kituba, French	25	French
Anyi, Baule, Bete, Manding, Senufo, French	60	French
Lingala (10%), Kongo, Luba, Mongo, Kiswahili, French	23	French
Afar, Somali, French, Arabic	54	Arabic, French
Arabic	49	Arabic
Bubi, Fang, English, Spanish	22	English, Spanish
Tigrinya, Amharic, Afar (Arabic, English, Italian)		
Amharic, Afar, Oromo, Sidamo, Somali, Tigrinya	65	Amharic
Fang-Mbeti (35%), Shira-Punu, French	37	French
Wolof, Mandinka, Fulani, English	61	English
Asante, Fante, Ewe, Ga, Dagombe, English	36	English
Fulani, Malinke, Susu, French	64	French
Creole, Balanta, Bijago, Fulani, Portuguese	45	Portuguese

KENYA	Nairobi	29	42 (59)
LESOTHO	Maseru	2	4
LIBERIA	Monrovia	3	
LIBYA	Tripoli	5.4	
MADAGASCAR	Antananarivo	13.5	1 (3)
MALAWI	Lilongwe	10	8 (14)
MALI	Bamako	10	
MAURITANIA	Nouakchott	2.3	
MAURITIUS	Port-Louis	1.1	
MOROCCO	Rabat	28.5	
MOZAMBIQUE	Maputo	18	24
NAMIBIA	Windhoek	1.6	(21)
NIGER	Niamey	9	

Kikuyu (20%), Dholuo (14%), Luhya (13%), Kikamba (11%), Kalenjin (11%), English, Kiswahili	22	Kiswahili, English
Sesotho, English	29	Sesotho, English
Kpelle, Bassa, Creole/Merico, Vai, English	60	English
Arabic	24	Arabic
Malagasy (98%), French	54	Malagasy, French
Chichewa/Chinyanja (50%), Chitumbuka; Ciyao (19%), English	44	English, Chichewa
Bambara, Dogon, Fulani, Manding, Senufo, Songhai, Tamasaq, French	69	French
Wolof, Berber, Soninke, Fulani, Arabic	62	Arabic
Creole (94%) Hindi (50%), English, French	17	English, French
Arabic, Berber	56	Arabic
Imakwa (28/38%), Xitsonga (12/24%), Portuguese	60	Portuguese
Herero, Kavango, Ovambo, Nama	(43?)	English
Hausa, Fulani, Kanuri, Songhai, Tamasheq, French	86	French

NIGERIA	Abuja (Lagos)	111	400
RWANDA	Kigali	6.5	1 (3)
SÃO TOMÉ	São Tomé	0.13	
SENEGAL	Dakar	8.6	
SEYCHELLES	Victoria	0.08	
SIERRA LEONE	Freetown	4.7	
SOMALIA	Mogadishu	9	
SOUTH AFRICA	Pretoria; Cape Town; Bloemfontein	40.5	25–80
SUDAN	Khartoum	29	
SWAZILAND	Mbabane	0.95	1 (4)
TANZANIA	Dar es Salaam	29	150 (127)
TOGO	Lomé	4.3	
TUNISIA	Tunis	9	

Hausa, Fulani, Yoruba, Igbo, Efik-Ibibio, English	43	English
Kinyarwanda, French	40	Kinyarwanda, French
Portuguese Creole, Fang, French		Portuguese
Wolof, Serer, Diola, Fulani, Manding, Creole, French	67	French
French Creole, English, French	21	English, French Creole
Temne, Mende, Creole, French	69	French
Somali, Arabic	76 (1990)	Arabic, Somali
isiZulu (23%), isiXhosa (18%), Afrikaans (14.4%), Sepedi (9%), English (8.6%), Setswana (8%), Sesotho (7.7%)	18	Afrikaans, English, isiZulu, isiXhosa, isiNdebele, Sepedi, Sesotho, Setswana, siSwati, Tshivenda, Xitsonga
Arabic, Dinka, Pari	54	Arabic
Siswati, English	23	English, Siswati
Kiswahili (5% as a primary language but 95% as a second language), Kisukuma (12%), English	32	Kiswahili, English
Ewe, Grusi, Gurma, French	48	French
Arabic, French	33	Arabic

UGANDA	Kampala	19	41
ZAMBIA	Lusaka	9.5	40
ZIMBABWE	Harare	11.2	8+ (19)

SOURCES: Sow and Abdulaziz, in Mazrui (1993: 533–548); Hartman (1990); the Africa Institute (1998); World Bank Group publication (n.d.)

Luganda (16%), Kiswahili, Lango-Acholi, Lusoga, English	38	English
Chibemba (19%), Chinyanja (11%), Lozi, Tonga, English	22	English
Chishona (67%), isiNdebele (15%), English	15	English

Index